RETHINKING THE GULAG

RETHINKING THE GULAG

Identities, Sources, Legacies

EDITED BY
ALAN BARENBERG
AND
EMILY D. JOHNSON

INDIANA UNIVERSITY PRESS

This book is a publication of

Indiana University Press
Office of Scholarly Publishing
Herman B Wells Library 350
1320 East 10th Street
Bloomington, Indiana 47405 USA

iupress.org

© 2022 by Indiana University Press

All rights reserved
No part of this book may be reproduced or utilized in any form or by any means, electronic or mechanical, including photocopying and recording, or by any information storage and retrieval system, without permission in writing from the publisher. The paper used in this publication meets the minimum requirements of the American National Standard for Information Sciences—Permanence of Paper for Printed Library Materials, ANSI Z39.48–1992.

Manufactured in the United States of America

First printing 2022

Library of Congress Cataloging-in-Publication Data

Names: Barenberg, Alan, editor. | Johnson, Emily D., editor.
Title: Rethinking the Gulag : identities, sources, legacies / edited by
  Alan Barenberg and Emily D. Johnson.
Description: Bloomington, Indiana : Indiana University Press, [2022] |
  Includes bibliographical references and index.
Identifiers: LCCN 2021033530 (print) | LCCN 2021033531 (ebook) | ISBN 9780253059628 (hardback) | ISBN 9780253059611 (paperback) | ISBN 9780253059604 (ebook).
Subjects: LCSH: Labor camps—Soviet Union—History. | Forced labor—Soviet Union—History. | Prisons—Soviet Union—History. | Prisoners—Soviet Union—History.
Classification: LCC HV9712 .R48 2022 (print) | LCC HV9712 (ebook) | DDC 940.54/050947—dc23
LC record available at https://lccn.loc.gov/2021033530
LC ebook record available at https://lccn.loc.gov/2021033531

CONTENTS

Acknowledgments vii

1. Introduction: Gulag Studies since the Archival Revolution / *Alan Barenberg and Emily D. Johnson* 1

PART I. *Identities*

2. Religious Identity, Practice, and Hierarchy at the Solovetskii Camp of Forced Labor of Special Significance / *Jeffrey S. Hardy* 19

3. Censoring the Mail in Stalin's Multiethnic Penal System: The Use of Languages Other Than Russian in Soviet Inmate Correspondence / *Emily D. Johnson* 43

4. "Who Are You in Life?": The Gulag Reputation System and Its Legacies Today / *Gavin Slade* 67

5. The *Real* Gulag: Commentary on the "Identities" Section / *Lynne Viola* 91

PART II. *Sources*

6. "They Won't Survive for Long": Soviet Officials on Medical Release Procedure / *Mikhail Nakonechnyi* 103

7. Applying Digital Methods to Forced Labor History: German POWs during and after the Second World War / *Susan Grunewald* 129

8. Framing Gulag Memoirs: A Distant Reading / *Sarah J. Young* 155

9. Researching the Gulag in the Era of "Big Data": Commentary on the "Sources" Section / *Judith Pallot* 181

PART III. *Legacies*

10. The Role of Nature in Gulag Poetry: Shalamov and Zabolotsky / *Josephine von Zitzewitz*   197

11. "I Would Very Much Like to Read Your Story about Kolyma": Georgii Demidov, Varlam Shalamov, and the Development of Gulag Prose, 1965–67 / *Alan Barenberg*   220

12. The Necropolis of the Gulag as a Historical-Cultural Object: An Overview and Explication of the Problem / *Irina Flige, Translated by Josephine von Zitzewitz*   243

13. Sites and Sounds of the Camps: Commentary on the "Legacies" Section / *Alexander Etkind*   273

14. Afterword / *Alan Barenberg and Emily D. Johnson*   284

Index   295

ACKNOWLEDGMENTS

THE ROOTS OF THIS COLLABORATION lie in the Hoover Institution's annual Summer Workshop on Authoritarianism, which was a model in its promotion of broad-ranging discussions and in bringing together academics from different disciplines and corners of the world (including the editors). We wish to thank Paul Gregory, Mark Harrison, Stephen Kotkin, fellow workshop participants, and the staff at the Hoover Institution and Library for their support and encouragement throughout the years. Financial support for this project was provided by the Office of the Vice President for Research, the Office of the Provost, the College of Arts and Sciences, and the Department of Modern Languages of the University of Oklahoma; the Office of the Provost, the College of Arts and Sciences, and the Department of History of Texas Tech University; the Buena Vista Foundation; and the Big XII Faculty Fellowship. This work would not have been possible without the support of our respective academic departments and colleagues. Thanks are due to the staff at Indiana University Press for shepherding this project to completion. In particular, Jennika Baines championed this book from the very beginning. Steven Barnes, Polly Jones, and the anonymous readers for this volume provided timely and insightful feedback. We wish to acknowledge the perseverance and good cheer shown by our contributors while facing the challenges of a global pandemic. Last but not least, we are grateful to our families for their patience and encouragement throughout the process of completing this volume.

RETHINKING THE GULAG

ONE

INTRODUCTION

Gulag Studies since the Archival Revolution

ALAN BARENBERG AND EMILY D. JOHNSON

THE PUBLICATION OF ALEKSANDR SOLZHENITSYN'S *The Gulag Archipelago* in 1973, almost fifty years ago, launched Gulag studies as an academic discipline. Although memoirs, fiction, poetry, and histories describing Soviet places of imprisonment had been in limited circulation since the 1920s, Solzhenitsyn gave a name and powerful interpretive framework to the Soviet system of labor camps and prisons. He used *Gulag*, the acronym for the Main Administration of Camps (*Glavnoe upravlenie lagerei*), a central agency in charge of administering sites of internment between 1930 and 1960, to refer to the entire complex of Soviet carceral institutions. This vast network of spaces of confinement, Solzhenitsyn explained in the introductory sections of the first volume of *The Gulag Archipelago*, extended across the length and breadth of the Soviet Union. At any moment, walking down the "crooked streets" of their lives, Soviet citizens might, he suggested, pass "walls and fences made of rotting wood, rammed earth, brick, concrete, iron railings" that concealed one of the system's outposts. "Well-disguised" and hidden from view, these sites had swallowed up millions of Soviet citizens between the 1920s and the 1950s. In Solzhenitsyn's description, the Gulag was "an almost invisible, almost imperceptible country" inhabited by a caste of prisoners with distinctive customs and characteristics, a tribe he identified as *zeks*, using the Russian abbreviation for the word *prisoner* (*zakliuchennyi*).[1] These unfortunates circulated endlessly through sites of interrogation, torture, and confinement, including many geographically remote and climatically harsh locations, until they died or had the good fortune to be released. Although scholars have challenged certain parts of Solzhenitsyn's conception of the labor camp system, including the degree to which carceral

1

spaces were isolated from the rest of Soviet life, his work has remained foundationally important to the field of Gulag studies, and his metaphors continue to shape the thinking of academics from an entire range of scholarly disciplines who work on this topic.

Solzhenitsyn was able to convey a sense of the scale and horrors of the Soviet carceral system through both literary metaphor and an accumulation of first-person testimony, but he did not have access to official statistics on the size and composition of the camp population, mortality rates, or the precise number and locations of sites of confinement. In fact, in the preface to *Gulag Archipelago*, Solzhenitsyn expressed doubts that such data would even become accessible and suggested that his lack of access to official archives had affected the form of his work, encouraging him to write something generically idiosyncratic and literary as opposed to a pure history of the camp system: "I would not be so bold as to try to write the history of the Archipelago. I have never had the chance to read the documents. And, in fact, will anyone ever have the chance to read them? Those who do not wish to recall have already had enough time—and will have more—to destroy all the documents, down to the very last one."[2] Solzhenitsyn's bleakest forebodings as to the fate of official Soviet archives describing the camp system were, fortunately, not realized. Although, as we will explain later in this introduction, archival access remains a problem for Gulag researchers, in the early 1990s scholars gained access to at least some of the records that Solzhenitsyn dreamed of reading. On the basis of these sources, scholars now estimate that from 1930 to 1952, approximately 25 million people cycled through the system, which included prisons, labor camps, labor colonies that held low-level offenders and juveniles, and "special settlements" to which various populations were exiled based on class origin or national identity.[3] Official statistics state that 2.4 million people died in camps, colonies, and prisons—figures that do not include deaths in special settlements. This should be understood as the lowest conceivable estimate. Recent research has suggested that official mortality statistics were often manipulated with an eye toward minimizing death rates.[4]

Most Gulag survivors who went on to write about their experiences were, like Solzhenitsyn, members of the educated classes who were sentenced under political statutes such as the infamous article 58. As a result, such "political" offenders—a category that included many people who had no inclination to dissent and were arrested on sometimes fantastical fabricated charges—have always received disproportionate attention in Gulag studies. Scholars have often treated their experiences and perceptions as normative. However, in most places and periods, political offenders constituted a minority of the Gulag's population; labor camp inmates convicted of political crimes typically comprised between a quarter and a third of the total incarcerated population.[5] The largest segment of the Gulag's population consisted of *bytoviki*, ordinary people sentenced for petty offenses and violations of labor discipline that would not, in many cases, merit criminal charges in most other societies. This category included, for example, starving peasants arrested for gleaning grain in state-owned fields and employees who violated harsh labor laws by arriving late to work one too many times. In addition, the Gulag held a population of violent career criminals known as *urki* or *blatnye* who followed their own social norms and traditions. As discussed by Gavin Slade in his contribution to this volume, this narrow slice of the prisoner population exercised extraordinary influence over life in the Gulag. Such inmates enjoyed a privileged status in some periods and places and often exercised authority over other prisoners.

The number of prisoners held in the Gulag varied significantly over time. In 1929 there were only 76,523 prisoners in the RSFSR serving sentences longer than three years. In the early 1930s, as a result of crackdowns on real and potential dissenters that accompanied crash industrialization and collectivization, the number of inmates held in prisons, labor colonies, and labor camps ballooned: by October 1934, the Gulag held 685,000 prisoners. The incarcerated population increased dramatically again during the so-called Great Terror of 1937–38, when intensive repressive campaigns targeted Soviet elites, ordinary citizens, and social undesirables: by January 1, 1939, nearly 1.3 million prisoners were held in the Gulag. Despite the fact that arrests and sentences to terms in the Gulag remained common during the Second World War, the overall population held in labor camps, prisons, and colonies declined between 1941 and 1944, primarily due to dramatic increases in mortality resulting from food shortages and the mass release of prisoners to fight on the front lines. By January 1, 1944, the prisoner population had fallen to 1.2 million. However, it expanded rapidly again after the war as a result of new political actions such as the Leningrad Affair, Soviet attempts to pacify reoccupied territory, and harsh new criminal laws, including the draconian antitheft laws of 1947. The camp and colony population reached its all-time high in 1948–52, hovering between 2.3 and 2.5 million prisoners.[6] It began to decline dramatically following Stalin's death in March 1953, when large contingents of prisoners were released as part of reforms initiated by Stalin's successors, including, most importantly, Nikita Khrushchev.

The number of exiles held in the Gulag system also expanded rapidly in the 1930s and 1940s. The first and largest group consisted of so-called *kulaks* (wealthy peasants) who were forcibly deported as part of the war against the peasantry that accompanied the collectivization of agriculture. In all, nearly 2.2 million were exiled to the far north, Urals, Eastern Siberia, and Kazakhstan, the majority from 1930 to 1931. This was followed by a variety of deportations based on national criteria, often involving an attempt to move entire national groups from their homes to various parts of Siberia and Central Asia. More than half a million Poles, Ukrainians, Belarusians, Moldavians, Latvians, Lithuanians, and Estonians were exiled as part of Soviet operations to pacify territories occupied from 1939 to 1941 and again during the reoccupation at the end of the Second World War. During the Second World War, more than a million Soviet Germans and Finns were exiled because of their suspect national identity. Wartime deportations also affected the so-called punished peoples of the Caucasus who were accused of collaborating with the Germans: in 1943–44, nearly a million Karachai, Kalmyks, Chechens, Ingush, Balkarians, and Crimean Tatars were sent into permanent exile. In all, it is estimated that nearly 5.4 million people were exiled to special settlements from 1930 to 1953.[7] All prisoner and exile figures listed here are approximate: potential irregularities in the central statistics maintained by Soviet state agencies and scholarly debates regarding which categories of repressed individuals should be included in the count make it hard to provide a simple answer to the question of how many inmates the system held.

The sites in which prisoners and exiles were confined varied in terms of both location and living conditions. In the prisons where those arrested were held while they were under interrogation and awaiting sentencing, conditions were filthy and often crowded, with dozens of inmates pressed into cells designed to hold two or four people. Generally, inmates did not work before sentencing and had almost no opportunity to correspond with family members. The strict isolation prisons set up to hold inmates believed to be particularly dangerous following the imposition of their sentences were very different. There, inmates were often housed singly or in pairs in cells and again generally did not work. The degree to which inmates could interact with each other and correspond with relatives varied over time. Some detention units were located in isolated areas—for example, the Solovetskii Special Purpose Prison (STON) operated on the Bol'shoi Solovetskii Island from 1937 to 1939, after the closure of the notorious Solovetskii Special Purpose Camp (SLON), which had been based in this forbidding far northern site from 1923 to 1933. Other detention units—such as Vladimir Central, which remains the Russian Federation's largest prison as of this writing—were based in large urban centers.

The camps and colonies that held most Soviet prisoners, almost always with heavy labor requirements, also varied in the ways they were situated. Although most were located in remote, resource-rich areas where forced labor could extract hard-to-reach raw materials to help the Soviet Union reach industrialization targets, there were also clusters of confinement sites near major cities. What labor camps and colonies produced varied by location. In and around Moscow, prisoners might work on construction projects or in the kind of closed scientific research institution that Solzhenitsyn described in his novel *The First Circle* (*V kruge pervom*). In the distant reaches of Kolyma, in northeastern Siberia, they mined gold and other precious metals. In Western Siberia, in the area around the city of Novosibirsk, inmates performed a wide range of economic tasks, including assignments connected with agriculture and military production. Prisoners lived in barracks, tents, and dugouts, usually with their work brigades. The supply of food, clothing, and other necessities varied from camp to camp and over time but was at its worst in famine years and during the Second World War, when the entire Soviet population faced dire shortages of resources.

Special settlements that held entire families of exiles were located in the far north, Siberia, and Central Asia. Those confined in them were forced to undertake a variety of economic tasks and faced living conditions that were often at least as harsh as those in labor camps. As noted above, most had been sent into exile because they were deemed kulaks (rich peasants) or belonged to an ethnic group that was judged potentially disloyal.[8] Exiles were allowed to take only what they could carry to their new settlement sites, and they often found themselves deposited in undeveloped wilderness without any regular source of supplies. Prohibited from leaving and stripped of most civil rights, they struggled to survive largely by their own labor while simultaneously working to meet any production targets set for them in forestry work, mining, collective agriculture, or any other area to which they were assigned.

During the Second World War, an entire separate network of confinement sites emerged to hold prisoners of war. Known as UPVI, the Administration for Affairs of Prisoners of War and Internees (*Upravlenie po delam voennoplennykh i interovannykh*), and then, beginning in 1944, as GUPVI, the Main Administration for Affairs of Prisoners of War and Internees (*Glavnoe Upravlenie po delam voennoplennykh i interovannykh*), it was administratively separate from the Gulag system but borrowed many of its practices. GUPVI prisoners, like Gulag inmates, performed various kinds of forced labor with often inadequate supplies of food and clothing. Their communication with their families back home was both carefully monitored and strictly limited.

As this overview of the most significant types of Soviet detention sites suggests, this volume defines the Gulag inclusively, much as Solzhenitsyn used the term. All Soviet confinement sites drew, to a greater or lesser degree, on the practices first developed at the infamous Solovetskii Special Purpose Camp, which opened in 1923. Most prisons, camps, and special settlements faced similar pressures and challenges, which included shortages of basic supplies and personnel, pressure to reduce death rates and raise production, and concerns about secrecy and security. Therefore, we believe that considering them together makes methodological sense. For this reason, the present volume includes chapters that speak to the experiences of inmates in the early Solovetskii Special Purpose Camp and even the GUPVI network as well as in labor camps and colonies that were subordinate to the Main Administration of Labor Camps between 1930 and 1960. Additionally, some material on life in the Gulag's special settlements appears in Irina Flige's contribution to this volume, although this is not the primary focus of her chapter. Our hope is that this inclusive editorial approach will provide readers with a more complete perspective on the role that forced labor and detention sites played in Soviet society and will also serve to highlight the ways in which the field of Gulag studies has evolved in recent decades.

THE EVOLUTION OF GULAG STUDIES

The worldwide publication of Solzhenitsyn's *One Day in the Life of Ivan Denisovich* and *The Gulag Archipelago*, as well as works about the Gulag by other early authors such as Varlam Shalamov and Evgeniia Ginzburg, led to international recognition of the human rights abuses perpetrated by the Soviet state and fueled interest in study of the Soviet labor camp system. Literary scholars were particularly active in writing about the Soviet camp system in the 1970s and 1980s as they analyzed Solzhenitsyn's groundbreaking work along with other examples of Gulag fiction and memoirs.[9] Within the field of history, work in Gulag studies progressed more slowly, largely because of a lack of archival sources. There were some important historical studies of the Gulag such as Dallin and Nicolaevsky's *Forced Labor in Soviet Russia* and Robert Conquest's *Kolyma: The Arctic Death Camps*, which, like Solzhenitsyn's *Gulag Archipelago*, drew primarily on oral testimony and memoirs.[10] However, for the most part, historians released little on places of imprisonment per se in these early decades, choosing instead to focus on the terror and arrests—topics that were better covered by official Soviet publications such as newspapers and journals and in materials available in the Smolensk Regional Communist Party archive, a fund of documents that the German army captured during the Second World War and that the US Army subsequently seized during the German retreat.[11]

The partial opening of Soviet archives related to terror and the Gulag at the end of the 1980s dramatically changed the landscape of Gulag studies. Access to extensive government documentation including official orders, inspection reports, and interagency correspondence promised to allow historians to craft much more detailed accounts of the operations of Stalin's labor camps and prisons, as well as of the inmate experience. The wealth of official sources suddenly available encouraged many historians and social scientists to expect clear and specific answers to questions that had long interested them: How many prisoners were held in Stalin's Gulag in different periods of time, and how many died? Did Soviet leaders primarily view the Gulag as a source of slave labor, or was it largely intended to punish political enemies? How isolated were Gulag camps from the rest of Soviet society? Survivor testimony, memoirs, and the literary sources that had once constituted the primary forms of information available on the camp system were ill suited to answering these sorts of questions and hence came to be seen by many historians and social scientists as secondary in importance, valuable largely because they provided a window on subjective experience.

The archival revolution yielded and continues to yield answers to many important questions, but it also introduced new conceptual challenges. For example, state, regional, and local archives provided a wealth of statistical data on everything from prisoner mortality to the productivity of labor camp enterprises. However, it quickly became clear that many actors in the labor camp system had strong incentives to manipulate data, which rendered at least some numbers potentially less reliable. Similarly, archival documents revealed that the overwhelming majority of inmates in Stalin's prison and camp system were convicted of nonpolitical charges, and yet such nonpoliticals were much less inclined to leave personal accounts of their time in the Gulag than were politicals. Historians wondered how to best understand their experiences and what their presence in the labor camps in such large numbers said about the overall aims and functions of the Gulag as a system. Official archives also contained substantial documentation on the activities of the Camp Cultural Education Sectors, the units in labor camps and colonies that were charged with the reform or reforging (*perekovka*) of inmates into productive citizens who might one day rejoin the main body of Soviet society. Solzhenitsyn and many important Gulag memoirists tended to dismiss all attempts to redeem prisoners, and indeed all ideological content in the Gulag, as "an empty 'justification' for evildoing."[12] But new archival sources, as well as new historical approaches to the Soviet project that focused on Soviet subjectivity, made such an assumption less tenable and encouraged many scholars to see Bolshevik ideology and aspirations to remake and reform inmates through labor as more central to the mission of the camp system than was initially realized.[13] Additionally, archival sources on the Gulag said remarkably little about what happened to prisoners and exiles after release and about the long-term effect of mass incarceration on Soviet and post-Soviet society. How did the families of those who had died in the camps memorialize their dead, and how did those who survived terms in the Gulag navigate the challenges of social reintegration?

In recent years, scholars in the social sciences and literature as well as history have pioneered new methods and approaches with the aim of studying such questions, which are not easily answered using party and state documents. The use of mapping programs to analyze camp locations and labor assignments, including the pioneering efforts of Judith Pallot in the Gulag Maps project (see her commentary in this volume); the application of corpus analysis to the study of memoirs and other forms of survivor testimony; and efforts at comparative analysis of prisoner populations in Russia and other areas of the globe have all enriched our understanding of Stalin's Gulag. Work with new sources such as the private correspondence of labor camp inmates, the art and crafts that prisoners made in confinement, labor camp periodicals, the presentation albums prepared by labor camps for visiting dignitaries, memoirs and diaries of camp bosses and guards, and the physical remains of the camp system itself have also offered new perspectives on important questions. Personal correspondence can illuminate the lives of Gulag inmates who did not write formal memoirs. The efforts of descendants of terror victims and activists to memorialize former camp locations and execution and burial sites can help us understand the lasting effects of the Stalinist terror on Russian society. Diaries and memoirs created by camp bosses and prison guards can document the ways in which official statistics were sometimes manipulated in sites of confinement.

Increasing restrictions on access to key archival collections in Russia and Kazakhstan have also encouraged scholars to turn to new sources and approaches. The major repositories of state and party documents concerning the Gulag in Russia and most other post-Soviet states have never been completely open to scholars. Most post-Soviet governments have restricted access to at least some materials that were seen as potentially defamatory to living people, including, specifically, documents in police archives that would reveal the names of informants and the substance of their reports. However, in recent years researchers have encountered increasing barriers when trying to access Gulag-related materials in regional and local archives in Russia and Kazakhstan. Funds focusing on specific camps, such as the Karlag archives used by Steven Barnes in his 2011 study *Death and Redemption*, are now largely closed to researchers. As a result, in recent years more scholars have turned to archives in Ukraine, Latvia, Lithuania, and Estonia, where materials on the terror and the camps are more easily accessible. Such republican archives have been particularly helpful in understanding how central policies pertaining to terror and the labor camp system were implemented on the ground. They have also highlighted the role that national identity and the politics of nationality played in both arrests and in places of confinement.

Despite all the new archival materials and methods now available to scholars of the Gulag, some very fundamental issues remain unresolved, including how best to understand the factors that led to the Gulag's creation and the system's functions. For decades, researchers have debated which of the Gulag's aims were primary and which secondary. Was the Soviet Union's vast network of labor camps and colonies envisioned chiefly as a means of addressing labor shortages in specific industries and regions (that conveniently also provided a means of isolating perceived enemies), or was the rationale behind the system's creation mostly political (and were any economic gains through forced labor a secondary factor)? To what extent did traditional carceral aims fuel the system's growth? Archival materials that became available in the early 1990s offered some support for a variety of perspectives—economic, political, and carceral. For example, archival documents clearly showed that the spread of forced labor across the Soviet Union was connected to the drive to implement Stalin's first five-year plan in 1928–32. Arrests increased in times of perceived labor shortage; those repressed were dispatched to locations and industries deemed key to meeting the targets of the plan. In some cases, individuals with specialized technical expertise, such as geologists and mining engineers, seem to have been arrested because their skills were needed by production sites operated by the Gulag.[14] Yet, as Lynne Viola persuasively argues in her pathbreaking study of special settlements, *The Unknown Gulag* (2007), it would be a mistake to see the Gulag as solely economic in function. Archival documents show that the first great expansion of the Gulag, which coincided with the collectivization campaign of the early 1930s, came as a result of political decisions. Millions of so-called kulaks were dispatched to special settlements and camps with the explicit aim of breaking resistance to collectivization. Moreover, statistical information from the archives of the Main Administration of Labor Camps allowed researchers, beginning in the 1990s, to track shifts in prisoner populations more accurately over time. This showed definitively that the expansion of labor camp and colony rolls in some periods, including specifically the late 1940s and early 1950s, was due as much to harsher sentencing of those convicted of crimes like petty theft as to an increase in political repressions. Such facts remind us that the Gulag was not just a political and economic force in Soviet society: it also had carceral functions, which it exercised with cruel disregard for the suffering of inmates and their loved ones.

Perhaps scholars have struggled to reach a consensus on the primary aims of the Gulag as a system in part because Soviet repressive measures were often more improvisational and reactive than was once suspected. In many respects, as Viola suggests, the Gulag is best understood as the product of a state with a utopian vision of controlling society but little actual capacity to realize its ambitions. Thus, the frequent use of terror and incarceration represents a sign of state weakness rather than strength.[15] Regardless of what Soviet leaders hoped to achieve through the creation of the state's vast forced labor system, the Gulag's true legacy is not really roads, canals, and raw materials such as lumber—these quickly fell into disuse or were often left to rot in the snow. Nor is it absolute political control or the maintenance of perfect social discipline and order—the Soviet empire fell just as civilizations before it did, and disorder and corruption remained endemic throughout the Soviet period. As seen from a contemporary vantage point, almost fifty years after the publication of Solzhenitsyn's *Gulag Archipelago*, the most lasting legacies of the Soviet Union's hellish system of forced labor are instead, as many contributions to this volume will make clear, collective and individual trauma, abandoned graves, and broken lives. As Alexander Etkind argues in *Warped Mourning*, the Gulag ultimately yielded only loss, not economic and political gains.

VOLUME SUMMARY

This volume brings together examples of cutting-edge scholarship in Gulag studies with the aim of providing readers with a sense of where the field is today and where it is going. We hope that the chapters in this volume, which includes studies by researchers in history, literary studies, anthropology, and sociology, will serve as models for the use of new theoretical frameworks, research tools, and sources. We view this volume as an extended professional conversation in which scholars with different training and perspectives can exchange ideas and explore common interests and concerns. As the title suggests, our volume is divided into three sections. The first, "Identities," contains articles that look at discrete categories of penal detainees (religious inmates, career criminals, members of national minorities) whose experiences in Soviet labor camps and prisons were in key respects exceptional and who remain understudied for a variety of reasons. The second section, "Sources," provides examples of the way in which new materials can revolutionize our understanding of the Soviet penal system. The authors contributing to this section use new primary sources or fundamentally new tools and methods such as text mining to explore fundamental problems in Gulag studies. The third section, "Legacies," looks at the aftermath of the Soviet penal system, including the sites that have arisen to memorialize it, literary texts that describe it, and the folk beliefs and traditions it has inspired.

Because our volume is so interdisciplinary and includes the work of scholars employing radically different approaches, each section concludes with a commentary essay that draws together the section's principal chapters, situating them in the larger context of Gulag scholarship, much as a discussant's remarks on a conference panel might help to link a set of papers. For example, in her essay that concludes the "Identities" section, historian Lynne Viola ties together a chapter on the experience of religious inmates at the early Solovki labor camp by the historian Jeff Hardy, a study of the place in the labor camp of the thieves-in-law and the criminal reputation system that they created by the sociologist Gavin Slade, and work by literature specialist Emily Johnson on the private correspondence of inmates belonging to Soviet minority groups. Viola notes ways in which the work of all three authors speaks to the problem of Soviet subjectivity that has inspired so much scholarly debate in both Soviet studies as a whole and Gulag studies specifically. This scholarly conversation grew out of Stephen Kotkin's revolutionary idea that Soviet workers in the 1930s learned to "speak Bolshevik," thereby acquiring a new Soviet subjectivity, and began to see themselves as part of a new Stalinist civilization.[16] All three chapters in the "Identities" section, Viola notes, can be read as meditations on the extent to which such a Sovietization process succeeded in the context of Soviet labor camps: were prisoners in this exceptionally punitive environment really reforged through the experience of hard labor and the influence of the Camp Cultural Education Sector just as free Soviet workers were in the 1930s? Did their worldview and essential sense of self change over the course of their sentences so that they understood themselves as Soviet citizens, or did they continue to understand themselves primarily as members of a religious, ethnic, or cultural subgroup? Further, Viola emphasizes how each chapter drives home the improvisational nature of the day-to-day operations of the Gulag, one of the major shifts in Gulag studies since the archival revolution of the 1990s.

In her commentary piece for the "Sources" section of this volume, geographer Judith Pallot looks at how new quantitative methods and approaches drawn from the digital humanities are reshaping the field of Gulag studies. She notes the continued importance of debates about numbers in Gulag studies, praising the historian Mikhail Nakonechnyi specifically for his innovative study of the way in which the medical release process (*aktirovka*) was used to artificially lower labor camp death rates. She shows how historian Susan Grunewald uses GIS data to provide a new reading of the symbiotic relationship between the Gulag and GUPVI networks of labor camps in the late 1940s. Pallot also describes how literary scholar Sarah Young uses text mining to identify dominant themes and widely employed literary devices in Gulag memoirs, highlighting patterns that merit further study. All three scholars, Pallot notes, mix quantitative and qualitative analyses in their chapters, combining the hard work of creating and working through statistical or geographic information, or, in the case of Young's project, a textual corpus, with context-sensitive readings of Soviet history and culture. Such mixed approaches, Pallot argues, can allow researchers to triangulate problems that seem resistant to resolution and arrive at important new scholarly insights.

Cultural historian and literary scholar Alexander Etkind serves as the commentator for the "Legacies" section of our volume. In his essay, he emphasizes the importance of continued work on the Gulag, particularly given the growing influence in twenty-first-century Russia of revisionist accounts of the Soviet period that cast Stalin in positive terms and minimize the human rights abuses that occurred under his leadership. The "Legacies" section contains an article by historian Alan Barenberg that analyzes debates among labor camp survivors in the 1960s concerning how best to write about the Gulag, a chapter by literary scholar Josephine von Zitzewitz that shows how the nature poetry that Varlam Shalamov and Nikolai Zabolotsky wrote following their release from the Gulag comments on the labor camp experience, and a study by historical geographer and activist Irina Flige of the Gulag's necropolis—the complex of graves and cemeteries, marked and unmarked, that holds victims of Soviet repression. Etkind notes that each of these studies highlights the lasting damage inflicted by the Soviet carceral system. Each author shows how arrests and labor camps destroyed lives, scarred psyches, broke families apart, and eroded social institutions and traditions, leaving a legacy of trauma that continues to negatively affect post-Soviet societies today.

No single volume can claim to provide a comprehensive look at how Gulag studies has evolved since the archival revolution of the 1990s. Yet by drawing together these articles and commentaries from a variety of disciplines in the humanities and social sciences, we offer a look at where the field is today and where it is headed in the coming decades. Although Solzhenitsyn feared that the Soviet archives would yield little for researchers given the ample opportunity to destroy documents, in the last three decades these materials have generated new insights, sparked controversies, and taken researchers down paths of inquiry that had previously been closed. We feel certain that in coming decades, these sources, combined with new approaches to nonstate documentation such as oral histories, memoirs, letters, and fiction, will continue to transform our understanding of the Soviet carceral system and will help scholars do an even better job of chronicling the devastating human rights abuses of the Stalin period. Thinking hard and writing honestly about this terrible chapter in Soviet history seems particularly important given ongoing efforts to sanitize the past in multiple post-Soviet states. We hope that this book can contribute to larger productive conversations about the Soviet carceral system and the ways in which the repressive policies of the past continue to shape society and culture across the former Soviet Union today.

NOTES

1. Solzhenitsyn, *Gulag Archipelago*, 1:4, x.
2. Solzhenitsyn, 1:x.
3. Khlevniuk, "The Gulag and the Non-Gulag," 480.
4. For more on this debate, see Alexopoulos, *Illness and Inhumanity*, and Mikhail Nakonechnyi's contribution to this volume.
5. The exception to this rule was during and after the Second World War. During the war, many nonpoliticals were released to fight at the front. The share of politicals rose to record levels in 1946–47, largely as a result of large-scale amnesties that applied only to nonpolitical prisoners. Getty, Rittersporn, and Zemskov, "Victims of the Soviet Penal System," 1048–49.
6. Bezborodov, Bezborodova, and Khrustalev, *Naselenie Gulaga*, 35–38.
7. Cadiot and Elie, *Histoire du Goulag*, 22–23.
8. For more on this, see Polian, *Against Their Will*.
9. For example, Scammel, *Solzhenitsyn*; Monas, "GULag and Points West"; Dunlop, Hough, and Klimoff, *Aleksandr Solzhenitsyn*; Maclean, "Walls and Wire"; Lowe, "E. Ginzburg's *Krutoi Marshrut* and A. Aksenov's *Ozhog*"; and Oja, "Shalamov, Solzhenitsyn, and the Mission of Memory."
10. Dallin and Nicolaevsky, *Forced Labor in Soviet Russia*; Conquest, *The Arctic Death Camps*.
11. See, for example, Getty and Manning, *Stalinist Terror*.
12. Barnes, *Death and Redemption*, 9.
13. See, for example, Lahusen, *How Life Writes the Book*; Barnes, *Death and Redemption*; Draskoczy, *Belomor*; and Ruder, *Building Stalinism*.
14. On the relationships among forced labor, science, and specialized technical knowledge, see Siddiqi, "Scientists and Specialists in the Gulag."
15. Viola, *The Unknown Gulag*, 188–90.
16. Kotkin, *Magnetic Mountain*, 198–237.

BIBLIOGRAPHY

Alexopoulos, Golfo. *Illness and Inhumanity in Stalin's Gulag*. New Haven: Yale University Press, 2017.

Barnes, Steven A. *Death and Redemption: The Gulag and the Shaping of Soviet Society*. Princeton: Princeton University Press, 2011.

Bezborodov, A. B., I. V. Bezborodova, and V. M. Khrustalev, eds. *Istoriia Stalinskogo Gulaga*. Vol. 4, *Naselenie Gulaga: Chislennost' i usloviia soderzhaniia*. Moscow: Rosspen, 2004.

Cadiot, Juliette, and Marc Elie. *Histoire du goulag*. Paris: Editions La Découverte, 2017.

Conquest, Robert. *Kolyma: The Arctic Death Camps*. New York: Viking Press, 1978.

Dallin, David, and Boris Nicolaevksy. *Forced Labor in Soviet Russia*. New Haven: Yale University Press, 1947.

Draskoczy, Julie. *Belomor: Criminality and Creativity in Stalin's Gulag. Myths and Taboos in Russian Culture*. Boston: Academic Studies Press, 2014.

Dunlop, John B., Richard Hough, and Alexis Klimoff, eds. *Aleksandr Solzhenitsyn: Critical Essays and Documentary Materials*. New York: Macmillan-Collier, 1973.

Etkind, Alexander. *Warped Mourning: Stories of the Undead in the Land of the Unburied*. Cultural Memory in the Present. Stanford: Stanford University Press, 2013.

Getty, J. Arch, Gábor T. Rittersporn, and Viktor N. Zemskov. "Victims of the Soviet Penal System in the Pre-War Years: A First Approach on the Basis of Archival Evidence." *The American Historical Review* 98, no. 4 (October 1993): 1017–49.

Getty, J. Arch, and Roberta Manning. *Stalinist Terror: New Perspectives*. New York: Cambridge University Press, 1993.

Khlevniuk, Oleg. "The Gulag and the Non-Gulag as One Interrelated Whole." *Kritika: Explorations in Russian and Eurasian History* 16, no. 3 (August 29, 2015): 479–98.

Kotkin, Stephen. *Magnetic Mountain: Stalinism as a Civilization*. Berkeley: University of California Press, 1995.

Lahusen, Thomas. *How Life Writes the Book: Real Socialism and Socialist Realism in Stalin's Russia*. Ithaca, NY: Cornell University Press, 1997.

Lowe, David. "E. Ginzburg's *Krutoi Marshrut* and A. Aksenov's *Ozhog*." *SEEJ* 27, no. 2 (Summer 1983): 200–210.

Maclean, Hugh. "Walls and Wire: Notes on the Prison Theme in Russian Literature." *International Journal of Slavic Linguistics and Poetics* 24–25:253–63.

Monas, Sidney. "GULag and Points West." *Slavic Review* 40, no. 3 (Autumn 1981): 444–56.

Oja, Matt F. "Shalamov, Solzhenitsyn, and the Mission of Memory," *Survey* 125 (1985): 62–69.

Pallot, J. "The Topography of Incarceration: The Spatial Continuity of Penality and the Legacy of the Gulag in Twentieth- and Twenty-First-Century Russia." *Laboratorium: Russian Review of Social Research* 7, no. 1 (2015): 26–50.

Polian, Pavel. *Against Their Will: The History and Geography of Forced Migrations in the USSR.* Budapest: ACLS Humanities E-book, 2004.

Ruder, Cynthia. *Building Stalinism: The Moscow Canal and the Creation of Soviet Space.* London: I.B. Tauris, 2018.

Scammel, Michael. *Solzhenitsyn: A Biography.* New York: Norton, 1984.

Siddiqi, Asif. "Scientists and Specialists in the Gulag: Life and Death in Stalin's Sharashka." *Kritika: Explorations in Russian and Eurasian History* 16, no. 3 (August 29, 2015): 557–88.

Solzhenitsyn, Aleksandr I. *The Gulag Archipelago, 1918–1956: An Experiment in Literary Investigation.* Three volumes. Translated by Thomas P. Whitney. New York: Harper and Row, 1973–1978.

Viola, Lynne. *The Unknown Gulag: The Lost World of Stalin's Special Settlements.* London: Oxford University Press, 2007.

ALAN BARENBERG is the Buena Vista Foundation Associate Professor of History at Texas Tech University. He is author of *Gulag Town, Company Town: Forced Labor and Its Legacy in Vorkuta.*

EMILY D. JOHNSON is the Brian and Sandra O'Brien Presidential Professor of Russian at the University of Oklahoma. She is author of *How St. Petersburg Learned to Study Itself: The Russian Idea of Kraevedenie* and editor and translator of *Gulag Letters* by Arsenii Formakov.

PART I

IDENTITIES

TWO

RELIGIOUS IDENTITY, PRACTICE, AND HIERARCHY AT THE SOLOVETSKII CAMP OF FORCED LABOR OF SPECIAL SIGNIFICANCE

JEFFREY S. HARDY

ALTHOUGH THE SOVIET GULAG HAS been the subject of numerous publications since the opening of Soviet archives in the early 1990s, few scholars have investigated religious identity and observance in the Soviet carceral context.[1] To some extent, this reflects Gulag archival files, which devote very little attention to this subject. It also speaks to the interests of contemporary historians and literary scholars, who find questions of penal operation and the daily lives and writings of political prisoners more compelling. Yet, as made clear by numerous memoirs from both religious and nonreligious inmates, religion played a meaningful role in the lives of many Gulag prisoners. It offered spiritual nourishment amid stark deprivation, a worldview that helped make sense of incarcerated life, a means of social organization, and a wellspring of resistance to secular authorities.

This chapter investigates the experience of Russian Orthodox clergymen at the Solovetskii Camp of Forced Labor of Special Significance (SLON) in the 1920s. SLON was the largest and most important penal camp of the Soviet 1920s and the predecessor of the Gulag system of the 1930s. It was celebrated by Soviet propaganda as an experiment in reeducating criminals, class enemies, and political prisoners through labor and other means.[2] It served, therefore, as a model institution for the early Soviet regime at a time when penal policy was still being developed. It was also, of course, located on the Solovetskii Islands, the site of one of the most important monastery complexes in Russian Orthodoxy.[3] And it served as the primary destination for imprisoned religious authorities.

The improvisational nature of this camp, the religious context of its location, the large number of imprisoned clerics, and the schism in Orthodoxy in the mid-1920s helped shape the identity and experience of SLON's religious prisoners. Priests, monks, bishops, and higher-ranking clergymen entered an environment that was both familiar due to its religious significance and unfamiliar because of the nature of incarceration. Because of SLON policies that allowed a significant amount of religious worship and the brotherly communion of hundreds of like-minded clerics, the Orthodox community at SLON was able to create a vibrant ecclesiastical society that was constantly invigorated by a steady supply of new inmates. Rather than be "reeducated" by labor and other correctional devices, Orthodox clerics for the most part maintained their religious devotions. The schism of the Orthodox Church in the late 1920s, however, caused a divisive split in this imprisoned clerical community, with most of them joining the breakaway faction that opposed the conciliatory policies of Acting Patriarch Sergius. Ultimately, new policies of harsh repression against religious practice starting in 1929, including the transfer of most clerics to other camps in the early 1930s, destroyed SLON's Orthodox community.

BOLSHEVIK IMPROVISATION AND THE RELIGIOUS ENVIRONMENT

The Bolshevik regime came to power in 1917 with a general idea of how to remake society in the pursuit of socialism, but it lacked specific blueprints on a range of important issues. The immediate context of civil war and recovery in the late 1910s and early 1920s further ensured that the regime would enact policies that were often reactive and improvisational (not to mention contradictory) in nature.[4] For religious and penal policy this was certainly the case, with government policymakers, Communist Party officials, academics, secret police operatives, and prison officials trying to figure out how to reform society along Marxist lines.

As a case in point, repression against religious institutions and authorities was at times violent but also sporadic, with Soviet authorities trying to define how or if to preserve religious liberty while simultaneously ensuring the creation of a secular if not atheist society.[5] Soviet authorities disassociated the church from the state and stripped it of many of its traditional functions, including education, marriage, divorce, and the registration of newborns. Churches were destroyed or repurposed, property ownership was transferred from the church hierarchy to new lay associations, monasteries were closed, priests were arrested or executed, and the head of the Orthodox Church, Patriarch Tikhon, was placed under house arrest for his strident opposition to Soviet power. Government and Communist Party officials waged atheistic propaganda campaigns among the Soviet population in an effort to stamp out religious belief in favor of belief in science and human progress. In 1922, the Soviets even used clergymen sympathetic to socialist ideas to set up a rival Orthodox hierarchy called the Living Church or Renovationist Church, which duly pledged loyalty to the state and opposition to Patriarch Tikhon.[6] Yet amid this repression, the Soviet constitution declared the freedom of religious worship, and Soviet officials allowed many churches to remain open. Especially in the countryside, religious belief and practice remained widespread and unmolested through the 1920s.

Questions about what to do with criminals, class enemies, and other social deviants and how the Soviet system of criminal justice should differ from its tsarist predecessor and from the bourgeois systems of the West were also heatedly debated, resulting in a complex and at times contradictory patchwork of penal institutions, policies, and practices.[7] Some personnel and prisons were retained from the Old Regime, but the new context of Marxist ideology seemed to demand reforms, such as greater insistence on forced labor and the use of camp-style facilities that allowed for communal reeducation. Yet what precisely Soviet corrections should look like was the subject of academic debate and a bureaucratic turf war among the People's Commissariat of Justice, People's Commissariat of Internal Affairs, and the secret police. The creation of SLON on October 13, 1923, was part of this experimental phase of Soviet penology, designed as it was by the secret police as a model institution that would transform "the most socially dangerous" inmates through labor, education, and the power of the collective.[8] From just a few thousand inmates left over from the previous Northern Camps of Forced Labor, SLON quickly became the largest place of incarceration in the Soviet Union, with over ten thousand inmates on the islands by the late 1920s.[9]

The social makeup of these prisoners was quite varied, a result of wide-ranging Bolshevik repressive policies. As inmate Anton Klinger described, "In the Solovetskii camp you could find representatives of any nationality, any religion, any profession. Russians and citizens of all countries in the world, Orthodox Christians, Protestants, Lutherans, Catholics and Jews."[10] Among these, hundreds of religious leaders, particularly from Russian Orthodoxy, were incarcerated at SLON in the 1920s.[11] Some had been convicted according to Article 72 of the Criminal Code of the RSFSR, which forbade the distribution or storage of counterrevolutionary propaganda and mandated incarceration for at least one year. This article was interpreted broadly, according to the memoirs of one SLON inmate, with church officials sentenced under it for such things as "resisting the confiscation of church valuables," conducting "monarchist propaganda," "raising children in a religious spirit," and "defending pure Orthodoxy from the threat of the so-called 'living,' 'renovationist' and

Figure 2.1. Orthodox clergy in the Solovetskii camp. January 1923. From left to right: Aleksei Shishkin, Mitrofin (Grinev), Ilarion (Troitskii), Evgenii (Zernov), Zakharii (Lobov), Pavel Chekhranov; standing: Simeon Krasnov, Iliia Pirozhenko, Aleksii Trifil'ev, Vladimir Vologurin, Petr Falevich. Photo courtesy of Wikimedia Commons.

other 'churches.'"[12] Other clergymen fell under Articles 119 through 125, which explicitly laid forth crimes related to the separation of church and state.[13] On arriving at the Solovetskii Islands from the transit camp near Kem', imprisoned members of the Orthodox religious hierarchy entered a world that was in some ways familiar. A number of local monks continued to inhabit the monastery, relatively unmolested by SLON authorities. Imprisoned clergymen often lived together, they were permitted to wear their ecclesiastical garb, they paid customary deference to their spiritual superiors, and they greeted each with the traditional threefold kiss; "in short," one memoirist noted, "they did not in any way depart from the centuries-old traditions of their caste."[14] The privileges of associating together and wearing religious robes are on prominent display in a number of photographs from this era, some of which betray no indication of being taken in a prison camp (see, for example, fig. 2.1).[15] As elsewhere in the Soviet Union, SLON administrators in the mid-1920s were trying to maintain some balance between ensuring the guarantee of religious liberty enshrined in the Soviet constitution and "reeducating" prisoners through antireligious action. In this climate of uncertainty, the privileges granted to Orthodox clergymen no doubt helped them preserve their religious identities, both internally and in the view of other inmates and guards.

The physical environment of the camp, located as it was in a monastery complex, was also familiar and indeed comforting to religious authorities. Inmates were often housed in cells formerly occupied by monks, or in chapels or other religious buildings; religious architecture dominated the skylines, and the roads, canals, and other improvements on the islands had been built by monks over the preceding centuries. Religious prisoners, therefore, found themselves surrounded by tangible reminders of devotion to God, even as the Bolsheviks repurposed religious buildings, destroyed icons, whitewashed frescos, desecrated the relics of the founders of the monastery, and otherwise worked to destroy the most recognizable markers of this sacred space. Indeed, the Solovetskii Islands' cherished status as a place of pilgrimage made it not just familiar but desirable as the location of imprisonment among at least some of the clergy. As related by a young inmate who witnessed an old priest crying at the transit point at Kem', "It turned out that he was crying for joy, since he was going to die not anywhere in the taiga, but on the land made holy by Zosima and Savvatii [the fifteenth-century founders of the monastery]."[16]

Yet if the clerical community and monastic architecture were familiar from the clerics' prior experiences and helped enforce their religious identity, other aspects of prison life at SLON were unfamiliar. The psychological "pains of imprisonment" described by sociologist Gresham Sykes, stemming from deprivation of liberty, goods and services, autonomy, and security, certainly afflicted the clergy as they did other prisoners.[17] Archpriest Sergei Znamenskii, like many other inmates, filed appeals to the Moscow Committee of the Political Red Cross for food and money.[18] Inmate Ivan Zaitsev recalled one group of clerics that traveled with him to Solovki, noting that the experience of incarceration had made them "extremely depressed."[19] Similarly, when one "mother Veronika," apparently a nun with some authority, was placed in the penalty isolator for twenty-nine days, she found herself disinclined to pray. Faced with hunger and cold, she discovered to her dismay that "her spiritual state was in a very slavish dependence on her physical condition." She thought that she could stay strong in the face of overt anti-Christian torture, but faced with such "prosaic, everyday phenomena" as loneliness, hunger, and cold, her spiritual devotion waned.[20] Once released from the isolator, however, she was able to renew her faith in the company of other believers.

For some, a Christian worldview that interpreted imprisonment as fulfilling God's will helped mitigate these challenges. Among others, Archpriest Mikhail

Mitrotskii, who served in the fourth Duma in prerevolutionary Russia, viewed Bolshevik repression as "a test of faith. The weak and the faint-hearted will fall away. Then those who remain will be [the church's] support, as were the martyrs of the first centuries."[21] Some even took this acceptance of suffering to the extreme. As one blind, elderly monk expressed to a friend after receiving news of his release, "I don't know what I did to make God so mad that he punished me so little. I am unworthy, apparently, of the martyr's crown, oh, unworthy."[22] Ultimately, Orthodox theology and the monastic tradition of suffering in imitation of Christ helped many clergymen passively accept the unfamiliar burdens of incarceration.[23]

One aspect of incarceration that required special adjustment and that challenged clerical identity to some extent was the mandatory labor imposed by SLON authorities. According to inmate accounts, the clergy in the first few years of SLON's existence were typically given "general work" to perform, which meant hard physical labor, and they were required to work even on Sundays and religious holidays. While monks in the Orthodox tradition often performed some amount of physical labor as part of their daily routine, priests and higher-ranking clergymen were unconditioned for such work. By 1926, however, many of them had been given privileged jobs in Company No. 6, housed in the Solovki Kremlin, because they were, in the words of one inmate, "the most honest, the most accurate, the most good-natured, and the most conscientious workers of all the prisoners at Solovki."[24] As political prisoner Gennadii Andreev noticed, "Wherever completely honest people were needed—at warehouses, supply depots, in the distribution of packages—the priests were employed."[25] Yet for some clergymen, such positions of trust provided irresistible temptation in a world of intense scarcity. Archimandrite Feodosii, for example, recalled with shame pilfering food from the supply depot he was charged with guarding to stave off the pangs of hunger, even as other inmates went hungry.[26]

Carceral society also created a challenging social and cultural climate for Orthodox clergymen. Memoir accounts differ to some extent as to the level of overt repression faced by religious inmates compared with other prisoners at SLON, but they were certainly targeted for abuse by some SLON personnel. Klinger remembered that "the inexpressible oppression, violence and mockery of the Solovetskii administration fell with special fury precisely on the heads of imprisoned clergy.... With every word and every gesture, the Solovetskii secret policemen try to offend and outrage the imprisoned priests." He further noted that rations and packages belonging to the clergy were routinely stolen, they were surrounded by stool pigeons, they were prohibited from conducting worship services, and they were beaten if they made the sign of the cross.[27] Sozerko Mal'sagov gave a similar account, declaring that "although they are the group of prisoners most oppressed and degraded by the camp leadership, they are distinguished by the humility and stoicism with which they bear physical and moral suffering."[28]

Religious inmates often complained of the profanity and blasphemy of both guards and common criminals, in particular the use of the names of God and the Virgin Mary.[29] Some inmates would spit on crosses or tear them from the necks of believers and then stomp on them. Lay believer Zaitsev called the constant swearing and blaspheming in the central cathedral where they were housed "an orgy of distraught people" and lamented the "cynical-sacrilegious mockery of the feelings of believing Christians that took place in this building."[30] Boris Sederkhol'm recalled how one night the commander of SLON rode in a drunken state into the chapel housing inmates to harass them. Noticing that one old priest was mumbling to himself as they stood at attention, Sederkhol'm asked, "Are you not well, father? What's wrong?" To his queries the priest replied, pointing to the floor, "Oh Lord, Lord. Right here we are trampling the place of the holy altar, and such language we are hearing! The drunk madman—riding a horse in the holy temple." Even though the temple no longer served its religious function, the priest was aware that they were standing in a holy place and that the first SLON commander, Aleksandr Nogtev, was forcing the inmates to thus commit blasphemy.[31]

Such persistent abuse of religious sensibilities no doubt had a detrimental psychological effect. Nikolai Kiselev-Gromov, a SLON administrator, recalled an old priest who went mad in the penalty isolator after being beaten for taking offense at the blasphemous language used by guards during a search.[32] In his memoir, Archimandrite Feodosii even confessed to using rude language with the convoy guards (as he later expressed in his memoir, "May the Bolsheviks be damned.")[33] The nature of camp society and the installation of many clergymen in positions of trust also meant the occasional moral quandary. Acting as informants for the administration was certainly a constant pressure, even if most inmates failed to include such things in their memoirs. Other situations arose that tested the ability to judge morally ambiguous situations. Feodosii, while working as a night watchman, for instance, faced the question of whether to allow inmate women to surreptitiously rendezvous with their lovers outside the barracks. Ultimately, he chose not to prevent or report them, preferring compassion and conscious rule breaking over Orthodox notions of obedience and sexual morality.[34]

RELIGIOUS PRACTICE

Given the repressive environment of the labor camp and the avowedly secular orientation of the Bolshevik regime, one might expect religious worship to be forbidden at SLON. Actual practice, in fact, varied over the course of the 1920s—a result of continued improvisation and confusion in Bolshevik penal and religious policy. According to memoirist Ivan Zaitsev, Commander Nogtev at first allowed religious worship by the local nonincarcerated monks and did not expressly forbid inmates from attending services but then refused to issue passes to those who desired to leave their cells to attend. The imprisoned clergy, meanwhile, were expressly forbidden from attending. When Fedor Eikhmans replaced Nogtev in 1925, however, he decided to allow the imprisoned clergy to begin attending services.[35] For the following three to four years, camp officials permitted liturgical worship at a small chapel in the cemetery, the only religious building that had not been appropriated for the needs of the camp. There, local monks, along with the incarcerated clergy, would perform daily services, complete with an inmate choir, after the working day was over. Due to the hundreds of clergy imprisoned on Solovki, each only rarely had the chance to perform worship services. Archimandrite Feodosii reported performing the liturgy only around ten times in just over two years. Starting in late 1928, the clergy were prevented from conducting the liturgy, although they were still allowed to meet in the chapel to pray.[36]

Church holidays at SLON merited special observation. Memoirist Arnol'd Shaufel'berger and others reported that holiday liturgical ceremonies at the cemetery church were "very celebratory" in nature.[37] When these were prohibited, the incarcerated clergy often performed clandestine holiday ceremonies and celebrations. Archpriest Pol'skii recalled secret Easter services in 1926, which were held in a supply depot overseen by Hegumen Pitirim (Krylov) from Kazan' and other clerics. At the moment when Ivan Popov, a well-known professor from the Moscow Spiritual Academy, was giving a talk, camp commander Fedor Eikhmans arrived for an unannounced inspection. On finding the group of clergymen assembled, he demanded to know, "What kind of a meeting is this?" Father Pitirim explained that it was an Easter gathering, and this explanation was apparently sufficient, as the commander left them in peace. Pol'skii suggests, credibly, that the camp commander was satisfied with the labor that Pitirim and his associates were performing and did not want to disturb the delicate balance between the secular authorities and the religious inmates.[38]

Pavel Chekhranov likewise recalled how in 1926, he and other inmates celebrated Easter in a clandestine fashion while incarcerated at SLON's transit camp on Popov Island and how this strengthened their faith and sense of community. The camp was overcrowded, religious observance was forbidden, and the clergymen discussed how they could observe the holiday in such conditions. This proved to be no simple task, however, and the discussions ultimately ended in disagreement. Two inmates, including Archbishop Ilarion, decided to hold Easter services in the unfinished bakery, which had no roof, windows, or doors and was therefore exposed to the elements. The others resolved to worship on the top bunks of a barrack. Chekhranov joined the first group "so that at least during these minutes [of worship] I won't have to hear swearing." While other inmates turned a blind eye, they slipped out of their barracks, reached the bakery undetected, and began the Easter liturgy. For Chekhranov, the words of the ritual had special meaning in their state of confinement, particularly the recounting of Israelite suffering in Egypt due to the obstinacy of the Pharaoh, who refused to release the Israelites from bondage. When they reached the chorus of "Christ is risen," Chekhranov related, "I didn't know whether to cry or laugh from joy." After finishing the services undetected, they celebrated the next day with coffee and pieces of Easter bread (*kulich*) that had been smuggled in from the local clergy at Kem'. Remembering this Easter service later, Chekhranov decided that even though it was "by starlight, without miter or vestments, it was most precious to the Lord."[39] Whether held in the approved cemetery church or in secret, holiday services in companion with fellow clerics clearly had a positive impact on the construction of a durable spiritual community at SLON.

Orthodox clergy also experienced the divine and strengthened their faith-based community by sharing prophetic visions with their fellow clerics and with lay believers. One bishop shared a vision he had on a starry Christmas Eve in which the stars gathered into the shape of a crown that descended to the earth while growing in brightness until they hovered over the common graves that held the bodies of dead martyrs. This sense that the spiritual world, which he characterized as "larger and more real than the visible world," surrounded them and occasionally was made manifest to them spurred this bishop to increased devotion.[40] Archimandrite Feodosii likewise recounted a "prophetic vision" he had one night in 1927 while on guard duty. He saw a mother on her deathbed, surrounded by brothers and sisters. She was given an icon and with it blessed Feodosii twice; she died while pronouncing a third blessing. His interpretation of this dream was that he would live for two years on the Solovetskii Islands and then die in the third (although in hindsight he realized that he would simply be taken from Solovki in the third year). This dream, though seemingly tragic for him, caused him to remember his old "holy" mother and to cry out, "Glory to God!"[41]

In addition to worship services and miracle stories as focal points of community building, the Orthodox clergy served one another as counselors and confessors. Many memoirists recalled the compassionate ministering of Archbishop Ilarion. As one priest who spent several days in close contact with him described, "These inspiring daily discussions with Lord Ilarion greatly tempered our unhappy life at Kem', especially my own."[42] Feodosii recalled that in 1927 and 1928, the inmates housed in the Kremlin benefited from their communion with Archbishop Petr, although not frequently, since many were eager but time was always lacking.[43] Andreevskii recalled that Bishop Viktor was endlessly warm to those who sought his spiritual guidance, giving comfort to those in need. He regularly received packages from his home parish but always distributed them to other inmates. He specialized in ministering to the common criminals, those in for petty theft and similar infractions.[44] Inmate Vladimir Zotov recalled Father Vladimir (Lozina-Lozinskii) performing a baptism for a fellow inmate and receiving a stay in the penalty isolator as punishment. When told not to conduct any more baptisms, he replied to the commander, "As a priest I cannot refuse to conduct ordinances for a believer."[45] And Boris Shiraev devoted several pages of his documentary novel to the long-suffering ministering of Father Nikodim, who served as teacher and confessor to common criminals.[46] That SLON officials allowed such spiritual communion to continue through the 1920s certainly speaks to contradictory penal policies that gave religious inmates important tools to combat the repression they faced.

In a few accounts, which of course cannot be verified, memoirists even recalled successful ministering efforts among SLON authorities. Inmate Shaufel'berg, for instance, recalled that an Orthodox priest who worked in the camp office often heard confessions from local Communists and gave them blessings. One priest even had the opportunity to baptize the infant of one of the top camp commandants, Barinov, because his wife was a convinced believer who often attended church services.[47] Pol'skii likewise recounted an instance where one of his guards, who often listened to Pol'skii and other clerics talking and who occasionally argued with them about religion, eventually had a change of heart. He secretly confessed to Pol'skii and accepted communion. As Pol'skii remarked on recalling this, "Examples like this are very joyful. The soul is real, and it turns out that the image of God in it is indestructible even for these half-beasts, half-people who are called *chekists*."[48] Certainly such miracles, as they were received and reported among the believing, demonstrated to them God's continued concern with his true followers and helped build a community of faith.

Clergymen employed in SLON's medical institutions were in a position to minister not only to the living but to the sick and dying. Performing last rites was considered an essential ordinance in Orthodoxy, and Bishop Maksim, serving as a doctor during a typhus epidemic in 1929, ensured that he was there to sanctify each death. As one eyewitness reported, "He closed the eyes of everyone who died, folded their arms over their chests and for a few moments he stood silently, not moving. Apparently, he was praying."[49] In a "comical incident" related by Mechislav Leonardovich that likewise illustrates the ministering mission of Orthodox clerics, he and clergyman Protopopov from St. Petersburg were attending to the sick in the midst of an epidemic in 1925. One evening Leonardovich discovered a patient without a pulse, and Protopopov, after checking for a heartbeat, said, "He's dead, the poor guy!" He then proceeded to pray over the body and made the sign of the cross before sending him to the morgue. To Leonardovich's surprise, an hour and a half later, around midnight, he went into the hall and found the dead man crawling toward him. Spooked, he called Protopopov, who, when he saw the struggling man, pulled out an icon and started to pray. The two then helped the man up; when he asked how he ended up in the morgue, they begged his forgiveness. Over the proceeding weeks, they helped him make a full recovery.[50]

Another example illustrates how proper Christian burials continued to be important for the imprisoned Orthodox clergy, both to guide a departed soul to heaven and to participate in a communal witness of faith. When Archbishop Petr died in 1929, his associates asked permission for a celebratory funeral, with singing, prayers, and a proper cross over the grave. It appeared that this would be approved, and they began digging the grave, but suddenly the authorities ordered Petr's body to be flung into the mass grave near the hospital where he died and covered with dirt. Multiple appeals went unheeded, so the clergy secretly gathered at the mass grave at night to pay their last respects to their departed leader. To their surprise, they found that the mass grave had not been covered up yet, and Petr's body was lying in a nightshirt at the bottom. According to Feodosii's account, "Spitting on all the prohibitions of the bosses, we triumphally clothed the master in a monastic robe and hood, put on the vestment and belt, placed a cross, a rosary, and a Bible in his hands, and loudly conducted the singing. There were twenty people gathered, they gave speeches, and then lowered the holy remains into the grave, raised a cross and placed an inscription on it, and then departed 'wailing and beating our chests' (Luke 23:48)." This deed apparently went unnoticed or at least unpunished, but a few months later an order was given to turn all the graveyard crosses into firewood.[51]

THE CHURCH HIERARCHY

Although communal worship services, shared visions, and various forms of communal and private ministering helped create a vibrant religious society among Orthodox clerics at SLON, church-state pressures developing outside the labor camp worked to splinter the imprisoned church hierarchy. Officially, the Orthodox clergy imprisoned at Solovki kept their ecclesiastical rank but were removed from their pastoral positions when they were arrested; they thus did not belong to the formal hierarchy of the church and were, moreover, in only infrequent contact with church headquarters in Moscow. In such conditions, they elected their own leadership and organized an informal church council that operated independently.[52] Starting with his arrival in February 1924, the elected leader of the Orthodox clergy at SLON was Archbishop Evgenii (Zernov), formerly of the Blagoveshchensk bishopric. Evgenii continued in this position until his release in 1926, when he was succeeded by Archbishop Prokopii (Titov) of Kherson and Odessa. After Prokopii's release in November 1928, the imprisoned clergy chose Archbishop Petr (Zverev) of Voronezh and Zadonsk as their leader, but he died just months later from typhus.[53]

This elected leadership, however, often did not represent the highest spiritual authority at SLON. In the conditions of hierarchical uncertainty that the prison camp environment created, the highest-ranking clergyman, Archbishop Ilarion (Troitskii), refused a formal leadership role. Ilarion, imprisoned at SLON from 1924 to 1925 and again from 1926 to 1929, was well known as Patriarch Tikhon's secretary and adviser and had gained widespread recognition for his attacks on the Living Church, the Bolshevik regime's attempt to splinter the Orthodox hierarchy. He was thus recognized by most imprisoned clerics at SLON as their de facto spiritual leader, and they often sought his advice and blessing.[54] According to political prisoner Oleg Volkov, even "the camp administration involuntarily treated this prominent man with respect and allowed him to live solitarily and in peace."[55]

Perhaps not surprisingly, given the nature of the prison camp environment and the intense pressures on the Orthodox Church in the Soviet Union at large, at times there were quarrels among the Orthodox clergy at Solovki. Sometimes these were simply a function of camp-level rivalries and patronage networks. Archimandrite Feodosii recalled how at one labor detail where he was instructed to introduce American-style accounting, there was a rivalry between the commander and chief accountant, and he and fellow inmate Archpriest Grinevich ended up on opposite sides. The two ranks—archimandrite and archpriest—were roughly equal (the former belonging to the "black clergy" of Orthodox monasticism and the latter belonging to the "white clergy" that served as priests in parish churches), leaving no easy way for the situation to be resolved. On seeing this, Feodosii quit his position and asked for reassignment rather than be put into conflict with Grinevich.[56]

Other arguments among the Solovki clergy were more religious in nature. Feodosii recalled that some of the priests resented the bishops because the latter devoted more energy to serving the laity than the lower-ranking members of the priesthood.[57] Sometimes clergymen argued over the meaning of the new Bolshevik regime. As explained by Andreevskii, who witnessed several heated discussions between two clerics, Bishop Maksim and Bishop Viktor, Maksim "was a pessimist and was preparing for the difficult trials of the last days, not believing in the possibility of a rebirth of Russia. But the Right Reverend Viktor was an optimist and believed in the possibility of a short but bright period, as a final gift from heaven for the tortured Russian people."[58] Personality conflicts such as these in the pressure-cooker environment of the labor camp strained relations among the clergy.

Some conflicts, however, were more serious in nature. In 1929, not all approved of the election of Archbishop Petr as head of the Orthodox clergy. Petr's friend, Archimandrite Feodosii, tried to help with his accounting duties to give him more time to minister, but other clergymen—Bishop Grigorii and Archpriest Pospelov—prevented this. Moreover, Feodosii recalled, Deacon Leliukhin "informed about our meetings and conversations." Petr's opponents then succeeded in getting him transferred to share a cell with Bishop Grigorii, "his enemy," and Leliukhin unceremoniously threw Petr's belongings out onto the street. This was, according to Feodosii, "an unheard-of scandal at Solovki. The entire body of believers was worried." At this point, the majority of high-ranking clergymen took Petr's side, "and bishop Grigorii was left on his own." Archpriest Pospelov even bowed down to the earth in front of Petr, begging for forgiveness. But, according to Feodosii, "forgiveness was not given." As Feodosii wrote, recalling this episode, "This is a difficult memory. The human weaknesses of the leadership came out in full force. It was bitter."[59] Other memoirists, in fact, chose to omit this conflict in their remembrances, leading readers to wonder what other clerical conflicts are now forgotten. Feodosii's account is far from unbiased, but the fact that lower-ranking clergymen could act in such open opposition to an archbishop demonstrates the potential for hierarchical breakdown in the repressive and at times alienating environment of the labor camp.

The largest source of tension among the clergy at SLON in the 1920s, which almost certainly played a role in the actions directed against Archbishop Petr, was the question of whether conciliation with the Bolshevik regime was possible. As already mentioned, some Orthodox clerics joined the state-sponsored Living Church, which by 1927 claimed control over around 20 percent of all parishes but was already declining in popularity.[60] At Solovki, this issue of conciliation manifested itself in part by the presence of a few clergymen of the church. Klinger recalled one former Living Church bishop who had become disillusioned with it and had attempted to return to Orthodoxy. As part of his repentance process, he revealed the close relationship between the alternative church and the secret police, for which he was reportedly convicted of "revealing state secrets." At SLON, however, his penance was not accepted by the Orthodox clergy, and he was therefore shunned by the other prisoners and tormented by the guards.[61] Feodosii also recalled two members of the Living Church clergy who ended up at Solovki. One, Zav'ialov, tried to inform on the Orthodox clergy but was not able to do much harm. But the other, Gamaliuk, "was a scoundrel of the highest order" who ultimately had to be bought off to keep him from making trouble.[62]

Patriarch Tikhon's death in April 1925 and the subsequent election of the more conciliatory Metropolitan Sergius as acting head of the church revived an already contentious debate on the issue of reconciliation. In part to prevent further schism and in part to lessen state repression against the church, Sergius, while in prison in 1926, agreed to allow state interference into church affairs in exchange for official recognition of the Orthodox Patriarchy.[63] At SLON, such moves in the direction of conciliation with the state were disturbing to many who continued to view Soviet power as an express manifestation of the Antichrist. In May 1926, some of the imprisoned clergy, including archbishops Evgenii and Prokopii, along with Professor Ivan Popov of the Moscow Spiritual Academy, composed a letter affirming Tikhon's hardline approach toward the Bolshevik regime. But there was considerable disagreement as to how strident a tone to take in the letter. Archpriest Pol'skii, a staunch advocate of "preserving the dignity" of the church and of suffering repression and death rather than colluding with the state, complained that the majority of other high-ranking clerics did not accept his uncompromising position. After his long and strident draft of the "Epistle of the Solovetskii Bishops" was widely criticized, with one bishop accusing him of wanting to die "as if to the accompaniment of music," he lamented that "the majority want to conduct negotiations with the authorities in the hope of a positive result. They think that it is not necessary to die, that no one requires this, that they can get by without it." In the end, Pol'skii remembered, "My draft was not accepted, it was seen as impractical, but is hope of agreement [with the authorities] really practical?"[64]

Ultimately, the lengthy "Epistle of the Solovetskii Bishops," while perhaps more conciliatory than Pol'skii would have liked, still staked out a firm stance against the Bolshevik regime. Addressed to the government of the USSR and dated June 7, 1926 (Easter Day), it criticized the state for guaranteeing religious liberty but simultaneously repressing religious authorities and other believers. It directly condemned the Living Church for abandoning Christian principles and for lying to the world about the state of religious affairs in Russia, and it declared that "the Orthodox Church will never enter this unworthy path." In the end, the message was clear: "The Orthodox Church does not believe in loyalty to the Soviet state."[65] Widely circulated in Russia and abroad, this epistle served as a warning to Sergius to continue to follow the oppositional stance of Tikhon (that Tikhon significantly moderated his anti-Soviet stance in 1923–25 was often forgotten by Orthodox opponents of Bolshevism).

After a months-long imprisonment, however, Metropolitan Sergius issued his infamous declaration of conciliation on July 29, 1927, which declared, "We want to be Orthodox and at the same time recognize the Soviet Union as our civil motherland, whose joys and successes are our joys and successes and whose failures are our failures."[66] When this was read at SLON, many of the imprisoned clergy accepted it as God's will and remained loyal to the hierarchy. They quickly became known (as elsewhere in Russia) as "Sergiusites." According to Andreevskii, a lay member who opposed them, the Sergiusite bishops also became more conciliatory with SLON authorities and in return were treated better by the guards.[67]

A number of high-ranking clergymen imprisoned at SLON, however, opposed Sergius and took on the name "Josephites," after Metropolitan Joseph of the Leningrad episcopate, who staunchly opposed conciliation with the Soviet regime.[68] They also referred to themselves as members of the "Catacomb Church," a dissenting movement within Orthodoxy that was created in 1922 to oppose all cooperation with Soviet authority.[69] The ranks of the Josephites at SLON swelled in the late 1920s, as most clerics incarcerated in the aftermath of Sergius's declaration were Josephites. These then distributed three more epistles from Solovki noting their opposition to Sergius.[70] Archbishop Ilarion tried to maintain a middle ground, condemning Sergius's declaration and often joining with the Josephites for worship services but also maintaining communication with Sergius as the head of the church.[71]

This compromise by Ilarion opened space for new leaders to emerge among the Josephite clergy: Archpriest Nikolai (Piskanovskii), who served as confessor for the breakaway movement, Bishop Maksim (Zhizhilenko), and especially Bishop Viktor of Viatsk (Ostrovidov). Viktor had been sent to Solovki in 1928 to serve a three-year term for his strident opposition to Sergius and to Soviet power. As described by inmate Dmitry Likhachev, a lay believer who was sympathetic to the Josephite position, Viktor "was very cultured and owned printed works on theology, but in appearance reminded one of a rural parish priest.... He tried to help everyone and, what really mattered, was able to, so that everyone was well disposed toward him and believed what he said." And although he worked with the Bolshevik regime to some extent, being tasked with laboring as a bookkeeper on the state farm (and occasionally pilfering food to give to his subordinates), Viktor refused to sacrifice his religious principles. When the SLON commander ordered all Orthodox clerics to shave their beards off like the other inmates in 1929, he was among the resisters and was therefore forcibly shaved.[72] In this manner, although lower in ecclesiastical rank than Ilarion and others, Viktor managed through the force of his personality to become the de facto leader of the Josephite clerics imprisoned at SLON in 1929–30.

One immediate point of contention when the schism occurred on Solovki concerned church services. Refusing to accept the liturgy performed by Sergiusites, Viktor and most other imprisoned clerics stopped attending services at the cemetery church that was operated by the local Sergiusite monks.[73] Rather, Viktor began to invite Josephite clerics, including Archbishop Ilarion, and a few select lay believers to a meadow or a forest clearing or occasionally a remote building at night to conduct secret worship services of the "Solovetskii Catacomb Church."[74] For Easter services in 1929, for instance, they gathered in a fish-drying building in the forest, using a secret knock at the door to evade detection. Candles and icons made out of paper were brought, and they successfully concluded the sacred liturgy.[75] Bishop Viktor and other Josephite clerics even conducted secret ordinations of "catacomb" bishops, cementing their break from the Sergiusite hierarchy.[76]

The stark tension between Josephites and Sergiusites is evident in an incident related by the lay Josephite Andreevskii. On one occasion Archbishop Antonii, a Sergiusite, asked to talk with Andreevskii about the latter's visit to Sergius as part of a delegation that protested the 1927 declaration. Bishops Viktor and Maksim counseled Andreevskii to receive a blessing from Antonii only if the latter expressed solidarity with the Catacomb Church. After a two-hour discussion, at the end of which Antonii professed his continued loyalty to Sergius, Andreevskii, as instructed, interrupted Antonii's parting blessing and abruptly left. On hearing what had happened, Maksim approvingly declared, "The Soviet and the Catacomb Church are incompatible. The secret, monastic, catacomb Church has anathematized the 'Sergiusites' and those who are with them."[77] By the late 1920s, therefore, the Orthodox hierarchy at Solovki had decisively split along the Josephite-Sergiusite line that was affecting Orthodoxy throughout Russia. But whereas the majority of clergymen outside of the camps remained loyal to Sergius, those incarcerated at SLON by 1929 mostly rejected his accommodationist stance.[78]

CONCLUSIONS

During the several years of the Orthodox council at SLON, religious identity, observance, and hierarchy played important roles in the lives of Orthodox inmates, although they were heavily conditioned by the specificities of the forced-labor camp. The contradictory penal policies concerning religion, combined with the historical religious surroundings and the "pains of imprisonment," created conditions of uncertainty and repression where inmates grappled with depression and with various moral quandaries but where sociability and formal liturgical observance ultimately strengthened spiritual bonds. Certainly, compared with the Gulag camps of the 1930s–1950s, there was a surprising amount of religious observance and communion among the imprisoned clergy. To a great extent, these conditions helped religious inmates endure the coercive nature of imprisonment, the antireligious propaganda and intentional sacrilege perpetrated by SLON authorities, and the large presence of nonreligious common criminals. The internal splintering of the Orthodox hierarchy after the death of Patriarch Tikhon, however, caused serious discord among the Orthodox clergymen at SLON, with the imprisoned Catacomb clergymen ultimately providing significant moral authority to the Josephite movement across Russia.

Starting in 1929, with the Stalin Revolution in full swing, SLON authorities initiated a renewed policy of repression against the Orthodox clergy. Priestly robes were confiscated, short hair and clean-shaven faces were mandated, hard labor was imposed, and many clerics were sent to the more primitive penal outpost on the nearby island of Anzer. Then, in the early 1930s, as Gulag camps multiplied in the Far North and Siberia, the large cohort of Orthodox bishops and priests was broken up, scattered to various penal institutions and places of exile. Never again would such a large body of Orthodox clerics be imprisoned in one location for such an extended period of time. Only at the special camp section for non-Orthodox Christians at Dubravlag in the late 1950s and early 1960s would a carceral spiritual community resemble the one created at SLON.[79]

In his memoir, Boris Solonevich recalls a conversation with an imprisoned Orthodox priest who wondered at the harsh repression meted out against the Orthodox Church. As the priest expressed, "You know, it's kind of funny, but they are so afraid of us, old men. . . . As someone once said, the most explosive material in the world is ideas and faith."[80] This statement is certainly validated by this initial foray into the religious history of the Soviet Gulag. SLON authorities and Orthodox clerics clashed on a number of issues as their seemingly incompatible worldviews came into conflict in this place of detention and deprivation. Still cautious and unsure as to the limits of antireligious repression, SLON authorities found themselves unwilling or unable to prevent the creation of a vibrant and mutually reinforcing spiritual community among imprisoned Orthodox clerics. Yet the "explosive material" of faith also contributed to the rupture of this community, as Sergiusites and Josephites clashed over the issue of conciliation with Soviet power. Additional research into how inmates experienced religion in the "Gulag archipelago" will no doubt shed valuable light on this conflict of ideas between believers and jailers and among believers themselves as well as on other aspects of the internal social and spiritual lives of Soviet inmates. The Gulag ultimately was not only a place of suffering and death; for many, it was a place of faith and communion.

NOTES

1. For notable exceptions, see portions of Solzhenitsyn, *Gulag Archipelago*; Applebaum, *Gulag*; Baran, *Dissent on the Margins*; and Hiatt, "Sedition and the Sacred."

2. David-Fox, *Showcasing the Great Experiment*, 148–58.

3. For more on the Solovetskii Islands and its labor camp, see Robson, *Solovki*; Brodskii, *Solovki: Labirint preobrazhenii*; Solzhenitsyn, *Gulag Archipelago*, 2:25–70; and Gullotta, *Intellectual Life*.

4. For a good sense of this confusion see Kotkin, *Stalin*, 227–32.

5. Peris, *Storming the Heavens*, 19–98; Keller, *To Moscow*, 31–106; and Husband, "Godless Communists."

6. Roslof, *Red Priests*.

7. Solomon, "Soviet Penal Policy"; Jakobson, *Origins of the Gulag*.

8. Kokurin and Petrov, *GULAG*, 29–30; Brodskii, *Solovki: Dvadtsat' let*, 49–50.

9. Smirnov, *Sistema ispravitel'no-trudovykh lagerei*, 317.

10. Klinger, "Solovetskaia katorga," in Umniagin, ed., *Vospominaniia solovetskikh uznikov*, 1:104. The majority of memoirs on imprisonment at SLON were written in the late 1920s and 1930s and published in newspapers and journals outside of Russia. These have recently been reproduced in a multivolume collection edited by Viacheslav Umniagin and published by the Solovetskii Monastery. Citations in the chapter come from this easily accessible collection.

11. SLON authorities reported on October 1, 1927, that there were 119 inmates with "clerical rank." Over the course of the 1920s, around 80 bishops and archbishops and 400 lower-ranking clerics spent time at SLON. Soshina, *Na Solovkakh*, 21, 196–97.

12. Klinger, "Solovetskaia katorga," in Umniagin, ed., *Vospominaniia solovetskih uznikov*, 1:105; Mal'sagov, "Adskii ostrov," in Umniagin, ed., *Vospominaniia solovetskih uznikov*, 1:401; Osipova, "V iazvakh svoikh," 50–51.

13. Rayner, *Criminal Code*, 30–31.

14. Sederkhol'm, "V razboinnom stane," in Umniagin, ed., *Vospominaniia solovetskih uznikov*, 1:702.

15. Many additional photographs of Orthodox clerics appear in Umniagin, *Vospominaniia*.

16. Quoted in Gullotta, *Intellectual Life*, 78.

17. Sykes, *Society of Captives*, 63–83.

18. Soshina, *Na Solovkakh*, 158–60. See additional letters from priests' wives on 163–67. For more on the Political Red Cross, see Galmarini, "Defending the Rights."

19. Zaitsev, "Solovki," in Umniagin, ed., *Vospominaniia solovetskih uznikov*, 2:207–9. Others, however, especially after a period of adjustment to camp life, exuded joy and compassion. Andreev, "Solovetskie ostrova," in Umniagin, ed., *Vospominaniia solovetskih uznikov*, 3:171; Andreevskii, "Na Kommunisticheskoi katorge," in Umniagin, ed., *Vospominaniia solovetskih uznikov*, 3:295.

20. Vtorova-Iafa, "Avgorovy ostrova," 40.

21. Volkov, "Pogruzhenie vo t'mu," in Umniagin, ed., *Vospominaniia solovetskih uznikov*, 3:238.

22. Andreevskii, "Na Kommunisticheskoi katorge," in Umniagin, ed., *Vospominaniia solovetskih uznikov*, 3:295.

23. Reznikova, *Pravoslavie na Solovkakh*, 14.

24. Robson, *Solovki*, 221; Zaitsev, "Solovki," in Umniagin, ed., *Vospominaniia solovetskih uznikov*, 2:262; Klinger, "Solovetskaia katorga," in Umniagin, ed., *Vospominaniia solovetskih uznikov*, 1:79; Likhachev, *Reflections*, 94.

25. Andreev, "Solovetskie ostrova," in Umniagin, ed., *Vospominaniia solovetskih uznikov*, 3:126. See also Volkov, "Pogruzhenie vo t'mu," in Umniagin, ed., *Vospominaniia solovetskih uznikov*, 3:237.

26. Feodosii, "Moi vospominaniia," in Umniagin, ed., *Vospominaniia solovetskih uznikov*, 3:77–78, 81–85, 88.

27. Klinger, "Solovetskaia katorga," in Umniagin, ed., *Vospominaniia solovetskih uznikov*, 1:105.

28. Mal'sagov, "Adskii ostrov," in Umniagin, ed., *Vospominaniia solovetskih uznikov*, 1:401.

29. Olekhnovich, "V kogtiakh GPU," in Umniagin, ed., *Vospominaniia solovetskih uznikov*, 5:555.

30. Zaitsev, "Solovki," in Umniagin, ed., *Vospominaniia solovetskih uznikov*, 2:223, 262.

31. Sederkhol'm, "V razboinnom stane," in Umniagin, ed., *Vospominaniia solovetskih uznikov*, 1:692.

32. Kiselev-Gromov, *S.L.O.N.*, 47.

33. Feodosii, "Moi vospominaniia," in Umniagin, ed., *Vospominaniia solovetskih uznikov*, 3:80, 99.

34. Feodosii, in Umniagin, ed., 3:77–78, 81–85, 88.

35. Zaitsev, "Solovki," in Umniagin, ed., *Vospominaniia solovetskih uznikov*, 2:264–65.

36. Feodosii, "Moi vospominaniia," in Umniagin, ed., *Vospominaniia solovetskih uznikov*, 3:96. The chapel was finally closed for good in 1932. Reznikova, *Pravoslavie na Solovkakh*, 10.

37. Shaufel'berger, "Solovki," in Umniagin, ed., *Vospominaniia solovetskih uznikov*, 1:649–50; Rozanov, *Solovetskii kontslager' v monastyre*, 249.

38. Pol'skii, "Publikatsii o Solovkakh," in Umniagin, ed., *Vospominaniia solovetskih uznikov*, 2:71–72.

39. Chekhranov, "Dve tiuremnye Paskhi," in Umniagin, ed., *Vospominaniia solovetskih uznikov*, 1:713–15.

40. Vtorova-Iafa, "Avgorovy ostrova," 45.

41. Feodosii, "Moi vospominaniia," in Umniagin, ed., *Vospominaniia solovetskih uznikov*, 3:83–84.

42. Feodosii, in Umniagin, ed., 1:713.

43. Feodosii, in Umniagin, ed., 1:91.

44. Andreevskii, "Vospominaniia o episkope Viktore," in Umniagin, ed., *Vospominaniia solovetskih uznikov*, 3:331.

45. Brodskii, *Solovki: Dvadtsat' let*, 230.

46. Shiriaev, *Neugasimaia lampada*, 249–70, 357–59; Rozanov, *Solovetskii kontslager' v monastyre*, 255.

47. Shaufel'berger, "Solovki," in Umniagin, ed., *Vospominaniia solovetskih uznikov*, 1:650.

48. Pol'skii, "Publikatsii o Solovkakh," in Umniagin, ed., *Vospominaniia solovetskih uznikov*, 2:80.

49. Andreevskii, "Episkop Maksim Serpukhovskoi," in Umniagin, ed., *Vospominaniia solovetskih uznikov*, 3:334. Bishop Maksim would soon thereafter be arrested for conducting religious ordinances and was executed in 1931. Soshina, *Na Solovkakh*, 26.

50. Leonardovich, "Na ostrovakh pytok i smerti," in Umniagin, ed., *Vospominaniia solovetskih uznikov*, 1:614–15.

51. Feodosii, "Moi vospominaniia," in Umniagin, ed., *Vospominaniia solovetskih uznikov*, 3:98. According to a different account, the authorities initially

had his body put in a common grave but later gave permission for a separate burial. Brodskii, *Solovki: Dvadtsat' let*, 237.

52. Reznikova, *Pravoslavie na Solovkakh*, 23.

53. Pol'skii, "Publikatsii o Solovkakh," in Umniagin, ed., *Vospominaniia solovetskikh uznikov*, 2:72; Feodosii, "Moi vospominaniia," in Umniagin, ed., *Vospominaniia solovetskikh uznikov*, 3:91.

54. Klinger, "Solovetskaia katorga," in Umniagin, ed., *Vospominaniia solovetskikh uznikov*, 1:106; Solonevich, "Molodezh' v GPU," in Umniagin, ed., *Vospominaniia solovetskikh uznikov*, 2:385–86; Kureishi, "Piat' let v sovetskikh tiur'makh," in Umniagin, ed., *Vospominaniia solovetskikh uznikov*, 2:135; V. N. I., "Solovetskii kontslager'," in Umniagin, ed., *Vospominaniia solovetskikh uznikov*, 3:59; Nikona, "So slov ochevidtsa . . . ," in Umniagin, ed., *Vospominaniia solovetskikh uznikov*, 3:53.

55. Volkov, "Pogruzhenie vo t'mu," in Umniagin, ed., *Vospominaniia solovetskikh uznikov*, 3:248.

56. Feodosii, "Moi vospominaniia," in Umniagin, ed., *Vospominaniia solovetskikh uznikov*, 3:86.

57. Feodosii, in Umniagin, ed., 3:99.

58. Andreevskii, "Vospominaniia o episkope Viktore," in Umniagin, ed., *Vospominaniia solovetskikh uznikov*, 3:331.

59. Feodosii, "Moi vospominaniia," in Umniagin, ed., *Vospominaniia solovetskikh uznikov*, 3:91–93.

60. Freeze, "Counter-Reformation in Russian Orthodoxy," 306.

61. Klinger, "Solovetskaia katorga," in Umniagin, ed., *Vospominaniia solovetskikh uznikov*, 1:107.

62. Feodosii, "Moi vospominaniia," in Umniagin, ed., *Vospominaniia solovetskikh uznikov*, 3:99.

63. Shkarovskii, "The Russian Orthodox Church," 369–70.

64. Pol'skii, "Publikatsii o Solovkakh," in Umniagin, ed., *Vospominaniia solovetskikh uznikov*, 2:76–78.

65. "Obrashchenie Solovetskikh episkopov," 102–7.

66. Cited in Shkarovskii, "The Russian Orthodox Church," 370.

67. Andreevskii, "Episkop Maksim Serpukhovskoi," in Umniagin, ed., *Vospominaniia solovetskikh uznikov*, 3:337–39.

68. Brodskii, *Solovki: Dvadtsat' let*, 217; Osipova, "Skvoz' ogn' muchenii," 14–15.

69. Shkarovskii, "The Russian Orthodox Church," 377–78.

70. Reznikova, *Pravoslavie na Solovkakh*, 26–27.

71. Sources on Ilarion are mixed, with some memoirs placing him in the Josephite camp while Orthodox accounts claim that he remained fully loyal to Sergius. Ioann, *Tserkovnye raskoly*, 128–29.

72. Likhachev, *Reflections*, 167–68, 173.

73. Brodskii, *Solovki: Dvadtsat' let*, 240; Likhachev, *Reflections*, 170.
74. Andreevskii, "Vospominaniia o episkope Viktore," in Umniagin, ed., *Vospominaniia solovetskih uznikov*, 3:330–31.
75. Andreevskii, "Katakombnye bogosluzheniia," in Umniagin, ed., *Vospominaniia solovetskih uznikov*, 3:312–13.
76. Andreevskii, "Episkop Maksim Serpukhovskoi," in Umniagin, ed., *Vospominaniia solovetskih uznikov*, 3:336–39.
77. Andreevskii, in Umniagin, ed., 3:339.
78. Ioann, *Tserkovnye raskoly*, 195–236
79. Baran, *Dissent on the Margins*, 82–85.
80. Solonevich, "Molodezh' v GPU," in Umniagin, ed., *Vospominaniia solovetskih uznikov*, 2:385.

BIBLIOGRAPHY

Applebaum, Anne. *Gulag: A History*. New York: Doubleday, 2003.
Baran, Emily. *Dissent on the Margins: How the Soviet Union's Jehovah's Witnesses Defied Communism and Lived to Preach about It*. New York: Oxford University Press, 2014.
Brodskii, Iurii. *Solovki: Dvadtsat' let osobogo naznacheniia*. Moscow: ROSSPEN, 2002.
———. *Solovki: Labirint preobrazhenii*. Moscow: Novaia Gazeta, 2017.
Chirkov, Iu. I. *A bylo vse tak. . . .* Moscow: Politizdat, 1991.
David-Fox, Michael. *Showcasing the Great Experiment: Cultural Diplomacy and Western Visitors to the Soviet Union, 1921–1941*. Oxford: Oxford University Press, 2012.
Freeze, Gregory L. "Counter-Reformation in Russian Orthodoxy: Popular Response to Religious Innovation, 1922–1925," *Slavic Review* 54, no. 2 (Summer 1995): 305–39.
Galmarini, Maria. "Defending the Rights of Gulag Prisoners: The Story of the Political Red Cross, 1928–38." *Russian Review* 71, no. 1 (January 2012): 6–29.
Gullotta, Andrea. *Intellectual Life and Literature at Solovki, 1923–1930: The Paris of the Northern Concentration Camps*. Cambridge, UK: Legenda, 2018.
Hiatt, Kathleen. "Sedition and the Sacred: The Political Repression of Religious Figures in Stalinist Ukraine, 1930–1955." PhD diss., Indiana University, 2016.
Husband, William B. *"Godless Communists": Atheism and Society in Soviet Russia, 1917–1932*. DeKalb: Northern Illinois University Press, 2000.
Ioann. *Tserkovnye raskoly v russkoi tserkvi 20-x i 30-x godov XX stoletiia*. Sortavala, Russia: Izdanie Sortaval'skoi knizhnoi tipografii, 1993.

Jakobson, Michael. *Origins of the Gulag: The Soviet Prison Camp System, 1917–1934.* Lexington: University Press of Kentucky, 1993.
Keller, Shoshana. *To Moscow, Not Mecca: The Soviet Campaign against Islam in Central Asia, 1917–1941.* Westport, CT: Praeger, 2001.
Kiselev-Gromov, N. *S.L.O.N.: Solovetskii les osobogo naznacheniia.* Arkhangel'sk, Russia: Tur, 2009.
Kokurin, A. I., and N. V. Petrov, eds. *GULAG: Glavnoe upravlenie lagerei, 1918–1960.* Moscow: Mezhdunarodnyi fond "Demokratiia," 2000.
Kotkin, Stephen. *Stalin: Paradoxes of Power, 1878–1929.* New York: Penguin, 2014.
Likhachev, Dmitry S. *Reflections on the Russian Soul: A Memoir.* Budapest: CEU Press, 2000.
"Obrashchenie Solovetskikh episkopov," *Sever,* 1990, no. 9:101–7.
Osipova, I. I. *"Skvoz' ogn' muchenii i vodu slez...": Goneniia na Istinno-Pravoslavnuiu Tserkov'.* Moscow: Serebrianye niti, 1998.
——— . *"V iazvakh svoikh sokroi menia...": Goneniia na Katolicheskuiu Terkov' v SSSR.* Moscow: Serebrianye niti, 1996.
Peris, Daniel. *Storming the Heavens: The Soviet League of the Militant Godless.* Ithaca, NY: Cornell University Press, 1998.
Rayner, O. T., trans. *The Criminal Code of the Russian Socialist Federative Soviet Republic.* London: H.M.S.O., 1925.
Reznikova, Irina. *Pravoslavie na Solovkakh: Materialy po istorii Solovetskogo lageria.* Saint Petersburg: Memorial, 1994.
Robson, Roy. *Solovki: The Story of Russia Told through Its Most Remarkable Islands.* New Haven, CT: Yale University Press, 2004.
Roslof, Edward E. *Red Priests: Renovationism, Russian Orthodoxy, and Revolution, 1905–1946.* Bloomington: Indiana University Press, 2002.
Rozanov, Mikhail. *Solovetskii kontslager' v monastyre, 1922–1939 gody.* Vol. 1. N.p.: Izd. Avtora, 1979.
Shiriaev, B. N. *Neugasimaia lampada.* Moscow: T-vo rus. khudozh., 1991.
Shkarovskii, Mikhail V. "The Russian Orthodox Church versus the State: The Josephite Movement, 1927–1940," *Slavic Review* 54, no. 2 (Summer 1995): 365–84.
Smirnov, M. B., ed. *Sistema ispravitel'no-trudovykh lagerei v SSSR, 1923–1960: Spravochnik.* Moscow: Zven'ia, 1998.
Solomon, Peter H., Jr. "Soviet Penal Policy, 1917–1934: A Reinterpretation." *Slavic Review* 39, no. 2 (June 1980): 195–217.
Solzhenitsyn, Aleksandr. *The Gulag Archipelago, 1918–1956: An Experiment in Literary Investigation.* Three vols. Translated by Thomas P. Whitney. New York: Harper & Row, 1974–1978.

Soshina, Antonina Alekseevna. *Na Solovkakh protiv voli: Sud'by i sroki, 1923–1939.* Moscow: Izdatel'stvo TSM, 2014.

Sykes, Gresham. *Society of Captives: A Study of a Maximum Security Prison.* Princeton, NJ: Princeton University Press, 1958.

Umniagin, Viacheslav, ed. *Vospominaniia solovetskikh uznikov.* Five vols. Solovki: Izdanie Solovetskogo monastyria, 2013–2018.

Vtorova-Iafa, O. "Avgorovy ostrova." *Istina i zhizn'*, no. 10 (1995): 32–47.

JEFFREY S. HARDY is Associate Professor of History at Brigham Young University. He is author of several articles and one book, *The Gulag after Stalin.*

THREE

CENSORING THE MAIL IN STALIN'S MULTIETHNIC PENAL SYSTEM

The Use of Languages Other Than Russian in Soviet Inmate Correspondence

EMILY D. JOHNSON

"But those from other countries, they didn't let them write; they weren't allowed. They didn't have permission. Because, if you didn't know how to write in Russian, well, there just wouldn't be any letters.... For instance, the Baltics, Latvia.... If you could write in Russian, then you wrote.... If you didn't, then what could you write? They didn't let you write."

—Labor camp survivor from
Western Ukraine, 2009 interview

"Happy, as always after having received mail from you, I returned to the dormitory. A fellow from Riga stopped by. I wrote a letter for him to send home (he doesn't know Russian)."

—Letter from the political prisoner Arsenii Formakov to his wife,
Anna Ivanovna Formakova, April 10, 1945

IT IS COMMON FOR STALIN-ERA labor camp and prison survivors to report in memoirs and interviews that regulations in their places of confinement prohibited them from corresponding in languages other than Russian.[1] Internal evidence in many surviving examples of labor-camp correspondence from the period, including the letter I cite above, also supports the view that prisoners could use the official camp mail system only if they—and their correspondents— could write in Russian.[2] As a result, researchers who work on the Soviet labor camp system or the purges that targeted minority groups within the Soviet Union have sometimes suggested that Stalin-era correspondence rules completely barred inmates from writing in languages other than Russian.[3]

In fact, however, the situation regarding language policy in the Soviet Union's labor camps and prisons as it pertained to the private correspondence of inmates is not as clear as such a blanket statement might suggest. Centrally issued regulations governing prisoner mail in the Soviet Union allowed for correspondence in the state's minority languages in both the early 1920s and throughout the Stalin period. Moreover, for the late 1930s and the 1940s, elaborate instructions for processing such mail exist in the archives of the NKVD, MVD, and the Gulag itself. This, of course, does not mean that the system functioned as it was supposed to: in many places, local camp officials probably did ban inmates from sending mail in languages other than Russian with an eye to simplifying operations. Censors may also have chosen to toss or burn letters written in unfamiliar languages. Camp inspection reports show that in at least some locations and years, mail written in languages other than Russian languished for long periods because of a lack of translators or was never delivered.[4]

The fact that mail composed in Russian moved much more efficiently might, in and of itself, have led many inmates to view writing in other languages as either pointless or de facto banned. Inmates learned much of what they knew about camp rules from each other: camp officials did not offer a detailed orientation to new arrivals on the ins and outs of camp life. A poster listing basic rules was supposed to hang in every barracks, but these, NKVD reports indicate, were often stripped off and used as smoking paper or defaced in ways that necessitated their removal by camp officials.[5] Regarding correspondence, such posters would, in any case, have told inmates at most how many letters they might hope to send a month or year and offered a bare bones list of the topics inmates were, in theory at least, not allowed to address in letters (e.g., the geographic location of the camp, work assignments, or the schedules that governed camp life). I have not found a single poster that mentions language.

Despite all the obstacles, prisoners did write letters in their native languages. They threw illicit letters written in their own languages from trains and tried to smuggle them out of investigative prisons before they left the republics in which they lived.[6] They exchanged handmade greeting cards written in languages other than Russian with sweethearts they met in camp and passed letters out of camp with free laborers, hoping that, in an area with many special settlers and exiles who spoke their language, an extra letter in Lithuanian or Latvian would not attract attention.[7] They also, in at least some cases, managed to write home in their native languages through the legal camp mail system. Repositories located in former Soviet republics such as the Museum of the Occupation of Latvia in Riga contain collections of camp correspondence in national languages, including some letters that are clearly marked with camp censorship stamps and/or blacking in a way that suggests they passed through the regular camp mail.[8] Moreover, even archives that do not have complete letters in national languages often contain pieces of correspondence that, although largely written in Russian, incorporate words, phrases, or entire passages in another Soviet language.

This article looks at surviving samples of inmate letters written wholly or partly in a variety of the Soviet Union's minority languages (Ukrainian, Udmurt, several dialects associated with Islamic minorities in the Soviet South, Latvian, and Lithuanian).[9] I argue here that by writing letters in their native tongues or even adding small snippets of text in a minority language to pieces of Russian-language correspondence, inmates did not simply aim to facilitate communication with relatives who may not have had a solid command of Russian. Their choice of language also reflects other factors, including a desire to establish a feeling of emotional closeness with those back home and efforts to lay claim to what they perceived as their authentic national selves and voices. As scholars at the Museum of the Occupation of Latvia note, the efforts of minority prisoners to correspond in languages other than Russian despite real obstacles suggest that they experienced profound "longing for... communication in their native language."[10] The use of Soviet minority languages in correspondence can also potentially read as resistance against both Russification and/or Sovietization, including the forms of "reforging" that were supposed to take place in camp. Describing the non-Russian political prisoners with whom he served camp sentences during the late Soviet period, Grigorii Petrovich Kutsenko, the head of the Kyiv Society of Political Prisoners and the Repressed, noted in a 2009 interview, "None of the prisoners wanted to write in Russian although they understood, they knew [that corresponding in any other language would lead to long delays]. If you were convicted because you were a Lithuanian, then you wanted to be a Lithuanian, and you wanted to address your children and your loved ones in Lithuanian."[11] Some Stalin-era inmates doubtless chose to write in languages other than Russian out of similar oppositional and nationalistic convictions.[12] However, even in illicitly mailed letters, few Stalin-era prisoners risked explicitly voicing oppositional sentiments. Minority inmates could, however, articulate longing for home and family in letters with little risk, and often such emotional notes coincide, in their correspondence, with attempts to employ a national language for self-expression.

Of course, the idea that languages are easily defined and stable entities and that "native" speakers use them in a consistent way throughout their adult lives is as much of an artificial construct as the notion of national identity.[13] A number of the letters that I will discuss in this article feature dialects that combine elements drawn from multiple Soviet languages. Did the prisoners who wrote such letters speak in these creole forms in their home communities before imprisonment, or did their language usage evolve as the result of years spent in multiethnic camps where Russian represented a lingua franca and pidgin forms abounded? Certainly, some inmates came from areas where a "hybrid dialect" was spoken: although Soviet linguists and ethnographers tried to draw clear dividing lines between the languages that the state officially recognized and promote what they deemed normative speech forms, in many regions of the USSR, as both Francine Hirsch and Yuri Slezkine show, ethnic identities were underdeveloped and/or in flux at least until the 1930s, and speech forms were slow to standardize.[14]

Even inmates from less linguistically diverse environments may, however, have begun employing mixed language forms in camp: evidence suggests that prisoner speech often changed in confinement in ways that may have facilitated the blending of languages and multilingual communicative acts. Non-native Russian speakers generally grew more fluent in Russian in camp; in memoirs, former inmates sometimes recall growing rusty in a native tongue by the end of a long sentence. Camp educators helped inmates with low literacy levels acquire new writing skills in either Russian or, depending on the site and period, in a dominant regional language that may or may not have corresponded to what they spoke at home. Inmates learned Russian-language criminal slang and Gulag-specific terminology in camp and, with the help of the camp's Cultural-Education Sector, often acquired the skill of speaking Bolshevik if they had not mastered it before arrest. Many prisoners would have struggled to describe the world of the camp without relying on the new vocabulary they had acquired within it: their prearrest lives offered no clear analogue and hence no obvious words for some aspects of Gulag reality; new facility in writing one or more languages might change how an inmate communicated with those at home. Later sections of this article will show ways in which hybrid language usage in Stalin-era prisoner correspondence reflects both evolving patterns of ethnic and linguistic identity in the Soviet Union as a whole and the Gulag's potential as a site for language learning, language loss, and linguistic transformation.

The source material I am examining in this article is both hard to find and difficult to work with, so my sample is relatively small; it includes examples of correspondence by twenty-four Stalin-era inmates. In some cases, determining which language an inmate used constituted a challenge: in addition to dialectical variation, orthographic and grammatical errors, poor handwriting, and the use of scripts that were officially abandoned by the 1930s complicated my efforts to secure translations. Relatively few examples of inmate correspondence in languages other than Russian have reached the best-known repositories in Moscow and St. Petersburg, including, specifically, the Memorial archives. Such letters tend instead to be found in provincial areas of the Russian Federation with large minority populations and also, of course, in former Soviet republics. Even in such places, finding non-Russian-language letters that clearly and unequivocally passed through the labor camp censorship system, as evidenced by camp censorship stamps and/or blacking marks, is challenging. For this project, I examined letters that traveled both legally and illicitly as well as some pieces of correspondence that cannot definitively be categorized. I included both archival documents and printed letters, provided they were published in the language(s) in which they were written as opposed to in translation.

In order to provide a clearer context for the documents I examine, I preface my discussion of individual letters with an account of the ways in which correspondence written in languages other than Russian was supposed to be processed in the camps in various periods and places. Because these regulations were implemented so imperfectly in local areas, they represent an excellent example of the larger issues of enforcement that plagued the camp system as a whole. As Steven Barnes notes, centrally issued Gulag and NKVD directives were often "altered, ignored, or undermined" by local camp administrations because they were contradictory or unrealistic given shortages of materials and personnel.[15] The idea that letters in all the Soviet Union's languages could be censored by the state's far-flung and underfunded camp system was never realistic. It is not surprising that the rules and procedures I describe below were often disregarded.

RULES AND PROCEDURES

When, following the October Revolution of 1917, the Bolshevik government assumed control of Russia's places of confinement, it left many procedures pertaining to the daily life of inmates that dated back to the Tsarist era effectively unchanged. Necessity doubtless played a role in this. Amid the turmoil of the revolution and later the civil war, stabilizing the system emerged as a key priority.[16] Provincial penal institutions, tenuously controlled from the center in the first years following the October Revolution, continued to rely on late-imperial codes unless newer directives clearly contradicted them. Another factor also promoted continuity in prison/labor camp procedures: prominent revolutionaries had, in many cases, spent time in Tsarist penal institutions and had internalized the rhythms governing prison life in the imperial period.[17] While early Bolshevik officials tried to implement a number of broad reforms to correctional policies, they seem to have accepted many basic routines involved in the operation of the prison system unquestioningly.

For the most part, early Bolshevik orders pertaining to prisoner mail and specifically to correspondence in languages other than Russian follow this general pattern. Like their immediate prerevolutionary predecessors, early Bolshevik authorities generally allowed prisoners to correspond with their loved ones (provided, of course, they could secure writing implements and paper) but subjected all incoming and outgoing mail to inspection, by and large concentrating censorship work in local institutions.[18] The prison warden himself or a deputy he selected for the task had responsibility for reviewing the letters of prisoners already sentenced for crimes. In the case of individuals held in connection with ongoing investigations, the administrative unit conducting the inquiry could choose to inspect all mail and could also curtail a prisoner's correspondence privileges if this seemed in the interest of the case.[19] Local control over the censorship of prisoner mail was so clearly established as a principle that, in the 1920s, central administrative bodies in Moscow occasionally rebuked local camp and prison bosses for unnecessarily forwarding private prisoner correspondence for inspection.[20] With the exception of international mail (prisoners could still send letters abroad to some extent during the 1920s) and the correspondence of certain high-profile political offenders, whose mail was censored in Moscow at the main VChK/GPU headquarters before being passed on to the Political Red Cross or the postal system for delivery, mail censorship was supposed to take place on site.[21]

For the most part, this principle of local control seems to have applied even to correspondence in languages other than Russian: camp bosses and prison wardens were expected to find translators and manage on their own. For instance, memoirs indicate that on Solovki in the 1920s, Vladimir Krivosh-Nemanich, a Serbian linguist who had served the Russian state in a variety of colorful capacities, including as a cryptographer and as the supervisor of the tsar's private library, was often called on by the camp censorship office to translate letters. Neither his status as a foreigner nor his political conviction—he was sentenced to Solovki for spying—disqualified him from such assignments: he knew, according to some sources, as many as forty languages.[22]

In camp locations with less cosmopolitan populations than Solovki, censoring mail in languages other than Russian caused complications that in some respects recall the struggles faced by Tsarist officials in far-flung locations in Siberia when processing the foreign-language mail of prominent exiles.[23] Perhaps because finding appropriate translators for all the languages that prisoners might use was not feasible in many camps, correspondence in languages other than Russian does appear to have been banned in some places of confinement even in the 1920s, when correctional regimes were generally more permissive in regard to correspondence privileges than in later decades. The files of the organization E. P. Peshkova: Pomoshch' politicheskim zakliuchennym (E. P. Peshkova: Aid for Political Prisoners) in GARF are interesting in this respect. Although this fund contains records that show some prisoners were able to send letters written in languages other than Russian—even in some cases correspondence that went abroad—it also reports on bans.[24] One letter sent from Peshkova's offices to the relative of a prisoner in 1926, for instance, notes, "I enclose the letter we received from you for L. E. Tsyrul'nikov, an inmate in the Suzdal camp, and inform you that it cannot be forwarded to him ... because correspondence with inmates can only be conducted in the Russian language."[25]

In the 1930s and 1940s, as the system of control over prisoner correspondence grew progressively more formalized, the translation of non-Russian letters remained primarily the responsibility of local camp officials. Failures to provide translation services and ensure the timely delivery of prisoner mail in languages other than Russian emerged as a point of concern in the labor camp system in the early 1930s amid the Union-wide campaign to foster the development of national identity among smaller "national minorities" (*natsmeny*). Often isolated in special national-minority brigades and barracks, supposedly under the theory that this would help them become more nationally conscious, Central Asian prisoners struggled to access camp services, including the legal mail system, because of language barriers.[26] In Dmitlag (Moscow region) in the early 1930s, as a step toward resolving such problems, special legal and correspondence bureaus were set up to provide assistance to minorities in their own languages. Translating letters, memoranda, inmate files, and newspaper articles between a variety of Soviet national languages and Russian represented an established part of camp life.[27] Nonetheless, orders suggest that the processing of correspondence for this contingent remained a problem because of a lack of qualified censors.[28] This only exacerbated more general deficiencies in the camp's postal units: orders issued in response to inspection reports from the 1930s often describe huge backlogs of undelivered letters and packages at camp outposts in Dmitlag—a fact that, as officials acknowledged, hurt inmate morale.[29]

The special instructions issued to camp censors in 1939 and 1947 largely codified the system for processing inmate mail in languages other than Russian that I outline above. Both the 1939 and 1947 instructions note that if a camp censorship department received a letter in a language that none of the censors knew, the camp should find a free laborer who could translate, or, failing that, a prisoner might be given the duty with the approval of the camp security office.

Inmates used as translators should, instructions warned, be sworn to secrecy and informed that they bore legal responsibility for the accuracy of their translations. Moreover, they were confined to mechanical translation: they were to have no part in deciding whether to pass or confiscate letters; such decisions represented the responsibility of the censor.[30] In a sign of how important such translators were to operations, instructions warned camps not to transfer prisoners used as translators to other outposts or camps unless someone else could be found to do the job.[31]

Using prisoners as translators in censorship offices was common throughout the Stalin period. In fact, when official reports, memoirs, and interviews with camp survivors mention translators, they are almost invariably inmates. Although the 1939 instruction banned using those convicted of counterrevolutionary crimes in such positions and the 1947 decree stipulated that only inmates convicted of "petty and insignificant crimes" could serve as translators, these restrictions seem to have been regularly ignored.[32] As late as the early 1950s, political criminals were occasionally employed not just as translators but even as censors in some camps.[33] Even if prisoners were not formally designated as censors, they might de facto take on such a role. Milja Tamm, an Estonian labor camp survivor sentenced as a political offender, reports in a memoir that while held in Kengir in the early 1950s, she translated letters in Estonian and German for the censor and eventually became so trusted that she no longer had to produce written translations: "They left it to me to cross out anything I considered unsuitable. Of course, it did not look right if a letter went out without some 'crossings out.'"[34] Tamm notes that because of her work in the censorship department, some of the other Estonian inmates in the camp "began to label me a Communist. I had no alternative. I think everyone in such a situation would look to survival."[35]

An inmate who was perceived as working closely with the camp's security apparatus might easily, as Tamm hints above, be labeled an informant, a dangerous identity in camp, particularly in the postwar era when hardened military veterans and partisans from newly reoccupied areas, including the Baltics and Ukraine, were absorbed into the camp system. Camp reports from the late 1940s and early 1950s are filled with accounts of the murder of informants.[36] Camp security officers struggled to recruit informants from among inmates labeled as Ukrainian nationalists as well as prisoners from the Baltic republics and Belarus.[37] Evidence from postwar camp inspection reports and orders suggests that camp officials also struggled to recruit translators from these populations probably both because inmates feared being suspected of serving as informants and because these areas had been forcibly annexed to the Soviet Union so recently, which would have made finding qualified translators more complicated. When inspection reports reference mail backlogs and failure to deliver correspondence in languages other than Russian because of an inability to find translators, often the Baltic languages are referenced specifically. For example, a report describing the state of Peschanlag (Karaganda, Kazakh SSR) in 1951 notes, "Letters and packages that arrived addressed to prisoners in the camp were distributed to them in a timely fashion with the exception of letters written in German, Latvian, Estonian and Lithuanian, which did not reach addressees because there were no censors capable of translating the texts of letters in the aforementioned languages. It was not possible to find such translators on site."[38] Since labor camps seem not to have tracked the volume of prisoner correspondence in languages other than Russian separately, it is hard to gain a sense of the volume of correspondence that camps received in languages other than Russian.[39]

Central decrees do sometimes acknowledge the possibility that it might not always be possible to find a qualified translator for a specific language in a given camp outpost or prison. For instance, the rules issued in 1946 for processing the correspondence of those sentenced as hard labor convicts (*katorzhniki*) suggested that, if no appropriate translator could be found, letters should be sent to the Prison Section (*Tiuremnyi otdel*) of the MVD in Moscow or one of its regional equivalents for translation.[40] Since letters then needed to be returned to the original penal site for censorship before being sent to their addressees, this unwieldy process, each stage of which involved separate paperwork and a new opportunity for the letter to be mislaid, led to substantial delays.[41] Backlogs in processing mail and evidence of carelessness in recruiting translators or reviewing their work could lead to write-ups in inspection reports and sanctions, and yet the camps were chronically understaffed, and the employees they did manage to recruit, particularly for poorly paid posts such as camp censor, were generally not well educated. Given the inherent difficulties in trying to process mail in the Soviet Union's diverse languages in distant camp outposts using local manpower, it is understandable that camp staff sometimes forbade inmates to write in languages other than Russian even if that were not required by the instructions issued in Moscow.

THE USE OF LANGUAGES OTHER THAN RUSSIAN IN INMATE CORRESPONDENCE

Even though some camps forbade prisoners from corresponding in languages other than Russian and, in others, censorship delays discouraged such efforts at communication, at least some Gulag inmates in the Stalin period managed to send home letters that were wholly or partly composed in Soviet minority languages. The factors that led inmates to write in minority languages varied and included both practical and emotional considerations. First and most obviously, corresponding in languages other than Russian allowed prisoners to more directly convey information to primarily non-Russian-speaking correspondents. Vasilii Kharitonovich Vasilenko's choice of language in the letters he sent home was most likely motivated by such practical considerations.

Vasilenko was from a farming community where Ukrainian probably constituted the primary communicative medium. He was working as the chair of the inspection commission at a collective farm in Tsepki, in Gadiachskii district of the Poltava oblast, when he was arrested in 1937—shortly after, family accounts suggest, he had tried to expose the misuse of state property by the farm's management. Sentenced to five years in a labor colony for low-level offenders, he was held in Molotovsk (Severodvinsk) in the Arkhangelsk region, where he worked in both a tailoring workshop and outside on construction projects. Released to serve on the front lines during World War II, he died in battle in March 1944. During the years that Vasilenko spent in the Arkhangelsk region, he wrote home in Ukrainian, sending letters filled with planting advice and requests for updates on the harvest and the health of specific farm animals.

Although some of these letters clearly passed illegally, the way in which others traveled cannot be determined with absolute certainty. They do not bear censorship stamps or signatures, but sometimes such marks were applied to envelopes, which in this case have been lost. Moreover, censorship protocols in labor colonies were often lighter than in camps and prisons.[42] Internal evidence within the Vasilenko correspondence suggests that he made use of both legal and illicit channels of communication and that he sent home, in addition to letters, either small sums of money or some other form of support. Notably, at the end of a letter dated May 24, 1939, that presumably passed illegally, Vasilenko wrote, "My dearest Marusia, I wasn't able to send off this letter today, so I wanted to add just a few words to it. When you receive a letter that has something enclosed in it from me, don't list everything that you received. Instead just note that you received a very valuable letter, and everything will be clear to me."[43]

Ukrainian was spoken widely enough in the Soviet Union and is close enough to Russian in its written form that finding translators should have, at least theoretically, presented less of a challenge for camps. Udmurt, the native language of Nikolai Grigor'evich Kutiavin, would doubtless have created more problems. The correspondence that survives from the four years Kutiavin spent in labor camps reveals some of the complex emotional factors that affected language choices in prisoner letters.

Kutiavin was a peasant with a primary education who was working on a collective farm in the village of Udino in the Iarskii region of Udmurtiia at the time of his arrest in 1932. He received a five-year sentence under article 58 and was sent first to Balakhlag (Nizhegorod region) and then in 1935 to Vetlag (Moscow-Kursk railway, Sukhobezvodnoe station), where he passed away in 1936. Most of the correspondence he sent home to his family during the years of his confinement probably passed officially: although the four letters that survive do not bear censorship marks or stamps, two of the letters list his camp's name and official mailing address, and one references its bimonthly mail collection days.[44] For the most part, Kutiavin wrote home in simple Russian marred occasionally by grammar and spelling errors. One lengthy letter to his wife and children dated April 25, 1935, however, includes an extended passage written mostly in Udmurt but with occasional interpolated Russian words. Although from the standpoint of the information it contains about life in Vetlag, this letter differs little from the Russian-language correspondence that Kutiavin penned, it is notably more emotional. In the section of the letter that is written mostly in Udmurt, Kutiavin describes his reaction to a recent letter from his brother-in-law:

> Now I will write in Udmurt. I received the letter and I was so happy. I read it and I was so upset. I started crying. He writes that [my] father-in-law and mother-in-law have already died. Now I will never see them again. He writes that [my] children are really suffering. They can't even send a package. But the letter I received made me so happy because I learned how you are faring. I really want to know where my children are living: in whose house [are they living] and what are they eating; who has taken them in?[45]

Did Kutiavin switch languages midletter because such heartfelt sentiments required expression in the language he associated with home and family life? This letter, which, unlike much of the rest of Kutiavin's correspondence, does not reference the camp directly or contain an official return address, may well have traveled illegally, but the fact that it opens in Russian and switches to Udmurt only after a paragraph of text suggests that the choice of language reflects something other than means of transmission. None of the Russian-language letters that Kutiavin sent is as personal in tone or accords so little space to discussions of the mechanics of camp life. In the Udmurt passage, Kutiavin merely says about himself, "I too am living badly. They don't give us much bread, it's not enough, and they make us work a lot. But what can you do? There's nothing to be done. So far, I am well, and I can work so long as God gives me strength. Perhaps someday I will get [back] to you. Be well. Write me a letter."[46] Again, emotional notes predominate here. In this letter, we do not hear that Kutiavin is working as a carpenter or learn how much money he has in his account, as we do in his Russian-language letters, and we do not hear questions about the harvest; instead, we hear longing for home and family.

Yet it is important to note that if Kutiavin reached for Udmurt as a means of expressing emotion, his use of this language seems imperfect. The Russian words that are interpolated into his Udmurt sentences—*letter, package, all the same, only, healthy* (*pis'mo, posylka, vse-taki, tol'ko, zdorov*)—suggest that he may have been more comfortable writing in Russian. This would not be surprising given that Udmurt written culture remained underdeveloped at least until the 1920s: the first Udmurt-language newspaper did not appear until 1914 and, like Kutiavin's letters, featured interpolated Russian words and phrases.[47] Until Soviet nation-building efforts created significant numbers of Udmurt schools and cultural organizations and standardized the Udmurt alphabet in the mid-1920s and early 1930s, literacy in the language was low.[48] Kutiavin probably received most of his primary education in Russian and had more experience writing in that language. He may have been particularly inclined to shift to Russian when referencing articles and concepts that had outsize importance in the Gulag (*package, letter, health*) since he experienced this world largely in Russian.

Letters written primarily in Russian but with interpolated words from a national language are at least as common as texts like the Kutiavin letter I describe above, featuring a minority language peppered with occasional Russian words. Even if prisoners could not regularly correspond in their national languages, they sometimes managed to include at least isolated words and phrases in their native tongue in Russian-language letters that passed legally. In some cases, prisoners added fragments of native language to their letters because this allowed them to compactly convey information that would have been less clear in Russian. For example, when Ignas Urbaitis wrote the name of a popular Lithuanian stationary store, the Press Foundation (*Spaudos fondas*), in Cyrillic in one of his letters, clarity was probably a primary consideration. Place names, book and periodical titles, and the names of organizations often appear in minority languages, either in the original script or in Cyrillic, within letters otherwise penned in Russian.[49] Occasionally prisoners used minority-language phrases as a kind of code in the hope of evading camp or military censorship. Arsenii Formakov, for instance, slipped the phrase "guards are on the watch towers" in Latvian into a letter he composed between January 1 and January 7, 1945, and dispatched illegally.[50] Such efforts at subterfuge were high risk and seem to have been relatively rare. Even if sent illicitly, letters, as many inmates would have known, could be intercepted in the secret censorship units that operated within Soviet postal stations or, during the war, by military censors.

Often, isolated phrases and sentences in minority languages in letters that otherwise are written in Russian seem intended to convey emotion as opposed to information. In this sense, such passages reflect in miniature some of the tendencies I highlighted in the lengthy Udmurt passage from the Kutiavin letter I cited above. A letter sent home to Mamadysh in the Tatar ASSR by Mirsaid Mustafich Khasanov (1900–44), a former senior agronomist and party member who was serving an eight-year term at the Mes'iu camp outpost in Sevzheldorlag, Komi ASSR, provides an excellent example of this phenomenon. Although largely written in Russian, the letter, which is dated November 7, 1943, contains a very faint line in Arabic script in one margin and a single Arabic-script word below Khasanov's signature. The Arabic-script margin note duplicates and underscores a command provided in Russian above it: "Sajida and Yankaz! Write to me more frequently."[51] Although Khasanov was Tatar ethnically, the line in Arabic script contains a mixture of linguistic elements. The name Sajida is spelled with a hard Tatar *j*, and yet much of the rest of the sentence is in what appears to be Azerbaijani. The spelling of the word *write* (*khaṭ*) is odd, and the word for *more frequently* (*chashche*) is transliterated Russian. Most likely Khasanov, who was born in 1900, had only limited writing skills in his native language. Notably the Arabic script that he employed had ceased to be used for either Azerbaijani or Tatar by the 1930s as a result of a Soviet Latinization campaign. The intake form that Khasanov's son completed when he donated the letter to the Moscow branch of Memorial lists Khasanov as having a higher education and from a petty bourgeois class background. Perhaps he learned Arabic script in childhood, but most of his education probably took place in Russian. The single Arabic-script word that appears below Khasanov's signature simply repeats his name.

Simple as they are, the small notes that Khasanov appended in non-Russian script are potentially important as markers of identity that underscore his emotional ties to his home community and nationality. In making these notes, he stepped outside of a Russian-language context and reached for other forms of belonging, associated perhaps with the world of childhood and family, despite the fact that his writing skills in Arabic were relatively primitive and he was Russified enough that his "native language" reads as a kind of creole that blends elements drawn from a variety of Soviet languages.

Did the blended language that Khasanov employed in the marginal note he appended to his letter really reflect the dialect he spoke at home with his family, or had his speech evolved as the result of years spent in the multiethnic labor camp system? In memoirs, camp survivors have commented on the unique speech forms that emerged in mixed-ethnicity work brigades and barracks. For example, describing patterns of language usage he observed in Kengir during the postwar period, A. E. Feldman writes, "The camp produced its own unique language. The western Ukrainians, of which there were a great many in the camp after the war, took advantage of the fact that their speech could be understood and did not want to speak Russian, instead using only Ukrainian. Foreigners and residents of Central Asia, who did not know Russian at all, gradually learned their language and thought that it was Russian. In general, most of the inhabitants of the camp spoke in a wild mixture of words from different languages, which they took for Russian."[52] Nonetheless, the language of home—or what they at least perceived as the language of home—exerted an enormous pull on many inmates. Familiar words, including specifically endearments and relationship terms remembered from home, often slip into inmate letters and sometimes are connected with feelings of longing. The Ukrainian poet Mikhailo Dray-Khmara, for example, wrote home to his wife and daughter from the Partisan mine and camp site in a letter dated October 14, 1936, "I am waiting for letters from my daughter [*dotsen'ki*]. I am often sad because I do not hear her favorite word 'tatunia.'" The Ukrainian words for *daughter* and *papa* in an otherwise Russian-language letter here clearly evoke the desire for togetherness.

SHIFTS IN LANGUAGE USAGE OVER TIME

Despite the pull of their native languages, if they corresponded with their families for any length of time, non-Russian Gulag inmates who began writing in minority languages often gradually drifted to the exclusive or almost exclusive use of Russian as they moved to locations that were more geographically distant from their home republics and as immersion in the multiethnic camp system, where Russian served as the lingua franca, further Russified them. Such shifts in language over time reflect the very real pressures of camp rules and censorship norms as well as greater facility in writing in Russian.

The letters of Sagdulla Khalmuradovich Khalmuradov from the archive of the Moscow Memorial society provide an example of this trend. Khalmuradov was a prominent Uzbek educator who, in the 1930s, helped found the House of Scholars (*Dom uchenykh*) in Tashkent and also served as the first director of the educational-pedagogical publishing house of the Uzbek Soviet Socialist Republic. Arrested in 1938, he was held in an investigative prison in Tashkent, internal evidence from his correspondence suggests, and then, after receiving

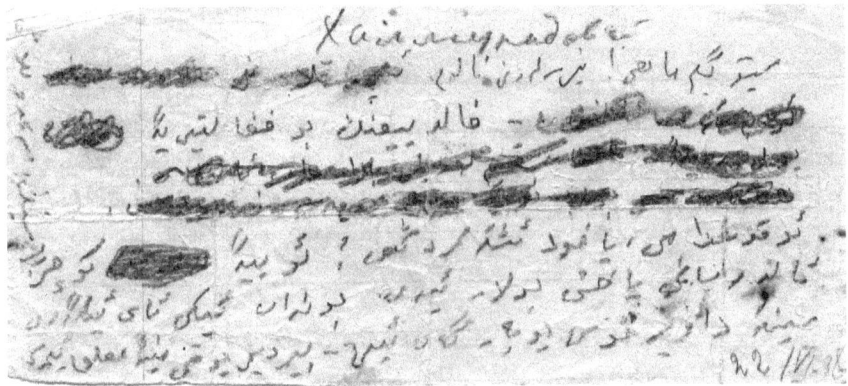

Figure 3.1. Note from Sagdulla Khalmuradovich Khalmuradov to his wife, dated June 6, 1938. Penciled response on the back of an inventory list with some apparent censorship marks. The text reads, "Dear Makhi, I got the things.... In terms of Khaldiev's actions.... Are you in school or have you started work? It would be good if you moved [him/her/yourself?] into your own house. Two months ago I sent you a document granting power of attorney, but I don't know if it was passed on to you or not. Yours, Sagdulla." Memorial Archive, Moscow f. 1, op. 1, d. 4995, l. 2.

a ten-year sentence, was moved to the Verkhne-Ural'sk prison early in 1939. He corresponded with his wife from there before being transferred to Vladivostok in May 1939. In the last letter he sent home to Tashkent in July 1939, Khalmuradov referenced a likely move to Bukhta Nagaeva and also noted that he had "become very weak recently as a result of prison, transfers between prisons, and the conditions of transport [to the Far East]."[53] Most likely, Khamuradov died shortly after sending this final letter, although no death date is listed in his Memorial file.

The collection of letters that survives from Khalmuradov's imprisonment in 1938–39 is written in a mixture of Russian and a Central Asian dialect that combines elements of Uzbek and Uyghur.[54] The file includes three small and heavily censored notes that Khalmuradov exchanged with his spouse while in the investigative prison in Tashkent, all of which were written in the couple's native dialect and on scraps of paper (see, for example, fig. 3.1). Like many notes exchanged between family members and prisoners in investigative prisons, these scraps of paper resemble something between a letter and an inventory list and doubtless were passed back and forth along with packages of clothing and food carried to the prison by Khalmuradov's spouse and with the laundry and unneeded goods she picked up. The first note is typical. On one side of a scrap of paper, Khalmuradov's wife listed what she had brought and what she had received and elliptically noted that the family remained "in the house that you saw." On the reverse, Khalmuradov explained that he could not get her a receipt showing that he had received the funds she'd tried to transfer (though he did receive the money) and enjoined her not to give up her studies and to follow the advice of her younger brothers.[55] In areas where minority languages were widely spoken, prisons did not need to search for translators and had no reason to press prisoners to communicate in Russian. Although, strictly speaking, prisoners and their relations were not supposed to use the inventory lists submitted with packages (and signed by prisoners to show receipt) to convey personal messages, often this rule was flouted, particularly in the provinces.

Aside from the inventory notes, the Khalmuradov file includes two communications on pieces of cigarette paper, also in Khalmuradov's native dialect, that were written in summer 1939, when Khalmuradov was being transported to Vladivostok from the Verkhne-Uralsk prison. "My beloved Makhi Aftab! Are you doing well? We were moved from the Ural prison and are heading towards the Far East. Don't be surprised if you don't get any word for a while.... I will write when I am settled."[56] Presumably, Khalmuradov wrapped these notes in some sort of cover that provided the family's address and threw them from the cattle car in which he was riding, and someone picked them up and mailed them. Likely train routes between Verkhne-Ural'sk and Vladivostok pass close to or through Kazakhstan, so perhaps the notes were picked up by someone who could read Khalmuradov's language. It is not clear if the two pieces of cigarette paper were sent together or separately. The messages on both are similar.

The letters that Khalmuradov sent home from both the Verkhne-Uralsk prison and the Far East were, on the other hand, written in Russian, suggesting Khalmuradov believed that corresponding in his native language was either banned or futile from these locations. He expressed himself fluidly in Russian but with some obvious grammatical and spelling mistakes, particularly in the earlier pieces of correspondence.[57] Although the sample is small (five letters in Khalmuradov's dialect, seven in Russian, written over a period of about a year), which complicates any effort to generalize, one might argue that Khalmuradov's written Russian improved over the course of his sentence. Certainly, immersion in the labor camp system, where Russian functioned as the dominant language of communication, had this effect on other inmates. For example, prisoners from the Baltics and other Western areas that were absorbed into the Soviet Union in the 1940s who arrived at their places of interment with limited knowledge of Russian generally acquired working proficiency in the language over time.[58]

Of course, a prisoner's choice of language in letters sent home was determined not only by local mail and censorship conditions and individual communicative ability; prisoners also considered the language skills of their addressees when choosing how to write, and such decisions were sometimes fraught, particularly in the case of children. In her memoir, Helgi-Alice Päts, the daughter-in-law of Estonian president Konstantin Päts, describes her efforts to locate and correspond with her two children during her internment in a labor camp in Turinsk in the 1940s. Her account shows us how the language competencies of both an interned parent and a child could change during a period of separation and how this could affect language choices in letters:

> In time I received word that my sons were at different orphanages in Ufa. I sent my first letter, in Estonian, to my older son Matti, believing that by now he had learned to write. And finally, I received a long-awaited reply from him. He had drawn on the paper even a picture of Toompea palace with a blue-black-white flag.... Matti wrote already with some Russian letters and when I finally replied to him a month later, I told him to write me in Russian because that's what he was using in school. I was allowed to write once a month. I was forgetting Estonian, and it would have become difficult to understand his letters.[59]

Here both mother and son seem to be suffering from a kind of linguistic amnesia, perhaps partly as a result of trauma. When, in June 1946, Päts was released after five years of imprisonment as part of the general amnesty announced in connection with the end of World War II, she went to Ufa to collect her older boy; the younger son had died during her internment. "Toward me ran the son who was still alive. He was now already thirteen years old. I embraced him and through the tears that covered my face, I said: 'My dear son, I have come for you.' He looked at me and said a single Estonian word, 'Forgot.' After that we spoke in Russian."[60] Language mattered profoundly to many inmates because it was intimately tied to their sense of self and their relationships with their loved ones and communities. Immersion in Stalin's multiethnic labor camp system and separation from family members could potentially erode language skills just as it made it difficult to maintain relationships.

LANGUAGE IN THE "PRISON OF PEOPLES"

In their work on Soviet nationalities policy, Yuri Slezkine, Francine Hirsch, and Terry Martin have all showed in different ways how the Bolshevik state worked in the 1920s and 1930s to foster the advancement of the minority nations it perceived as underdeveloped through a program of "compensatory nation-building" that involved the creation of alphabets, schools, periodicals, cultural institutions, and national literatures as well as preferential hiring and admissions practices.[61] Despite its reputation as "a prison of peoples" and "breaker of nations," the Soviet state, these scholars remind us, worked diligently to cultivate national identity at least in the case of the peoples it chose to recognize, effectively according each a "separate room" within the "communal apartment" of Soviet society as a whole.[62]

In some limited respects, we see this general Soviet policy of minority nation advancement within the Gulag: particularly in the 1930s, during the drive to foster national consciousness among the national minorities, labor camps might aptly be described as sites of nation-building. Camps like Dmitlag, Belbaltlag (Medvezh'ia gora), and Karlag (Karaganda region, Kazakh SSR) had translation bureaus, minority language periodicals, and cultural and educational programs for Central Asian prisoners. Even as they starved, froze, and were worked to death, prisoners were exhorted to pursue various forms of self-development in their national cultures and languages.

Yet in other key respects, the essential realities of life in the Gulag often complicated efforts by Soviet minorities to live their lives in accordance with their evolving national cultures and to realize Soviet doctrines of national development: non-Russian inmates often struggled to obtain accommodations they were supposed to be receiving, including specifically the right to access services in their native languages. In what really was a "prison of peoples," there were rarely "separate rooms" for the various nationality groups. Prisoners could and did try to cling to those who shared their language or place of origin, and *zemliachestva* (support networks based on a shared region of origin; compatriotship), a phenomenon that Gavin Slade discusses in his chapter for this volume, played an important role in the lives of some of those interned in the Gulag. However, for the most part, inmates were thrown into mixed barracks and brigades and immersed in a world where Russian—albeit often broken Russian—represented the only way to get things done. Given this reality, it is understandable that many inmates perceived labor camps and prisons as sites of Russification as much as Sovietization.

The letters that labor camp inmates managed to send home in their minority languages or in a mixture of Soviet languages provide us with an important window on this aspect of Soviet life. In them we see inmates reaching for native languages as a means of expressing love and longing even if they could not write in them perfectly, but we also see them sometimes slowly giving up efforts to write in a national language in the face of practical constraints or as Russian gradually became their primary means of communication. Dispersed in archives and private collections throughout the former Soviet republics and Russian provinces, such documents represent an important resource for studying the experiences of minority populations in the Gulag. Hopefully, over time, such material will become more readily available, and broader studies of minority language communication in the labor camp system that chart where and when inmates could most easily access the legal mail system will become possible. The national boundaries that divide Russia from other former Soviet republics often circumscribe scholarship on the Soviet labor camp system in a way that is unfortunate. Archives and museums located in different countries and operating in different national languages cannot always collaborate easily and do not necessarily know about each other's scholarship and collections. Work on the experience of specific national groups often takes place in isolation. Generalizing about Gulag correspondence on the basis of solely Russian collections is potentially misleading, and yet expanding beyond this framework and looking more broadly at the experience of non-Russian internees presents real challenges. Much, however, can be gained by working with non-Russian materials and collections.

NOTES

I would like to thank Jeff Hardy for his suggestions for improving this article. A preliminary version of this chapter was presented at a conference on "The Politics and Pragmatics of Translation in the USSR: The Daily Life of Language in a Multi-National Empire" at Columbia University's Harriman Institute. The copyright to the Formakov letter dated April 10, 1945, belongs to Stanford University. The original letter can be found in the Arsenii Ivanovich Formakov papers, Box 1, Folder 1, Hoover Institution Archives, Stanford University.

1. For example, Sabbo, "Gibel'nyi etap," 37; Jameikis, *Only Eleven Came Back*, 89; Juciute, *Footsteps in the Death Zone*, 173, 256.

2. On language restrictions on correspondence mailed into Soviet labor camps, see, for example, the letter that Ignas Urbaitis sent his son Algirdas dated March 14, 1947: "Write me a letter or a postcard in your own hand. If you cannot answer because of your weak knowledge of Russian, ask your mother to help you." Virtual Museum of the Gulag.

3. For example, Kuodyte and Tracevskis, *Siberia*, 37; Plioplys, "Letters from Siberia, Part 3," "Hope and Spirit."

4. For example, State Archive of the Russian Federation (GARF), fond(f.) R-8360, opis'(op.) 1, delo(d.) 8, list(l.) 81; GARF, f. R-9407, op. 1, d. 1488, l. 189; Dulatbekov, *Osoblagi*, 406, 416; see also Zhemkova and Kozlova, *Pravo perepiski*, 106–7.

5. For an example of a sheet of rules, see GARF, f. 9401s, op. 1a, d. 234, ll. 60–61. On the defacement of posters, see GARF, f. 9413s, op. 1s, d. 125, l. 75.

6. For example, *Estonia, 1940–1945,* 323; Justina Jonauskaite, "Pis'mo na loskute tkani"; *Soviet Deportations in Estonia,* 203–4.

7. For an example, see *Latvijas Okupacijas muzeja GadaGramata. 2000,* 334–35. On the circulation of Estonian-language correspondence in areas with many exiles, see Oispuu, "Collection and Processing," 21–26.

8. See, for example, the letter sent by Janis Dreimanis to his cousin Marte Peterson in Riga from Inta, which is dated October 25, 1951. Neither the letter nor the envelope has a censorship stamp, but a line that, judging by the context, described hard conditions in camp is blacked out. Museum of the Occupation of Latvia, Osnovnoi Muzeinii Fond (OMF) 16988/1/1. See also the letter that Bernards Upmanis sent Antonina Upmane, his mother, from Iagrinlag in Molotovsk in March 1946: Museum of the Occupation of Latvia, OMF 1439. It has a military censorship stamp and provides Upmanis's official return address, which suggests the letter traveled legally.

9. When I use the term *minority language* in this article, I mean Soviet languages other than Russian.

10. *Latvijas Okupacijas muzeja GadaGramata. 2000,* 335.

11. Kutsenko was arrested in 1984 and was sentenced to four years in a labor camp under article 78. He was finally released in January 1988.

12. As an act of resistance, Iurii Dombrovskii reportedly wrote to his mother in Latin, thereby sending his camp security officer on a wild goose chase in search of a potential translator: Arman Malumian, "I dazhe . . . ," 214–15.

13. Hirsch, *Empire of Nations,* 145–86.

14. Hirsch, 145–86; Slezkine, "The USSR as a Communal Apartment," 427–33.

15. Barnes, *Death and Redemption,* 2.

16. Adams, *The Politics of Punishment,* 194–95.

17. Jakobson, *Origins of the Gulag,* 34, 18.

18. See, for instance, GARF, f. A-353, op. 2, d. 837a, ll. 4–5.

19. Compare with the description of prerevolutionary prison censorship in Skipton and Michalove, *Postal Censorship,* 1:185, 187, 210.

20. For instance, GARF, f. 4042, op. 10, d. 8, ll. 163–64.

21. Regarding international mail, see GARF, f. 4042, op. 10, d. 8, ll. 99–104. On the role of the Political Red Cross in forwarding inmate correspondence, see GARF, f. R-8409, op. 1, d. 179, ll. 20–30. For complaints regarding delays associated with processing mail in Moscow, see GARF, f. R-8419, op. 1, d. 8, ll. 88–88 ob.

22. Zdanovich and Izmozik, *Sorok let na sekretnoi sluzhbe;* Solovieff, *School for Tchekists,* 62–63; Brodskii, *Solovki,* 84.

23. M. N. Gernet reports that an English-language letter mailed from New York to Chernyshevsky in his Viliuisk exile was sent from Iakutia to Irkutsk for translation and then forwarded on to the Third Section in St. Petersburg, where it remained. *Istoriia tsarskoi tiur'my,* 2:302.

24. GARF, f. R-8409, op. 1, d. 108, l. 125.
25. GARF, f. R-8409, op. 1, d. 106, l. 113.
26. Barnes, *Death and Redemption*, 93–95.
27. GARF, f. R-9489, op. 2, d. 5, ll. 459–59 ob.
28. GARF, f. R-9489, op. 2, d. 51, l. 23–23 ob.
29. See, for example, GARF, f. R-9489, op. 2, d. 20, l. 6.
30. GARF, f. 9401, op. 1a, d. 37, l. 95; GARF, f. 9401, op. 1a, d. 225, l. 116 ob.
31. GARF, f. 9401, op. 1a, d. 37, l. 95.
32. GARF, f. 9401, op. 1a, d. 37, l. 95; GARF, f. 9401, op. 1a, d. 225, l. 116 ob.
33. Rossi, *Spravochnik po Gulagu*, 2:276–77.
34. Tamm, "An Evil Wind," in Lie et al., *Carrying Linda's Stones*, 266–67.
35. Tamm, in Lie et al., 267.
36. See, for example, Dulatbekov, *Osoblagi*, 400, 407.
37. Dulatbekov, 143.
38. Dulatbekov, 406; see also 416.
39. Dulatbekov, 387.
40. GARF, f. 9413, op. 1, d. 70, l. 105.
41. In the post-Stalin period, Ukrainian political prisoners protested such a system because the delays it entailed limited their contact with the outside world. See the note about Sviatoslav Karavanskii in "Politzakliuchennye i ssyl'nye" and the note about Nikolai Rudchenko in "Mordovskie lageria."
42. On the censorship of mail for prisoners in labor colonies, see GARF, f. 9401s, op. 1, d. 558, ll. 342–43.
43. Memorial Archive, Moscow, f. 1, op. 3, d. 698, ll. 2–3.
44. Memorial Archive, Moscow, f. 1, op. 2, d. 2563, l. 5, l. 6 ob.
45. Memorial Archive, Moscow, f. 1, op. 2, d. 2563, l. 4, l. 8. Translation provided by Kutiavin's son Nikolai Grigor'evich in 1990, when the letters were transferred to Memorial.
46. Memorial Archive, Moscow, f. 1, op. 2, d. 2563, l. 4, l. 8.
47. Vakhrushev, "Nachalo knigoizdatel'skoi deiatel'nosti," 1261–62; Egorov, "Frazeologiia v informatsionnom pole," 19–21.
48. Vasil'eva and Vorontsov, "Natsional'naia shkola v Udmurtii," 70–76.
49. See, for example, Drai-khmara, *Tvori* 630, 640–41, 643.
50. Formakov, *Gulag Letters*, 94.
51. Memorial Archive, Moscow, f. 1, op. 3, d. 5453, l. 5. I am grateful to Amel Khalfaoui, Alexander Jabbari, Gershon Lewental, and Samuel and Mieka Hodgkin for their help in translating these notes.
52. Dulatbekov, *Osoblagi*, 741.
53. Memorial Archive, Moscow f. 1, op. 1, d. 4995, l. 24.
54. The non-Russian sections of the letters were translated by Rakhmon Inomkhojayev. Thanks to him and Paul Foster for their help.

55. Memorial Archive, Moscow f. 1, op. 1, d. 4995, l. 1.
56. Memorial Archive, Moscow f. 1, op. 1, d. 4995, ll. 4–5.
57. Memorial Archive, Moscow f. 1, op. 1, d. 4995, ll. 15, l. 16 ob., l. 23 ob.
58. See, e.g., the memoirs of Helgi-Alice Päts, in Lie et al., *Carrying Linda's Stones*, 230.
59. Päts, in Lie et al., 230.
60. Päts, in Lie et al., 233.
61. Slezkine, "The USSR as a Communal Apartment," 414.
62. Hirsch, *Empire of Nations*, 3, 5; I. Vareikis and I. Zelenskii, *Natsional'no-gosudarstvennoe razmezhivanie Srednei Azii*, 59 as cited in Slezkine, "The USSR as a Communal Apartment," 415.

BIBLIOGRAPHY

Adams, Bruce F. *The Politics of Punishment: Prison Reform in Russia, 1863–1917*. DeKalb: Northern Illinois University Press, 1996.

Barnes, Steven A. *Death and Redemption: The Gulag and the Shaping of Soviet Society*. Princeton, NJ: Princeton University Press, 2011.

Brodskii, Iurii. *Solovki: Dvadtsat' let osobogo naznacheniia*. Moscow: Rossiiskaia politicheskaia entsiklopediia; ROSSPEN, 2002.

Drai-Khmara, Mikhailo. *Tvori*. Kyiv: Naukova Dumka, 2015.

Dulatbekov, Nurlan Orynbasaruly. *Osoblagi v Kazakhstane: Stepnoi, Peschanyi, Lugovoi, Dal'nii*. Almaty: Karagandskii universitet "Bolashak," 2014.

Egorov, A. V. "Frazeologiia v informatsionnom pole gazetnogo teksta (na primere udmurtskikh gazet vremen Pervoi mirovoi voiny)." *Ezhegodnik finno-urgorskikh issledovanii* (2014): 17–22. https://cyberleninka.ru/article/v/frazeologiya-v-informatsionnom-pole-gazetnogo-teksta-na-primere-udmurtskih-gazet-vremen-pervoy-mirovoy-voyny.

Estonia, 1940–1945: Reports of the Estonian International Commission for the Investigation of Crimes Against Humanity. Tallinn: Estonian Foundation for the Investigation of Crimes Against Humanity, 2005.

Formakov, Arsenii. *Gulag Letters*. Edited and translated by Emily D. Johnson. New Haven, CT: Yale University Press, 2017.

Gernet, M. N. *Istoriia tsarskoi tiur'my*. Third edition. Five volumes. Moscow: Gos. Izdat iuridicheskoi literatury, 1960–63.

Hirsch, Francine. *Empire of Nations: Ethnographic Knowledge and the Making of the Soviet Union*. Ithaca, NY: Cornell University Press, 2005.

Jakobson, Michael. *Origins of the Gulag: The Soviet Prison Camp System, 1917–1934*. Lexington: University of Kentucky Press, 1993.

Jameikis, Stasys. *Only Eleven Came Back: An Eyewitness Account of Survival*. Translated by Regina Share. Hobart: Baltic Research Foundation, 2017.

Jonauskaite, Justina. "Pis'mo na loskute tkani." Virtual Gulag Museum. Accessed June 1, 2021. http://www.gulagmuseum.org/showObject.do?object=506421&language=1.

Juciute, Elena. *Footsteps in the Death Zone*. Huntington Beach, CA: GEM Publishing, 2001.

Kuodyte, Dalia, and Rokas Tracevskis. *Siberia: Mass Deportations from Lithuania to the USSR*. Vilnius: Genocide and Resistance Research Centre of Lithuania, 2004.

Kutsenko, Grigorii Petrovich, interview by Emily D. Johnson, 2009.

Labor Camp Survivor from Western Ukraine, interview by Emily D. Johnson, 2009. The subject was held in Ukhta from 1945 to 1949 and requested anonymity.

Latvijas Okupacijas muzeja GadaGramata. 2000. Komunistu un Nacistu Juga. Riga: Latvijas 50 gadu okupacijas muzeja fonds, 2001.

Lie, Suzanne Stiver, Lynda Malik, Ilyi Joe-Cannon, and Rutt Hinrikus, eds. *Carrying Linda's Stones: An Anthology of Estonian Women's Life Stories*. Tallinn, Estonia: Tallinn University Press, 2009.

Malumian, Arman. "I dazhe nashi slezy. . . ." In *Soprotivlenie v gulage: Vospominaniia. Pis'ma. Dokumenty*, edited by Semen Samuilovich Vilenskii, 212–16. Moscow: Vozvrashchenie, 1992.

Martin, Terry. *The Affirmative Action Empire: Nations and Nationalism in the Soviet Union, 1923–1939*. Ithaca, NY: Cornell University Press, 2001.

"Mordovskie lageria," *Khronika tekushchikh sobytii*, no. 51 (December 1, 1978). http://hts.memo.ru/.

Oispuu, Leo. "Collection and Processing of Personal Data of Repressed Persons," *Communist Crimes in Estonia: Additional Name List, 1940–1990. Supplements for Books R1–R7*, ed. Leo Oispuu. Tallinn: Estonian Repressed Persons Records Bureau, 2010.

Plioplys, Audrius V. "Hope and Spirit." Accessed June 1, 2021. https://www.hopeandspirit.net/category/moving-pictures/.

"Politzakliuchennye i ssyl'nye," *Khronika tekushchikh sobytii*, no. 7 (April 10, 1969). http://hts.memo.ru/.

Rossi, Zhak. *Spravochnik po Gulagu*. Translated by Natal'ia Gorbanevskaia. Second ed. Two vols. Moscow: Prosvet, 1991.

Sabbo, Hilda. "Gibel'nyi etap." In *Arkhivy pamiati: Nikogo ne zabyt'; nichego ne zabyt'*, edited by Liudmila Glushkovskaia, 37–39. Tallinn, Estonia: Estonskii kul'turnyi tsentr, 2013.

Skipton, David M., and Peter A. Michalove. *Postal Censorship in Imperial Russia*. Two vols. Urbana, IL: J. H. Otten, 1989.

Slezkine, Yuri. "The USSR as a Communal Apartment, or How a Socialist State Promoted Ethnic Particularism." *Slavic Review* 53, no. 2 (Summer 1994): 414–52.

Solovieff, E. I. *School for Tchekists: An Authentic Memorandum of a Latvian Citizen Who Spent Seven Years in a Soviet Russian Labor Camp*. Sanford, FL: Latvian Former Railroadmen Organization in Exile, 1983.

Soviet Deportations in Estonia: Impact and Legacy. Articles and Life Histories. Tartu, Estonia: Tartu University Press, 2007.

Vakhrushev, A. A. "Nachalo knigoizdatel'skoi deiatel'nosti na udmurtskom iazyke." *Izvestiia Samarskogo nauchnogo tsentra Rossiiskoi Akademii Nauk* 5, no. 7 (2009): 1259–62. https://cyberleninka.ru/article/n/nachalo-knigoizdatelskoy-deyatelnosti-na-udmurtskom-yazyke.

Vareikis, I., and I. Zelenskii. *Natsional'no-gosudarstvennoe razmezhivanie Srednei Azii.* Tashkent, Uzbekistan: Sredne-Aziatskoe gosudarstvennoe izdatel'stvo, 1924.

Vasil'eva, O. I., and V. S. Vorontsov. "Natsional'naia shkola v Udmurtii: Istoriia i sovremennost'." *Ezhegodnik finno-ugorskikh issledovanii* (2013): 70–84. https://cyberleninka.ru/article/n/natsionalnaya-shkola-v-udmurtii-istoriya-i-sovremennost.

"Virtual Museum of the Gulag." Accessed June 1, 2021. http://www.gulagmuseum.org/start.do?language=1.

Zdanovich, A. A., and V. S. Izmozik. *Sorok let na sekretnoi sluzhbe: Zhizn' i prikliucheniia Vladimira Krivosha.* Moscow: Iks-Khistori, 2007.

Zhemkova, Elena, and Alena Kozlova. *Pravo perepiski: Sviaz' voli i nevoli: O pis'makh, posylkakh i svidaniiakh zakliuchennykh sovetskikh tiurem i lagerei.* Second expanded edition. Moscow: Agey Tomesh, 2017.

EMILY D. JOHNSON is the Brian and Sandra O'Brien Presidential Professor of Russian at the University of Oklahoma. She is author of *How St. Petersburg Learned to Study Itself: The Russian Idea of Kraevedenie* and editor and translator of *Gulag Letters* by Arsenii Formakov.

FOUR

"WHO ARE YOU IN LIFE?"

The Gulag Reputation System and
Its Legacies Today

GAVIN SLADE

RECENT GULAG SCHOLARSHIP HAS BEGUN to pay more attention to the lives of the common criminals of the camp system, challenging the largely negative presentation of these prisoners in the numerous Gulag memoirs written by political prisoners.[1] Mark Vincent has recently argued that the elaborate rules, rituals, and practices associated with common criminals, and in particular the hierarchies they produced, were a manifestation of *prisonization*, a term that describes prisoner adaptations to the deprivations associated with imprisonment—the loss of liberty, security, and sex. The unwritten rules that governed these hierarchies dictated "the most intricate details of [daily life] ... impacted relationships with other social groups ... profoundly affected day-to-day operations of the camps, [yet] remain marginalized in Gulag historiography."[2] This marginalization is partly due to the relative rarity of historical sources on common criminals in the Gulag. Official reports tend to lump these prisoners together as "criminal-bandits" or "criminal elements" while memoirs place them "beyond the bounds of humanity."[3]

This chapter aims to speak to both issues: the need for greater theorization of the role of common criminals in the Gulag and the lack of data on this issue. In the first two sections below, I lend support to Vincent's observation that the norms, practices, and rituals of common criminals had an immense impact on the daily life of all the Gulag's inhabitants. I also, however, reconceptualize these social forms. Instead of casting criminal society as a subculture that enabled individual socialization into the communal prisoner environment, as Vincent did, I suggest that the unwritten rules and practices of the common criminals were a form of prisoner self-governance. Shifting conceptually from subculture to governance allows us to theorize the elaborate cultural forms—tattooing, jargon, nicknaming, songs—as mechanisms for positioning prisoners in a hierarchy. This hierarchy was a strictly policed and near-universal caste system.[4] The crucial governance function that the caste hierarchy performed was the provision of timely, credible information about individual prisoners, a prerequisite for producing trust and thus the coordination of prisoner activity. In other words, what we see as a subculture was in fact a reputation system that touched all prisoners in the Gulag regardless of whether they were political or common prisoners or whether they acquiesced to their hierarchical position and recognized the broader system.

In the final section, I argue that fragments of this reputation system still exist and that data from present-day interviews with prisoners and former prisoners can help us understand how the system worked in the Soviet Gulag. As such this chapter speaks as much to the "Legacies" section of this edited collection as to the "Identities" section. To reveal these legacies, I utilize data from four former Soviet countries: Georgia, Lithuania, Moldova, and Kyrgyzstan. This chapter makes no claim that the prison systems of these four independent countries are identical to the Gulag nor that they are identical to each other. Yet, as Judith Pallot argues, there are aspects of carceral life that have remained "remarkably constant" in this part of the world since the 1930s, and "listening to prisoners' talk today can draw attention to punitive aspects of the everyday Gulag that have been hitherto overlooked."[5] I aim to demonstrate the truth of this remark by showing how present-day prisoners in the former Soviet Union use a reputation system formed in the Gulag to find reliable answers when asking each other the question "who are you in life?" (*kto ty po zhizni?*).

REPUTATION SYSTEMS

The tattoos, unwritten rules, jargon, nicknaming, card games, and songs that make up the culture of the common criminals of the Gulag—the so-called thieves' world—have been the object of study since the inception of the camp system in the 1930s. The most recent scholarship on the Gulag's criminal subculture argues that it should be understood not only as an often violent normative order that facilitated predation on certain prisoner groups but also as a sociopsychological response to the conditions of the Gulag that produced survival-oriented adaptations and built collective identities based on shared values.[6] This section switches the emphasis away from culture and a focus on values and toward the governance functions of subcultural norms and practices in the Gulag. I argue that the subculture's primary governance function was to facilitate the spread of credible information throughout the camp system.

Paul Milgrom, Douglass North, and Barry Weingast have used the concept of a *reputation system* to explain how credible information is managed in low-trust, impersonal settings. In this section, I will define this term and review its application to prison settings before applying it to Gulag prisoner society.

Milgrom, North, and Weingast examined the transmission of information about trader reputation during an explosive trade boom in the medieval period that resulted in the creation of more impersonal trading networks.[7] As European medieval trade became geographically dispersed and traders' reputations harder to establish, cheating became much easier. In order to facilitate trade in these circumstances, a reputation system was created that collected and distributed information about individual traders' identities and past behavior. Traders empowered some merchants to act as private judges to resolve disputes and "to transmit *just enough* information to the right people in the right circumstances to enable the reputation mechanism to function effectively for enforcement."[8] This institution, the law merchant and its enforcers, had the means to damage the reputations of individual traders and those associated with them, which deterred dishonesty. For the law merchant institution to work, traders had to mutually monitor each other, report cheating, and contribute to its maintenance.

Prisoners, just like traders, benefit from cooperation; exchanging scarce goods can decrease the pain of imprisonment and produce profits for those who govern prison trade.[9] In prison, cooperation is ensured easily enough when populations are small and the turnover of prisoners in the system is low. Prisoners in such conditions maintain an inmate code of honor that shames those who cheat. Those who breach the code are easily shunned and ostracized by the others. In small prison populations, breaches of the code are directly observable. It is not necessary to develop special practices of oversight or rules on monitoring to prove when a breach has occurred and to decide on what punishment should follow. The inmate code is enforced by all prisoners and as such is a decentralized system of informal governance.[10]

Just as with medieval trading networks, once prison societies begin to increase in size and complexity, incentives emerge to develop centralized governance structures that will regulate behavior and enable cooperation. Prison gangs are one type of centralized informal structure. They are hierarchical corporate entities that manage prisoner interactions through strict rules enforced through centralized decision-making.[11] Gangs emerged in the US in the second half of the twentieth century due to a huge increase in prison populations, a decrease in the average age of prisoners, and the expansion of prison drug markets.[12] Under these conditions, formal penal administrations struggled to produce the licit governance required to provide security, regulate disputes, and police and suppress illicit markets. Thus, in the US a demand for governance increased among prisoners, and, in response, gang formations began to emerge.[13] These gang formations developed collective reputations for violence as well as, in many cases, order and justice. Individuals affiliated with gangs benefited from this collective reputation. Information about an individual could be inferred from gang membership status, provided this status could be effectively communicated. For the system to function, this status had to be prohibitively difficult to mimic, or mimicry had to carry a credible threat of severe punishment.

The law merchant and prison gangs are alike in that they produce centralized governance, defined here as the protection of property rights, the undergirding of transactions and trade, and the coordination of collective action for mutual benefit.[14] They do this by raising the costs on cheating through managing information about individuals and groups and sanctioning cheating and the faking of identity; this is the essence of a reputation system. For the system to run, these governance providers must be able to collect and manage information at a low cost, ensure that decisions are actually honored and punishments enacted, and minimize their own cheating.[15]

Forms of informal prisoner governance can be discerned in Tsarist and early Soviet prisons where informal hierarchies of prisoners, divided by a diverse range of subcultural categories and crime types, were already evident.[16] As the Soviet prison population expanded in the early 1930s, these hierarchies solidified and began to be policed by groups of prisoners known as thieves-in-law (*vory-v-zakone*, best translated as "thieves-professing-the-code"; hereafter I will use the term *thieves* as shorthand) and the *blatnye* (singular *blatnoi*).[17] All thieves were blatnye, but not all blatnye were thieves; those prisoners who oversaw whole camps, individual barracks, or prisoner detachments on behalf of the thieves were considered blatnye.[18] Some middle-ranking castes were not blatnye but still lived according to the thieves' code. Lower castes were made up of those prisoners who worked, political prisoners, and outcasts (*obizhennye*). The caste position of a prisoner determined his rights and obligations within the system and had a significant impact on his reputation as an individual. The boundaries of the castes were maintained by cultural markers—knowledge of jargon and the thieves' code, skill in cards, maintenance of a nickname, tattoos—and policed by the blatnye, who could punish fakers. The punishment function was centralized and monopolized at the top of the prisoner hierarchy. The blatnye held thieves' courts that judged those who broke the thieves' law and determined demotion and promotion in the hierarchy. Vincent reports that punishment unsanctioned by the elite caste was prohibited.[19]

As with any system of governance, compliance was secured through appeals to appropriateness and instrumentality. The thieves presented themselves as opponents of a vicious and oppressive state. Gulag survivor Bernhard Roeder writes that "everywhere and incessantly the system praises the hero of socialist labor, the pioneer, the robot-like worker, the machine man amidst his machines; but in their hearts the people love the elite criminal [the *blatnoi*], the strong, free man."[20] Such high-caste criminals could be providers of useful services: information transmission, the judging of disputes between prisoners, punishing wrongdoers through demotion down the ranks of the caste system, and the collection and redistribution of resources.

Political prisoners made up a tiny fraction of the overall prison population and could not opt out of the informal stratification system of the common criminals. As memoirs attest, political prisoners had no choice but to interact with the common criminals, and those interactions were structured by the infinitely more powerful position that the latter held. Similarly, those who worked, the so-called *muzhiki* and *bytoviki*, also became part of this informal system whether they actively embraced it or not. Thus, the hierarchies had a "near-universal character."[21] To achieve this universality, the thieves depended on the bulk of common criminals to comply and support the caste system.

Why did this reputation system emerge and develop, and how did it achieve this near universality across the camps of the Gulag? The resilience of a reputation system is defined by the specific context in which it operates. Prison characteristics that impact the efficient creation and maintenance of reputation systems include the architectural design of prisons, the degree of control maintained by prison guards and their corruptibility, and the frequency of prison transfers.[22] Where prisoners are kept in communal living conditions, prison guards are scarce and corruptible, and transfers between prisons are frequent, a reputation system will emerge more quickly and be easier to maintain. The Gulag had just such conditions: a lack of formal governance that produced a consequent demand to informally control violence in collectivist living quarters, corruption and the growth of trade on black markets, the formal use of a community responsibility system that made prisoner work detachments responsible for the productivity of individual prisoners, the seemingly ubiquitous presence of state-recruited informants, and frequent prisoner transfers. These conditions produced very strong incentives among prisoners to create the social institutions required to run a reputation system and very low barriers to that system's maintenance and regulation. The next section will examine each of these conditions in turn and show how, taken together, they allowed for the formation and spread of the reputation system.

EXPLAINING THE EMERGENCE AND EXPANSION OF THE GULAG REPUTATION SYSTEM

A lack of formal control over the prison environment is a necessary condition for the emergence of prisoner governance. Accounts of the early Gulag attest to the dearth of effective formal governance and the corresponding corruption and violence in the camps. In his study of the Vorkutlag camp complex, Barenberg cites an NKVD report from 1942 that complained that "zonification," the process of walling prisoners into "zones" and placing them under guard, had never taken place in many parts of the camp: "a whole series of camp subdivisions completely lack a zone ... prisoners are never under guard."[23] Moreover, many prisoners had the right to move around freely without escort, and others were permitted to live outside the camp entirely. In one official report on the Ukhta-Pechora camp from 1938, 95–96 percent of the camp had been left unguarded.[24] In the prisoner accommodation blocks, "it is impossible to establish order, demand discipline or, most important, exercise control."[25] According to Khlevniuk's data, by January 1, 1939, the overall ratio of guard to prisoner was 1:9. This 1939 ratio tells only part of the story, however: around 8 percent of the guards at that time were themselves prisoners employed by camp administrations, and half the guards were armed so they could man the perimeter fences as opposed to working with prisoners inside the camps.[26]

In such conditions where formal governance mechanisms were lacking, insecurity and victimization were widespread among the prisoners, and this produced a demand for greater certainty and effective protection. The thieves were both producers of violence and protectors from it. In the 1930s, "gang crime spread ... the cruelest and most aggressive criminals increased their influence terrorizing the political prisoners, and often imposing their own rules."[27] In a memo from Krasnoyarsk camp dated December 8, 1939, guards were found to consort with "repeat criminals," and it was observed that "brigandage, robberies, theft, hooliganism, knifing, open resistance ... gambling, drinking ... flourish in the camp. Gangster and criminal elements undermine camp discipline." One prisoner by the name of Kopka, "an active bandit and disrupter," instead of being assigned to isolation, was appointed head of the team of juvenile prisoners.[28]

As Kopka's case suggests, camp guards often failed to separate prisoners by their official categories. Alexopoulos, examining prisoner complaints and official investigations of violence at Pechorlag in 1952, also finds that prisoners were not segregated in any way, leaving them vulnerable to the coercive influence of the most hardened criminals. She writes that "the balance of power at the camp had shifted in favor of the most violent prisoners... gangs of inveterate criminals who followed the 'thieves' law'."[29] Arbitrary violence from the camp administration was also frequent; Khlevniuk refers to the "lawlessness and arbitrary rule" of the camp administrations.[30] The few investigations that were carried out by Soviet authorities revealed sickening violence against the prisoner population and a systematic lack of procedural compliance.

As well as violence, corruption was ubiquitous. Supplies intended for the prisoners were routinely stolen by guards to be sold on black markets.[31] Heinzen's study of corruption in the Gulag reports that graft had reached "outrageous proportions" and become so embedded that anticorruption measures were not seriously undertaken.[32] Shortages were common, and illicit markets for a range of goods and services emerged. For the whole of 1939, of the overall amount assigned to the camps, only 54 percent of cotton cloth, 62 percent of blankets, and 26 percent of felt boots were actually supplied to prisoners.[33] In Pechorlag in 1952, official reports found that food was lacking or limited and that "prisoners could not go to their worksite because they lacked footwear."[34] Illicit markets for gambling were also commonplace.[35] As Shalamov recalls, "Every night in the camp the criminal element gathered to play cards."[36] The thieves held a special position in this regard, regulating the games and ensuring debt collection. These illicit markets for scarce goods, services, and entertainment required governance. The thieves at once preyed on and governed these markets, resolving disputes, excluding and punishing cheaters, and managing access.

Even where prisoners had been "zoned," they still lived in intensely communal conditions that produced insecurities. Kharkhordin has systematically studied the emergence of the collective or team of workers (*kollektiv*) as one of the building blocks of the Soviet economic and social system.[37] The collective was also a method to establish prisoner-led order in the chaotic prison conditions described above. Prisoner detachments worked and lived together in communal quarters known as barracks. The purpose of the detachments was to realize a "full system of self-governance."[38] Such collectives ran on a community responsibility system: the group was punished for the failures and transgressions of its individual members. For prisoners, then, it was important to know and try to control which newcomers joined any particular collective and how they behaved once part of a work team. This system thus incentivized intense information collection and mutual monitoring among prisoners, or what Piacentini and Slade call the "polyopticon" of all watching all.[39]

The role of the blatnye as monopolists of informal governance gave them leverage over other prisoners, which in turn afforded them privileges from the prison administration. Barnes discusses how this "coddling of the thieves" created bitterness for political prisoners such as Solzhenitsyn.[40] The blatnye could refuse to work in return for assurances that other prisoners would be kept in order. However, ensuring informal order, while in the interests of the camp administration, did not mean that the blatnye shared information with the administration about prisoners; this was forbidden by the thieves' code. To gain information, prison administrators set up an agent network under the auspices of a special subdivision of the national Gulag administration known as the Third Department. In 1935, an official order was issued that complained of "the frequent exposure" of Third Department agents and the need to set up more secure systems of communication.[41] Heinzen reports that by 1947, 7 percent of prisoners in the Gulag were informers.[42] Hardy puts this number for prisons in Soviet Estonia in the 1950s at 12 percent.[43] The formal policy of recruiting informers increased the incentives for prisoners to obtain credible information about each other. The greater the formal pressures to inform on fellow prisoners, the more efficient the informal system of uncovering and punishing informers had to be. Thus, the thieves' code placed clear prohibitions on informing and lying about one's identity. Severe punishments including death could ensue for giving information to the state.[44]

To establish the veracity of status and identity claims, a consensus on the mechanisms to credibly communicate reputation was vital. This was in part due to the frequency of prisoner transfer from camp to camp. As Gambetta argues, it is costly to continually reprove one's social status, particularly if this status is based on one's capacity for criminality and violence.[45] Prisoner transfers both facilitated the uniformity of informal mechanisms for transmitting reputation and multiplied the opportunities to credibly threaten sanctions for infractions wherever a prisoner was detained in the camp system. In 1939, for example, of the 1.3 million people in the camps, 240,000 were transferred between camps and 56,000 were transferred from camps to colonies or prisons.[46] Thus, in that year, a full 23 percent of the camp population was in motion between penal institutions, and even this figure does not include newcomers being transported into the camps and those leaving the system. During the war years 1941–45, intercamp transfers increased.[47] The result was that the thieves' norms, the informal caste system, and its attendant rituals spread across the space of the Gulag along the train lines and roads. Transportation arteries linked the camps into "a fairly integrated system" that provided a source of contacts for criminals and opportunities to promote common interests.[48] Varese cites a number of examples from the archives of prisoners escaping informal punishment by transferring camps only to be punished in their next location, or arriving in camps and faking a criminal reputation only to be eventually found out and punished.[49] These remarkable cases show coordination across vast distances.

The frequency of transfer, then, incentivized Gulag prisoners to ensure that reputations traveled with them as they moved. There were two main mechanisms to do this credibly. Firstly, tattoos and hard-to-fake demonstrated subcultural knowledge—argot, card playing, nicknaming, songs—became an efficient way to transmit criminal history and caste status. The Gulag famously produced a tattooing culture more extensive and communicative than the cultures of other prison systems.[50] Secondly, notes and messages—known as *ksiva, maliava*, or *progon*—were passed through the system. A 1939 report from a prison in Krasnoyarsk states that there was "practically no cell isolation ... by use of threads, cords, ropes and even planks prisoners systematically pass correspondence, objects and products from one cell to another. Meetings between prisoners from different cells during transfers became common practice."[51] The credibility of information passed in the notes was guaranteed through the use of jargon (*fenia*) and the signatures of the relevant blatnye, the faking of which would be severely punished.

Due to the conditions noted above, prisoners in the Gulag had many incentives and opportunities to gain and share information on each other. There was always the possibility that the blatnye could cheat, yet they had incentives not to abuse the power they possessed over the prisoner population. As a small minority, the blatnye relied on compliance from those lower down in the hierarchy. Those in the lower castes could challenge abuse of the system through the established channels of communication. Just like any prisoner, in communal conditions blatnye had nowhere to hide. The thieves could be subjected to "uncrowning" (*razkoronovanie*)—that is, to having their status removed and being downgraded through the castes based on decisions made by other thieves. Other thieves had a strong incentive to downgrade untrustworthy or abusive status holders as the collective reputation of their caste depended on individual thieves acting appropriately. The so-called Bitches' War that occurred in the camps from 1948 to 1953 can be interpreted as an extreme example of the thieves policing themselves. This "war" pitted the thieves against so-called bitches who more loosely interpreted the thieves' code.[52] The bitches were deemed to have breached fundamental precepts of thievish behavior, as many had gone to the front to fight for the Soviet state during the Second World War. With the support of the prison administration the bitches won, yet they continued to maintain the thieves' practices and the hierarchical system of castes.

In summary, stringent prisoner castes, the boundaries of which were policed by full-time regulators at the top of the system, can be understood as a reputation system. In the conditions of the early Gulag, it would have proven impossible for a prisoner to have efficiently and reliably uncovered the standing and past behavior of other prisoners in any given camp. Yet this information would have been crucial for survival: the prison population was growing quicker than prison administrations could govern, there was little segregation of prisoners and conflicts were common, informants were seemingly everywhere, and one prisoner could be punished formally for another's fecklessness. The incentives to create informal institutions that could reduce uncertainty by producing reliable means of establishing identity were overwhelming. Thus, Gulag prisoner society produced castes that had collective reputations. The collective reputations of the castes were common knowledge and easy to find out. An individual's reputation was grounded in their caste status. In order to prevent inmates from falsely claiming a high caste status, the system needed regulation and policing; this is where the blatnye and thieves found their niche. Collectivist living conditions, corruption, and prisoner transfer provided the opportunities for these actors to spread their influence across the whole prison system.

To be sure, the benefits of the reputation system that developed were not distributed equally. The provision of governance by the blatnye served them and their followers, often at the expense of others. Political prisoners, for example, could disavow the thieves' norms, but their identities and reputations were still collected and distributed by the reputation system; the stories of conflict and abuse during encounters with the blatnye that pepper political prisoner memoirs are understandable only if status were easily uncovered and could not be easily faked or hidden. The system of criminal governance that emerged was not a public good provided to all equally; illness, deprivation, victimization, and death were more prominent among certain groups, particularly political prisoners and those at the bottom of the criminal status hierarchy.

In the post-Stalin period, the conditions described above changed.[53] Smaller and more easily managed colonies became more common than large camps, and prisoner numbers significantly declined. Smaller colonies increased the efficacy of formal prison governance, reducing the demand for informal prisoner order. Smaller working groups of prisoners were instituted, including the detachment or *otriad* system, in which a dedicated detachment head ostensibly oversaw prisoner work and educational activities. Formal institutions of prisoner self-governance were strengthened. The pressure of fulfilling the Gulag's economic goals was lifted, and penal policy turned toward rehabilitation. This last change in the measurement of prison performance weakened incentives for violence by the prison administration and collusion with the informal thieves' hierarchies to increase productivity and maintain order. Moreover, prison transfers decreased, and criminals were more likely to be held in colonies nearer to their homes than had been the case in the Stalin period.

Despite these changes, concerns about prisoner "gangs" continued. The reform of criminal and penal codes had the effect of intensifying the relative proportion of hardened criminals in the colonies; 53 percent of the prison population were recidivists by 1960 compared to 25 percent in 1956. In 1957, camp and transit points were, according to one MVD report, "ruled" by these recidivists and gangs.[54] Soviet criminologists openly recognized the problem of the thieves' subculture in scholarly publications such as Monakhov's 1957 monograph on the subject. Nevertheless, Hardy writes that by the early 1960s, violence and disturbances in the colonies were falling and that "the mass phenomenon of organized criminal gangs within the Gulag [had] largely disappeared."[55]

However, while the conditions that had led to the emergence and expansion of the criminal reputation system had fundamentally changed and violent gangs were under control, the cultural and social forms of the thieves' hierarchies remained part of prison life. Émigré writer Valery Chalidze's 1977 book *Criminal Russia* argues exactly this: "despite official claims, the underworld has survived to this day, especially that sector of it known as the thieves' world which deserves to be regarded as a social institution since it has its own internal cohesion and ethical code."[56] What is more, in the 1950s and 1960s, the criminal subculture became visible within Soviet society. By the 1980s, the depth of the influence of criminal subculture on Soviet young people was openly acknowledged and linked to "group crime," the form of illegal behavior that later came to be known as organized crime.[57]

The connection between the Gulag subculture and the protection rackets that emerged in the late 1980s and 1990s has also been well established. The speed with which the thief-in-law networks expanded outside of the former Soviet region into Europe and America in the 1990s should perhaps not be all that surprising: the reputation system's norms and practices that enabled criminals to coordinate across the huge expanses of the Gulag served organized criminals very well in globalized illegal markets. Meanwhile, the prison colonies of the former Soviet republics went through crisis: prison populations increased as government budgets collapsed, and prison officers, underpaid and humiliated by the expansion of prisoners' rights, became harder to recruit. Corruption became rampant. In many places in the former Soviet Union, prisoners again were left to fend for themselves. In the next section, using prisoner interviews from the present day, I show that in the post-Soviet period prisoners fell back on the coordination mechanisms of the criminal reputation system to manage their survival.

THE REMNANTS OF THE GULAG REPUTATION SYSTEM IN POST-SOVIET PRISONS

This section is based on 139 interviews with prisoners, former prisoners, and prison staff in four former Soviet countries: Lithuania, Georgia, Moldova, and Kyrgyzstan. The interviews were conducted as part of a research project on prisoner society in male prisons—known still as colonies—since the collapse of the Soviet Union. Each case study was chosen with an eye to highlighting variation in the degree of prison reform that has occurred in the post-Soviet region—in particular, a reduction in collective barrack confinement and an increase in cell-based confinement. The data reveal that the reputation system formed in the Gulag still exists to varying degrees across all four cases, but it is most robust where prison reform has progressed more slowly. In these terms, Moldova and Kyrgyzstan were the two cases of most minimal reform. Thus, for consistency, I will draw mainly on data from these two cases in this section.

There are, of course, significant differences between the Gulag and colonies in Kyrgyzstan and Moldova. The colonies in these two countries still maintain "industrial zones" where prisoners work. Yet this work is not required by law as it was in Soviet times, and the number of work placements is limited. Moreover, there is no group of prisoners in these prisons who are identifiable as political prisoners according to the specific article of the criminal code they were convicted under, as there had been in Soviet times. Despite the differences, I will show that there is a constant: the Gulag reputation system described above still exists, albeit in altered form. This section briefly describes this system and then analyzes the functions it serves: the suppression of ethnic or regionally based gang formation, the monopolization and control of violence, the maintenance of caste boundaries, and the timely transmission of information about identity. The section draws attention to how prison conditions in Kyrgyzstan and Moldova are in many ways similar to those of the Gulag. These conditions include collective living, underresourcing and understaffing, and a continuation of the use of informants for managing the prison system. Where respondents are cited, names have been changed in line with guarantees of anonymity.

Across the four countries of the research project, a caste hierarchy in prisons still exists. At the top remain the thieves, usually very few in number and often not physically in prison. Prison leaders known as *polozhentsy* defer to the thieves and lead a devolved hierarchy. Underneath them, overseers, or *smotriashchie*, monitor individual barracks and various areas of prison such as the work zone or the canteen. The common prisoners, *muzhiki*, work and contribute to the thieves' mutual aid fund known as the *obshchak*; they make up the majority of prisoners in most prisons. Beneath them, irregulars (*neputi* or *neputevye*), who have breached the code or otherwise do not follow it; goats (*kozly*), who are often uncovered informants; and untouchables (*obizhennye*) all live outside the thieves' "understandings." In Moldova and Lithuania, a new caste known as, respectively, skiers (*lizhniki*) and elephants (*slony*) has emerged, consisting of those who actively resist the thieves' system.

In the present day, these hierarchically organized subcultural categories compete with other prisoner group affiliations. Prisoners may share regional and ethnic identities that can compete with or supersede the categories assigned by the prison subculture. This is not new: histories of the Gulag note how, in the postwar period, the influx of large numbers of prisoners from nationalist groups, particularly from Ukraine and the Baltic States, shook up prisoner society.[58] Nationalists were not interested in the solidarity of prisoners and instead agitated for their own national group interests. Following the nationalist movements in the Soviet republics in the 1980s and some of the ethnic conflicts that have occurred since the collapse of the Soviet Union, we might expect prisoner society to be completely broken up along ethnic lines today.

Interviews show that the principle of compatriotship (*zemliachestvo*)—that is, associating with someone from the same "soil"—is indeed a basis for discovering a prisoner's identity based on mutually shared contacts.[59] However, *zemliachestvo* is used to facilitate the reputation system rather than replace it. In my interview data, particularly in Moldova and Kyrgyzstan, prisoners actively subordinate local, ethnic or national identities to their criminal caste status within the informal governance system. In Kyrgyzstan, for example, one explicit rule concerned a prohibition on the creation of what respondents called *blok*, translated straightforwardly as a group or bloc. This term refers to any group of prisoners that has formed and excludes others based on an identifying feature such as ethnicity or place of birth.

Blocs are considered a threat to the principle of subordination to the thieves' hierarchy. Prisoners are encouraged to organize socially according to their hierarchical caste, known informally as "suits" (*masty*, as in cards), rather than by forming groups based on ethnicities, regions, towns or even parts of town. These rules on forming blocs demonstrate an overt intention to control prisoners' social affiliations and to prevent alternative concentrations of power from emerging. The rhyming phrase in Russian "to live not by regions, but by suits" came up in several interviews, including one with a respondent in Kyrgyzstan, originally a Kabardian from the North Caucasus region of Russia:

> "I mean, bloc that is unthievish [*bliadstvo*] there [in prison] ... if you have three, four, five guys from Pokrovka [a region of Bishkek] who want to get together for example, that is a *blok*. If that's the case, they'll reach out from the elite caste [*obshchak*] and say "what's this with you five?" ... No compatriotship [*zemliachestvo*], no, only [organize] by the understandings [informal code] ... We live in suits, not by regions but by suits [*ne po oblastiam, a po mastiam*]."[60]

The quote shows that in Kyrgyzstan the caste system remains the key mechanism for organizing prisoner society. It is possible that similar informal rules existed during the time of the Gulag, explaining the relative lack of ethnic gangs in the Soviet prison system.

To enforce these informal rules the reputation system continues to utilize violence. Violence is directed downward through the hierarchy to the lowest groups. These groups suffer much worse deprivation than other prisoners. The permanent possibility of being cast out into the lower categories strengthens the upper castes by creating relationships of dependency on the caste system for security and goods, whether foodstuffs or illicit substances. Moreover, violence is used to maintain the caste system's boundaries between groups. This can result in separated living arrangements and punishments for those who ignore these boundaries. As one Moldovan prisoner from the lowest caste explained "if a common prisoner [*muzhik*] is coming, you must stand against the wall and let him through and not look at him. If you do not do this, you will be beaten."[61] An important coda to this remark is that the physical punishment could not just be enacted by anyone; before any punishment could be carried out, those in the higher caste had to review the evidence substantiating the offense. Such reviews can be done efficiently as the divisions between zones, sectors and dormitories are practically meaningless: the main limits on prisoner movement and monitoring are imposed by the informal, as opposed to formal, authorities. The lowest castes, however, still live separately. For example, in Cricova No. 15, a colony holding the only thief-in-law in prison today in Moldova, 100 of the 600 total prisoners were untouchables held in a separate sector.

The separation of castes is produced by both informal and formal means. When a prisoner first enters the reception unit of a prison colony, known as "quarantine," information is already circulating about the prisoner's caste status through informal channels. The information arrives at the colony from the remand prison ahead of the prisoner. The central remand prisons, in the case of Moldova Chisinau #13 and in Kyrgyzstan Bishkek #1, act as switchboards directing information through the penal system. Prisoners move in and out of these prisons as they are transferred. A respondent with experience of both Soviet and post-Soviet Kyrgyzstani colonies discussed how he communicated with authoritative prisoners in a separate colony some distance away to resolve a dispute in the 1990s:

> When they transfer someone to remand [*SIZO*], all the notes [*maliava*] get sent through with them and then whoever is being sent out from remand to Pokrovka [colony], my note goes with them.... [the resolution] takes 10 days, sometimes two weeks ... the note gets answered and sent back with the next transfer [*etap*].[62]

From the other end of the age spectrum, one respondent, a juvenile in Moldova's juvenile detention facility Goian #10, was sent temporarily to Chisinau #13 as punishment for his part in a riot. He explained:

> those of us who follow the understandings, we show interest in each other, actually we are interested in what is happening in the prison in general and outside the prison. When I was in Chisinau #13, I collected information to bring back to Goian about who will be coming here, who they are, and what is happening elsewhere in the prisons ... we can understand who should be an untouchable or who is already an untouchable.[63]

Transmitting information face to face and through written notes increases the credibility of the information received. In the present day, however, cell phones are also extremely common in dormitory barracks. As one respondent put it, "there is communication everywhere. In the cells there are telephones; every person has a phone. In the quarantine, the criminal leader will be able to talk to you and ask you 'who are you in life' [*kto ty po zhizni*]? You can't hide it."[64] The question "who are you in life?" and variations on this theme ("who can you live with?") is a normative and subcultural one; the intention is to uncover the attitude to the thieves' code, willingness to live by its rules, and whether you have breached the thieves' code in the past. Respondents gave revealing examples of this:

> "This one guy made out he was a first timer, but actually he had been inside before, and he had been selling drugs in prison. If you are a dealer [*bariga*], then you are an irregular [*neputevye*] ... so he was downgraded, he became an irregular.... Information will always get to us. He hadn't been inside [in Kyrgyzstan], but actually in Tashkent [Uzbekistan]. You see, it got to us from there. But you have to have the evidence, you can't just go after

someone... there was a group of guys [in Tashkent] who could confirm it [that the prisoner had been a dealer] for us."[65]

Independent drug dealing in prisons had been banned by a thieves' decree (*progon*) around 2008 in Kyrgyzstan. An attempt to cover up breaches of the rules in this case failed, even though the information had to travel across state borders. Attitudes to the code, type of crime, references about behavior from those outside prison, and behavior within prison, all contribute to the positioning of the prisoner within the hierarchy. This position is often decided before the prisoner has left "quarantine" to "move up" (*podnimat'sia*), in the jargon of the *blatnye*, into the communal life of the colony itself. Once a categorization is made in quarantine, this plays a significant role in dormitory and sector allocation within the colony. In both Kyrgyzstan and Moldova, it was reported by both prisoners and staff that prison guards also asked the question "who are you in life?" as an informal part of their formal processing of new arrivals. Thus, formal and informal processes mix together in allocating and categorizing prisoners.

As in the Gulag, prison departments today in Kyrgyzstan and Moldova struggle to hire enough guards and to resource penal institutions properly. In 2016, the prison department budget met only 35 percent of the needs of Kyrgyzstan's prisons.[66] Thus, there is a large black market in Kyrgyzstan for basic essential goods. In Branesti colony in Moldova, of 184 working prison staff in 2017, only 46 uniformed guards worked within the prison walls, and only 11 such guards were on duty at any one time. The biggest cadre (69 officers) within the staff of Branesti were guards assigned to the perimeter fence and armed with automated weapons. In such circumstances, as in the Gulag, governance within the walls of the colony is left up to the prisoners.

Due to underfunding, instead of dividing and increasing the segregation of prisoners to diminish the thieves' norms and their influence, Branesti reduced the number of sector walls within the colony from ten sectors in 2007 to six sectors in 2017. Sectors are physical divisions within a colony made up of detachments (*otriadi*). Prisoners are grouped within a detachment which is assigned to a sector. By reducing the number of sectors, the prison administration in Branesti produced greater numbers of prisoners per sector, roughly one hundred per sector in 2017 versus sixty per sector in 2007. This leads to less physical division of prisoners and thus more direct contact between them. As a consequence, information gathering, monitoring and control of prisoners through the caste system is easier. Similarly, in Kyrgyzstan, respondents referred frequently to *khod*, roughly translated as mobility in the colony, that gave every prisoner access to any other. As one respondent said:

"[The prison administration] have them [internal sector walls], but they don't close them ... when we were inside [2001–2008] there was nothing, there was no regime whatsoever. There is the possibility to stop mobility [*khod*] but it isn't used. It was in the Soviet period, they had the sector [*lokalka*] walls, but, when we were in there, there was a mutual agreement between the staff and prisoners."[67]

The structural hinderances to the maintenance of the reputation system in Kyrgyzstan and Moldova are minimal and are to some degree reminiscent of the processes of zonification and dezonification of the Gulag era.

To manage these minimally staffed, open spaces of the post-Soviet prison colony, prison administrations in Kyrgyzstan and Moldova still use the Soviet system of informants. In Moldova, prisoners are formally recruited as informants by the operative division within a colony, paid a basic salary for their services, and expected to provide regular and credible information on indiscretions within the prison. Negative attitudes to informing are expressed by prisoners today in Moldova and Kyrgyzstan. In both countries, when prisoners go to the administrative zone in the colony, whether to visit a doctor, attend a family visit or see a social worker, they must go in pairs. The reason for this is that the operative officers are also situated within the administrative zone. To ensure that prisoners are indeed visiting the doctor and not informing, a credible witness is required who reports back to overseers among the prisoner body. Through this mechanism it is ensured that mutual monitoring extends to all areas of the colony, particularly those dominated by staff presence. Just as in Soviet times, the role of informants within the prison system sows high levels of distrust among prisoners. To develop the trust needed to coordinate activities for mutual advantage, prisoners require strong prohibitions on snitching. The prisoner hierarchy produces such prohibitions. It also streamlines evidence gathering, decision making and efficient sanctioning to produce a credible deterrent to informing.

In Georgia and Lithuania prison administrations have vigorously attempted to disrupt the reputation system among prisoners. Such reforms include separating high caste members in bespoke high security prisons, extra sanctions for those professing the thieves' code, increasing the number of sectors within colonies, increasing the number and power of staff, and even attempting (but failing) in Lithuania to scrap the system of informants for keeping order. These reforms have had varying effects on prisoner society, often bringing about disorder as staff attempt to implement greater control and prisoner society reorders itself, generating information through other, often more violent, means.[68] Otherwise, in all four cases the basic conditions for the formation of an institutionalized reputation system are still present to some degree. Thus, while this chapter does not demonstrate that the colonies of Kyrgyzstan or Moldova today have the exact same conditions as the Gulag, in general, prisoners still face age-old coordination problems for which residues of the old Gulag reputation system still find a purpose.

To summarize, across the four cases I researched, prisoner numbers remain high by international standards.[69] Prisons are often poorly funded, with low levels of staffing and high levels of corruption.[70] Prisoners still live in communal conditions in colonies poorly divided by sectors and managed through formal networks of informants. Transfers, and particularly movement between remand prisons and colonies, remain frequent. As long as these conditions persist, the reputation system formed in the Gulag will continue to frame the social lives of prisoners across the former Soviet Union.

CONCLUSION

In 2011, the Russian Minister of Justice, Aleksander Konovalev, reporting to a Duma committee on the current Russian penal system and plans for its reform, identified a peculiar feature of the system: "[there exists the dominance of] criminal leaders who try to spread the thieves' idea. The widespread nature of the criminal culture ... is clearly a product of the collective system of holding prisoners."[71] This chapter has shown that this "criminal culture" is both a legacy of the Gulag and a source of prisoner identity: a reputation system. The chapter explicated how the formation of this reputation system was linked to the conditions of the Gulag. Beyond the collective living conditions identified by Konovalev, conditions conducive to institutionalizing a reputation system in the Gulag included the size of the penal system, frequent transfers between camps, understaffing, interprisoner and guard violence, corruption, and the extensive use of informants. All these factors contributed to producing an organized system of information transmission that enabled prisoner self-governance.

Certainly, the reputation system was dangerous to political prisoners as they were involuntarily subjected to it; the system in fact facilitated their victimization. The accounts of political prisoner memoirists have left the impression that a clear us-and-them divide existed between political prisoners and common criminals belonging to this system of collective beliefs. As Barnes argues, this division might not have existed so neatly in reality, as political prisoners could utilize the informal institutions and networks of contacts developed by the common criminals.[72] Granted, the memoirs of political prisoners certainly characterize the world of the thieves as one of violence, extortion, and inhumanity. Shalamov describes a "corrupting power" over "hundreds of thousands of people who have been seduced by the ideology of these criminals [thieves] and have ceased to be people."[73] It is easy to empathize with the horror political prisoners must have felt on coming into contact with a society of hardened criminals that had developed intricate cultural codes. Nonetheless, to understand that society, it is not enough simply to draw attention to its horrifying aspects. Rather, this chapter has focused on the practical and instrumental purposes the criminal culture served.

Prisoner governance provides certain public and club benefits, often as a collective response to extreme conditions of victimization and deprivation.[74] Read sympathetically, the thieves-in-law can be understood as a survival-oriented social unit aimed at the organization of consumption in conditions of extreme scarcity, rather than as an economic unit aimed at dominating a market for protection.[75] One consumption item that had become increasingly scarce, uncertain, and therefore valuable was credible information about one's immediate social milieu. In response to these deprivations, the Gulag birthed a sophisticated reputation system, the remnants of which prisoners throughout the former Soviet Union still employ.

NOTES

The author would like to thank the two anonymous reviewers as well as Matthew Light for their helpful reflections and comments on drafts of this chapter. The chapter has been much improved thanks to their engagement.

1. Vincent, *Cult of the "Urka"*; Kuntsman, "'With a Shade of Disgust'"; Alexopoulos, "A Torture Memo."
2. Vincent, *Cult of the "Urka,"* 13.
3. Ginzburg, *Journey into the Whirlwind*, 12, 101.
4. I use the concept of *caste* here not in the sense of immutable hereditary standing but in the broader sense of a strictly policed division of society based on difference in rank and prestige. I use this concept since it is also used in the common speech of prisoners in the former Soviet Union in the early twenty-first century to refer to one's hierarchical position in prisoner society.
5. Pallot, "Gulag as Crucible," 683, 693.
6. Vincent, *Cult of the "Urka."*
7. Milgrom, North, and Weingast, "The Role of Institutions."
8. Milgrom, North, and Weingast, 3. Italics in original.
9. Sykes, *Society of Captives*, 63–84.
10. Sykes and Messinger, "The Inmate Social System," 5–19.

11. Butler, Slade, and Dias, "Self-Governing Prisons," 2.
12. Skarbek, *Social Order of the Underworld*, 41.
13. Skarbek, 49–51.
14. Skarbek, 5.
15. Milgrom, North, and Weingast, "The Role of Institutions," 3.
16. Varese, *The Russian Mafia*, 145–66.
17. Chalidze, *Criminal Russia*, 71; Varese, "Society of Vory-v-Zakone," 515–38; Slade, *Reorganizing Crime*, 11–17; Gurov, *Krasnaia mafia*, 25–26.
18. It is worth noting, since the *blatnye* managed information, that the name itself, coming from the Russian *blat*, has connotations of mutual knowledge and reciprocal relations.
19. Vincent, *Cult of the "Urka,"* 198.
20. Roeder, *Katorga*, 91.
21. Roeder, 110.
22. Butler, Slade, and Dias, "Self-Governing Prisons," 4–5.
23. Quoted in Barenberg, *Gulag Town, Company Town*, 40.
24. Khlevniuk, *The History of the Gulag*, 120.
25. Quoted in Khlevniuk, 122.
26. Khlevniuk, 222.
27. Khlevniuk, 180.
28. Quoted in Khlevniuk, 232–33.
29. Alexopoulos, "A Torture Memo," 166.
30. Khlevniuk, *The History of the Gulag*, 39.
31. Applebaum, *Gulag*, 97; Barnes, *Death and Redemption*, 54; Khlevniuk, *The History of the Gulag*, 208.
32. Heinzen, "Corruption in the Gulag," 245.
33. Khlevniuk, *The History of the Gulag*, 208.
34. Alexopoulos, "A Torture Memo," 171.
35. Vincent, *Cult of the "Urka,"* 158–89.
36. Quoted in Varese, "Society of the Vory-v-Zakone," 520.
37. Kharkhordin, *The Collective and the Individual*.
38. Kharkhordin, 102.
39. Piacentini and Slade, "Architecture and Attachment," 182.
40. Barnes, *Death and Redemption*, 89.
41. Barnes, 98–99.
42. Heinzen, "Corruption in the Gulag," 468.
43. Hardy, "Informant Networks in the Estonian Gulag," 419.
44. Varese, "Society of the Vory-v-Zakone," 516.
45. Gambetta, *Codes of the Underworld*, 78–111.
46. Khlevniuk, *The History of the Gulag*, 153.
47. Bacon, *The Gulag at War*, 113–16.

48. Varese, "Society of the Vory-v-Zakone," 525.
49. Varese, "Society of the Vory-v-Zakone."
50. Lambert and Christ, *Russian Prison Tattoos*.
51. Quoted in Vincent, *Cult of the "Urka,"* 156.
52. Barnes, *Death and Redemption*, 155–201
53. This paragraph is based on Hardy, *The Gulag after Stalin*, 58–96.
54. Hardy, 87.
55. Hardy, 92.
56. Chalidze, *Criminal Russia*, 34.
57. Slade, *Reorganizing Crime*, 12–17.
58. Barnes, *Death and Redemption*, 155–201.
59. Slade, "Violence as information, 937–55;" Pallot, Piacentini and Moran, *Gender, Geography and Punishment*, 197–218.
60. Interview with Zaur, 35, Bishkek, Kyrgyzstan.
61. Interview with Dan, 45, Soroca Colony, Moldova.
62. Interview with Mirlan, 60, Bishkek, Kyrgyzstan.
63. Interview with Ivan, 17, Goian colony, Moldova.
64. Interview with Victor, 30, Branesti colony, Moldova.
65. Interview with Vasily, 38, Novopokrovka, Kyrgyzstan.
66. Public Defender's Office of Kyrgyzstan, *Human Rights in Kyrgyzstan*, 172.
67. Interview with Vasily, 38, Novopokrovka, Kyrgyzstan.
68. Slade, "Violence as Information," 937–55.
69. Slade, "A Return to 'Gulags'?," 185–204.
70. Butler, Slade, and Dias, "Self-Governing Prisons," 1–18.
71. Quoted in Pallot, "Gulag as Crucible," 709.
72. Barnes, *Death and Redemption*, 89.
73. Shalamov, *Kolyma Tales*, 411.
74. Roth and Skarbek, "Prison Gangs and the Community Responsibility System."
75. McDonnell, "Budgetary Units."

BIBLIOGRAPHY

Alexopoulos, Golfo. "A Torture Memo: Reading Violence in the Gulag." In *Writing the Stalin Era: Sheila Fitzpatrick and Soviet Historiography*, edited by Golfo Alexopoulos, Julie Hessler, and Kiril Tomoff, 157–76. New York: Palgrave MacMillan, 2011.
Applebaum, Anne. *Gulag: A History*. New York: Doubleday, 2003.
Bacon, Edwin. *The Gulag at War: Stalin's Forced Labour System in the Light of the Archives*. London: Palgrave Macmillan, 1994.

Barenberg, Alan. *Gulag Town, Company Town: Forced Labor and Its Legacy in Vorkuta*. New Haven, CT: Yale University Press, 2014.

Barnes, Steven A. *Death and Redemption: The Gulag and the Shaping of Soviet Society*. Princeton, NJ: Princeton University Press, 2011.

Butler, Michelle, Gavin Slade, and Camila Nunes Dias. "Self-Governing Prisons: Prison Gangs in an International Perspective." *Trends in Organized Crime* (2018): 1–16.

Chalidze, V. *Criminal Russia: Essays on Crime in the Soviet Union*. New York: Random House, 1977.

Dan (45). Interview by Gavin Slade, Soroca Colony, Moldova, 2017.

Gambetta, Diego. *Codes of the Underworld: How Prisoners Communicate*. Princeton, NJ: Princeton University Press, 2011.

Ginzburg, Eugenia. *Journey into the Whirlwind*. San Diego: Houghton Mifflin Harcourt, 2002.

Gurov, Aleksandr. *Krasnaia mafiia*. Moscow: Samotsvet, 1995.

Hardy, Jeffrey S. *The Gulag after Stalin: Redefining Punishment in Khrushchev's Soviet Union, 1953–1964*. Ithaca, NY: Cornell University Press, 2016.

———. "'A Very Important Yet Complicated Matter': Informant Networks in the Estonian Gulag, 1952–1964." *Russian History* 44, no. 2–3 (2017): 411–48.

Heinzen, James. "Corruption in the Gulag: Dilemmas of Officials and Prisoners." *Comparative Economic Studies* 47, no. 2 (2005): 456–75.

Ivan (17). Interview by Gavin Slade, Goian colony, Moldova, 2017.

Kaminski, Marek M. *Games Prisoners Play: The Tragicomic Worlds of Polish Prison*. Princeton, NJ: Princeton University Press, 2018.

Kaminski, Marek M., and Don C. Gibbons. "Prison Subculture in Poland." *Crime and Delinquency* 40, no. 1 (1994): 105–19.

Kharkhordin, Oleg. *The Collective and the Individual in Russia: A Study of Practices*. Berkeley: University of California Press, 1999.

Khlevniuk, Oleg V. *The History of the Gulag: From Collectivization to the Great Terror*. New Haven, CT: Yale University Press, 2004.

Kuntsman, Adi. "'With a Shade of Disgust': Affective Politics of Sexuality and Class in Memoirs of the Stalinist Gulag." *Slavic Review* 68, no. 2 (Summer 2009): 308–28.

Lambert, Alix, and Mary Christ. *Russian Prison Tattoos: Codes of Authority, Domination, and Struggle*. Alglen, PA: Schiffer, 2003.

Ledeneva, Alena V. *Russia's Economy of Favours: Blat, Networking and Informal Exchange*. Cambridge: Cambridge University Press, 1998.

McDonnell, Erin Metz. "Budgetary Units: A Weberian Approach to Consumption." *American Journal of Sociology* 119, no. 2 (2013): 307–50.

Milgrom, Paul R., Douglass C. North, and Barry R. Weingast. "The Role of Institutions in the Revival of Trade: The Law Merchant, Private Judges, and the Champagne Fairs." *Economics and Politics* 2, no. 1 (1990): 1–23.
Mirlan (60). Interview by Gavin Slade, Bishkek, Kyrgyzstan, 2015.
Pallot, Judith. "The Gulag as the Crucible of Russia's 21st-Century System of Punishment." *Kritika: Explorations in Russian and Eurasian History* 16, no. 3 (2015): 681–710.
Pallot, Judith, Laura Piacentini, and Dominique Moran. *Gender, Geography, and Punishment: The Experience of Women in Carceral Russia*. Oxford: Oxford University Press, 2012.
Piacentini, Laura, and Gavin Slade. "Architecture and Attachment: Carceral Collectivism and the Problem of Prison Reform in Russia and Georgia." *Theoretical Criminology* 19, no. 2 (2015): 179–97.
Public Defender's Office of Kyrgyzstan. *Human Rights in Kyrgyzstan*. Bishkek, 2016.
Roeder Bernhard. *Katorga: An Aspect of Modern Slavery*. London: Heinemann, 1958.
Roth, M. Garrett, and David Skarbek. "Prison Gangs and the Community Responsibility System." *Review of Behavioral Economics* 1, no. 3 (2014): 223–43.
Shalamov, Varlam. *Kolyma Tales*. Harmondsworth: Penguin, 1995.
Skarbek, David. *The Social Order of the Underworld: How Prison Gangs Govern the American Penal System*. Oxford: Oxford University Press, 2014.
Slade, Gavin. *Reorganizing Crime: Mafia and Anti-Mafia in Post-Soviet Georgia*. Oxford: Oxford University Press, 2013.
———. "A Return to 'Gulags'? Explaining Trends in Post-Soviet Prison Rates." In *The Political Economy of Punishment Today*, edited by Dario Melossi, José A. Brandariz García, and Máximo Sozzo, 203–22. London: Routledge, 2017.
———. "Violence as Information during Prison Reform: Evidence from the Post-Soviet Region." *British Journal of Criminology* 56, no. 5 (2016): 937–55.
Sykes, Gresham M. *The Society of Captives: A Study of a Maximum Security Prison*. Princeton, NJ: Princeton University Press, 2007.
Sykes, Gresham M., and Sheldon L. Messinger. "The Inmate Social System." *Theoretical Studies in Social Organization of the Prison* (1960): 5–19.
Varese, Federico. *The Russian Mafia: Private Protection in a New Market Economy*. Oxford: Oxford University Press, 2001.
———. "The Society of the Vory-v-Zakone, 1930s-1950s." *Cahiers du Monde Russe* 39, no. 4 (1998): 515–38.
Vasily (38). Interview by Gavin Slade, Novopokrovka, Kyrgyzstan, 2015.
Victor (30). Interview by Gavin Slade, Branesti colony, Moldova, 2017.
Vincent, Mark. *Cult of the "Urka": Criminal Subculture in the Gulag, 1924–1953*. PhD diss., University of East Anglia, 2015.
Zaur (35). Interview by Gavin Slade, Bishkek, Kyrgyzstan, 2015.

GAVIN SLADE is Associate Professor of Sociology at Nazarbayev University, Kazakhstan. His most recent project was a comparative study of prison gangs under conditions of reform in Lithuania, Moldova, Georgia, and Kyrgyzstan, the results of which were published in the *British Journal of Criminology*, *Theoretical Criminology*, and the *European Journal of Criminology*. His current project (www.gulagshadow.org) concerns societal and elite attitudes, perceptions, and cultural consumption of prisons in the former Soviet Union, funded by the Economic and Social Research Council of the UK.

FIVE

THE *REAL* GULAG

Commentary on the "Identities" Section

LYNNE VIOLA

THE GULAG LOOMS LARGE IN the history of the Soviet Union. Under Stalin, it became a vast network of penal institutions that stretched across the country and housed millions of people. Yet until the last ten years or so, our knowledge of the Gulag system was fairly limited and shaped more by assumption than actuality. The source base we relied on was also relatively limited, confined largely to the very rich intelligentsia memoirs as long as archives were not open.

Scholars of the totalitarian model, which long dominated the Western historiography on the Soviet Union, posited an unwarranted equivalency between the Gulag and the Nazi camp system, in both cases privileging an ideal camp type (in the singular) based on strict state control, overwhelming guard power, uniformity, and harsh discipline. This view was reinforced with the publication of Aleksandr Solzhenitsyn's *The Gulag Archipelago* and his novella *One Day in the Life of Ivan Denisovich*. The novella was set in one of the postwar strict regime camps (*osobye lageri*, 1948–54) that housed the most "politically dangerous" prisoners; Solzhenitsyn's own camp experience was also, in part, based on internment in a strict regime camp. That setting proved conducive to understanding the Gulag as a totalitarian institution.

New research has broadened our definition of the Gulag to extend beyond the labor camps described by Solzhenitsyn and others to include institutions such as "labor colonies" and "special settlements." Further, it has revealed that Soviet confinement sites changed and adapted over time.[1] In fact, it is almost impossible to describe the system, as it was in continual administrative flux. As we learn more about individual camps, it has become clear that the camps were highly diverse despite sharing rules and regimens that, at times, remained little more than paper constructs, impossible to implement and not suitable for local conditions. No two camps were entirely alike. The sector of the economy that each camp served very much defined its basic setup and the lives of its prisoners. Individual "Gulag bosses" could also put their personal imprint on a camp.[2] And the geographic location of a camp could determine such life and death issues as the availability of food and medical supplies, the quality and quantity of camp personnel, and relations with the surrounding free population.

The new research on the Gulag has benefited from the partial opening of Soviet archives and the appearance of a huge number of new memoirs, many of them written by ordinary people rather than the political prisoners who produced most examples of the genre before the fall of the Soviet Union. The three chapters under consideration exemplify the new research, drawing on a range of sources, including new memoirs, archival collections, and oral history. Yet while most of the new research has been about institutions, these chapters are very much about the prisoner experience, pushing the boundaries of our understanding of religion, language, nationality, and informal institutions in the Gulag. The section as a whole is a contribution to our understanding of prisoner identities, demonstrating that the striking diversity of Gulag institutions was mirrored in the varied identities of its inhabitants.

Jeffrey S. Hardy turns our attention to the largely unexplored topic of religion in the camps. Using newly available memoirs, he focuses his study on the Russian Orthodox clerics imprisoned in the 1920s on the Solovetskii islands, home to one of the largest and most important monasteries of northern Russia. Solovki (for short) served, as Hardy notes, as a kind of improvisational laboratory for penal reform in the still vegetarian era of the 1920s.

Hardy writes that in this period the Soviet authorities were attempting to balance the official "guarantee of religious liberty" and the ideological reeducational purposes of incarceration. Although life was by no means easy, and camp authorities were not liberal, Russian Orthodox clerics were able to create a vibrant religious community on Solovki, not unlike the virtual universities described by former prisoner and later noted literary critic Dmitry S. Likhachev, who served a term on Solovki (1928–31) while in his twenties.[3] As Hardy notes, clerics wore ecclesiastical garb, maintained church hierarchy, conducted the liturgy, celebrated religious holidays, and were housed together, serving "one another as counselors and confessors." In part, these patterns of autonomy derived from prerevolutionary prison traditions, when different strata of prisoners banded together in real or virtual communities. These traditions lingered, probably through neglect, sometimes even into the mid-1930s, as the Yugoslav communist Ante Ciliga recalled regarding the communities of different groups of political prisoners.[4]

As the 1920s progressed, the Solovki regime became harsher and more restrictive. The decline in the status and position of the Orthodox clerics reflected the ongoing upheaval in the Russian Orthodox church. The predominant mindset among clerics on Solovki, following Patriarch Tikhon, was one of nonrecognition of the Soviet state. This stance had been challenged, both within Solovki and especially outside of it, by members of the "living church," which sought accommodation with the state. By the late 1920s, according to Hardy, the community on Solovki was broken up, and clerics were moved to far harsher and more desolate places of incarceration.

Hardy's study is a first foray into the topic of religion in the camps. As such, it joins a rich new historiography on the Russian Orthodox church and religion.[5] Religious identity did not disappear on entry into the camps. The clerics under study never learned to "speak Bolshevik"—that is, adopt the language of the new Soviet state in order to navigate life in the camp—and had leeway to continue living Orthodox lives.[6] This study suggests the need for further research on religion in the camps in later years. We know, for instance, that large waves of peasants entered the special settlements and the camps in the 1930s, constituting the largest component of the incarcerated population.[7] Many, especially women, maintained their religious beliefs. These historically neglected women can sometimes be glimpsed in the background of the memoirs of political prisoners, especially in cases when they defied the authorities.[8] The entry of large numbers of non-Soviet prisoners from the Baltic, Eastern Europe, and western Ukraine on the eve of and after the war also presents researchers with an opportunity to study religious identity. As Hardy warns us, this kind of research is not easy, given the relative archival silence on the subject. Still, there has been a huge number of memoirs published since the fall of the Soviet Union, written by people from all walks of life.

In addition to providing us with new insights into the lives of Orthodox clerics on Solovki, Hardy's work reminds us of the improvisational nature of the early camps: the authorities did not succeed in exercising full control even in the relatively contained area of Solovki, and, importantly, pockets of relative autonomy remained amid the horrors. Hardy also shows the evolution of the detention site on Solovki as the camp system took shape and became (officially) the Gulag in 1930.[9] One cannot help but wonder what types of materials exist in the archives of the FSB on the history of Solovki.

Emily D. Johnson's work takes us directly into the Gulag of the 1930s and 1940s. By exploring camp correspondence written in non-Russian languages, a highly original route into questions of identity, she is able to delve into prisoners' language use and the instability of language over time. Johnson notes that "centrally issued regulations governing prisoner mail in the Soviet Union allowed for correspondence in the state's minority languages." These official regulations were in line, at least in the early years, with the state's efforts "to foster the development of national identity among smaller 'national minorities.'" And places like Dmitlag and Karlag, with large camp populations, "had translation bureaus, minority language periodicals, and cultural and educational programs" for some non-Russian nationalities. This finding corresponds with Hardy's finding that the Soviet state, at least on paper, attempted to follow, in his case, its policies on religion and nationality.

At the same time, Johnson shows how actuality differed from state policy and how important the role of local camp authorities was in determining practice. Some local camp authorities banned the use of other languages in prisoner correspondence. Elsewhere, authorities made use of prisoners, even political prisoners who were forbidden from these types of activity, to translate (and censor!) their fellow prisoners' letters. In part, these practices evolved locally because of the sheer impossibility of securing translators for the myriad languages of the Soviet Union. Johnson also shows how prisoners worked around local prohibitions by smuggling letters out of the camp, throwing letters from trains while in transport, and slipping in occasional phrases in their native language within letters written in Russian.

Importantly, Johnson also shows how Russian became the lingua franca of the multiethnic camp system. Many inmates learned or improved their Russian over time. This was especially the case in the postwar period, when large numbers of people from the Baltics and Eastern Europe entered the system. As they learned Russian, their letter writing changed. At the same time, occasional slippage allowed sentiments in the native language, which, according to Johnson, most often were used to convey emotions. Gulag jargon, in Russian, also entered their letters as a language of its own developed in the camps. The centrality of Russian, Johnson argues, was what led "many inmates [to perceive] labor camps ... as sites of Russification as much as Sovietization."

Johnson's chapter is a fascinating foray into language and identity. As Hardy did for religion, she demonstrates the persistence of national identity in the camp as well as its gradual erosion. She also reminds us of the sheer diversity of the Gulag—a multiethnic universe that requires further research. Finally, she shows the gulf between policy and actuality as local camp authorities often determined the contour of specific camps.

Gavin Slade's work focuses on the world of the criminal (*vory-v-zakone*), a topic that has received relatively little attention in the historiography. Our understanding of criminals comes largely from memoirs by members of the intelligentsia who, uniformly, describe the criminals or thieves as subhuman, out of control, and violent. Slade instead turns our attention to the subjects of reputation, prisoner self-government, and the vast information networks created and maintained by the criminals, which stretched all over the Soviet Union. Set within a comparative framework that includes literature on the power and reach of gangs in US prisons as well as the reputation system developed by medieval traders, his analysis shows how Soviet criminals maintained a reputation and disciplinary system based on hierarchy and personal history. Slade also takes his study into the present with a series of interviews, exploring the continuity of the criminal reputation system in the prisons of Moldova and Kyrgyzstan today (where cell phones strengthen the system!).

As in the studies by Hardy and Johnson, context is a key to understanding. This vast reputation system, according to Slade, emerged in response to "a lack of formal governance and a relative lack of control over violence in collectivist living quarters, corruption and the growth of trade on black markets, the formal use of a community responsibility system that made prisoner work detachments responsible for the productivity of individual prisoners, the seemingly ubiquitous presence of state-recruited informants, and frequent prisoner transfers." Memoirs by political prisoners often claimed that camp officials ceded considerable authority to the criminals because Bolshevik theory deemed them "socially near" to the working class. Slade's work helps us understand how and why this occurred. Reputation was important in the world of the Gulag. The question of "who are you in life?" allowed fellow criminal inmates to know who they were dealing with, as did tattoos, jargon, and the notes that passed through the system during transport. The rule of criminals, according to Slade, protected (criminal) property rights, secured transactions, and facilitated both collective action for mutual benefit and a range of services. It provided a governing infrastructure, however lawless, in the poorly run and inadequately guarded camp system. And camp authorities cast a blind eye on this informal institution as long as relative order prevailed.

Slade contributes to our understanding of the complexities of the Gulag system. Criminals combined to form their own culture within the camps, one that was self-sustaining, seemingly ubiquitous, and powerful. Criminals in the Gulag often did not "speak Bolshevik" in their day-to-day interactions, creating instead an alternative language and culture that drew from prerevolutionary practices and life on the outside. It would be interesting to know more about the defense mechanisms used by other noncriminal prisoners against this system. Slade mentions the existence of the work collective, which seems to have served as an alternate community. Likewise, after the war, groups of prisoners from the same nations and regions often came together in communities known as *zemliachestva* for self-preservation and belonging.

Slade, like Hardy and Johnson, portrays the internal life of the camps in ways that would hardly be familiar from the earlier totalitarian model. The *real* Gulag functioned poorly, was highly disordered, lacked sufficient personnel, and contained a world within that often was divided by community, belief, and ethnicity. The population of the Gulag, in many ways, reflected the population of the Soviet Union. Both these populations could be characterized as being in constant flux, traumatized, and exhibiting complex and fluid identities shaped by war, revolution, and repression as well as generation, gender, ethnicity, and status.[10]

As Johnson reminds us, the Gulag was a multiethnic institution. It was also a socially complex institution, with a population dominated by peasants. Historians have largely neglected the Gulag's peasant population in spite of their numbers in the various institutions of the Gulag. Because most of the deported "kulaks" were sent to special or labor settlements, this population has not been seen as part of the Gulag, defined narrowly as labor camps. The special or labor settlements were part of a large and complex system that contained enormous variation among types of penal incarceration. Roughly half of the Gulag population, writ large, were *not* in labor camps. Women also made up a large part of the Gulag in both exclusively women's and mixed-gender camps as well as in special and labor settlements. Yet the study of gender in the Gulag still awaits its historian.

Criminals, laborers, political prisoners, white-collar criminals, non-Russian prisoners, and foreigners were also among the Gulag's inhabitants. While some of these prisoners may have "spoken Bolshevik," especially while writing appeals to authority, such language was far from universally adopted in everyday life and in correspondence with the outside world. Non-Russian prisoners, who often found just speaking Russian challenging, may have been particularly slow to absorb the nuances of Soviet rhetoric. Prisoners not only spoke a number of languages, real and figurative, but they also presented fluid and evolving identities. And many prisoners remained stubbornly and bravely anti-Soviet.

The Gulag, like the Soviet Union itself, was subject to basic laws of history. Context, contingency, and chronology helped shape the system. The Gulag was dynamic, changing radically over time from the experimental Solovki camp that Hardy discusses, to the peasant Gulag of the 1930s, to the terrible war years when mortality reached a high point, to the postwar years when an array of seasoned veterans from various fronts and various nationalities became prisoners. Chronology, or periodization, matters when discussing the Gulag because it was anything but a static institution. Too often, historians have based their generalizations on the camps of the late 1930s. Likewise, contingency was important. This was especially so in the case of the deportation of the kulaks, when planning for the special settlements coincided with the deportations and developed "on the fly" (*na khodu*).[11]

Context also mattered. Slade demonstrates this well when he explains why and how criminals came to, in a sense, administer the camps. Situated in an undergoverned and vast country with limited infrastructure and subject to explosive growth, Moscow did not have the resources to fulfill its ideological and political missions. According to regulations, the inhabitants of the Gulag were supposed to be controlled by a staff of just over 300,000. For example, in 1946, the total complement of Gulag workers was 330,438 people, with only 295,124 of these positions actually filled, leaving over 10 percent of jobs vacant. Roughly 100,000 of this number were guards, the majority of whom were not members of the Communist Party. The percentage of women among staff was very small except for during the war years, when women and older reserve NKVD cadres filled vacancies in the Gulag. Even after the war ended, the Gulag continued to struggle to fill vacant positions. In February 1949, out of a total of 337,474 staff positions, only 276,661 were filled.[12] The Gulag administration was never able to fully staff the camps and settlements. Moreover, the cadres sent to serve in the camps were the worst of the worst. Most were poorly educated, and few were party members. The Gulag therefore had to depend on prisoners, even—against the rules—political prisoners, to staff some specialist jobs and also to work as guards.[13]

In the end, the prisoners serving terms of hard labor in the Gulag suffered more from sheer neglect and negligence than from strict regimes and harsh oversight. Although scholars have often compared Soviet and Nazi concentration camps, the comparison is facile given the many different types of camps and penal institutions in both systems. In the case of the Soviet penal system, living and working conditions varied widely, as did the degree of control and regimentation. The special/labor settlements generally had a commandant in charge (though sometimes one commandant served several settlements) but nothing more in the way of guards or barbed wire. Escapes, especially in 1930 and 1931, occurred in the tens of thousands. The camps varied widely depending on whether a camp was strict regime. Smaller, remote subcamps were often virtually autonomous, cut off for months at a time in winter or during the spring thaw and left unstaffed because of shortages of cadres. Barbed wire and high-intensity lighting were deficit items, and escapes, though at lower numbers than in the special settlements, also occurred in numbers higher than historians expected to see.[14]

Moscow was known for its almost aesthetic planning—detailed and impossible to fulfill. The periphery was known for its singular inability to fulfill Moscow's plans, whether due to sheer (usually material) inability, corruption, or unwillingness. There was a massive disconnect between policy and implementation, as these chapters by Hardy, Johnson, and Slade all demonstrate. The price of this disconnect came in prisoners' health, safety, and, most importantly, lives.[15] This is, of course, not to say that Moscow's intentions were benign. Moscow was fully aware of the limitations of undergovernment and the fate of prisoners in the Gulag.

NOTES

1. For some examples, see Barnes, *Death and Redemption*; Barenberg, *Gulag Town, Company Town*; Bell, *Stalin's Gulag at War*; Hardy, *The Gulag after Stalin*; Alexopoulos, *Illness and Inhumanity*; Johnson, ed. and trans., *Gulag Letters*; Ruder, *Building Stalinism*; David-Fox, ed., *The Soviet Gulag*.

2. For the impressions of one Gulag boss, see Kaple, ed. and trans, *Gulag Boss*. Also see Chistyakov, *Diary of a Gulag Prison Guard*.

3. Likhachev, *Reflections on the Russian Soul*, 98–9, 121–26, 136–38, 146.

4. Ciliga, *Russian Enigma*, 209–37.

5. For discussions of this historiography, see Werth, "Lived Orthodoxy," 849–65; and Wagner, "Religion in Modern Russia," 151–68. Thanks to Francesca Silano for these references.

6. This term is from Kotkin, *Magnetic Mountain*, 220–22.

7. See Viola, *Unknown Gulag*.

8. For one example, see Ginzburg, *Journey into the Whirlwind*, 412–13.

9. For a discussion (with documents) of the birth of the Gulag, see Krasil'nikov, "Rozhdenie GULAGa."

10. Viola, ed., *Contending with Stalinism*, 3–9.

11. Viola, *Unknown Gulag*.

12. Petrov and Vladimirtsev, eds., *Karatel'naia sistema*, 257–8, 163–4, 277–84, 355–58.

13. Beria attempted to end this practice. On January 1, 1939, 25,000 prisoners worked as guards; by September 1, 1940, only 2,650 did. Petrov and Vladimirtsev, eds., 34, 44–8.

14. For information on conditions in the special settlements, see Viola, *Unknown Gulag*. For conditions in subcamps, see Kaple, *Gulag Boss*. In addition, many of Varlam Shalamov's *Kolyma Tales* were set in such satellite camps.

15. Viola, "Aesthetic of Stalinist Planning."

BIBLIOGRAPHY

Alexopoulos, Golfo. *Illness and Inhumanity in Stalin's Gulag*. New Haven, CT: Yale University Press, 2017.
Barenberg, Alan. *Gulag Town, Company Town: Forced Labor and Its Legacy in Vorkuta*. New Haven, CT: Yale University Press, 2014.
Barnes, Steven A. *Death and Redemption: The Gulag and the Shaping of Soviet Society*. Princeton, NJ: Princeton University Press, 2011.
Bell, Wilson T. *Stalin's Gulag at War: Forced Labour, Mass Death, and Soviet Victory in the Second World War*. Toronto: University of Toronto Press, 2019.
Chistyakov, Ivan. *The Diary of a Gulag Prison Guard*. Translated by Arch Tait. London: Granta, 2016.
Ciliga, Ante. *The Russian Enigma*. Translated by Fernand G. Fernier, Anne Cliff, Margaret Dewar, and Hugo Dewar. London: Ink Links, 1979.
David-Fox, Michael, ed. *The Soviet Gulag: Evidence, Interpretation, and Comparison*. Pittsburgh: Pittsburgh University Press, 2016.
Ginzburg, Eugenia Semyonovna. *Journey into the Whirlwind*. Translated by Paul Stevenson and Max Hayward. New York: Harcourt Brace Jovanovich, 1967.
Hardy, Jeffrey S. *The Gulag after Stalin: Redefining Punishment in Khrushchev's Soviet Union, 1953–1964*. Ithaca, NY: Cornell University Press, 2016.
Johnson, Emily D., ed. and trans. *Gulag Letters: Arsenii Formakov*. New Haven, CT: Yale University Press, 2017.
Kaple, Deborah, ed. and trans. *Gulag Boss: A Soviet Memoir*. New York: Oxford University Press, 2011.
Kotkin, Stephen. *Magnetic Mountain: Stalinism as a Civilization*. Berkeley: University of California Press, 1995.
Krasil'nikov, S. A. "Rozhdenie GULAGa: Diskussii v verkhnikh eshelonakh vlasti: Postanovleniia Politburo TsK VKP (b), 1929–1930." *Istoricheskii arkhiv* no. 4 (1997): 142–56.
Likhachev, Dmitry S. *Reflections on the Russian Soul: A Memoir*. Translated by Bernard Adams. Budapest: CEU Press, 2000.
Petrov, N. V., and N. I. Vladimirtsev, eds. *Istoriia Stalinskogo Gulaga*. Vol. 2, *Karatel'naia sistema: struktura i kadry*. Moscow: Rosspen, 2004.
Ruder, Cynthia A. *Building Stalinism: The Moscow Canal and the Creation of Soviet Space*. London: I.B. Tauris, 2018.
———. *Making History for Stalin: The Story of the Belomor Canal*. Gainesville: University of Florida Press, 1998.
Varlam Shalamov. *Kolyma Tales*. Translated by John Glad. London: Penguin, 1994.
Viola, Lynne. "The Aesthetic of Stalinist Planning and the World of the Special Villages." *Kritika: Explorations in Russian and Eurasian History* 4, no. 1 (2003): 101–28.

———, ed. *Contending with Stalinism: Soviet Power and Popular Resistance in the 1930s*. Ithaca, NY: Cornell University Press, 2002.

———. *The Unknown Gulag: The Lost World of Stalin's Special Settlements*. New York: Oxford University Press, 2007.

Wagner, William G. "Religion in Modern Russia: Revival and Survival." *Kritika: Explorations in Russian and Eurasian History* 15, no. 1 (2014): 151–68.

Werth, Paul W. "Lived Orthodoxy and Confessional Diversity: The Last Decade on Religion in Modern Russia." *Kritika: Explorations in Russian and Eurasian History* 12, no. 4 (2011): 849–65.

LYNNE VIOLA is University Professor at the University of Toronto. She is author of *The Unknown Gulag: The Lost World of Stalin's Special Settlements* and *Stalinist Perpetrators on Trial: Scenes from the Great Terror in Soviet Ukraine*.

PART II

SOURCES

SIX

"THEY WON'T SURVIVE FOR LONG"

Soviet Officials on Medical Release Procedure

MIKHAIL NAKONECHNYI

ALMOST EVERYTHING THAT WE KNOW about official Gulag mortality and release statistics in 1930–55 is derived from the summary reports of its central administration, published in the 1990s. According to these sources, of the 17–18 million prisoners who entered the system between 1930 and 1955, 1.7 million perished. In other words, 90 percent of the detainees survived their custodial terms while only 10 percent died.[1] Scholars are divided concerning the reliability of this official data. Some historians tend to accept the above-mentioned figures as more or less reliable, and some doubt them. The former ("the believers"), representing the authoritative view, defend (with a few caveats) the ultimate veracity of the central accounting. Their main argument is predicated on the assumption that the classified and "functional" nature of the camp mortality and release data safeguards it from any kind of serious falsifications. The outnumbered latter ("the skeptics") hypothesize that death rates were artificially deflated by mass discharges of terminally ill "goners" via early release on medical grounds. Many of these former inmates died soon after release, but camp doctors consciously excluded these fatalities from medical registries. To illustrate the most eloquent examples of this stark polarity, Viktor Zemskov, the most radical of the believers, qualified central statistics as "absolutely precise" while Golfo Alexopoulos recently argued that they "can only be interpreted as inadequate."[2] She was the first to produce, in 2017, the only estimate based on archival documentation that constitutes an alternative to the "official" death toll of 1.7 million: 6 million dead, combining "official" mortality and alleged "unregistered" deaths of medically discharged invalids after release. Alexopoulos calculated 30 percent death and 70 percent survival rates from 1930 to 55. Although there has been a shift toward a more critical view on the Gulag mortality data since the 1990s, many influential historians (e.g., Wheatcroft, Barnes, Barenberg, Zemskov) continued even in the 2000s and 2010s to view official figures as, if not perfect, at least generally reliable.[3] Hence, claims concerning the prevalence of "release to die" practices have often been received skeptically or even ignored due to a variety of factors. First, there is still an insufficient understanding of its temporal and spatial spread. Second, the nascent scholarship of medical release (Alexopoulos) builds predominantly on the central NKVD-Gulag records. The records of local penal institutions and of the two other institutions involved in administering the procedure, the Procuracy and the Ministry of Justice (MIu), remain almost totally neglected.[4] Their interaction with the Central Gulag Administration remains unclear.

This chapter seeks to contribute to the abovementioned historiographical debate and address at least some of the described deficiencies. It aims to elucidate how medical release functioned throughout the penal system over a long time frame. I specifically concentrate on the role of the center and its interplay with the periphery.[5] So far, we have only Alexopoulos's interpretation of the question. In her view, firstly, deception via release was systematic, ubiquitous, and highly coordinated by the upper echelons of the NKVD for dozens of years with the aim of masking the "destructive capacity" of the system. Secondly, this policy's carefully orchestrated application grew exponentially over time from 1930 up to 1953, peaking in the late 1940s and early 1950s (ostensibly the deadliest period in the Gulag's existence, though less is known about it).[6] The present chapter strives to confound and significantly revise this exposition.

Here I try to handle the following dilemmas: if medical release was indeed a machination (at least occasionally), should we construe it as exclusively low-level deception to delude the central apparatus (analogous to the more well-known inflation of production output, the infamous "tufta")?[7] Or, on the contrary, was the top administrative echelon of all three relevant agencies (not just the Gulag) deliberately acting as an accomplice or even a catalyst in the manipulation of statistics? Or was there a conflict of interest between the Gulag, the Ministry of Justice, and the Procuracy around medical release and the distortion of mortality data? To answer these questions, I analyze the top and bottom tiers of bureaucratic hierarchies through their horizontal and vertical interactions.

The principal contention of this chapter is that high-level and low-level interest in falsifying the data via medical release converged during catastrophes but diverged considerably (although not entirely) in more ordinary times. Furthermore, I contend that the duplicitous facet of early release on medical grounds became ubiquitous during crises (1932–33, 1941–45, 1946–47) while in more normal periods (1930–31, 1934–36, 1939–41, 1948–55) it receded. In this exegesis, I considerably deviate from Alexopoulos's argument, which suggests that its application increased over time. To corroborate my principal claim, I offer new evidence from the archives: the voices of Soviet bureaucrats themselves. In newly discovered documents, officials (voluntarily or involuntarily) concede the existence of exactly such a deceptive scheme. The present chapter provides for the first time a systematized sample of such confessions, semiconfessions, and circumstantial affirmations by employees of three bureaucratic superstructures involved in medical release—the Gulag, the Ministry of Justice, and the Procuracy. By doing so, I endeavor to delineate the degree of dissemination of these peculiar acknowledgments across multiple temporal, spatial, and institutional variables. In order to properly articulate the circumstances behind officials' slips of the tongue, each of them is embedded within the broader historical context. The present chapter is divided into four substantive parts. I start with a note on methodology and sources. The next subsections correspond to the three principal bureaucratic actors in medical discharge. I conclude by adumbrating my own interpretation of the role of the center in the deception.

A NOTE ON METHODOLOGY AND SOURCES

At first glance, the extraction of officials' confessions concerning the manipulation of camp mortality data looks like an intractable methodological conundrum. There are two conspicuous impediments. First, functionaries left only a handful of ego documents such as memoirs and diaries. The few that are available understandably lack any candid attestations of this kind. Furthermore, we do not have any trial materials pertaining to the Gulag's high-ranking doctors and administrators (in contrast, for example, with the Nazis or even the NKVD circa 1937–38), where such testimonies theoretically could be present.[8] Second, the only representative corpus of official materials at our disposal is the internal documents of the pertinent agencies.

These sources are problematic for several reasons. Medical discharge was obfuscated with—using Stephen Wheatcroft's apt term—a certain "façade of legality."[9] According to Articles 457, 458, and 462 of the RSFSR Criminal Procedural Code, a severely ill inmate could be freed before the expiration of their sentence.[10] The procedure included three stages: invalid certification in the penal establishment via special commission (so-called *aktirovka* or *aktirovanie*— i.e., issuing an administrative act of invalid certification), confirmation by the procurator, and the final decision on early release (made by a court). After release, the ex-inmate was supposed to be transferred into the care of relatives, a civilian hospital, an invalid house, or administrative exile. Overwhelming evidence indicates that relatives were often absent, and hospitals habitually refused to accept the discharged. As a result, ex-cons died en masse immediately after formal release without even leaving the camp premises. Thousands of additional deaths from starvation and exposure to the elements occurred in train stations and railcars during exhausting return journeys from the camps. Nevertheless, official Soviet discourse never openly admitted that Gulag invalids were deliberately "released to die."[11] Indeed, on the surface, it looked like a purely technical process, an innocuous variation of parole with humanitarian undertones. This semblance of external orderliness is extremely difficult to penetrate. Alexopoulos encountered a similar recalcitrant problem in her pioneering work. She notes, "The Gulag's internal data on medical discharges ... was highly opaque."[12]

Other complicating factors include the Stalinist bureaucracy's proclivity toward the compartmentalization of sensitive information and multilayered secrecy, which was especially stringent with regard to excess deaths of any kind.[13] Moreover, in the "formal" edifice of Soviet agencies, prisoner death rates were supposed to be lowered by conventional therapeutic or prophylactic means, not through deceptive contrivances.[14] Inevitably, functionaries engaged in self-censorship. They were hesitant to forthrightly declare in written form that granting freedom to nearly dead inmates would improve mortality statistics—even in internal memoranda. Consequently, many classified reports on medical discharge are formulaic, purposely ambiguous, and uninformative.[15]

To circumvent these limitations, I use institutional triangulation to cross-reference communication between and within three bureaucracies over a long time frame. During 1930–53, the agencies in question hired tens of thousands of employees. Hence, probability theory makes any deceitful scheme impossible to conceal: information leaks in complex systems are ineluctable, especially under pressure. This chapter argues that the propensity to falsify the data increased during disasters, accompanied by the worst resource deficits and the highest death rates. Therefore, focusing on catastrophic periods (the war, national famines) helps pinpoint direct "confessions." Besides, a fresh multi-institutional perspective allows us to examine the main questions of this chapter through the prism of both inter- and intrabureaucratic conflicts at the center and periphery. Hence, in addition to the central archives (State Archive of Russian Federation, State Military Archive), I utilize several local ones: the state archives of the Samara, Arkhangel'sk, Tambov, and Novosibisk regions as well as the Party archive of the Perm region.

THE GUITU NKU/GULAG NKVD

The penal system served as a starting point in the process of aktirovanie. The director of the Gulag, the minister of the interior, and their deputies in the main NKVD-MVD apparatus defined general policy. The technical implementation of the procedure was entrusted to a pair of departments within the central Gulag: the Sanitary department (SANO), an embedded health service, and the Allocation and Distribution department (URO/OURZ), a statistical and labor allocation subdivision.[16] Their lower tiers were responsible for identifying inmates sick with "grave and incurable illness" vis-à-vis special commissions.[17] The present subsection aims to provide evidence for each of the described administrative levels of the Gulag as well as the Main Administration of Corrective-Labor Establishments (GUITU), an almost unstudied civilian penal structure under the jurisdiction of the Commissariat of Justice (NKU) in 1930–34.[18]

The earliest hints of the use of medical release to manipulate mortality statistics can be traced to the catastrophic 1932–33 famine. The prison-industrial complex was severely affected: both OGPU and NKU branches were deluged with emaciated prisoners. Registered Gulag mortality in 1933 skyrocketed to 15 percent.[19] Every sixth prisoner died— in absolute terms, more than seventy thousand people in just one year. The death toll for the GUITU subsystem is yet unknown. Bits and pieces of evidence suggest that the situation there was even worse than in the more prioritized OGPU camps.[20]

Formally, mass death in detention was not tolerated in Moscow. Camps were forced to comply with strictly defined quotas of "acceptable" morbidity/mortality rates.[21] Those who managed to report declining death rates were lauded and motivated with institutional recognition (even awards). The outliers were scapegoated and occasionally investigated.[22] These inspections ended in the arbitrary prosecution of officials.[23] Meanwhile, centralized supply was severely reduced in 1933.[24] As a result, the localities found themselves in an almost inextricable predicament: they had to adhere to blatantly impracticable central demands to lower soaring death rates quickly without any resources. Otherwise, they faced prosecution.

The abovementioned factors incentivized the penal periphery to devise clandestine self-serving schemes to provide expected figures and deflect blame. Thus, the director of the administrative sector of Western Siberia region penitentiaries Emets attempted to pacify the higher-ups with a remarkable explanation for the exponential rise of mortality under his jurisdiction (January–April 1932). While in the first four months of 1931 there were only 137 prisoner fatalities in 18 NKU penitentiaries in the region, in January–April 1932 the number swelled to 992 deaths.[25] A total of 319 out of 992 cases (32.1 percent) passed away due to "general emaciation."[26] Emets explicitly claimed that NKU tardiness contributed to the crisis. The attempts of the penal administration to get rid of "inconvenient" dying and ill prisoners through aktirovka failed because of red tape in the criminal justice system, which delayed the process up to two months. In Emets's words, "Such groups of prisoners caused a significant death rate."[27]

Essentially, a functionary complained that the sluggishness of the courts exacerbated the mortality indicator under his purview. Emets implied that if discharges had been executed more quickly, this would have lowered the death index. This is confirmed at the end of the memo by the set of measures that a GUITU bureaucrat offered to alleviate the crisis. Among other more standard enhancements (like the improvement of diet and treatment), he underscored, "Diminution of mortality in the corrective-labor establishments in the near future will happen due to ... persistent and systematic demands that the judicial authorities apply Article 458 to invalids ... for whom conditions of detention in ITU [corrective-labor establishments] could have deleterious consequences and increase mortality."[28]

Another example emanates from the Gulag circa 1935–36, the least deadly years of the decade. At some point in 1936, a chief doctor of the prison-industrial complex, Isaak Grigorievich Ginzburg, the first head of the Gulag SANO, submitted a report to Matvei Davydovich Berman, director of the system. The memorandum was brimming with institutional self-laudation and praised the decline of death rates in prisons and colonies (so-called MZ, *mesta zakluchenia*) of the RSFSR. According to Ginzburg's data, while the death rate was hovering around 2 percent in 1934, it decreased to just 1.26 percent in 1935. Explaining this positive change for 1935, the top-echelon physician pronounced:

> In comparison with the previous year, we should take into account that in 1934 releases under article 458 were practiced more widely—and in the case of gravely bedridden patients with transfers to civilian hospitals, and this mortality was not registered in the places of detention anymore.
>
> If, despite that, the percent of mortality dramatically declined, this fact should be attributed to improvements in
> a) the general state of MZ
> b) the conditions of detention
> c) the medical setting.[29]

This evidence suggests that Ginzburg clearly understood two facts. First, aktirovka was directly linked to the registered death index. Second, those released on medical grounds, at least in part, died after discharge, artificially lowering death rates in places of confinement. Remarkably, Ginzburg openly reported this to Berman. Ginzburg's note also may serve as an indication of the partial unreliability of low camp mortality figures for the noncrisis years 1934–35.

The next piece of evidence pertains to the war years, which were characterized by the worst death rates historically: roughly one million inmates expired in 1941–45. In addition to prisoners, the Gulag exploited other "contingents" during the war. One of the most prominent comprised "mobilized" internees of the "labor army" (*trudovaia armiia*).[30] It consisted of several ethnic minorities (most notably, Volga Germans and peoples of the Central Asian republics) deemed too "suspicious" to be enlisted into the armed forces but still exploited for the war effort in the rear in the ambiguous status of "labor soldiers." They lived and worked alongside prisoners in the same camps. The labor army drew extensively on Gulag theory and praxis in the development of its organizational principles. It had its own variation of aktirovanie (called "demobilization due to sickness"), which was sometimes applied, as shown below, with equally deceptive intent.[31]

The combination of deaths and medical releases in the labor army had become so large-scale by 1941–42 that it seemed all too likely that newly acquired "labor capital" might be squandered in just a few months.[32] This forced the Gulag leadership to enjoin local officials not to proceed with aktirovka without getting its approval in each case (April 1942). In one inquiry for such authorization (dated October 20, 1942), the commander of Solikamstroy Boikov and the head of its URO Olehnovich called for Nasedkin's "urgent sanction" to demobilize 184 invalids. The rationalization was straightforward: the lack of food and the coming winter could increase mortality.[33]

Although Solikamstroy's petition was denied, massive discharges of emaciated internees continued unabated during 1942—occasionally without the permission of the center.[34] In order to get rid of invalids, local administrators took risks and broke the chain of command. This may serve as an indication of how desperate the situation was on the ground at the time. As a result, the NKVD temporarily rescinded medical demobilization entirely in October 1942 in a futile attempt to preserve the workforce. Recorded mortality rates ballooned even higher. Local camps immediately issued frantic pleas asking the Gulag center to reinstate the procedure. In one case, the deputy commander of Volzhlag, captain of state security Zaikin, sent a distressed request to Gulag director Nasedkin on December 15, 1942. Zaikin noted that because of the ban on discharge, 450 invalids were stranded in the camp. He insisted that "the question of the demobilization of those designated as invalids [*aktirovannye*] needs to be resolved in the most urgent manner." According to the commandant, "Taking into account the fact that mortality among invalids has reached thirty cases in November . . . I request your order to immediately demobilize the invalids."[35] I argue that Zaikin was frustrated with his inability to remove dying internees from the statistical records of his camp because the increased death rates that resulted guaranteed trouble for him and his subordinates.

The Gulag leadership, regularly briefed on negative dynamics of health indicators across the system, was sympathetic to pleas like Zaikin's. However, the final decision on the reintroduction of aktirovanie in the labor army rested on the minister of the interior, Lavrentii Pavlovich Beria. Consequently, to justify its reinstatement to his own superiors, Gulag chief Nasedkin produced a missive on December 18, 1942, two months after he himself prohibited medical discharge of *trudarmeitsy*. Its line of argumentation is revealing. The Gulag director frankly utilized the catastrophic increase of registered mortality to make his case. According to Nasedkin, while deaths decreased somewhat in a few local administrations, mortality soared in the ill-famed forestry camps and Bakalstroi. In conclusion, the Gulag chief noted, "to avoid a further increase of mortality and the number of invalids, I would recommend implementing the demobilization of German invalids now."[36] Beria acquiesced.[37] Beginning in December 1942, medical releases of Volga Germans resumed.

The whole episode is indicative of the general ambivalence of the high-level NKVD toward the application of aktirovanie during catastrophes. On the one hand, its massive use wasted the workforce of Volga Germans, whom the NKVD had taken great pains to deport, supply, and concentrate. Moscow officials were concerned that camp doctors, easily susceptible to corruption, squandered the labor force by releasing prisoners or internees whose health had not degenerated completely and who still could be potentially exploited in the camp economy.[38] Moreover, local camps often freed ill prisoners whom central command considered too dangerous from a state security standpoint (e.g., political prisoners and recidivists). Occasionally, the authorities even "hunted" for survivors among the medically released with the intention of reincarcerating them.[39]

On the other hand, aktirovka helped keep soaring mortality down. In addition, it allowed camps to economize precious resources and helped preserve the limited capacity of camp hospitals to heal those inmates with at least slim chances of recovery and return them to production rather than wasting time on terminal cases. The NKVD could not decide which imperative held more priority—hence the contradictory, haphazard policy. Importantly, Nasedkin was not afraid to break the "façade of legality" and advertise the impact of aktirovanie on registered mortality as a cogent argument to higher NKVD brass. This deduction raises another question: Were Nasedkin's immediate higher-ups in the NKVD hierarchy (at the ministerial level) also aware that medical discharge was being used to artificially lower mortality statistics?

This can be addressed via dissection of a report by senior URO inspector Nechaev and deputy head of the production department of ULLP (Main Administration of Forestry Camps) Engalychev. The pair of plenipotentiaries was sent to investigate the deadly Viatlag forestry camp that housed both prisoners and labor army internees. Their scathing memo, dated July 3, 1943, was addressed to Beria's right hand and curator of the Gulag in the central NKVD apparatus, Deputy Minister of the Interior Vasilii Vasil'evich Chernyshev.[40] The value of the memorandum for the purpose of this chapter is enhanced by handwritten markings left by Chernyshev. Commenting on the seemingly positive downward trend in recent months before their inspection, Nechaev and Engalychev forthrightly confessed, "If we analyze the data of the Sanitary department of the camp on mortality among the mobilized, at the first glance, it may seem that, starting with February 1943, the growth of terminal cases somewhat stabilized and began to wane. But in reality these indicators are just statistical data because the camp demobilized 1,308 people due to various ailments, predominantly those who were emaciated and afflicted with vitamin deficiency disease, who were, in the majority of cases, gravely ill and would have produced a high death rate for this period had they remained in the camp."[41] Chernyshev drew a line in the margin and wrote next to it, "Correct!"[42] This exclamation confirms that Beria's deputy was conscious of two facts: those released were on the brink of death, and medical discharges heavily distorted objective camp mortality statistics. It is instructive how inspectors used the expression *just statistical data* to describe the superficial nature of registered figures.

Valuable evidence can be inferred from reports of local doctors in 1943–45. In August 1943, the head of the medical-sanitation department of the Tambov regional labor colonies (OITK) Chernysheva (alongside commandant Popov) complained about the sudden illness of the regional judge and the sluggishness of her subordinates "who postponed for considerable periods of time the aktirovanie of those known to be hopeless [*zavedomo beznadezhnye*] invalids."[43] The adjective *hopeless* unequivocally suggests that the head doctor understood the terminal condition of the candidates for discharge. Delays inevitably increased recorded mortality, presenting the penal medical service under her command in an unfavorable light to the senior officials. In another instance, Chernysheva informed the central apparatus that out of eleven total prisoner deaths in February 1944, five were officially certified invalids. OITK doctors tried to set these ailing prisoners free, but "two of them were denied release ... although they had alimentary dystrophy in an irreversible phase."[44] The word *irreversible* denotes that Chernysheva and her colleagues were specifically targeting at least some nearly dead inmates for the procedure.

The final piece of evidence for the penitentiary system came to light due to one of many conflicts of interest between the Gulag and the Ministry of Justice. On September 7, 1947, the head of URO and Gulag director deputy German Markovich Granovskii sent an inquiry to the chief of the directorate of the camp courts, Dobronravov. According to Granovskii, the commander of the regional labor colonies of Vladimirskaya oblast' Kuznetsov complained of the systematic delays of the regional court while processing materials pertaining to medical release under Article 457 of the Criminal Code. When Kuznetsov tried to approach the chairman of the judiciary, a certain Gridneva, with a request to expedite the review, the judge responded that there were no established terms for the consideration of such cases. Therefore, Gridneva replied, they would be resolved when the court had time for them. Granovskii asked Dobronravov to intervene and force the judiciary to process the materials faster. For the present discussion, it is important that a top-echelon bureaucrat offered a revealing justification as to why judicial inaction was so detrimental from his point of view. According to Granovskii, "As a result of the delay in processing these cases in the regional court, in July 1947 alone there were four deaths among those eligible to be released due to ill health and whose materials were already in the court."[45]

In the final analysis, how can we interpret Granovskii's intervention and link it to the rest of the evidence? First, it shows that the URO director was cognizant of invalids' mortality. In that respect, we can add him to the cohort of exalted NKVD-MVD officials who were, as we have determined, privy to this knowledge: his boss, the seventh Gulag director Nasedkin, the third Gulag director and deputy minister of the interior Berman, the chief of SANO Ginzburg, as well as the deputy minister of the interior and sixth Gulag director Chernyshev. Moreover, Granovskii's message (1947) becomes suggestive and even symptomatic if we contextualize it with the earlier cases of Emets (1932) and Chernysheva (1944). These incidents were separated from each other by many years and concern random penal officials of various affiliations and ranks (subaltern camp doctor, midlevel officer, and top administrator). Nevertheless, they manifest almost identical patterns: the penal bureaucracy in various years was clashing with the criminal justice system over the expeditious consideration of invalids' cases. The reason was the same in all three instances:

candidates for release died too early due to unwanted red tape, exacerbating registered mortality in the Gulag's zone of responsibility. Exactly the same phenomenon was discovered by Alexopoulos, who found several additional examples where officials complained that "high rates of mortality were attributed to their inability to release prisoners in a timely manner."[46]

THE PROCURACY

The Soviet Procuracy—a powerful bureaucratic competitor of the NKVD-MVD—served as an idiosyncratic external check on the Gulag's operations starting in the early 1930s. The inspection mechanism worked via a dedicated department of oversight over places of confinement in Moscow and special camp procurators on the ground.[47] Despite the availability of a vast amount of materials, the camp Procuracy remains one of the least researched agencies of the Stalinist state. Importantly, it played a crucial, albeit totally unstudied, oversight function in the execution of the medical release process. After an invalid was approved for release via a commission of penal officials, his case file was transferred for procuratorial review before going to the court for the final ruling. The camp procurators were also obliged to participate in court sessions on early release on medical grounds. If, for some reason, the procurator decided that the prisoner did not meet the criteria for discharge, he had a legal right to override the decision of the camp or judicial authorities (issue a "protest").

If we take the declared goals of the camp Procuracy at face value, it can be assumed that its materials may provide an invaluable insight into the skewing of mortality data. First, procurators were required to investigate egregious cases of prisoner mass death and punish responsible officials.[48] Second, they were supposed to detect all suspicious machinations with accounting. Finally, by their very purpose, the camp procurators epitomized "socialist legality" and, in theory, were antagonistic to the Gulag. However, the actual picture that emerges from archival documents is far more ambivalent. The fundamental problem is the structural, almost ubiquitous corruption that plagued the camp Procuracy under Stalin from its inception. Although formally working for a rival agency, the camp procurators habitually were in cahoots with, or even subjugated to, the local NKVD administration. Jeffrey Hardy noticed this phenomenon during the Khrushchev era.[49] Under Stalin, this proclivity tended to be even more pronounced.

This situation led to the three unequal patterns in procuratorial behavior in relation to supervision of aktirovanie. In rare instances, intransigent maverick procurators exposed the distortion of mortality statistics via the use of medical release, although this did not necessarily guarantee criminal prosecution of the guilty parties.[50] I would argue that such precedents were aberrational. The second scenario was far more pervasive: an average procurator tersely reported on supervision over the process. Content-wise, such reports, as a rule, gravitated toward dry, often quantitative forms devoid of any mention of the invalids' state of health.[51] However, some procurators understood that the medically released were on the brink of death and wrote about this openly without any attempt at obfuscation. For instance, the procurator of Birlag (Khabarovsk region), Mikhailov, noted in his report to Moscow from January 24, 1942, about invalids designated for discharge: "In order to double-check their health condition, I personally travelled into camp divisions, inspected all the invalids and was convinced that they will not survive for long if they are set free."[52] Finally, as we shall see below, a substantial proportion of procurators shared the agenda of their camp administration and acted as accomplices to the Gulag officials in the "release-to-die" practice.

Thus, procurator Mikhail Isaevich Khelemskii informed Moscow that the regional penal system released 6,751 invalids in 1943. According to Khelemskii, "Because of this and other measures, we managed to achieve a sharp reduction in the mortality rate in the regional UITLiK [Administration of Camps and Colonies] and Arkhlag NKVD." As evidence, Khelemskii included the following mortality figures for the regional UITLK in 1943: 1.36 percent in the first quarter; 1.32 percent in the second quarter; 1.07 percent in the third quarter; and 0.89 percent in the fourth quarter. In Arkhlag, mortality had fallen from 0.6 percent in the first half of 1943 to 0.4 percent in the second half.[53] Khelemskii's report offers several points to consider. First, it becomes clear that the putative decline of the death rate occurred—at least partly—due to the release of invalids and not necessarily because prisoners there were supplied or treated better. Second, the intended audience for Khelemskii's report is very important. It was sent to Vladimir Pavlovich D'iakonov, deputy procurator of the USSR and head of the department of oversight over places of detention. Notably, Khelemskii considered it appropriate to frankly dissect the role of the procedure in mortality diminution to one of the highest functionaries in the entire Procuracy. Tellingly, the UITLiK procurator did not depict it to his boss as subterfuge. On the contrary, Khelemskii accentuated his own participation in the process and lauded himself for its revitalization.[54] This suggests that at least some local procurators and the head of the department of oversight over places of detention were complicit in the distortion of mortality data. The following case of Procurator Bubnov of Sevpechlag helps to substantiate this interpretation. As soon as the situation began to normalize in 1944, local camp administrations were dissuaded from the massive application of aktirovanie, and, starting in spring 1944, the number of freed invalids decreased significantly. In some localities, it dropped to zero.[55] One such camp was Sevpechlag, tasked with railroad construction in Komi Autonomous Republic. In October 1944, its procurator, Bubnov, sent a communication to the Sevpechlag commandant, Barabanov, and his own Moscow boss, D'iakonov. The procurator complained about the "abnormal state of affairs" with medical release in the camp. Beginning in March 1944, Sevpechlag had failed to discharge even a single invalid. On May 29, 1944, the procurator advised the camp administration to resume the practice. Although five months had passed since this reminder, Bubnov bemoaned, it continued to be ignored. The procurator also personally approached Deputy Commandant Artamonov and admonished him many times about the necessity of initiating the procedure. Artamonov promised to address the issue but did nothing.

It is important to highlight that the principal argument in favor of the reintroduction of aktirovanie, formulated by Bubnov, was to counter increasing prisoner mortality.[56] The procurator finished his communiqué by urging Sevpechlag's commandant to compel the heads of SANO and OURZ to "proceed immediately" with medical release. The issue was important enough to be supervised by Deputy USSR Procurator D'iakonov directly. On December 14, 1944, he telegraphed Bubnov with a request to inform him about the concrete measures Sevpechlag had taken to implement aktirovka.[57] In response, the commandant's deputy, Artamonov, furnished a detailed report directly to D'iakonov that described Sevpechlag's reinvigorated efforts to release invalids.[58]

What can we glean from this episode? In theory, Bubnov was supposed to prosecute penal officials for high mortality and statistical manipulations. In practice, the Sevpechlag procurator himself was an active participant in data distortion, with the full approval and supervision of his Moscow boss. Quite paradoxically, the camp procuracy (both central and local) was apparently even more concerned with the artificial reduction of death rates in Sevpechlag than was its own passive NKVD administration. Importantly, Bubnov's behavior was not a deviation by the standards of his department. His emphasis on urgency is consonant with almost identical requests for the intensification of medical releases "to avoid mortality" from other procurators, including Dmitlag deputy procurator Chernezkii (1935), Novosibirsk procurator Kondrashev (1944), Azerbaijani UITLiK procurator Khelemskii (1945), and Uzbekistani UITLiK procurator Fedorovich (1945).[59] In Fedorovich's and Khelemskii's cases, D'iakonov played the same supervisory role as in the Sevpechlag incident.[60]

I would argue that these examples elucidate a peculiar convergence of the institutional interests of the Gulag and the camp Procuracy, which, to date, has found insufficient reflection in scholarship on camp mortality statistics. It is important to underscore that the tasks of the camp procurators included oversight over mortality reduction measures, especially during wartime. The procurator was seen as an efficacious overseer when the camp under his supervision demonstrated a downward mortality trend. In some rare instances, high death rates could even lead to demotion and other career trouble.[61] In this context, the Procuracy acted as an adviser to Gulag officials, encouraging them to tweak the statistics in a desirable direction for both agencies.

THE MINISTRY OF JUSTICE

Separate camp courts were organized by a Decree of the Central Executive Committee and Council of People's Commissars on November 17, 1934.[62] The rationale was similar to the deliberations behind the establishment of the camp Procuracy: the penitentiary system had become so large that it required its own judicial organs. For the present discussion, it is important to note that in addition to regular criminal proceedings, the second main prerogative of the camp court system was the consideration of medical release cases.

The court represented the last stage in the entire procedure. It wielded the legal power to issue so-called judicial determinations (*sudebnoe opredelenie*) on discharge.[63] The latter could be either negative or positive, depending on a set of variables. According to Galina Ivanova, the proclaimed independence of the camp courts was feigned to a large extent.[64] With an obvious parallel to the Procuracy, penal justice often (but not always) fell under the sway of the NKVD-MVD. Not surprisingly, this influence pervaded medical release cases as well. As the judge of Ukrainian UITLiK Zhlobin complained in 1948, only the MVD had tangible influence in the process while the courts and procurators were powerless.[65] It can be presupposed that this dependency made some camp judges susceptible to distorting mortality rates via aktirovanie in the economic or political interests of the Gulag. But the "façade of legality," as a rule, prevented the judiciary from being overly candid in acknowledging this complicity in official correspondence.[66]

Nevertheless, institutional bickering and frictions again help to extract evidence otherwise camouflaged behind formalities. The first set of clues revolves around the perennial battle against so-called red tape (*volokita*) in medical release.[67] A memo sent by Pashutina, the head of the directorate of the camp courts, on August 6, 1948, to USSR Minister of Justice Konstantin

Table 6.1. Time spent processing selected medical release cases by administrative tier, 1947–April 1, 1948

	0–5 days	6–10 days	11–20 days	>20 days
Commission	513 (13.3%)	809 (20.9%)	985 (25.9%)	1554 (40.3%)
Procuracy	1744 (45.3%)	1299 (33.6%)	441 (11.4%)	337 (9.7%)
Court	1991 (51.8%)	700 (18%)	880 (22.8%)	290 (7.4%)

Source: GARF, f. R-9492, op.5, d. 42, l. 224.

Petrovich Gorshenin can serve as an example. If the director of the Gulag URO, Granovskii, castigated the courts for delays and resultant deaths in 1947, Pashutina returned the favor and accused NKVD-MVD commissions of exactly the same "sin." To lend credence to her claim, she submitted the following data, contained in table 6.1, to the minister.

According to Pashutina, red tape, especially prevalent on the level of camp commissions, had led to a "very serious consequences—the mortality of the prisoners."[68] After providing statistical data on deaths for several localities, the head of the Camp Courts Directorate furnished concrete examples of such incidents. In the Molotov region, the prisoner Egorov was diagnosed with TB of the lungs on January 1, 1948. The central commission of the UITLiK processed his case file almost a month later, on January 21. Then the case got stuck in the Procuracy for half a month, until the procurator finally transferred Egorov's file to the camp court on March 1. When, at long last, members of the court arrived at the regional hospital, it was discovered that Egorov had passed away on February 2.[69] On January 16, the local medical commission of the same hospital certified another prisoner, M. M. Kudriashov, as suffering from a "grave incurable malady."[70] The central commission of UITLiK "freed" Kudriashov on February 6, 1948, while the procurator yielded his sanction even earlier—on February 2, 1948. When the court convened to process his case, the judges were informed that Kudriashov had died on February 2, 1948. Both incidents were not aberrational. Pashutina concluded that "analogous red tape, leading to the deaths of prisoners, was allowed in the instance of prisoner Votinov and other cases."[71]

Pashutina's memo confirms three things. First, some of those designated for discharge during 1947–48 were nearly dead or dying. Second, the head of the directorate considered this fact to be important enough to inform the minister of justice about it. Third, top judicial authorities viewed administrative delays causing these deaths as unacceptable ("very serious consequences"),

Table 6.2. Diagnoses of medically released invalids in Azerbaijani regional labor colonies (UITLiK), first half of 1948

Diagnosis	Absolute Number	Percentage (%)
Alimentary dystrophy	265	60.9
Tuberculosis	77	17.8
Diseases of the internal organs	55	12.8
Diseases complicated by senility	19	4.3
Invalidism that led to total disability	5	1.1

Source: GARF f. R-9492, op.5, d.34, l. 69.

exactly as the Procuracy and NKVD-MVD did in the examples cited above. This is remarkable intrabureaucratic congruency. As a result, during 1947–48 the central Ministry of Justice issued several categorical orders (some signed by the deputy minister of justice) to expedite aktirovka and fight red tape in various localities.[72]

Evidence can also be gauged from the analysis of expressions employed by camp court judges. On August 5, 1948, Frolov, the chairman of the Azerbaijani UITLiK camp court, furnished a breakdown of diagnoses of those medically released from the colonies of the republic (see table 6.2). The camp judge left a revealing comment under this table: "It is necessary to emphasize that the early release of prisoners convicted of serious crimes was applied only when the inmates were in hopeless condition and on their death beds [*iavliaiutsia smertnikami*]."[73] Translating this passage into English is tricky. The word *smertnik*, employed by Frolov, can be translated as "condemned to death." Semantically it suggests that at least some of those released, in the judge's exegesis, were on the verge of dying, and he clearly understood this fact.

Frolov continued to utilize this vocabulary in regular monthly court reports. According to them, even in "normal" 1949, when medical releases radically decreased and conditions in the camps somewhat improved, prisoners in the Azerbaijani colonies, mostly charged for theft under the draconian laws of 1947, were released with dystrophy diagnoses. Thus, Lyafitova Sakkina Abbas Kizsi received five years of deprivation of liberty for stealing one turkey from a collective farm. She spent four months in the colony and was set free with the following description: "suffering from third-grade alimentary dystrophy, cachexia, the condition is hopeless." Petr Maksimovich Marushin received ten years of deprivation of liberty for stealing two kilograms of flour but served only one year of his sentence. He was discharged with ascites in "hopeless condition."[74] TB was also widespread. Tagiev Hussien Aga Mamed Ogly received a five-year sentence for stealing a suitcase and spent two years, two months behind bars. He was released from the colony with "multiple tuberculosis lesions of the glands with suppuration, decay, and fistulas."[75] Hussien Guli Aga Ogly Mamedov was sentenced to five years of deprivation of liberty for stealing three sheaves of barley from a collective farm. He spent seven months in the colony and was set free with "stage three dystrophy coupled with diarrhea" in "extremely grave condition."[76] As we can see, the majority of the invalids released in "non-catastrophic" 1949 from the Azerbaijani colonies were characterized with unequivocal "extremely grave/hopeless" adjectives by the camp judiciary. Moreover, in another report to Moscow, Frolov made probably one of the bluntest confessions to the use of aktirovka to distort mortality rates ever recorded. On January 1, 1949, he wrote to Pashutina, the head of the directorate:

> 186 people ... were freed from serving their sentence in the third quarter. The overwhelming majority of them were in hopeless condition. The majority of those who were released in the past were in an analogously hopeless condition. Apparently, this can explain the fact that parolees prone to crime do not return to places of confinement; they die soon after release. In some cases, the court considers medical discharge of inmates solely because they end up in hopeless condition.... Recently, people have been discharged [*aktiruiutsia*] only when their state of health becomes obviously hopeless. Maybe we should change this practice in the sense that we should implement aktirovanie before the onset of such a state—i.e., in order to preserve people?... All these questions deserve attention because the current practice of early release justifies itself solely in a sense that it reduces mortality in places of confinement. And that's it.[77]

Apparently, Frolov's disarming candor seemed excessive to the central directorate's taste. First, Pashutina left handwritten symbols near the judge's statements—a question mark near "they die soon after release" as well as a question mark and exclamation marks near the affirmation that medical discharge reduced death rates.[78] I would hypothesize that these symbols conveyed her displeasure. Second, Pashutina responded personally to Frolov's report on February 7, 1949, with a series of critical remarks. Among other things, she succinctly qualified his assertion that "all the prisoners" are in a hopeless condition and die soon after release as "wrong."[79] Notably, Pashutina did not explain why she believed this. Nevertheless, immediately after this somewhat unfounded critique, she provided the following advice: "If in selected cases, nominations for the early release of prisoners, suffering from grave incurable illness or totally disabled, are delayed through the fault of administration for a long time, raise this question officially before the republican Minister of the Interior."[80]

Essentially, she insisted that Frolov should fight red tape in the MVD to avoid the registration of invalids' death. In his report, the judge had noted that two cases were dropped from review by the judiciary: one prisoner had died four days before the file reached the court and the other right on the day of the court session concerning his release.[81]

How can we reconcile the apparent contradiction in her response? I contend that Pashutina's reaction, on the one hand, demonstrates a revitalized "façade of legality." What was acceptable to claim openly in the catastrophic year 1947, which occasioned massive discharge of invalids, became more politically sensitive in "normalized" 1949. To contextualize, around this time (1948–49) the central policy regarding aktirovka took another U-turn: officials were dissuaded from using medical release (just as in May 1944), and the number of those freed shrank to marginal values.[82] On the other hand, we know that Pashutina was already well informed about the correlation between red tape and "undesirable" mortality among candidates for discharge. Essentially, Pashutina chastised her subordinate for his bluntness but provided the local judge with advice on how to avoid early deaths during the process of aktirovanie.

Meanwhile, Frolov was not the only camp judge who claimed that those medically released died very soon after discharge. On February 11, 1949, Gubanov, the chairman of the Western Kazakhstan UITLiK camp court, made a peculiar inquiry to Pashutina. According to the adjudicator, the Aktubinsk regional court processed fifty-three medical release cases during 1948. All fifty-three prisoners were "freed a long time ago and had dispersed in all directions across the Soviet Union." After a protest by the republican procurator, the Supreme Court of KazSSR had repealed these determinations: the regional court did not have jurisdiction over inmates of the Gulag. All fifty-three case files were diverted to the camp court for new consideration. Gubanov wondered, "I ask you to clarify how to proceed with such cases: should we consider them in absentia or initiate a search, take the released into custody in order to bring them to court, and only then review the cases? It is possible that out of the fifty-three people freed, a fraction has already died."[83] If we assume for the sake of argument that officials did not realize the terminal condition of those released through aktirovanie, why then did Gubanov express this concern to Pashutina, although less than a year had passed since the invalids' discharge?

CONCLUSION

This chapter provided several key insights. One pertains to the temporal and spatial scope of the use of aktirovanie to artificially depress death rates.

Although it is hard to assess the precise degree of its pervasiveness, officials in random local camps—from Pechora to the Moscow region—conceded the practice's influence on registered statistics as early as 1932 and as late as 1949. Especially instructive is an almost identical rationalization behind the regular demands to expedite the procedure (to "avoid mortality") that was espoused by diverse representatives of formally independent bureaucracies through the years. These newly discovered cases are concordant with analogous separate incidents of red tape causing deaths found by Alexopoulos, Bell, and Ivanova. Furthermore, in addition to the Gulag proper, including prisoners and labor army contingents, we discovered that aktirovanie was practiced in the GUITU NKU subsystem in 1932–34, probably the most obscure island of the Soviet penal archipelago to date. This fact suggests that its registered mortality, which is still unknown as of 2018, is understated as well. It also indicates that, despite the revelations of the 1990s, we are still very far from having an accurate estimate of the excess deaths caused by the Soviet system of incarceration. Whereas this chapter did not focus specifically on the quantification of additional fatalities among released invalids, I propose in my unpublished PhD dissertation a preliminary estimate of an additional 800,000 to 850,000 deaths of released "certified invalids" (aktirovannye). This raises the death toll directly caused by the results of Gulag incarceration to 2.5 million (prisoners only). This figure, although not definitive, is substantially different from the only two estimates based on archival evidence found in the literature to date: 1.7 million (the official figure) and 6 million (Alexopoulos's estimate).[84] As this chapter suggests, while one should not simply accept the official Gulag death rate as accurate, one must also be careful about estimating an overall death rate (in Alexopoulos's case, 30 percent) without considering the uneven application of aktirovanie over time and across places of incarceration. My fundamental argument is that the overwhelming majority of the invalids released during periods of crisis (such as war and famine) should be considered additional deaths that were omitted from central records to deliberately lower mortality rates. However, in more "normal" times, the use of medical releases to manipulate mortality data was much lower; therefore, we should not necessarily assume that most medical releases should simply be added to the official prisoner mortality figures.

The second insight that this chapter offered is the unexpectedly active role of the local and central camp Procuracy (and, to a lesser extent, the camp courts) in the manipulation of inmate mortality statistics. The unique relationship between the Gulag and the Procuracy in this regard has received no scholarly attention so far. Donald Filtzer, writing about the territorial Procuracy, perspicaciously noted, "This was an almost schizophrenic institution. It was responsible for ensuring the preservation of legality within an essentially lawless system."[85] I would argue that this assertion is even more suitable to the procuratorial department of oversight over places of detention. The confluence of institutional imperatives generated curious "patron-client" relations between the supervisory agents and the NKVD administration. Both bureaucracies, although formally antagonistic, had to report low or declining mortality rates to appear effective and successful. But in crisis periods, this was a nearly unattainable goal without accounting fraud. On the one hand, the camp Procuracy acted as a competitor of the NKVD, from time to time punishing its officials for high mortality and occasionally exposing falsifications in recordkeeping. On the other hand, it could operate as the Gulag's closest ally in the suppression of registered mortality via aktirovka even at the highest level. This intrinsically contradictory interaction certainly extends our understanding of the protean, often opportunistic nature of oversight as well as the Janus-faced "socialist legality" under Stalin's rule.

The third—and principal—insight concerns the agency of the central administration in the manipulation of mortality statistics. I attempted to understand whether the "release-to-die" practice was a variation of low-level fraud or if the center sanctioned and encouraged the deception. The empirical data demonstrates that such an either/or binary logic is too crude and suggests a rather paradoxical interim answer. I would characterize the central intervention not as sustained collusion but as a situational cover-up. Simply stated, the top echelon of all three agencies under the external pressure of national catastrophes was occasionally (but not always) complicit in mortality data distortion.

This discovery certainly compounds entrenched preconceptions about malfeasance in the Gulag. Under prevailing assumptions (formulated due to overconcentration on economic fraud), it is habitually presented as endemic to low-level tiers but not Moscow (with the sole exception of Alexopoulos's argument). I contend that medical "tufta" was far more complex in its motivations/incarnations and cannot be properly understood via this classic principal-agent dichotomy. However, it would be an oversimplification to construe it as a monolithic, meticulously coordinated interbureaucratic conspiracy of the higher-ups. On the contrary, medical release was often the result of ad hoc improvisation. Further, it was a frequent cause of reciprocal scapegoating.

I argue that it was not a rigid scheme, unanimously and assiduously enforced from the top to the bottom according to the universal blueprint over the decades, as Alexopoulos seems to contend. Rather, the deceptive facet within the procedure was mercurial, depending on the place and especially the time period: it became far more egregious during national disasters, as in 1932–33, 1941–44, and 1946–47. When the underfunded system faced a critical mortality crisis that it could not mitigate quickly by conventional means, its central apparatus employed medical release as an emergency measure. As soon as the situation reverted back to ordinary, as in 1934–36, 1939–41, 1944–46, and 1948–53, high-level stimulus to tweak the data via releases receded. The center, concerned with workforce preservation, fulfillment of the production plans, and state security, tended to curtail medical release in favor of more standard medical measures to improve conditions and return the custodial population to work. In this deduction, I also considerably depart from the second point of Alexopoulos's exegesis on the radical worsening of conditions in the late 1940s and early 1950s. I have not found evidence supporting the hypothesis that this period witnessed historically high rates of medical releases, which hid the deadliest period of the Gulag's operation.

Overall, it can be concluded that the deceptive facet constituted only one vector among heterogeneous political, legal, and economic ones, which defined ever-changing policy toward invalids in the Gulag over the years, and it was not always the most puissant. Nevertheless, examples from "normal" 1935–36 and 1949 indicate that the use of aktirovka to artificially depress mortality statistics probably never disappeared completely but was blended into more regular medical activity on a smaller scale and confined to the lower administrative levels.

Lastly, this corollary can be used to decipher the broader contentious problem of Gulag medicine and invalids. In the historiographical dimension, this tension is lucidly evident in recent juxtapositional scholarly interventions by Dan Healey and Alexopoulos.[86] Michael David-Fox observed that "differences between the two treatments are impossible to ignore."[87] While the former focuses on efforts by camp doctors, however limited, to return ailing inmates into the camp economy, the latter emphasizes their attempts to conceal the "destructive capacity" of the Gulag through the discharge of invalids. I would argue that both scholars are correct to some extent. One interpretation does not necessarily nullify the other, but its meaningful applicability is strongly predicated on the concrete locality and especially temporal period. In my view, the multifarious Gulag medical sphere is best understood as evolving over time and through its innate contradictions (described in this chapter), not monocausal universalistic explanations.

NOTES

1. Getty, Rittersporn, and Zemskov, "Victims of the Soviet Penal System," 1041.

2. Zemskov, "Politicheskie repressii," 119; Alexopoulos, *Illness and Inhumanity*, 15.

3. Barnes, *Death and Redemption*; Barenberg, *Gulag Town, Company Town*; Wheatcroft, "The First 35 Years of Soviet Living Standards," 29.

4. However, one should note the important contribution by Galina Ivanova, who is the first and the only scholar to date to employ materials of the MIu to briefly describe postwar medical release. See Ivanova, *Istoriia GULAGa*, 414–17.

5. By the center, I mean the central apparatuses of the Gulag, Procuracy, and Ministry of Justice (MIu), not the Politburo or Sovnarkom.

6. Alexopoulos, *Illness and Inhumanity*, 157.

7. Alexopoulos, 154. On "economic tufta," see Heinzen, "Corruption in the Gulag," 456–75.

8. Historians of the Great Terror, for instance, have the opportunity to scrutinize the deceptive practices via the testimonies of the NKVD officials purged in 1939–40. See Viola, *Stalinist Perpetrators on Trial*.

9. Wheatcroft, "The Scale and Nature of Stalinist Repression," 1151.

10. And analogous articles in republican codes. For example, in the Azerbaijani code it was Article 445; in the Ukrainian code, Article 389. See State Archive of the Russian Federation (GARF), fond (f.) R-9492, opis' (op.) 5, delo (d.) 58, list (l.) 2 and f. R-9492, op. 5, d. 53, l. 229.

11. Nakonechnyi, "'Factory of Invalids,'" 55–189.

12. Alexopoulos, *Illness and Inhumanity*, 152.

13. For instance, see the usage of the euphemism *black* (*chernye*) to designate deaths in an already classified medical report of the Privoszhskii ITL in 1943. GARF, f. R-9407, op. 1, d. 343, l. 4. In the ciphers of URO, mortality was occasionally replaced with the euphemism *unloading*. GARF, f. R-9414, op. 1, d. 1143, l. 5.

14. For a representative "formal" rationale, see GARF, f. R-9414, op.1a, d. 619a, l. 3.

15. For a typical procuratorial report, see GARF, f. R-8131, op. 37, d. 3816, l. 49. For an example from the MIu, see GARF, f. R-9492, op. 5, d. 67, l. 158. For an example from the GULAG, see GARF, f. R-9414, op. 1a, d. 363.

16. For the URO role in medical release, see GARF, f.R-9414, op. 1, d. 1143, l. 453. For SANO, see GARF, f. R-8131, op. 37, d. 1626, l. 90. Nakhapetov, *Ocherki istorii sanitarnoi sluzhby*, 61–63.

17. For the earliest 1930 iteration of the process, see GARF, f. R-9401, op. 1A, d. 1, l. 17. On invalids, see Healey, "Lives in the Balance," 527–56.

18. Khlevniuk estimates eight hundred thousand prisoners there as of May 1933 (stock figure) in *Khoziain*, 167.

19. Bezborodov, Bezborodova, and Khrustalev, eds., *Naselenie Gulaga*, 477.

20. For mortality in some penitentiaries of GUITU in 1932, see the State Archive of Novosibirskaia oblast' (GANO), f. 47, op. 5, d. 166, l. 87; For 1933, see Khlevniuk, *Khoziain*, 168.

21. On quotas, see Alexopoulos, *Illness and Inhumanity*, 105–6; Krasil'nikov, *Spetspereselentsy*, 10.

22. Alexopoulos, *Illness and Inhumanity*, 154.
23. For a wartime example, see Perm GASPI (Permskii State Archive of Social-Political History), f. 105, op. 8, d. 94, l. 57.
24. On the 1933 ration, see the Russian State Military Archive (RGVA), f. 37837, op. 23, d.1, l. 83. I thank K. M. Aleksandrov for bringing this document to my attention. The GUITU norm for 1933 can be found in GARF, f. R-5446, op. 14a, d. 745, l. 22.
25. GANO, f. R-47, op. 5, d. 163, l. 3. A figure of typhus-related deaths from Emets's report was published in Isupov, "Epidemii sypnogo tifa," 91.
26. GANO, f. R-47, op. 5, d. 163, l. 4.
27. GANO, f. R-47, op. 5, d. 163, l. 50ob.
28. GANO, f. R-47, op. 5, d. 163, l. 60ob.
29. GARF, f. R-9414, op. 1, d. 2740, ll. 20–200b.
30. On the general history of the labor army, see German and Kurochkin, *Nemtsy SSSR*.
31. GARF, f. R-9479, op. 1, d. 147, ll. 118–19.
32. Kirillov and Matveeva, "Trudmobilizovannye nemtsy," 627–55.
33. GARF, f. R-9414, op. 1, d. 1157, l. 160.
34. GARF, f. R-9414, op. 1, d. 1157, ll. 156, 158.
35. GARF, f. R-9414, op. 1, d. 1157, l. 150.
36. GARF, f. R-9414, op. 1, d. 1157, l. 148.
37. GARF, f. R-9414, op. 1, d. 1157, ll. 145–46.
38. For an example of these concerns, see GARF, f R-8131, op.37, d. 2055, ll. 9–10.
39. GARF f. R–8131, op.37, d.799, l. 145.
40. GARF, f. R-9414, op.1, d. 1183, ll. 35–43.
41. The last sentence was quoted in German and Kurochkin, *Nemtsy SSSR*, 118. Here, the quotation is presented in full.
42. GARF, f. R-9414, op. 1, d. 1183, l. 42.
43. State Archive of Tambovskaia oblast' (GATO), f. R-3957, op. 2, d. 42, l. 22.
44. GATO, f. R-3957, op. 2, d. 61, l. 6.
45. GARF, f. R-9492, op. 5, d. 15, l. 83–83ob.
46. Alexopoulos, *Illness and Inhumanity*, 155.
47. For the typical camp Procuracy report, see the State Archive of Samarskaia oblast' (GASO), f. R-2596, op. 1, d. 1998, ll. 1–30.
48. For example, see Perm GASPI, f. 105, op. 8, d. 94, ll. 90–103.
49. Hardy, *The Gulag after Stalin*, 98.
50. GARF, f. R-8131, op. 37, d. 2498, l. 148.
51. For example, see camp procurators' reports on Sevpechlag (GARF, f. R-8131, op. 37, d. 2053, l. 69); Ivdel'lag GARF, f. R-8131, op. 37, d. 2059, l. 140); Khabarovskoe UITLiK (GARF, f. R-8131, op. 37, d. 1627, l. 213); Solikamlag

(GARF, f. R-8131, op. 37, d. 2064, l. 66); Cheliabmetallurgstroy (GARF, f. R.-8131, op. 37, d. 2066, ll. 150–51); Svobodlag (GARF, f. R.8131, op. 37, d. 2033, l. 60); Bogoslovlag (GARF, f. R-8131, op. 37, d. 2035, l. 108); Volzhlag (GARF, f. R-8131, op. 37, d. 3842, l. 183); Servurallag (GARF, f. R-8131, op. 37, d. 2045, l. 67); Tagillag (GARF, f. R-8131, op. 37, d. 2528, ll. 15–16); Usol'lag (GARF, f. R-8131, op. 37, d. 2036, l. 125); Karlag (GARF, f. R.-8131, op. 37, d. 2526, l. 279); Noril'lag (GARF, f. R-8131, op. 37, d. 2063, l. 36); Nizhneamurlag (GARF, f. R-8131, op. 37, d. 2041, l. 1180b.).

52. GARF, f. R-8131, op. 37, d. 799, l. 110.

53. GAAO, f. 5865, op. 2, d. 11, ll. 54–55. Khelemskii's report was quoted for the first time in Mel'nik, "Iagrinskii ITL," 216–44.

54. State Archive of Arkhangel'skaia oblast'(GAAO), f. 5865, op. 2, d. 11, l. 52.

55. GARF, f. R-9414, op. 1, d. 1146, ll. 26–26ob.

56. GARF, f. R-8131, op. 37, d. 2053, l. 171.

57. GARF, f. R-8131, op. 37, d. 2053, l. 172.

58. GARF, f. R-8131, op. 37, d. 2053, l. 175.

59. Alexopoulos, *Illness and Inhumanity*, 156; Bell, *Stalin's Gulag at War*, 61; GARF, f. R-8131, op. 37, d. 2523, l. 15; GARF, f. R-8131, op. 37, d. 2482, l. 78.

60. GARF, f. R-8131, op. 37, d. 2523, l.18; GARF, f. R-8131, op. 37, d. 2482, l. 79.

61. High mortality in Unzhlag was one of the reasons why its procurator, Abrosimov, lost his post and got demoted in September 1942. See GARF, f. R-8131, op. 28, d. 97, ll. 13–130b.

62. GARF, f. R-428, op. 3, d. 23, l. 1.

63. For examples, see GASO, f. R-4958, op. 17, d. 6; GARF, f. R-9492, op. 5, d. 30, ll. 11–12ob.

64. Ivanova, *Istoriia GULAGa*, 397.

65. GARF, f. R-9492, op. 5, d. 21, ll. 249–50.

66. See reports of camp courts of Novosibirskaia UITLiK (GARF, f. R-9492, op. 14, d.145); Viatlag (GARF, f. R-9492, op. 14, d. 157); Nyroblag (GARF, f.-9492, op. 14, d. 165); Ivdel'lag (GARF, f. R-9492, op. 14, d. 158)

67. Ivanova, *Istoriia GULAGa*, 417.

68. GARF, f. R-9492, op.5, d.42, ll. 224–225.

69. GARF, f. R-9492, op.5, d.42, ll. 224–225.

70. GARF, f. R-9492, op. 5, d. 42, l. 225.

71. GARF, f. R-9492, op. 5, d. 42, l. 225.

72. For example, see GARF, f. R-9492, op. 5, d. 32, l. 20.

73. GARF, f. R-9492, op. 5, d. 34, l. 70.

74. GARF, f. R-9492, op. 5, d. 58, l. 124.

75. GARF, f. R-9492, op. 5, d. 58, l. 135.

76. GARF, f. R-9492, op. 5, d. 58, l. 124.

77. Partly quoted in Ivanova, *Istoriia GULAGa*, 417.

78. GARF, f. R-9492, op. 5, d. 48, ll. 3–4.
79. GARF, f. R-9492, op. 5, d. 48, l. 8.
80. GARF, f. R-9492, op. 5, d. 48, l. 8.
81. GARF, f. R-9492, op. 5, d. 48, l. 6.
82. GARF, f. R-9492, op. 5, d. 48, l. 2.
83. GARF, f. R-9492, op. 5, d. 64, l. 6.
84. Nakonechnyi, "'Factory of Invalids,'" 323–36.
85. Filtzer, *Soviet Workers and Late Stalinism*, 177.
86. David-Fox, *The Soviet Gulag*.
87. David-Fox, 20.

BIBLIOGRAPHY

Alexopoulos, Golfo. *Illness and Inhumanity in Stalin's Gulag*. New Haven: Yale University Press, 2017.
Barenberg, Alan. *Gulag Town, Company Town: Forced Labor and Its Legacy in Vorkuta*. New Haven, CT: Yale University Press, 2014.
Barnes, Steven. *Death and Redemption: The Gulag and the Shaping of Soviet Society*. Princeton, NJ: Princeton University Press, 2011.
Bell, Wilson. *Stalin's Gulag at War: Forced Labor, Mass Death, and Soviet Victory in the Second World War*. Toronto: University of Toronto Press, 2018.
Bezborodov, A. B., I. V. Bezborodova, and V. M. Khrustalev, eds. *Istoriia Stalinskogo Gulaga*. Vol. 4, *Naselenie Gulaga: chislennost' i usloviia soderzhaniia*. Moscow: Rosspen, 2004.
David-Fox, Michael, ed. *The Soviet Gulag: Evidence, Interpretation, and Comparison*. Pittsburgh: University of Pittsburgh Press, 2016.
Filtzer, Donald A. *Soviet Workers and Late Stalinism: Labor and the Restoration of the Stalinist System after World War II*. Cambridge: Cambridge University Press, 2002.
German, A. A., and A. N. Kurochkin. *Nemtsy SSSR v "Trudovoi Armii": 1941–1945*. Moscow: Gotika, 1998.
Getty, J. Arch, Gábor T. Rittersporn, and Viktor N. Zemskov. "Victims of the Soviet Penal System in the Pre-War Years: A First Approach on the Basis of Archival Evidence." *The American Historical Review* 98, no. 4 (1993): 1017–49.
Hardy, Jeffrey S. *The Gulag after Stalin: Redefining Punishment in Khrushchev's Soviet Union, 1953–1964*. Ithaca: Cornell University Press, 2016.
Healey, Dan. "Lives in the Balance: Weak and Disabled Prisoners and the Biopolitics of the Gulag." *Kritika: Explorations in Russian and Eurasian History* 16, no. 3 (2015): 527–56.
Heinzen, James. "Corruption in the Gulag: Dilemmas of Officials and Prisoners." *Comparative Economic Studies* 47, no. 2 (2005): 456–75.

Isupov, V. A. "Epidemii sypnogo tifa kak faktor sverkhsmertnosti gorodskogo naseleniia Zapadnoi Sibiri (1932—1933 gg.)." *Ural'skii istoricheskii vestnik* 44, no. 3 (2014): 90–95.

Ivanova, G. M. *Istoriia GULAGa, 1918–1958: Sotsial'no-ekonomicheskii i politiko-pravovoi aspekty.* Moscow: Nauka, 2006.

Khlevniuk, O. V. *Khoziain: Stalin i utverzhdenie stalinskoi diktatury.* Istoriia Stalinizma. Moscow: ROSSPEN, 2010.

Kirillov, V. M., and N. V. Matveeva. "Trudmobilizovannye nemtsy na Urale: Sostoianie i novye aspekty issledovaniia problem." In *Nachal'nyi period Velikoi Otechestvennoi voiny i deportatsiia rossiiskikh nemtsev: Vzgliad i otsenki cherez 70 let*, edited by A. A. German, 627–55. Moscow: MSNK-press, 2011.

Krasil'nikov, S. A. *Spetspereselentsy v Zapadnoi Sibiri. Vesna 1933–nachalo 1938 gg.* Novosibirsk: Ekor, 1994.

Mel'nik, T. F. "Iagrinskii ITL v Molotovske," In *Katorga i ssylka na Severe Rossi*, edited by M. N. Suprin, 216–44. Arkhangel'sk: KIRA, 2006.

Nakhapetov, B. A. *Ocherki istorii sanitarnoi sluzhby GULAGa.* Moscow: ROSSPEN, 2009.

Nakonechnyi, Mikhail. "'Factory of Invalids': Mortality, Disability and Early Release on Medical Grounds in GULAG, 1930–1955." PhD diss., University of Oxford, 2020.

Viola, Lynne. *Stalinist Perpetrators on Trial: Scenes from the Great Terror in Soviet Ukraine.* New York: Oxford University Press, 2018.

Wheatcroft, Stephen. "The First 35 Years of Soviet Living Standards: Secular Growth and Conjunctural Crises in a Time of Famines." *Explorations in Economic History* 46, no. 1 (2009): 24–52.

———. "The Scale and Nature of Stalinist Repression and Its Demographic Significance: On Comments by Keep and Conquest." *Europe-Asia Studies* 52, no. 6 (2000): 1143–59.

Zemskov, V. N. "Politicheskie repressii v SSSR (1917–1990)." *Rossiia XXI*, no. 1–2 (1994): 107–24.

MIKHAIL NAKONECHNYI is a postdoctoral researcher at the Aleksanteri Institute, Finnish Centre of Russian and Eastern European Studies at the University of Helsinki. He works on the five-year project GULAGECHOES, which is funded by the European Research Council (ERC) and focuses on the construction of ethnic identities in the Soviet Gulag and post-Soviet prison systems.

SEVEN

APPLYING DIGITAL METHODS TO FORCED LABOR HISTORY

German POWs during and after the Second World War

SUSAN GRUNEWALD

FORCED LABOR PERVADED THE SOVIET Union. Various groups of society toiled under unfree conditions. Even free citizens had to work lest they be arrested under a variety of harsh labor laws. By the time Nazi Germany invaded the Soviet Union in summer 1941, the planned economy mobilized numerous categories of unfree laborers in the Gulag system. With the start of the war, a new group entered this continuum: prisoners of war. In 1939, with the Soviet invasion of Poland and the Winter War with Finland, the NKVD opened a new branch known as the Administration for Affairs of Prisoners of War and Internees (UPVI, or *Upravlenie po delam voennoplennykh i interovannykh*). In 1944, the increase of the POW population during the course of the Second World War resulted in the NKVD upgrading the UPVI into the Main Administration of Prisoners of War and Internees (GUPVI, or *Glavnoe upravlenie po delam voennoplennykh i interovannykh*).[1] As the name implies, this administration organized all aspects of POW life in the USSR from medical treatment, housing, clothing, and feeding to labor assignments. The UPVI/GUPVI ran its own series of camps specifically for POWs modeled after the NKVD's other camp system, the infamous Gulag. UPVI/GUPVI leaders took much of the infrastructure developed over ten plus years of the Gulag, such as medical evaluations and the ratio of rations to labor assignments, and applied it to their new charges.

Over the course of the Second World War, the UPVI/GUPVI system expanded to over four thousand camps across the Soviet Union. One particular battle dramatically shaped the administration. The Battle of Stalingrad (August 23, 1942–February 2, 1943) marked the turning point in the war not only for the Soviet Union but also for the German POWs. Prior to Stalingrad, the UPVI housed 10,528 Germans. In this battle alone, the Red Army captured 91,000 German soldiers and officers, including 22 generals. Many of these men died from a combination of the harsh weather, their poor physical condition, and poor Soviet planning. Soviet officials did not expect to take so many men, and the massive influx overwhelmed the UPVI's ability to provide its charges with shelter, medical supplies, and food.[2] By the end of the war, the Soviets held roughly 3 million POWs of German nationality. By December 1945, between deaths and repatriations of the ill or injured, this number decreased to about 1.5 million. Many of these men remained in Soviet captivity until they died or could no longer work.

The number of POWs continued to decrease until 1949, by which point only thousands of POWs remained on Soviet soil. The last men who remained in Soviet captivity from 1949 to 1956 were held for their potential as bargaining chips in the developing Cold War rather than for their labor contribution. In essence, they had fulfilled much of their economic utility but still served a political purpose for the Soviet government. It is important to note that some, but not all, of these last men to return had been tried and sentenced as war criminals. The filtration camps that helped assign POWs to labor tasks also made sure that the POWs had not been members of the SS or been involved in war crimes. Thousands of Germans went before military tribunals; those convicted served their sentences in the Gulag and not GUPVI labor camps.[3] Documents concerning the tribunals process are generally still classified. For the sake of simplicity and space limitations, this chapter focuses solely on German prisoners of war detained in GUPVI labor camps.[4]

The course of the war and postwar dictated not only the growth and decline of the UPVI/GUPVI but also its geographic distribution and work assignments. From its beginning, the UPVI operated forced labor camps. From 1943 to 1945, as the Red Army shifted from defensive to offensive fighting, it began to take increasing numbers of German captives, and so Soviet officials worked out policies regarding how best to utilize POW labor. With the end of the war in sight in spring 1945, Soviet leaders such as Stalin and Beria issued edicts explicating how POWs would be used in the reconstruction effort of the Soviet Union. The staggering economic and human damages of the war left the Soviet Union in dire need of reconstruction and labor. The state mobilized its able-bodied German POWs in the reconstruction effort for a variety of reasons. The captive Germans provided a convenient labor source in a country that had lost twenty-seven million citizens, according to conservative estimates.[5] They would also temporarily take the place of Soviet forced laborers who had either died amid the horrendous wartime camp conditions or been released to fight with the Red Army. Finally, POW labor provided an outlet for the vengeful feelings of the population, as many Soviet citizens desired to see their enemies punished and performing recompense for the suffering they had caused.

This chapter seeks to situate the POWs amid the vast range of forced labor in the Soviet Union during the 1930s and '40s. The first section of this chapter takes a temporal look at the evolution of labor policy vis-à-vis German POWs from the start of the war into 1946. The second section of the chapter examines the spatial and environmental aspects of the UPVI/GUPVI camp system. The chapter argues, based on both archival sources and geographic information system (GIS) mapping, that Soviet leaders consciously chose to keep able-bodied German POWs for labor after the end of the Second World War. Indeed, GIS mapping has led to a breakthrough because it allows us to analyze and illustrate the widespread use of POW labor in ways that would not be possible with traditional sources alone. As the mapping section of this chapter will show, this form of computer analysis challenges common notions about POW labor in the USSR and illustrates the unique roles that these men played in the overall forced labor system. Unlike many Soviet citizens confined within the Gulag system who were sent to perform hard labor in arctic regions of European Russia or in far Eastern Siberia, POWs were not as geographically isolated and were primarily used for high-priority reconstruction projects in major cities and key industries. The geographic distribution of GUPVI camps and the range of economic tasks that GUPVI inmates performed suggest that Soviet leaders saw the GUPVI system as having a different role than the better-known Gulag camps. This chapter will highlight the distinctive social, political, and economic functions of the GUPVI system within the larger context of Soviet forced labor.

FORCED LABOR AND GERMAN PRISONERS OF WAR

Scholars familiar with the history of forced labor in the Soviet Union know the details and debates surrounding the Politburo's creation of the Gulag in 1929. Oleg Khlevniuk contends that the Politburo created the Gulag in order to conserve state resources. The camps needed to replace the USSR's existing sites of confinement with a self-sustaining system through the colonization of remote regions and the development of local resource deposits.[6] Alan Barenberg also argues that the Gulag served as a means to populate distant, resource rich locations in need of labor.[7] Others, such as Galina Ivanovna and Michael Jakobson, have noted this policy did not emerge in a vacuum but was an extension of Tsarist penal policies of forced labor (*katorga*) and exile.[8] The system mobilized diverse contingents of prisoners. Common criminals such as murderers and rapists mixed with those arrested and sentenced for hooliganism or violating draconian labor laws that extracted harsh punishments for labor turnover, shirking work, and workplace theft.[9]

Political prisoners also counted toward the vast Gulag forced labor camp population. Aleksandr Solzhenitsyn, Robert Conquest, and Anne Applebaum have emphasized the fate of political prisoners in the system.[10] Although these authors have noted the system's emphasis on forced labor, they see it more as a means to segregate and exterminate undesirables from society. Their stances have largely been countered through research that shows that the Gulag employed labor as one way to potentially correct and reform citizens who had strayed from socialist ideals. Labor, as well as other forms of reeducation, would serve as the basis and metric for refashioning.[11]

Although disagreement about the motives of the Gulag abounds, scholars have been able to agree that the formation and expansion of the system correlated to the social and economic upheavals caused by industrialization, collectivization, and the Terror. For example, the Gulag system did not consist solely of forced labor camps. It also encompassed special settlements, which the NKVD created in the 1930s to mobilize hundreds of thousands of dispossessed kulaks, targeted in collectivization as undesirables and potential opponents to the state's plans.[12] Industrialization and collectivization also resulted in the mobilization of the Soviet Union's free populations. Reforms to the criminal code and new labor laws attempted to address labor shortages, turnover, and discipline, all worsened by collectivization and industrialization.[13] These laws meant that citizens had to work or they would be punished—and such punishments invariably included forced labor, whether within the Gulag system or outside it.

Over the course of the 1930s, Soviet officials worked out the ways in which Gulag labor would contribute to the economy. By 1940, forced labor camps prioritized two major labor tasks. The first of these tasks consisted of resource extraction. Forced labor dominated certain resource industries in this time period. Although scholars continue to debate the economics of this particular aspect of forced labor, there is no denying that Gulag inmates significantly contributed to industrialization. In 1940, the Gulag represented about 50 percent of the Soviet Union's nickel industry, close to 80 percent of the tin industry, 60 percent of the gold industry, and 40 percent of both the cobalt and chrome ore industries.[14] In 1940–41, the Gulag produced 12 to 13 percent of the USSR's timber.[15] The second major task of Gulag labor consisted of large-scale construction projects. Between 1931 and 1933, inmates constructed the White Sea–Baltic, or Belomor, Canal on time and under budget. Although the canal was too shallow to have any real military or economic utility and came at the cost of high mortality, the project nonetheless signaled to some in the state that forced Gulag labor could be used to successfully undertake massive construction projects. Following this "victory" of forced labor, the NKVD took on ever-more ambitious tasks for the state. In 1940–41, the Gulag accounted for 13–14 percent of the USSR's capital construction projects.[16]

Thus, by the start of the war, forced prison labor contributed greatly to the Soviet economy. This did not shift during the war, when labor became even more regimented across the free and unfree populations. During the war, Gulag inmates continued to participate in key resource industries as well as defensive production. They laid thousands of miles of railroad and road, constructed hundreds of miles of pipelines, and produced millions of rounds of ammunition, shells, grenades, bombs, and mines. The continued reliance on forced labor during the war years came at great cost. From January 1, 1941, to January 1, 1946, 932,000 inmates died—over half of the documented deaths in the system's entire existence.[17] As Mikhail Nakonechnyi notes in his chapter for this volume, this figure should probably be understood as a minimum: local camp bosses faced repercussions if death rates climbed too high and therefore had incentives to manipulate the mortality statistics that they reported to the center.

Between high mortality rates and releases of prisoners to fight for the Red Army, the war led to a significant decrease in the Gulag population. However, the war also led to the mobilization of new groups into the forced labor system, including Soviet citizens of German, Finnish, or Romanian descent, and German prisoners of war. With the influx of German captives after the Battle of Stalingrad, the highest levels of Soviet governance started to direct the labor mobilization of the POWs. In February 1943, Stalin decided the labor assignments of 140,000 POWs in his capacity as the chairman of the State Defense Committee. He ordered the UPVI to assign "40,000 men to the reconstruction of the Donbass and Rostov coal mines, 15,000 men for the construction of coal mines around Moscow, 20,000 men for reconstruction work in the city of Stalingrad." He broke up the remaining men into groups of 3,000 to 15,000 to work in construction industries, factories, power plants, and hydroelectric stations across the Soviet Union in places such as Astrakhan, Uzbekistan, and Kazakhstan.[18]

With the tide of the war shifting firmly into Soviet favor in 1944 and 1945, the role of German POW labor evolved. Over the course of 1945, top Soviet officials prioritized the assignments of the increasing number of German POWs. In April 1945, Lavrentii Beria, the commissar of internal affairs and state security, wrote a letter to Stalin asking what to do with the 97,487 German POWs taken on sections of the Belorussian and Ukrainian fronts. Stalin replied that these POWs were to be transferred to the control of the NKVD, which would then be responsible for distributing them to various economic commissariats. Stalin personally ordered that 37,600 and 28,000 POWs be assigned to the commissariats of coal and construction, respectively. In other words, roughly 67 percent of the group was to be assigned to those industries most in need of unskilled labor. Additional POWs were to be allocated to metallurgical, electrification, and other heavy and light industrial commissariats in smaller numbers, mainly in groups of 5,000 and under. Stalin also ordered a final group of 250 POWs for allocation to munitions commissariats.[19] Postwar planning continued with the aim of urban and industrial reconstruction.

Less than a month later, and just a few days prior to the final German capitulation, Soviet officials drew up more plans for the use of the POWs. As of May 5, 1945, Beria decided to send the majority of POWs to Russia, with additional large numbers distributed throughout Ukraine, Belorussia, Lithuania, Estonia, Karelo-Finland, Moldova, Armenia, Azerbaijan, Uzbekistan, and Georgia.[20] In addition to sending POWs to work in coal and construction, Soviet authorities also assigned them by the tens of thousands to aid in the reconstruction of specific cities, including Sevastopol, Orel, Bryansk, Riga, Minsk, Kiev, Stalingrad, Saratov, Taganrog, Zaporozhe, and Moscow.[21]

It was immediately clear that the Soviet officials intended to use German POWs for the postwar reconstruction of the economy. They kept only able-bodied POWs. In an economy of shortages, the state was not interested in allocating precious resources to support injured or weak German prisoners who would need care and were unable to work. The retention of physically fit German POWs amounted to reparations for the war just like the vast wealth of industries and other goods removed from the sections of Germany that Soviet forces occupied.[22] The men and machines served as both emotional trophies and economic recompense for the war. Economic utility could come only from those POWs in good physical standing, however. Thus, the first major wave of POW repatriations occurred immediately after the war. On May 4, 1945, the Red Army High Command stated that they had captured 3,180,000 German POWs.[23] Yet by May 17, 1945, there were 2,090,661 German POWs mobilized and spread out over 34 commissariats through 107 NKVD camps throughout the country.[24] Ill and injured POWs who were sent home to Germany because they were deemed unfit to work explain at least part of this drop. For example, one POW, Robert Otto, broke his leg in June 1945 and returned to Germany on a transport of 450 ill or injured POWs. His story reflects the Soviet approach to managing those who could not work in this immediate postwar period.[25] But not all the roughly 1 million men who had disappeared from GUPVI's prisoner rolls by mid-May 1945 returned home alive. Hundreds of thousands of German POWs doubtless died in Soviet captivity, although assessing the exact number is difficult. Scholars of the Gulag have noted that camp directors used prisoner transports and releases to lower or hide camp death statistics. Oleg Khlevniuk has stated that camp leaders placed the ill on trains, as those who died in transit did not count as a death for any particular camp. Golfo Alexopoulos and Mikhail Nakonechnyi have noted that camp leaders systematically released terminally ill prisoners in order to keep mortality rates low and as a cost-cutting measure.[26] It is probable that GUPVI officials borrowed these methods of statistical manipulation from their Gulag counterparts.

While Soviet leaders such as Stalin and Beria may have decided to which industries, regions, or cities the POWs would be deployed, it was up to local camp leadership to facilitate and organize the labor assignments. Filtration camps sent POWs from areas near the front to main camps, where local leadership housed and assigned them via contracts with local industries, a practice that was also very common for Gulag inmates.[27] The contracts outlined strict conditions for the POWs' labor and treatment. One such contract dated December 20, 1944, was concluded between Camp No. 27 in Krasnogorsk, on the outskirts of Moscow, and the nearby Victory of Labor Textile Factory. It stated that the textile factory could make use of fifty POWs until December 31, 1945. The factory would, at its own expense, arrange for daily transport between the camp and the factory and provide the POWs with a one-hour lunch break and food. The factory would also pay the camp for the POWs' work. If the prisoners exceeded their quotas, the factory would pay the standard bonuses, which would also accrue to the camp to help with its operating costs.[28]

In another contract from 1946, Ministry of Defense Factory No. 393 haggled with Camp No. 27 for more workers. One stipulation was that the factory had to erect barracks for the workers on loan from the camp.[29] This contract, like many others, illustrated the permeability of camp boundaries as POWs moved back and forth from camps to worksites. Although physical camps with gates, walls, and barbed wire existed, the loaning of POWs to industry meant that prisoners interacted with free Soviet labor on factory floors. In addition, some prisoners lived outside of camp boundaries as labor needs outweighed fears of escape or segregation. Contracts with local industries and the permeability of the camp system constituted key features of the Gulag system as well as the GUPVI, as Wilson Bell and Alan Barenberg have noted. In January 1935, for example, 20.5 percent of Siblag's prisoners worked as contracted laborers in nearby enterprises.[30] In the case of Vorkuta, prisoners worked among free citizens on contracts and lived outside of the camp zone not in return for their good behavior but for their ability to contribute to nearby mines and factories.[31]

The labor shortages of the war and postwar years led to desperation for workers as well as numerous labor disputes between enterprises. In its 1946 contract with Camp No. 27, Ministry of Defense Factory No. 393 noted that it already employed three hundred POWs, but it asked for an additional seven to eight hundred. In need of any possible worker, the factory stated that up to 20 percent of the POWs could be in the third labor category—that is, those who could work only short hours at light tasks due to physical impairment.[32] Any labor contribution, no matter how small, in the estimation of the factory's managers, was better than nothing. A variety of camps and commissariats wrote to the central GUPVI leadership begging for additional POWs in the way that Ministry of Defense Factory No. 393 did. In March 1946, for example, the commissar of civilian housing begged the GUPVI for one thousand laborers in Crimea but received only one hundred.[33] At other times, the GUPVI was so overwhelmed with requests that it took months to respond. Even the intervention of high-level ministers could not guarantee the receipt of workers or answers. In December 1945, the deputy minister of civilian housing construction of the RSFSR contacted V. V. Chernyshev, the deputy head of the NKVD. The letter remained unanswered, however, and another was sent in May 1946.[34] The ministry asked for five hundred POWs to work on one particular housing construction project. Despite the repeated pleading, and from the head of a ministry no less, only the deputy head of the GUPVI, Major-General Ratushchnyi, replied two weeks later, writing that all the POWs from the nearest camp, No. 319, were already employed and that he could not deliver the requested five hundred POWs.[35] The repeated requests reflected the extreme labor shortage of the postwar years, and the failure to supply the POWs to civilian housing construction attests to the continuing priority of heavy industry over consumer needs.

In addition to deciding where to send the POWs and what tasks they would perform, Soviet leaders also emphasized productivity. On July 2, 1945, Beria sent a directive to camp directors stressing that prisoners must be compelled to fulfill production targets. He also tasked camp directors with submitting monthly reports to the NKVD detailing the use of POW labor.[36] The directors needed to include the physical conditions of POWs and their labor assignments, plan fulfillment, and expenses and profits in the reports and send them to leading officials, including Stalin, Molotov, Beria, Malenkov, Bulganin, and Kaganovich.[37] The close tracking of the POWs' labor contribution and costs suggests that Soviet officials made an ongoing calculation about the worth of the prisoners to reconstruction. As with the Gulag, it is likely that numbers presented in these reports were manipulated. Nonetheless, these summary reports illustrate the importance that top Soviet officials placed on German POW labor.

As time progressed, the reports concerning German POWs began to assess their contribution to the Soviet economy. There were two types of reports: internal ones for the GUPVI leadership and ones that went from the GUPVI leadership to the top Soviet leadership. The head of the GUPVI, S. Kruglov, for example, sent a top-secret report to Stalin, Molotov, and Beria in June 1946 on the number and physical condition of the German POWs.[38] The report included information about how many POWs were ill, had been repatriated, or had died and detailed breakdowns of their labor deployments. According to the report, 1,408,817 German POWs were assigned to 42 of 43 possible labor assignments across a variety of industries. The roughly 1.4 million working German POWs represented 4 percent of the total free state-employed national population.[39] The majority of the POWs were assigned to the MVD, defense industries, or fuel and heavy industries. Roughly 17 percent of all POWs, or 239,510 men, worked for fuel and power industries. These deployments were aimed at the restoration of the power grid throughout the liberated territories as well as the energy sector as a whole. The next largest assignment for POWs was to defense-related industries, in which 16.9 percent of POWs, or 238,540 men, labored in June 1946. Close to 180,000 POWs worked for heavy industry and metallurgy, comprising 12.6 percent of the working German POWs. The MVD and transport industries each employed roughly 10 percent. The POWs working for the MVD most likely consisted of those assigned to labor tasks around the camps, those awaiting new assignments on loan to other ministries and industries, and those working on MVD economic projects such as the Volga-Don Canal and the Baikal-Amur Mainline.[40] Almost 7 percent worked for a variety of construction industries, and 4.5 percent worked for different sorts of food industries including fishing, grain procurement, and tractor production. The remaining 20 percent of the POW workforce was scattered across a variety of assignments including producing chemicals, paper, and textiles as well as a number of nondescript local organizations and light industries. Thus, 89 percent of the German POWs worked for various economic ministries, all in vital sectors of the economy.

The POW labor assignments for June 1946 illustrate the state's needs and priorities for postwar reconstruction in 1946: power, defense, heavy industrial construction, civilian housing construction, and transportation. The bulk of the POWs worked in coal and the construction of electric power stations. Many other POWs worked for metallurgical enterprises or in the construction of heavy industry, machine tools, and in heavy machine building. These industries were essential to the development of light industry and the consumer sector. Many POWs also worked to make building materials and to construct housing. A large number of POWs worked to build various forms of transportation in the USSR. While some produced motor vehicles, ships, or airplanes, 50 percent of POWs working for transportation-related industries worked for the Ministry of Railways, which faced the challenge of repairing and replacing bombed and destroyed tracks. These 74,627 POWs accounted for 5 percent of all German POW workers in June 1946.

The state's assignment of German POW labor in mid-1946 correlated directly with the damages sustained during the war. The Nazis had destroyed over 31,000 factories, 65,000 kilometers of railways, 4,100 train stations, 98,000 collective farms (*kolkhozy*), 1,876 state farms (*sovkhozy*), and 2,890 machine-tractor stations.[41] Donald Filtzer has stated that the destruction was so severe that the Soviet Union resembled a "defeated power" rather than the victor that it was. All totaled, the Soviet Union lost around 25 percent of its physical assets during the war.[42] In the years immediately following the war, reestablishing the rail networks, factories, and housing stock took priority. Economic reconstruction necessitated the reconstruction of heavy industry, the energy sector and mines, and vital transport networks. Thus, the state assigned POWs to key labor tasks that would allow for the revitalization of the national economy.

MAPPING OF GERMAN POW CAMPS

Archival sources present information concerning the highest-level policies of the Soviet Union regarding German prisoner of war captivity and labor, but they do not properly present the vast scope of POW integration into both the Soviet economy and geography. The following maps (figs. 7.1–7.4) plot the intersections between camp locations, resource deposits, industrial centers, and transportation hubs in the Soviet Union.[43] During and after the Second World War, 4,313 German POW camps operated throughout the territory of the entire Soviet Union, in every republic with the exception of Tajikistan. Most of these camps operated in the republics that had seen the fiercest fighting of the war. Figure 7.1 illustrates the locations of these camps throughout the entire Soviet Union.[44] Many of these camps also housed POWs of other nationalities such as Austrians, Romanians, Hungarians, Finns, and Japanese. Generally, Germans vastly outnumbered the other nationalities in camp populations. Camp documents clearly noted the different national compositions of their inmates. As the first map illustrates, many of the German POW camps were concentrated in

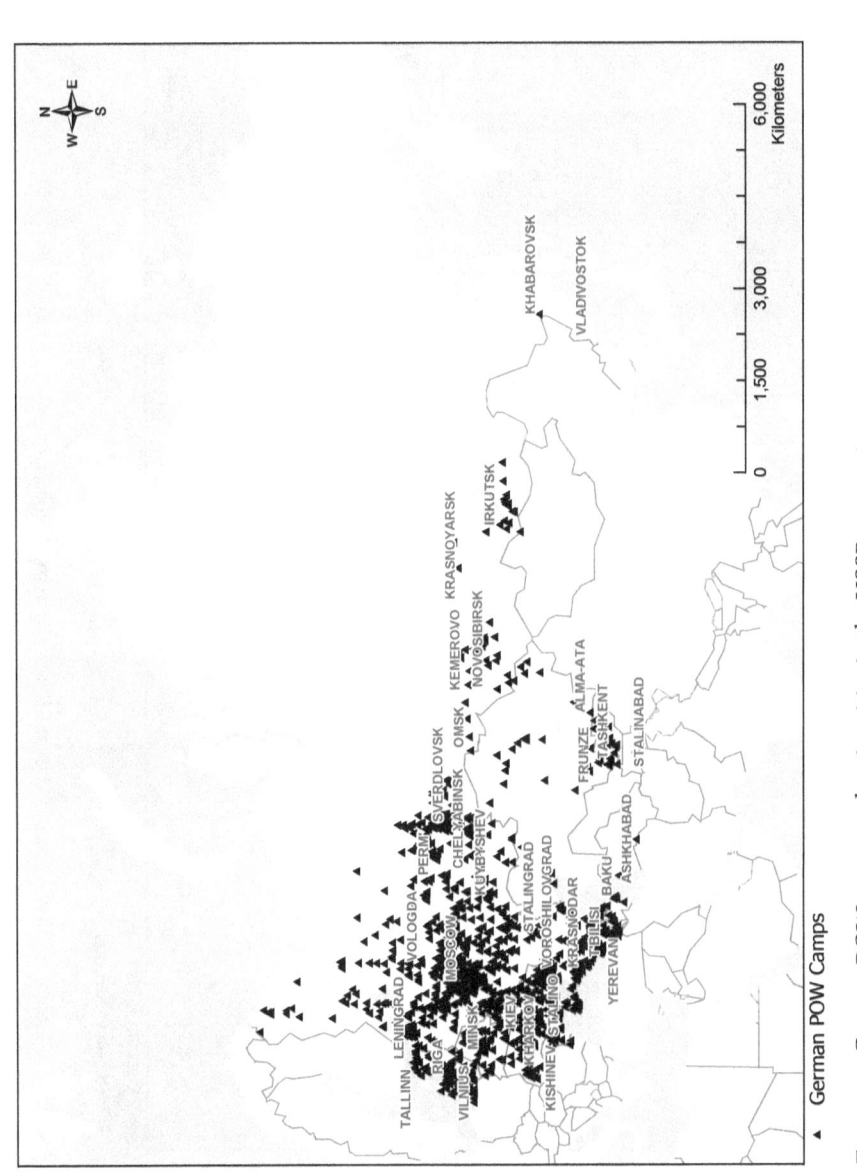

Figure 7.1. German POW camps and major cities in the USSR, 1941–56.

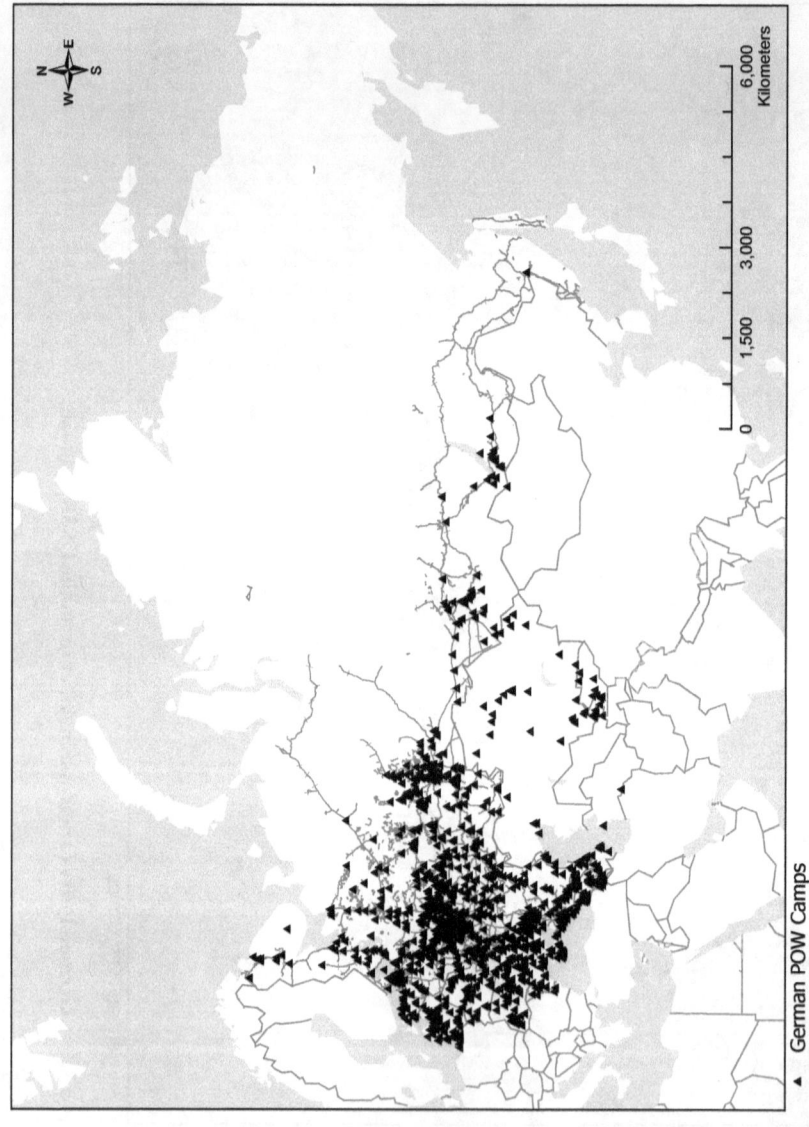

Figure 7.2. German POW camps in the USSR and Russian railroads, 1941–56.

areas formerly occupied by the Wehrmacht, indicating that the German POWs were deployed in the rebuilding of what they had destroyed. In addition to the practicalities of having the Germans engage in the restoration of some of the most badly damaged areas, these were also the places where the population had suffered the most directly. Watching the enemy perform reparations could also have served to improve the morale of the local population. Thus, POW labor in the European portions of the USSR and the RSFSR addressed both economic and emotional needs.

Of the 4,313 German POW labor camps located throughout the Soviet Union, 3,986 were in Belarus, Estonia, Latvia, Lithuania, Moldova, Russia, and Ukraine—the republics that were either wholly or heavily occupied by the Nazis. Of the total number of camps, 2,858, or 66 percent, were located in Russia. Although these camps were sited throughout both European and Asiatic Russia, they were concentrated primarily in areas that had seen fighting during the war, in the industrial centers in the Ural Mountains, and along the Trans-Siberian Railroad, as figure 7.2 illustrates. Of the Soviet republics that had not been the site of significant fighting, Kazakhstan had the highest number of camps. There, POWs worked in the coal industry.[45]

Many camps were located near population centers, which had often seen considerable wartime destruction, as well as close to key industrial sites in the Ural region. The placement of POW camps followed a pattern very different from that of Gulag camps. Comparing the locations of the German POW camps from 1941 to 1956 with those of Gulag camps in 1945 and 1946 from Judith Pallot's project *Mapping the Gulag* clearly illustrates this difference.[46] Her work shows that Gulag camps tended to cluster in the north of the RSFSR as well as in remote regions of western Siberia. As the mapping series in figures 7.1–7.4 shows, few to no POW camps existed in these inhospitable areas.

Digital mapping has altered many of the commonly held assertions taken from German sources about the POW camps. Most Germans associated the GUPVI camp system with Siberia and snow. However, mapping shows that most of the GUPVI camps operated outside of Siberia. Those that did operate in Siberia were outside the region's harshest climatic extremes. Whereas some Gulag camps existed in the Soviet Union's coldest places, figure 7.3 shows that this was not the case for the GUPVI system.[47] Although German POW camps did expose their inmates to temperatures more extreme than those of Germany, most of the camps existed in the more temperate European regions of the Soviet Union and Russia.

Herein lies one of the greatest differences between the GUPVI and Gulag systems. As Wilson Bell, Steven Barnes, and Alan Barenberg have noted, Soviet authorities tried, although often failed, to isolate Gulag inmates from the free population geographically due to concerns about the potential for prisoners to corrupt free populations.[48] However, Soviet authorities did not randomly choose the locations for Gulag camps solely as a means of punishment. Alan Barenberg has noted in his study of Vorkuta that a mixture of factors resulted in the camp's establishment, including the need to develop a rich coal basin in an inhospitable area and perform internal colonization of the vast expanses of the Soviet Union. For Vorkuta and other Gulag locations, forced prison labor enabled the state to address labor shortages in these remote regions while simultaneously isolating perceived internal enemies from potential bases of support.[49] While the locations of Gulag camps correlated to the harshest climates and most remote regions of the Soviet Union, the need to develop important extractive industries directed these placements rather than the desire to punish.

The difference in the concentrations of Gulag and GUPVI forced laborers likely stems from the conditions of the war. The German POWs needed to rebuild what they had destroyed, both from an economic standpoint and because of notions of vengeance. Employing them in the industrial and population centers of the Soviet Union accomplished both tasks. Additionally, Soviet authorities recognized that the POWs would either die or return to Germany. Unlike Soviet citizens, who could remain in remote regions around camps after release, the Germans could not be used to colonize the internal expanses of the Soviet Union. Although a handful may have remained, the overwhelming majority returned to the places in Germany where they had either enlisted in the army or been drafted.[50] Memoir accounts and returnee interviews also overwhelmingly state that the men desired to go home as soon as possible.[51] Had more been given the opportunity to stay, it is unlikely that many would have chosen to do so. Thus, employing the POWs in the population-rich and previously more developed regions of the Soviet Union outweighed concerns of escape, fraternizing with Soviet citizens, and punishment.

Most of the POW camps depicted in this series of maps opened during or after 1944, as the Red Army marched toward Berlin. The NKVD sent captured Germans to camps across the Soviet Union. The republics with the most and longest running camps were Belarus, Kazakhstan, Russia, and Ukraine. This is likely due to two factors: destruction and industry. Belarus, Russia, and Ukraine had been heavily damaged by fighting. Republics such as Armenia, Kyrgyzstan, Moldova, Turkmenistan, and Uzbekistan all had small numbers of camps that generally did not run for more than five years. This implies that the industries in these regions were not vital to the long-term restoration of the national economy. Additionally, as figure 7.4 shows, Ukraine, Russia, and

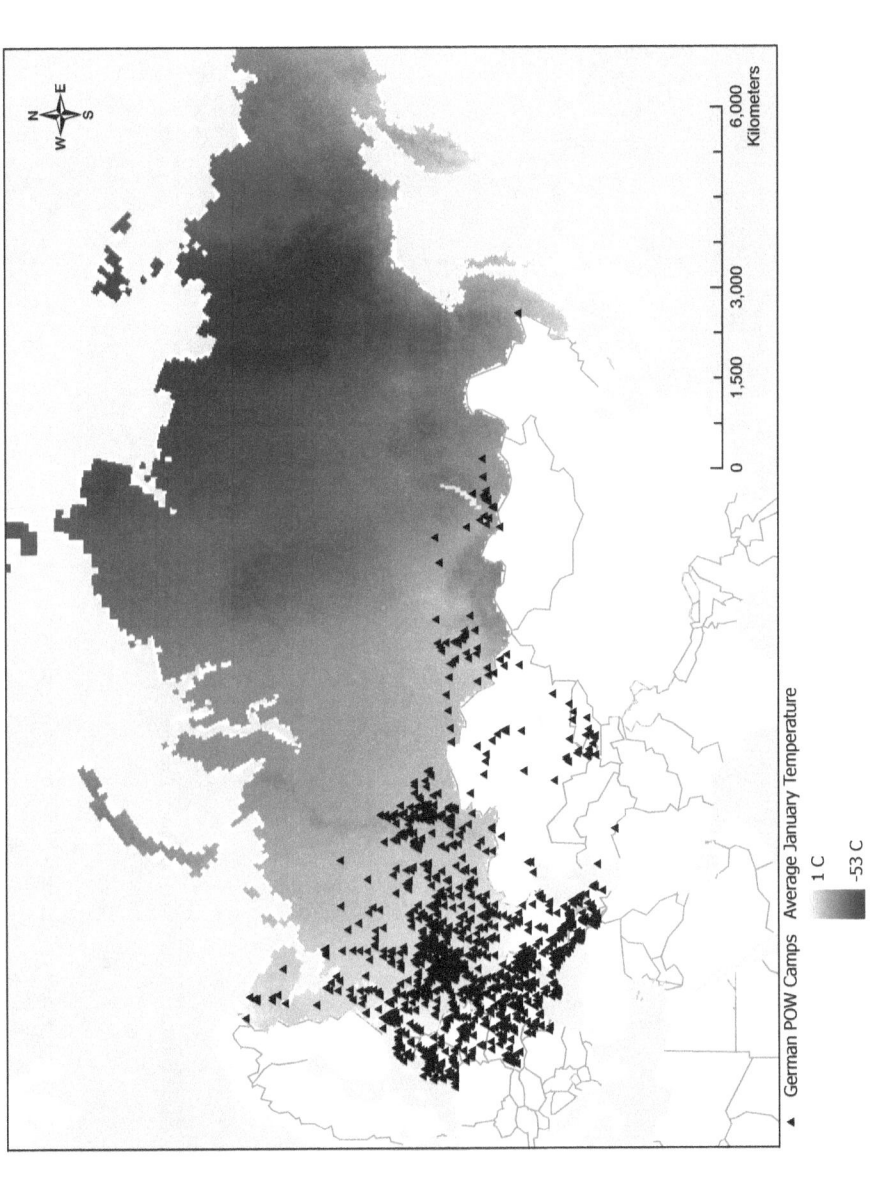

Figure 7.3. German POW camps in the USSR and average January temperature in Russia, 1941–56.

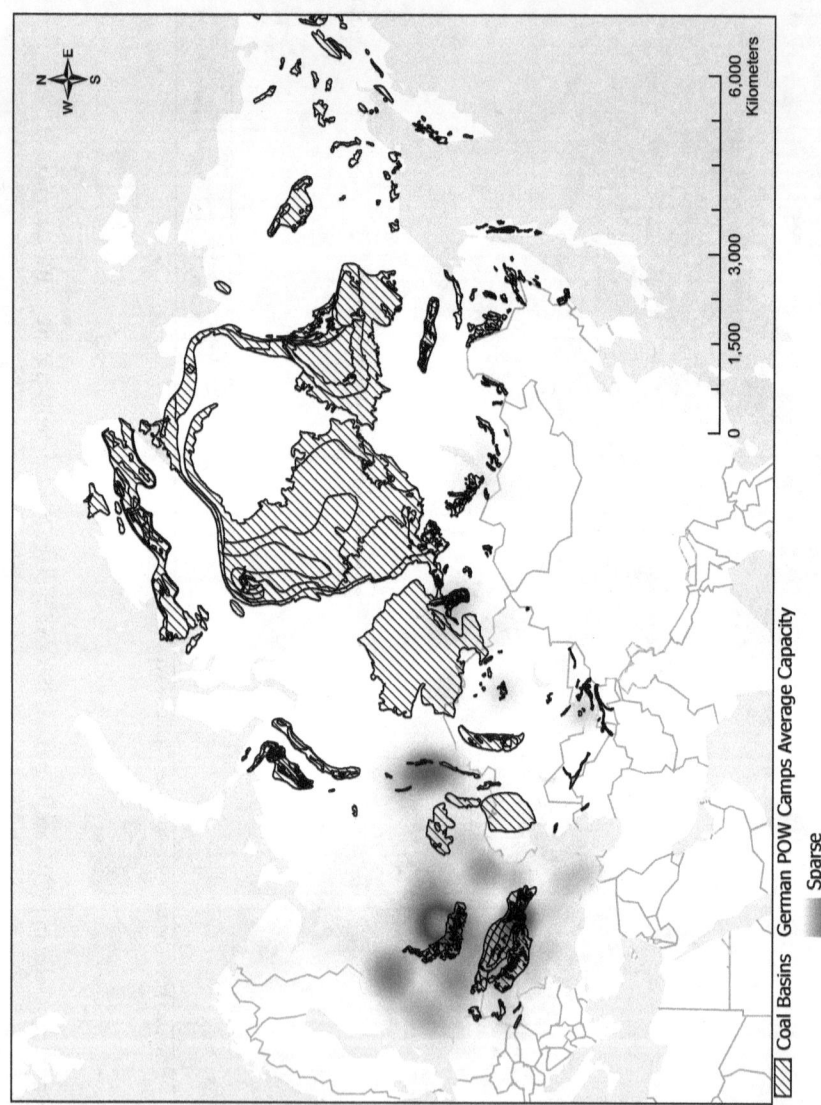

Figure 7.4. Average German POW camp populations, 1941–56.

Kazakhstan were the central sites for the Soviet coal industry, in which POWs were heavily mobilized.[52] This particular map depicts coal basins in relation to the average population density of camps.[53] Ukraine's rich coal fields, for example, were a major source of coal production for the entire Soviet Union, and many of the POWs incarcerated in this republic were employed in the coal industry. Almost three-quarters of all of the POW camps were located in coal-rich regions of Ukraine. Furthermore, large concentrations of POW camps were located around cities that existed due to coal extraction such as present-day Donetsk or Luhans'k, previously known as Stalino and Voroshilovgrad, respectively. The coal mines had been flooded or blocked by party activists as the Red Army retreated in order to deprive the invading Germans of their use. Later, the retreating Germans destroyed whatever sites they had restored. Coal was one of the foundational resources for the reconstruction effort. Beria and Stalin closely tracked the totals of German POWs and personally assigned them to specific commissariats, industries, or cities, and both clearly viewed coal as a priority.[54] GUPVI documentation that lists camps in coal-rich regions in Ukraine does so not only by the cities but also by the mines for which the inmates worked, further emphasizing the connection between POW labor and mining. For example, there were camps at mines 5, 6, 7, 8, 12, and 31 in Stalino (Donetsk) alone.[55] Finally, in addition to illustrating the close connection between POW camp locations and the coal industry, this map confirms that the majority of the German POWs labored in camps in the European territories of the Soviet Union and Russia. Whereas figures 7.1–7.3 clearly demonstrate that the majority of POW *camps* were located in the European territories of the Soviet Union and Russia, figure 7.4 confirms that this was also the case for the German POW population, since it also takes into account the population density of the camps.

The majority of the camps depicted in this mapping series closed between 1948 and 1950, which indicates that their use was largely related to postwar reconstruction. In general, the large-scale closure of camps between 1946 and 1949 coincided with progress fulfilling the country's All-Union Fourth Five-Year Plan, which ran from 1946 to 1950. It aimed to rebuild the USSR.[56] As the Soviet Union recovered from the ravages of war and territories that lay in ruin were rebuilt, camps closed, and their prisoners either returned home or were sent to areas that still required their economic contribution. Although restoration of the Soviet economy was not necessarily completed by 1950, substantial effort had been made to rebuild what had been damaged during the war. By that point, POW numbers had dwindled substantially, and their role in the economy became a secondary reason for their captivity. Their labor was still used, but they had become pawns in diplomatic negotiations of the Cold War. As tensions rose over the spread of Communism in Europe and Asia as well as the arms race, Western states used the POWs as another reason to condemn and pressure the Soviet Union. The West German press launched a massive campaign against the Soviet Union regarding the POWs. Representatives of the United States, Great Britain, and France privately wrote to Soviet officials regarding the POWs and publicly called for an investigation of the situation in the United Nations.[57] For unknown reasons, Soviet authorities ignored the political liability of POW incarceration. Perhaps they wished to assert their power and independent authority in the face of perceived bullying. Around this time, Soviet officials began to place increasing importance on reeducation efforts among POWs. While there had been propaganda and reeducation efforts among German POWs since the early stages of the war, such work became increasingly important amid growing Cold War tensions. Just as Gulag officials attempted to ideologically refashion their prisoners, so too did GUPVI leaders. Reports to the Politburo at this time included details about reeducation efforts in addition to data concerning labor productivity.[58]

The need to hold the POWs as a captive labor force also decreased in these later years as the Gulag population grew amid a new wave of postwar crackdowns. During the war years, many Gulag inmates either left the camps to fight for the Red Army or died. As the Gulag population decreased, the increasing POW population filled the gap. After the war, the opposite held true. With the cessation of hostilities, the number of German POWs could only decrease, whereas arrests led to the growth of the Gulag population. Indeed, this was the case from 1946 to 1948. The Gulag population increased from 601,000 at the beginning of 1946 to 809,000 in 1947 and then to 1.1 million in 1948. These jumps in population coincided with a wave of arrests and sentencings for "counterrevolution," violations of new antitheft laws implemented in 1947, and failure to comply with draconian labor laws that had been instituted in the '20s and '30s.[59]

CONCLUSION

Over the course of the 1930s, the Gulag system became an important part of the Soviet economy, which relied on forced labor for large-scale construction projects and the extraction of raw materials. While contemporary scholars continue to debate the economic effectiveness of prison labor as well as the larger purpose of the Gulag, research here shows that one important subset of the Soviet state's forced labor population, German POWs, was consciously deployed by the state to serve economic goals of reconstruction.

Data show that from their initial mass captures in 1943 through 1950 and the fulfilment of the Fourth Five-Year Plan, German POWs played an important role in the Soviet economy. Following Germany's capitulation on May 9, 1945, Soviet leaders forced German POWs to repair the massive destruction they had caused, which helped offset the enormous Soviet death toll of the war. While forcing German prisoners to rebuild the country they had destroyed was a distinct form of punishment with political meaning, the use of German POWs' forced labor was primarily motivated by economic needs. After releasing the ill or incapacitated, the NKVD dispersed the remaining 1,666,391 German POWs within an already established and functioning forced labor system, where they made definitive contributions. Soviet leaders such as Stalin, Beria, and Molotov were deeply involved in the deployment of the POWs, deciding their labor assignments and closely tracking their contributions. The significance of POW labor is further substantiated by the competition over and requests for their services. Appeals for workers from a variety of ministries as well as the details of labor contracts between camps and local industries reveal how necessary the POWs were to the economic projects of the country. Indeed, administrative directives regarding the German POWs were deeply and consistently motivated by economic concerns. The NKVD/MVD sought to get the highest possible levels of production from their POW population with the lowest resource investment.

Mapping analysis reinforces and details the economic contributions of the POWs. The geographic placement of the camps overwhelmingly lines up with what had been occupied territories that were ravaged by the war and with key industrial and resource centers. POW camps were not placed in harsh regions to punish, isolate, or exterminate the POWs but rather in areas where they could make substantial contributions to the economy. While forced labor may not have been as productive or cost effective as free labor, it contributed vitally to postwar reconstruction, especially amid the terrible shortage of men and women due to casualties of the war. Only after 1950, when the economy had stabilized and Soviet officials had repatriated most of the POWs did motivations shift, with the Soviet government holding the remaining prisoners for political rather than economic reasons.

NOTES

1. Kuz'micheva, *Skvoz' plen*, 10.
2. Kuz'micheva, *Skvoz' plen*, 12; Beevor, *Stalingrad*, 396; Werth, *Russia at War*, 533–40, 542.

3. Bourtman, "'Blood for Blood,'" 247–48, 259; Biess, *Homecomings*, 45; Kuz'minykh, *Voennyi plen i internirovanie*, 359–64; Epifanov, *Organizatsionnye i pravovye osnovy nakazaniia*, 234–44.

4. I discuss the different types of political detention and release of POWs in depth in my dissertation: Grunewald, "German Prisoners of War in the Soviet Union." Both this chapter and my dissertation examine those labeled as *nemtsy*—"Germans," as opposed to any other nationalities that fought for fascist Germany such as Austrians or allies such as Italians, Romanians, or Bulgarians. Soviet archival sources clearly delineate the differences between these nationalities, and I have chosen to focus on the largest group, the Germans, because they were the most significant and relatively easiest to follow through the documents.

5. Zubkova, *Russia after the War*, 20.

6. Khlevniuk, *The History of the Gulag*, xvi, 2, 9, 84.

7. Barenberg, *Gulag Town*, and "'Discovering' Vorkuta."

8. Ivanova, *Istoriia GULAGa*; Jakobson, *Origins of the Gulag*.

9. Solomon, *Soviet Criminal Justice*. See especially 194, 196, 299, and 301–5 for discussions about the increasingly severe criminal punishments for labor-related offenses and hooliganism over the course of the 1930s and 1940s.

10. Solzhenitsyn, *The Gulag Archipelago*; Conquest, *Kolyma*; Applebaum, *Gulag*.

11. Barnes focuses extensively on refashioning in *Death and Redemption*. Other scholars have also noted the relationship between labor, reeducation, and reform. See, for example, Bell, *Stalin's Gulag*, 44; Barenberg, *Gulag Town*, 82–83; Maddox, "Gulag Football," 510.

12. Viola, *The Unknown Gulag*, especially 149.

13. Solomon, *Soviet Criminal Justice*, 194, 196, 299, 301–5.

14. Gregory, "An Introduction to the Economics of the Gulag," in Gregory and Lazarev, eds., *The Economics of Forced Labor*, 8.

15. Bell, *Stalin's Gulag*, 10.

16. For a detailed analysis of the White Sea–Baltic Canal, see Morukov, "The White Sea-Baltic Canal," in Gregory and Lazarev, eds., *The Economics of Forced Labor*. Morukov notes in his chapter that the canal was indeed too shallow to offer true strategic help, but other nations did not know the depth of the canal and assumed it could indeed help the Soviet navy. Khlevniuk, *History of the Gulag*, 84; Bell, *Stalin's Gulag*, 10.

17. Bacon, *The Gulag at War*, 134–37; Bell, *Stalin's Gulag*, 9.

18. Russian State Military Archive (RGVA), fond (f.) 1p, opis' (op.) 9a, delo (d.) 8, list (ll.) 39–40.

19. State Archive of the Russian Federation (GARF), f. 9401, op. 2, d. 95, ll. 36–38.

20. GARF, f. 9401, op. 2, d. 95, ll. 366–67; GARF, f. 9401, op. 1, d. 2226, l. 199; GARF, f. 9401, op. 1, d. 2227, ll. 152–53.
21. GARF, f. 9401, op. 2, d. 95, l. 369.
22. On the removal of physical assets from Soviet-occupied Germany, see Naimark, *The Russians in Germany*, 141–204.
23. Borchard, *Die Deutschen Kriegsgefangenen*, 43.
24. GARF, f. 9401, op. 1, d. 2227, ll. 31–32; GARF, f. 9401, op. 1, d. 737, ll. 239–41; f. 9401, op. 1, d. 2227, l. 100.
25. Archive of the German Caritas Association (ADCV), 372.15 ( ) Fasz. 1 Bericht aus Russland von Herrn Robert Otto, 24 October 1945.
26. On the question of POW mortality statistics, see Gerlach and Werth, "State Violence—Violent Societies," 168–70. They report that officially 356,687 German POWs died in Soviet captivity between 1941 and 1956 but note that there are plenty of reasons to dispute this number including the variances in reported numbers of the captured and repatriated in official Soviet news releases as well as POWs who died after capture but before they could be registered. They report that over 800,000 German POWs could have died in Soviet captivity. Khlevniuk, *History of the Gulag*, 78. Alexopoulos, *Illness and Inhumanity*, 133.
27. Filtzer, *Soviet Workers and Late Stalinism*, 25–26; Bell, *Stalin's Gulag*, 10, 39; Barenberg, *Gulag Town*, 155, 305n31.
28. RGVA, f. 105p, op. 8, d. 16, ll. 7 and 70b.
29. RGVA, f. 105p, op. 10, d. 8, l. 68.
30. Bell, *Stalin's Gulag*, 39.
31. Barenberg, *Gulag Town*, 155.
32. RGVA, f. 105p, op. 10, d. 8, l. 68.
33. RGVA, f. 1p, op. 4i, d. 36, l. 13.
34. RGVA, f. 1p, op. 4i, d. 36, l. 34.
35. RGVA, f. 1p, op. 4i, d. 36, l. 33.
36. GARF, f. 9401, op. 1, d. 744, l. 27 in Zagorul'ko, *Voennoplennye v SSSR*, 618.
37. GARF, f. 9401, op. 2, d. 139, ll. 105–11; GARF, f. 9401, op. 2, d. 235, ll. 340–48.
38. GARF, f. 9401, op. 2, d. 137, ll. 366–77.
39. Clarke, *Soviet Economic Facts*, 23. Clarke gives a figure of thirty-two million state-employed workers in 1946. This does not account for forced labor.
40. Maier-Lutz, *Flußkreuzfahrten in Rußland*, 235; RGVA, f. 1/p, op. 10i, d. 1, l. 3.
41. GARF, f. 17, op. 125, d. 410, l. 72.
42. Filtzer, *Soviet Workers and Late Stalinism*, 13.
43. The following maps illustrate the approximate location of the German POW camps. The sourcebook, Chvatova, Austermühle, and Agentstvo, *Orte des Gewahrsams* lists the nearest village or city for each camp (i.e., Moscow, Russia; Yerevan, Armenia; etc.). The locations depicted in this map series are based on

the GoogleMaps latitude and longitude coordinates for each nearest settlement. They are not indicative of where each camp was actually located. Camps could have been contained within the city or on the outskirts. Both were common placements for camps.

44. I used the camps from Chvatova, Austermühle, and Agentstvo, *Orte des Gewahrsams*, 12–247, to look up approximate camp locations based on the villages or cities given. These All-Union maps represent 4,266 camps of the 4,313 listed in the book. Some camps could not be found either by an automated process with GoogleMaps or manually.

45. The Russian railroad information comes from Land Resources of Russia, "Transportation." The railroad lines depicted are those of modern Russia, though the basic rail lines, including the main lines of the Trans-Siberian Railway, existed long before the start of the Second World War. Regarding POWs working for coal industries in Kazakhstan, see GARF, f. 9414, op. 1, d. 328, ll. 28–33.

46. Pallot, "Distribution of Camps 1945–1946."

47. Average January temperature data was downloaded from Land Resources of Russia, "Climate."

48. Bell, *Stalin's Gulag*, 7, 63, 69; Barnes, *Death and Redemption*, 7, 14; Barenberg, *Gulag Town*, 41, 97.

49. Barenberg, "'Discovering' Vorkuta,'" 25–28.

50. See GARF, f. 9526, op. 6, d. 508, ll. 66–68 for an example of not only how Soviets tracked the number of those repatriated in a given convoy or period but also how they tallied how many Germans returned to which occupation zone of Germany.

51. See GARF, f. 9401, op. 2, d. 169, ll. 367–76 for examples of German POW reactions in May 1947 to the news that they would be held in Soviet captivity until December 1948. Soviet authorities polled the POWs to assess their reactions and presented this information to Stalin, Beria, Molotov, and Zhdanov. The information about continued incarceration depressed most of the Germans. Memoir accounts vary drastically in terms of tone, composition, and reaction to captivity, but every memoir is most descriptive in two parts: capture and release. Many memoirists expressed elation when given the news that they would be returned to Germany. See Kehler, *Einblicke und Einsichten*; Schuetz, *Davai, Davai!*; Rühle, *Die Ärzte von Stalingrad*; Fuchs, *Wer spricht von Siegen*; or Popp and Dulias, *Another Bowl of Kapusta* for examples of positive attitudes regarding release.

52. The coal data comes from Michael Brownfield et al., "Coal Quality and Resources of the Former Soviet Union."

53. For the purpose of this series, population density was calculated by taking the average of a camp's minimum and maximum capacity as listed in Chvatova, Austermühle, and Agentstvo, *Orte des Gewahrsams*. Some camps grew over

time; others shrank. It is unclear if camps tended to operate at, under, or over capacity. Of the 4,313 German POW camps listed in Chvatova, Austermühle, and Agentstvo, 76 had no information related to capacity; thus, those camps are not represented in the capacity heatmap.

54. GARF contains a number of documents in which Stalin himself ordered or tracked the assignments of the German POWs. See, for example, f. 9401, op. 2, d. 137, ll. 366–77; f. 9401, op. 2, d. 95, ll. 36–38; f. 9414, op. 1, d. 328, ll. 21–27, 28–33, 51-ob. A number of camps were excluded from these visualizations because they were listed as mining settlements around certain cities. These mining settlements were removed from the data set because there was no way of knowing where exactly they were located besides the nearest major city.

55. Chvatova, Austermühle, and Agentstvo, *Orte des Gewahrsams*, 224.

56. Zaleski, *Stalinist Planning*, 347.

57. The West German press featured many regional newspapers and magazines as opposed to one particular publication that was widely read across the territory. A scan of major news publications such as *Bild*, *Der Spiegel*, and *Frankfurter Allgemeine Zeitung* results in condemnation of the Soviet Union for continuing to keep the POWs. See Russian State Archive of Socio-Political History (RGASPI), f. 82, op. 2, d. 488, ll. 181–82; RGAPSI, f. 82, op. 2, d. 1168, ll. 75–80, ll. 113–18 for examples of Politburo correspondences concerning Western diplomats who questioned the detention of the POWs through private diplomatic letters as well as in front of the United Nations.

58. GARF, f. 9401, op. 2, d. 199, ll. 403–9. On reeducation of Gulag inmates, see Barnes, *Death and Redemption*, 57–58; Bell, *Stalin's Gulag*, 44; Barenberg, *Gulag Town*, 82–83; Maddox, "Gulag Football," 510.

59. Barnes, *Death and Redemption*, 157–159; Barenberg, *Gulag Town*, 59–63.

BIBLIOGRAPHY

Alexopoulos, Golfo. *Illness and Inhumanity in Stalin's Gulag*. New Haven, CT: Yale University Press, 2017.

Applebaum, Anne. *Gulag: A History*. New York: Doubleday, 2003.

Bacon, Edwin. *The Gulag at War: Stalin's Forced Labour System in the Light of the Archives*. New York: New York University Press, 1994.

Barenberg, Alan. "'Discovering' Vorkuta: Science and Colonization in the Early Gulag." *Gulag Studies* 4 (2001): 21–40.

———. *Gulag Town, Company Town: Forced Labor and Its Legacy in Vorkuta*. New Haven, CT: Yale University Press, 2014.

Barnes, Steven A. *Death and Redemption: The Gulag and the Shaping of Soviet Society*. Princeton, NJ: Princeton University Press, 2011.

Beevor, Antony. *Stalingrad: The Fateful Siege, 1942–1943*. New York: Penguin, 1999.

Bell, Wilson T. *Stalin's Gulag at War: Forced Labour, Mass Death, and Soviet Victory in the Second World War*. Toronto: University of Toronto Press, 2018.

Biess, Frank. *Homecomings: Returning POWs and the Legacies of Defeat in Postwar Germany*. Princeton, NJ: Princeton University Press, 2006.

Borchard, Michael. *Die deutschen Kriegsgefangenen in der Sowjetunion: Zur politischen Bedeutung der Kriegsgefangenenfrage 1949–1955*. Düsseldorf: Droste, 2000.

Bourtman, Ilya. "'Blood for Blood, Death for Death': The Soviet Military Tribunal in Krasnodar, 1943." *Holocaust and Genocide Studies* 22, no. 2 (Fall 2008): 246–65.

Brownfield, Michael, Douglas Steinshouer, Mikhail Povarennykh, Ivan Eriomin, Mikhail Shpirt, Yevgeny Meitov, Irena Sharova, Nina Goriunova, and Margarita Zyrianova. "Coal Quality and Resources of the Former Soviet Union: An ArcView Project." Last modified December 7, 2016. https://pubs.usgs.gov/of/2001/ofr-01-104/readme.htm.

Chvatova, Veronika, Ulrich Austermühle, and Rossija Archivnoe Agentstvo. *Orte des Gewahrsams von deutschen Kriegsgefangenen in der Sowjetunion (1941–1956): Findbuch; [Standorte von Kriegsgefangenenlagern, Arbeitsbataillonen, Friedhöfen sowie Einrichtungen des Frontlagernetzes; auf der Grundlage von Dokumenten der Kriegsgefangenenverwaltung aus dem Staatlichen Russischen Militärarchiv]*. Dresden: Stiftung Sächsische Gedenkstätten zur Erinnerung an die Opfer politischer Gewaltherrschaft, 2010.

Clarke, Roger A. *Soviet Economic Facts 1917–1970*. London: Macmillan, 1972.

Conquest, Robert. *Kolyma: The Arctic Death Camps*. New York: Viking, 1978.

Epifanov, Aleksandr E. *Organizatsionnye i pravovye osnovy nakazaniia gitlerovskikh voennykh prestupnikov i ikh posobnikov v SSSR 1941–1956 gg.* Moscow: Unity, 2017.

Filtzer, Donald A. *Soviet Workers and Late Stalinism: Labour and the Restoration of the Stalinist System after World War II*. Cambridge: Cambridge University Press, 2002.

Fuchs, Helmut. *Wer spricht von Siegen: der Bericht uber unfreiwillige Jahre in Russland*. Munich: A. Knaus, 1987.

Gerlach, Christian, and Nicolas Werth. "State Violence—Violent Societies." In *Beyond Totalitarianism: Stalinism and Nazism Compared*, edited by Michael Geyer and Sheila Fitzpatrick, 133–79. New York: Cambridge University Press, 2009.

Gregory, Paul, and V. V. Lazarev, eds. *The Economics of Forced Labor: The Soviet Gulag*. Stanford, CA: Hoover Institution, 2003.

Grunewald, Susan. "German Prisoners of War in the Soviet Union: Life, Law, Memory, 1941–1956." PhD diss., Carnegie Mellon University, 2019.

Ivanova, G. M. *Istoriia GULAGa, 1918–1958: Sotsial'no-ekonomicheskii i politiko-pravovoi aspekty*. Moscow: Nauka, 2006.

Jakobson, Michael. *Origins of the Gulag: The Soviet Prison Camp System, 1917–1934.* Lexington: University Press of Kentucky, 1993.
Kehler, Ernst. *Einblicke und Einsichten: Erinnerungen.* Berlin: Dietz, 1989.
Khlevniuk, Oleg V. *The History of the Gulag: From Collectivization to the Great Terror.* New Haven, CT: Yale University Press, 2004.
Kuz'micheva, I. P. *Skvoz' plen: Nemetskie voennoplennye v Sovetskom Soiuze.* Moscow: Sabashnikovykh, 2007.
Kuz'minykh, A. L. *Voennyi plen i internirovanie v SSSR (1939–1956 gody): Monografiia.* Vologda: Drevnosti Severa, 2016.
Land Resources of Russia. "Climate." Accessed June 4, 2021. http://webarchive.iiasa.ac.at/Research/FOR/russia_cd/climate.htm.
Land Resources of Russia. "Transportation." Accessed June 4, 2021. http://webarchive.iiasa.ac.at/Research/FOR/russia_cd/trans.htm.
Maddox, Steven. "Gulag Football: Competitive and Recreational Sport in Stalin's System of Forced Labor." *Kritika: Explorations in Russian and Eurasian History* 19, no. 3 (2018): 509–36.
Maier-Lutz, Edeltraud. *Flußkreuzfahrten in Rußland. Unterwegs auf Wolga, Don, Jenissej und Lena.* Berlin: Trescher, 2005.
Naimark, Norman M. *The Russians in Germany: A History of the Soviet Zone of Occupation, 1945–1949.* Cambridge, MA: Belknap Press of Harvard University Press, 1995.
Pallot, Judith. "The Distribution of Camps (*Lagerya*) in USSR, 1945–1946." Accessed July 7, 2021. https://www.gulagmaps.org/distriubution-of-camps-in-ussr.
Popp, Dianna M., and Gottfried P. Dulias. *Another Bowl of Kapusta: The True Life Story of a World War II Luftwaffe Fighter Pilot and P.O.W. in Russia.* Bloomington, IN: AuthorHouse, 2004.
Rühle, Otto. *Die Ärzte von Stalingrad: Genesung in Jelabuga: Kessel Stalingrad—Antifaschule für ein neues Deutschland—autobiographischer Bericht.* Berlin: Wünsche, 2007.
Schuetz, A. D. Hans. *Davai, Davai!: Memoir of a German Prisoner of World War II in the Soviet Union.* Fefferson, NC: McFarland, 1997.
Solomon, Peter H. *Soviet Criminal Justice Under Stalin.* Cambridge: Cambridge University Press, 1996.
Solzhenitsyn, Aleksandr Isaevich. *The Gulag Archipelago, 1918–1956: An Experiment in Literary Investigation.* New York: Harper & Row, 1974.
Viola, Lynne. *The Unknown Gulag: The Lost World of Stalin's Special Settlements.* Oxford: Oxford University Press, 2007.
Werth, Alexander. *Russia at War: 1941–1945.* New York: E. P. Dutton & Co., 1964.
Zagorul'ko, Maksim Matveevich. *Voennoplennye v SSSR 1939–1956: Dokumenty i materialy.* Moscow: Logos, 2000.

Zaleski, Eugene. *Stalinist Planning for Economic Growth, 1933–1952.* Chapel Hill: University of North Carolina Press, 1980.

Zubkova, Elena Iur'evna. *Russia after the War: Hopes, Illusions, and Disappointments, 1945–1957.* Armonk, NY: M. E. Sharpe, 1998.

SUSAN GRUNEWALD is the Digital History Postdoctoral Associate at the University of Pittsburgh World History Center. Support for her research has been provided by a Cohen-Tucker Dissertation Research Fellowship from the Association of Slavic, East European, and Eurasian Studies; two A. W. Mellon Foundation Digital Humanities Fellowships at Carnegie Mellon University; and a Travel and Research Grant from the Central European History Society.

EIGHT

FRAMING GULAG MEMOIRS

A Distant Reading

SARAH J. YOUNG

FOR SURVIVORS OF THE SOVIET labor camps, the imperative to remember and commit the experience of the Gulag to paper requires finding a form appropriate to the story they must tell. This question of form is apparent in Aleksandr Solzhenitsyn's subtitle to *The Gulag Archipelago* (*Arkhipelag GULag*), "an experiment in literary investigation," and in Varlam Shalamov's insistence in his essay "On Prose" (*O proze*), "I do not write memoirs. There are no memoirs in *Kolyma Tales*. I do not write tales either—or rather, I try to write not a tale, but something that would not be literature."[1] In creating hybrid forms and memoirs that are not memoirs, the most famous Gulag authors explicitly foreground the literary dimension as they confront the problem of representation and the difficulty of translating the traumatic experience of incarceration into words. The question of how this approach affects the form of Gulag memoirs more generally is the focus of this chapter.

In addressing questions like this, anecdotal evidence taken from a small selection of memoirs is insufficient. Yet examining this body of works on a wider scale is hampered by the enormous number of Gulag texts in existence, which is beyond the ability of a single researcher to study exhaustively, even if we consider only published narratives. A distant reading technique, however, has the potential to identify common approaches and larger patterns within this tradition. Some might object to this method on the grounds that it treats texts that testify to the most appalling, traumatic experience as if they were any other data to be processed. But the experience of reading and the practice of analysis of any kind are very different processes. Reading is emotional, particularly when dealing with subjects such as the Gulag, and, as Franco Moretti suggests, individual texts speak to us in a way that a corpus never can.[2] But analysis on any level is more detached, stepping back from our initial emotional experience of a work. Distant reading in fact lies at the opposite end of the same continuum as close reading, and these forms have more in common with each other than either has with reading as a private, emotional activity. Moreover, distant reading does not preclude close reading, as it often identifies the aspects of a text that require traditional analysis. Rather than moving us away from engagement with the material, it has the potential to bring us closer to it.

The Sakharov Center in Moscow, devoted to the history of political oppression and the human rights movement in the USSR, has curated an online database of Gulag memoirs that offers the opportunity to create a substantial corpus of texts for analysis.[3] In addition to 1,284 memoirs, it contains poetry (22), diaries (24), letters (58), interviews (59), and biographies (90), primarily from the Stalin era but also including 61 works devoted to the early postrevolutionary period and 91 texts concerning post-Stalinist imprisonment. Once duplicates and empty pages have been removed, the corpus consists of 457 full books, 113 extracts from books, 793 shorter memoirs from collections (some of which are also extracts), 153 journal publications, and 34 newspaper articles. The total word count is just over 43,800,000. While far from being a complete corpus, this is large enough to be representative. Although some other Gulag works are available elsewhere online, including Solzhenitsyn's books and Shalamov's stories, I have not appended these beyond restoring the full text in a few cases where an extract appears in the Sakharov archive; there are not sufficient numbers of additional texts to make any difference to results, and adding them risks reverting to the sort of cherry-picking that use of the corpus is intended to preclude.

Using the archive effectively means accepting the definition of a "Gulag memoir" that the Sakharov Center employs. This includes, for example, Nadezhda Mandel'shtam's memoirs, which scarcely touch on the Gulag itself (in the strict sense of the system of camps and forced labor) and deal primarily with her husband's arrest and its effects. Some might consider the scope of this too broad, reflecting Gullotta's wider category of "Soviet repression literature" rather than the subgenre of "Gulag literature."[4] However, there are two reasons for employing an inclusive rather than exclusive definition. The first is that the Gulag was not an isolated phenomenon. As studies by Alan Barenberg and Wilson Bell have shown, the labor camp system was porous and overlapped with other aspects of Soviet life.[5] For historians as much as survivors and their family members, the question of what the Gulag encompasses or excludes does not always have a straightforward answer. In the case of families who suffered multiple generations of repression, for example, or children who lost parents in the Gulag, a broad focus may offer the only possibility of recounting that story. Such texts may tell us little about the mechanics of incarceration, but as part of the collective voice bearing witness to the traumas of the Soviet period, their perspective on the wider impact of the Gulag is equally valid as an object of study and otherwise.[6]

The second reason relates to what Gulag survivors actually write about. Barenberg's essay in the current volume cites Shalamov's disquiet at how many memoirs (unlike his own stories) shied away from depicting the camps. Solzhenitsyn's *One Day in the Life of Ivan Denisovich* (*Odin den' Ivana Denisovicha*) may have been perceived as a watershed, turning the focus of Gulag texts to hard labor and life in the camps themselves, yet the emphasis of many memoirs has remained on the initiatory experience. Evgeniia Ginzburg's *Journey into the Whirlwind* (*Krutoi marshrut*, more literally translated as *An Arduous Journey*) is typical in this regard, as she devotes almost one-third of her two volumes of memoirs to events leading up to her arrest, the preliminary investigation (lasting approximately seven months), and two years of near solitary confinement in Iaroslavl' prison. Her transport to Kolyma and the subsequent fifteen years of hard labor and exile are given comparatively shorter treatment. Even *The Gulag Archipelago* does not turn its focus to the transport system or the camps themselves until three-quarters of the way through the first volume. Solzhenitsyn's long Gulag novels, *In the First Circle* (*V kruge pervom*) and *Cancer Ward* (*Rakovyi korpus*), are also notable for their substantial treatment of the periods prior to arrest and after release as well as of the world outside the camps. The tendency by Gulag narrators to downplay in relative terms the representation of existence within the labor camps could be interpreted as a traumatic lacuna, reflecting not only the pain of recalling that experience or committing it to paper but also "the attempt to bear witness to something that failed to be registered as it happened."[7] On the other hand, it could be viewed as a practical response to the problem identified by Dostoevsky in *Notes from the House of the Dead* (*Zapiski iz mertvogo doma*), of how to depict the sheer monotony of years spent in the camps and retain any sense of interest or readability.[8] The more eventful months surrounding arrest may simply be easier (both emotionally and intellectually) to fashion into a compelling story. In this sense, Shalamov's insistent focus on the camps is a less usual approach.

Whatever one's precise definition, the Sakharov Center corpus offers significant potential for analysis across different disciplines, opening up new possibilities for Gulag studies as well as research into aspects of Soviet life more generally. From a historian's point of view, one might use it to gather evidence on transport, work and living conditions, medical treatment, or attitudes toward criminals. For sociologists, the corpus would allow analysis and comparison of institutional or behavioral norms, both inside and outside the camps, including, for example, the effects of the Gulag on family dynamics. Considering the corpus as a textual whole, network analysis could identify links between memoirs of imprisonment in the same places, and text mining could produce maps of camps referenced in the works. For literary scholars, the corpus offers the opportunity to compare narratives about different areas of the Gulag or different periods of imprisonment; to explore gender differences; and to compare the use of language in letters, diaries, poetry, and memoirs or between depictions of the Gulag itself and the "non-Gulag" aspects of these texts. My starting point is the question of the genre of memoirs and how these texts frame themselves; content is never divorced from form, and the form therefore has significant implications for how we read the content of these works. By examining the prefatory materials of the texts (titles, authorial prefaces, and the opening paragraphs of memoirs in the corpus), I aim to identify the forms and conventions employed as authors seek modes in which to represent their experience of the Gulag and express their perspective on it. In doing so, I will show how literary categories come into play in our consideration of Gulag narratives and will assess the implications of these for our understanding of this body of texts as historical evidence.

The following analysis has primarily been conducted using *AntConc*, a free desktop concordance application.[9] Where the dictionary form of a word is given, searches were conducted on all variants. I defined categories through qualitative close reading and, where appropriate, assigned more than one category to texts. I do not claim that my classifications are either exclusive or exhaustive; the focus on genre and framing questions influenced my decisions, but other criteria for categorizing texts and titles are obviously possible. Translations are my own.

TITLES

While titles are often formulated with significant input from editors and others, they nevertheless play a crucial role in framing the text and directing the reader. Removing duplicates as well as headers and subtitles obviously inserted by editors of collections leaves a list of 1,337 titles, forming a corpus of 5,871 words overall and 2,814 unique words. The vocabulary of titles overall emphasizes optimism as much as the negative impact of the Gulag and suggests a desire to avoid sensationalism. Notably, life (*zhizn'*) is the second most common noun (after *memoirs*) in this micro-corpus, featuring eighty-five times in titles, with no negative modifiers. Death (*smert', mertvyi*), by comparison, appears only twenty times. Positive terms such as joy (*radost'*), light (*svet*), hope (*nadezhda*), and happiness (*schast'e/schastlivost'*) occur four, eleven, two, and seven times respectively. These may be small numbers, but they are similar to those alluding to the overwhelming suffering experienced in the camps, which we might expect to be more prominent. Hunger (*golod*) appears twice and cold (*kholod*) four times; suffering (*stradanie*) itself has three occurrences, as does grief/woe (*gore*); sorrow (*skorb'*) has five, grief/sorrow (*pechal'*) four, pain (*bol'*) five, and bitter (*gor'kii*) six. Words denoting terror and fear have a minimal presence: fear/terror (*strakh*) and to fear (*boiat'sia*) both appear twice, the latter prefaced with a negative pronoun (no other negatives modify subsequent terms discussed); other synonyms for fear are absent. Perhaps most strikingly, there are only fifteen references to Stalin/-ist in titles, seven to Article 58—the notorious article of the Stalinist penal code defining counterrevolutionary crimes—and four to the various incarnations of the Soviet security apparatus.

Breaking down the titles in this way enables us to identify some overall patterns, but viewing them as individual units is also integral to understanding their modes of framing the texts. Reading the titles thematically, I identified four fundamental categories. Five hundred fourteen directly advertise their status as Gulag memoirs while 450 allude to the subject matter indirectly (referring, for example, to suffering or memory, but without identifying the Gulag as the source of these). There are 103 poetic titles apparently unconnected to the main subject—for example, Alieva's "The Scent of Violets" (*Zapakh filiaki*).[10] Two hundred seventy-two neutral titles encompass generic definitions, such as the ubiquitous *My Memoirs* (*Moi vospominaniia*), and references to people, notably family members, in both cases without further elaboration. I will return to the role of generic markers below.

As table 8.1 shows, direct references to the Gulag take a number of forms.[11] Aspects of the author's case or sentence, such as Mindlin's *Full Face and Profile: [Article] 58-10* (*Anfas i profil': 58-10*), often elide with those that refer to time, as in Zoia Marchenko's *Seventeen Years on the Islands of the Gulag* (*Semnadtsat' let na ostrovakh GULAGa*). But reference to the spatial dimension alone is much more common. A distinctive geography arises, as journeys to or between camps emphasize the dramatic change or distance involved—for example, in "New York—Moscow—Siberia under Convoy" (*N'iu-Iork—Moskva—Sibir' po etapu*) by Blok-Baers. Alongside Kolyma (twenty-eight), it is no surprise to find that the major camp systems at Noril'sk (eight), Vorkuta (ten), and Solovki (twelve) feature strongly. However, Shirkolag (a camp in the Perm region devoted to the construction of the Shirokovskii hydroelectric power station),

Table 8.1. Direct references to the Gulag in memoir titles

Themes and References	Number of Titles
Spatial/locational	184
Identity	142
Case/sentence	76
Temporal	47
Experience	25
General	30
Other	30

with ten occurrences, is more prominent than its size or significance as a camp would imply, for reasons I discuss below. By contrast, Karaganda appears de-emphasized, with only two occurrences (although individual camps in the Karaganda system including Ekibastuz, Kengir, and the Akmolinsk Camp for Wives of Traitors to the Motherland, usually known by its acronym ALZHIR, do feature).

The other major thematic category of direct references to the Gulag in titles relates to questions of personal identity. Just over 70 percent of these refer to the designation imposed on authors by their experience of the Gulag. This relates for some to their cases or grounds for arrest—for example, Ermolaev's *Notes of an "Enemy of the People"* (*Zapiski "vraga naroda"*). In other instances, they refer to the identity associated particularly with incarceration: *Notes of a Political Prisoner* (*Zapiski politzakliuchennogo*) by Bolonkin; *Notes of a Goner* (*Zapiski dokhodiagi*) by Belousov. The remaining titles express degrees of continuity with the authors' prearrest identity, such as Aleksandrovskii's *Notes of a Camp Doctor* (*Zapiski lagernogo vracha*). As I will show, the formation and survival of identity plays a very significant role overall in framing these memoirs, in a number of different ways.

Indirect references to the Gulag appear in titles where the subject matter of the repressions is not overt but understood or else represented by a silence in the title. Categorization here is more elusive because these references are by their nature allusive. However, as table 8.2 shows, a number of themes stand out, of which three in particular merit further elaboration (the significance of literary references will be discussed in relation to prefaces below). Unsurprisingly, memory plays a major role in many titles, such as Zubovskii's *I Remember How It Was* (*Ia pomniu, kak eto bylo*). Overall, the titles corpus features

Table 8.2. Indirect allusions to the Gulag in memoir titles

Themes and References	Number of Titles
inexpressibility	87
life and spirit	85
memory	73
spatial	71
temporal	70
suffering and loss	47
fate	44
survival and return	34
cruelty and inhumanity of power	31
ideas, truth, and lies	24
we/many	21
literary references	10
other	13

twenty-five occurrences of memory (*pamiat'*) and seventeen of the verb *to remember* (*pomnit'*). Almost as prominent is not forgetting, with twenty-two instances of *to forget* (*zabyt'*), as in Abbas-Ogly's *I Cannot Forget* (*Ne mogu zabyt'*). Injunctions to survivors to remember and tell the story are also frequent, such as Tiurbeev's "This Cannot Be Forgotten" (*Takoe ne zabyvaetsia*) and Siniagovskii's "I Must Tell" (*Ia dolzhen rasskazat'*). The above titles also contain examples of one of the other major themes: inexpressibility. While a few texts explicitly indicate the difficulty of the task, such as Abushinov's "Impossible to Express in Words" (*Nevozmozhno vyrazit' slovami*), two overlapping devices are more common.[12] The first, appearing forty-two times, is the use of demonstrative pronouns: *And It Was in Those Days* (*I bylo v te dni*) by Ashkenazi; "This Is How It Was" (*Tak eto bylo*) by Irshtein—the latter also the title of a well-known collection of memoirs. The second involves the use of ellipses (forty-one occurrences, with a further twenty-six in poetic titles and those directly referring to the Gulag): "I Ask Myself . . ." (*I sprashivaiu sebia . . .*) by Vaza; Gridin's *We, Who Didn't Exist . . .* (*My, kotorykh ne bylo . . .*). These devices have two main functions. First, by leaving the root of the experience unsaid, they gesture toward the idea of "unspeakability" associated with trauma.[13] Second, they frame the subject matter as commonly understood, a reference that does not require specific explanation, implicitly positioning the Gulag as *the* defining experience of the Soviet century.

The use of demonstrative pronouns in titles such as *This Is How It Was* frames the Gulag as something inevitable, removing the perpetrators—and therefore questions of responsibility and agency—from the equation. That sense of inevitability is also apparent in the concept of fate, which features quite strongly, as in titles such as Akhtiamov's *In Defiance of the Blows of Fate* (*Naperekor udarom sud'by*) and Vaishvillene's *Fate and Will* (*Sud'ba i volia*). Indeed, fate (*sud'ba*) becomes a further keyword that enables the Gulag itself to remain unspoken, synonymous with its suffering and loss, and it is notable that this single word appears almost as frequently as all other types of reference to suffering considered together. At the same time, this recourse to fate suggests that suffering is expected, even accepted.

While direct references to the Gulag and indirect allusions that deliberately avoid naming the subject account for the majority of texts, the significant body of neutral titles, as I note earlier and as shown in table 8.3, includes many that refer solely to the genre of the work. In some cases, the author's fame renders a more explanatory title unnecessary, as in the memoirs of Nadezhda Mandel'shtam.[14] But such titles are also used by lesser-known writers, such as topographer Valerii Lisianskii, suggesting an attempt to avoid influencing the reader's response with further framing. That sense of classification according to the type of text in question extends to the entire corpus, as just under half of all titles and subtitles are labeled with generic markers: 659 in total. Excluding from consideration the 107 markers of other forms such as diaries, poetry, and letters, the genre identifiers of retrospective prose memoirs feature a large range of terms. *Memoir* (*Vospominaniia*) is by some distance the most common word in this micro-corpus, alongside other designations of life-writing, but a variety of terms occur that are normally used to signal degrees of fictionalization—for example, story (*povest'*), novel (*roman*), even detective story (*detektiv*). Some of these fictionalizing designations are modified by documentary (*dokumental'nyi*). The fact that so many memoirs have this sort of genre marker suggests a need to specify the type of text being presented. This already indicates an awareness that simply telling the story or relating the facts is never just that; there are always choices to be made in terms of both content and style. At the same time, including these types of markers also implies a degree of uncertainty, as though affirming the genre in the title will compensate for a lack of adherence within the text to generic boundaries or will direct the reader to approach the text in a particular way that might otherwise not be immediately obvious. The preoccupation with genre in titles spills over into prefatory material, to which we will now turn.

Table 8.3. Genre markers in the titles and subtitles of Gulag memoirs

Genre	Russian	Number of Titles
memoirs	vospominaniia	204
letters	pis'ma	60
notes	zapiski/zapis'	55
story/narrative	povest'/povestvovanie	46
history	istoriia	27
diary	dnevnik	26
story/tale/narrative	rasskaz	26
book	kniga	18
poetry	stikhi/stikhotvorenie	17
novel	roman	14
autobiography	avtobiografiia	16
documentary	dokumental'nyi	12
archive	arkhiv	11
chronicle	khronika	11
memoir	memuar	10
confession	ispoved'	9
pages	stranitsy	8
prose	proza	8
sketch	ocherk	7
evidence, testimonial	svidetel'stvo	7
biography	biografiia	6
article	stat'ia	6
(long) poem	poema	4
meditations	raszdum'ia	4
tragedy	tragediia	4
life story	zhizneopisanie	3
life	zhitie	3
notes	zametki	3
novella	novella	3
requiem	rekviem	3
reportage	reportazh	3
oral tale	skaz	3

(Continued)

Table 8.3. Genre markers in the titles and subtitles of Gulag memoirs (*Continued*)

Genre	Russian	Number of Titles
essay	*esse*	3
impression	*vpechatlenie*	2
statement	*zaiavlenie*	2
commentary	*kommentariia*	2
testimony	*pokazanie*	2
manuscript	*rukopis'*	2
self-portrait	*avtoportret*	1
detective story	*detektiv*	1
appeal, complaint	*zhaloba*	1
testament	*zaveshchanie*	1
comedy	*komediia*	1
confession	*pokaianie*	1
saga	*saga*	1
tragicomedy	*tragikomediia*	1
study	*etiud*	1

AUTHORIAL PREFACES

One hundred and nine full books in the Sakharov Center archive contain authorial prefaces, comprising a corpus of 73,340 words in total and 20,500 unique words. Using a combination of concordance analysis to identify keywords and their distribution and close reading of the prefaces to determine themes, I established a dozen common preoccupations (see table 8.4). I will discuss some of these (relating to family, history, archives, and the national theme) below, in the context of the openings of the memoirs proper, where they appear in similar ways. Across the prefaces themselves, while genre is not the most prevalent theme, it nevertheless features in almost 20 percent of texts. Olitskaia begins her short preface, "What should I title my memoirs?"[15] Some authors, such as Akhtiamov, make further attempts at more precise definition through identification of multiple genres: "This documentary-memoir story bears witness [*dokumental'no-memuarnia povest' svidetel'stvuet*] to how the social genocide of Leninist-Stalinist totalitarianism happened."[16] In shorter texts as well, a similar preoccupation is apparent, as in Ratushnaia's memoir: "What is this? A story? Tales? An essay? Or is it Memoirs? But after all memoirs are usually

Table 8.4. Themes in authorial prefaces to Gulag memoirs

Theme	Number of Prefaces	Percentage
personal	55	50
writing	46	42
duty	43	39
witnessing	32	29
family	26	24
history	24	22
memory	22	20
genre	21	19
literature	10	9
national	10	9
archives	5	5
spiritual	3	3

written by famous people."[17] The introduction of multiple genres also takes the form of *denial* of their relevance, as for Viktor Bulgakov: "Finally, the form. Is this a novel? No. A poem? No. A story? No. A Chronicle? Not at all. Memoirs? Absolutely not. A diary? Of course not. What, then? Above all, it's *akin* to letters."[18] Bulgakov's form of letters to the self is, however, more of an artificial construction than this implies. Moreover, the use of paralepsis here places the work simultaneously on the boundary of all these genres, to create, as Gary Saul Morson put it, "an entire text of uncertain status and exploit the resonance between two [or in this case, several—author's note] kinds of reading."[19]

This preoccupation with genre and the attempts by numerous authors to straddle multiple prose forms may be a reflection of the long-standing blurring of boundaries between memoir and fiction in nineteenth-century Russian literature, identified by Beth Holmgren: "while fiction 'digested' and transformed the memoir, the memoir absorbed and flaunted literary features."[20] Yet while one may easily identify the generic boundaries being crossed in (to give the most pertinent example) Dostoevsky's *Notes from the House of the Dead*, many of these twentieth-century Gulag texts, by contrast, read as straightforward memoirs, despite their ruminations on the subject of genre. In other words, they seem to be complicating something that does not at face value appear to be a significant problem.

The tendency to highlight the associations of memoirs with fictional forms also appears problematic in relation to the question of establishing authority that is usually at the forefront of survivors' testimony. Yet to a great extent, this relates to a common issue in narratives of trauma: the problem of how to put one's experience into words. As we have seen, allusions to the unspeakable in titles indicate that this is an issue for authors. A significant number of texts address this question through the theme of writing that appears in over 40 percent of prefaces. In many of these, the question of how to write or whether one has the ability—even the right—to do so is paramount.[21] Anatolii Marchenko, in the original preface to *My Testimony* (*Moi pokazaniia*), insists, "I do not consider myself a writer, and these notes are not an artistic work."[22] Similar denials of the author's artistic credentials are apparent elsewhere. Lev Polak notes, "I am not a writer, and I don't even have a humanities education."[23] Paradoxically, such attempts to distance themselves from literariness actually confirm these writers' participation in the tradition's artistic mores. For some, there is little choice, regardless of their own abilities, as in the opening lines of Zatmilova's short memoir of the SR Irina Kakhovskaia: "It's difficult for me to start these memoirs. I'm very well aware that not only do I have no literary talent, but I lack even the ability to represent people whose names belong, if not to the history of our country, then to the history of the revolution. But realizing that I am almost the only one left of those who knew them . . . love and respect for them forces me to begin my notes."[24] The process of writing can be emotionally painful, as theater director Nataliia Sats admits: "I'm writing this book—but I really don't want to. . . . In this book for the first time I'm writing about what I've always tried to tear out of my heart, brain, memory."[25] In other cases, the intellectual problems are at the forefront: "When you set about writing a book like this, probably the main difficulty is the selection of material."[26]

A significant number of authors use their prefaces to invoke the imperative to write as a duty before history, family, and fellow prisoners who did not survive (39 percent of prefaces), or to testify to what they saw and experienced (29 percent). At the same time, several survivors express concern about whether another memoir is actually superfluous. Lev Fink ponders, "Now this theme is reflected in hundreds of books, and therefore new doubts arise: won't my memoirs be lost in the general deluge, will they be interesting to the reader?"[27] Ratushnaia, who connects the problem to genre, hesitates for the same reason: "Do I need to write, when *The Gulag Archipelago* has already been written? But *The Gulag Archipelago* is not a story, or a novel; it's an encyclopedia, a monograph. Whereas I will talk only about those days, those events, which burned into my soul and stuck in my memory."[28] Fink also finds an affirmative answer: "Millions of people went down the road of the Gulag, but the destiny of each of them is their own, unique [*uchast' u kazhdogo iz nikh svoia, nepovtorimaia*]."

Boris Vail', in a memoir published in 1980 and therefore significantly before the "general deluge" of works devoted to the Gulag, comes to a similar conclusion in very similar terms: "But witnesses and participants in events give their own evidence, their own testimony.... From this point of view, not only are the works of Solzhenitsyn valuable, for example, but so are the memoirs of any prisoner of the Gulag. For if each person is an individual, then each person's worldview is also individual, unique, their own [*i videnie mira kazhdym chelovekom—lichnoe, nepovtorimoe, svoe*]."[29] That sense of the individuality of experience, which saves memoirs from homogeneity, indicates why a wider perspective on what constitutes a "Gulag memoir" is necessary.

The appeals by Vail' and Ratushnaia to Solzhenitsyn are part of a significant subset of prefaces. Polak refers to the talented, professional writers on the subject—Solzhenitsyn, Shalamov, Razgon, Ginzburg, Grossman—with whose works his own efforts should not be compared. Gershman frames his entire preface as a dialogue with Solzhenitsyn.[30] Overall, the prefaces contain 30 references to Solzhenitsyn and *The Gulag Archipelago* by 23 authors while in the full corpus a similar tendency to refer to Solzhenitsyn is apparent, with 2,282 references to the author in memoirs and 709 occurrences of *archipelago*, all but a handful of which allude directly or indirectly to Solzhenitsyn's magnum opus.

Indeed, it is notable that the prefaces contain fewer references to Lenin/-ism (22, by 14 authors) than to Solzhenitsyn. This suggests that the primary concern of this group of writers at least lies not with the ideology of the regime that unjustly imprisoned them—a conclusion one could also draw from the minimal reference to Stalin/-ism in the titles of the whole corpus. Rather, it implies a greater preoccupation with writing their own works into the literary tradition by highlighting their affinity with the most famous existing works and indicating the additional contribution they are making. Wider literary references in titles have the same effect. A small but significant number of indirect references to the Gulag take the form of titles that allude to other works. Allusions to Dostoevsky appear in titles such as Shiller's *Letters from the House of the Dead* (*Pis'ma iz mertvogo doma*), tying narratives of imprisonment in the Soviet context back to their nineteenth-century roots. Most such references are to Solzhenitsyn, however, including Bogdesko's *Circle after Circle* (*Krug za krugom*) and Aituganov's *Circles of Hell* (*Krugi ada*). Direct mentions of the Gulag in titles make similar allusions to Solzhenitsyn—for example, Sabinin's "Islands of the Gulag Archipelago in Kazakhstan" (*Ostrova arkhipelaga GULAG v Kazakhstane*).

While allusions to Solzhenitsyn significantly outstrip other literary references in titles and prefaces, the full corpus of 1,283 memoirs tells a somewhat different story. Overall, 276 texts by 261 authors refer to Solzhenitsyn (a further 12 cite *The Gulag Archipelago* without naming the author). At 21.5 percent of all memoirs, this is only slightly above the 19 percent of texts that refer to Dostoevsky (257 works by 244 authors). Both these figures, however, are dwarfed by the 32 percent of memoirs that make reference to Pushkin: 408 texts by 389 authors. While this predominance occasionally reflects Pushkin's own brief exile and his association with the Decembrist revolutionaries (whose ordeals in Siberia are invoked by 171 authors in 184 texts as a major precursor to the twentieth-century experience of incarceration), a perusal of the concordance list of 2,716 references to Pushkin confirms that the vast majority appeal to his name as the "founder" of Russian literature.

In turning away from the immediate circumstances of their writing to place their memoirs within a larger literary context through references to Russia's greatest writers and the hybridity of genre that flourished in nineteenth-century Russian literature, Gulag memoirists emphasize continuity, rather than rupture, in relation to literary form and history. This is at variance with the perspective of Holocaust memoirs, where the emphasis on historical rupture and the uniqueness of the trauma means the texts must also be unique, rendering past genres irrelevant. Indeed, the exception of surviving, in Primo Levi's terms, in itself makes every Shoah text exceptional.[31] By contrast, in terms of their literary form, Gulag narratives' adherence to existing literary trends and association of their own work not only with other survivors' texts but also with the apogee of Russian literary culture reflects the tenacious conception within the Russian intelligentsia of literature as a higher source of moral authority. While invoking the name and works of Solzhenitsyn allies memoirs to the wider project to document the Soviet labor camps that *The Gulag Archipelago* epitomizes, it is ultimately this broader range of literary and genre references that endows the texts with authority. This comes not only from having witnessed history in the making and survived the violence, cruelty, and oppression of the Soviet era but also, and perhaps primarily, from turning that experience into a work of literature.

OPENING SCENES

The examination of titles and authorial prefaces shows the extent to which artistic mores are at the forefront of survivors' considerations for their narratives. As they position their own memoirs as much in relation to Russian literary culture as to their historical context, they show a strong awareness of the significance of genre and a clear understanding of the problem of representation

Table 8.5. Themes in the first five hundred words of Gulag memoirs

Theme	Number of Texts	Percentage
Gulag experience	751	63
family background	346	29
memory	229	19
personal status	168	14
history	162	14
national story	80	7
setting/place	63	5
poetic/philosophical	45	4
other narratives	14	1

that is particularly acute when translating traumatic experiences into narrative. As these elements prove so prominent in the introductory framing of the texts, the final section of this chapter seeks to elucidate the factors that shape the texts themselves and how these relate to literary and genre contexts. While using the opening scenes of memoirs as the basis for analysis will not answer every question about the form of these texts, it can nevertheless tell us a good deal about how the authors envision their works and the different types of narratives they produce as a result. This analysis focuses on the first 500 words taken from every complete narrative and extracts from the beginning of works, creating a subcorpus of 1,188 texts with 581,003 words overall and 83,229 unique words. As with the authorial prefaces, I read each initial extract to identify themes and genres, supplemented by concordance analysis. The analysis that follows relates primarily to texts on the Stalin-era repressions, as these form the vast majority of memoirs in the corpus.

Reading the opening five hundred words of each text to assess the various types of framing that indicate different authorial emphases, assumptions, or ideas about the memoirs, I identified nine main categories. In each text, at least one and up to three of the themes in table 8.5 is explicitly highlighted. In some ways, the results are perhaps unsurprising: the majority of memoirs begin with some aspect of the author's own experience of the Gulag. I will return below to precisely what that involves and what aspects of the Gulag are endowed with most emphasis. Of the 37 percent of texts that do not begin with any direct reference to the author's journey through the Gulag, a significant number focus on describing the writer's family, often going back through several generations, or detail the author's education or work record. The stress here is primarily on the person rather than the experience. In other works, the lyrical evocation of a setting, whether of a camp or exile region or of the family home or native village or city, privileges responses to the wider world more generally and, in relation to recollections of the home, to the formation of the subject's identity as part of that, rather than the traumatic experience of incarceration. Many of these other texts, therefore, contain evidence of a desire by the authors to define themselves according to something other than their period of imprisonment and hard labor or the definition they were given by the Soviet security apparatus. This is one reason why a broad definition of Gulag memoirs, as discussed above, is appropriate.

Memory is unsurprisingly crucial, framing 19 percent of texts. A substantial number of these (41 percent) relate to general forms of looking back, inspired, for example, by a television program, reading another memoir, accessing one's own or one's family's records in the KGB's archives, or simply because of old age and a desire to set down the past for posterity. Rather more prominent, however, is the emphasis on childhood memory, which is reflected in almost all the remaining works in this category. Within these types of openings, recollections of a (usually) happy childhood prior to disaster striking the family are significantly more frequent than those detailing the disaster itself, accounting for 170 occurrences. The language of memory is privileged throughout these opening sections; *I remember* (*pomniu*) is by far the most common verb form after past tense forms of *to be* (*byt'*). With 448 occurrences, this is the 93rd most frequently used word in the subcorpus of the first 500 words. By comparison, *I remember* is the 191st most common word in the Sakharov Center corpus as a whole—still quite prominent, but below forms of *to speak* (*skazat'*), *to become* (*stat'*), and *to know* (*znat'*). Confirming the precedence given to early memories, positive instances of *I remember* (*pomniu*) in the first 500 words are connected to recollections of childhood 203 times while 108 occurrences refer to aspects of the repressions; other subjects of memory are comparatively insignificant. Thirty-three overlaps between the two major categories provide some vivid memories of both deportation and the arrest of parents.[32] In relation to traumatic events, however, the absence of memory can be as important as its presence. Of 93 occurrences of *I don't remember* (*ne pomniu*) and seven of *I barely remember* (*smutno/malo/plokho pomniu*), 37 refer to aspects of the repressions and 41 to aspects of childhood. Of the latter, slightly under half (18) refer to the absence of memory of close family members, as in the opening of Lisianskii's memoirs: "I was born in 1923, I do not know the date or month of my birth, I hardly remember my parents."[33] Thus, while in the positive sense childhood is overall granted greater significance within memory than the Gulag, even

Table 8.6. Historical subjects in the first five hundred words of Gulag memoirs

Historical Subject	Number of Texts	Percentage
imperial Russia	2	1.2
revolution	17	10.3
repressions	62	37.6
war	58	35.6
post-Stalin	11	6.6
general	15	9

where trauma caused by the repressions has removed memory, representation of that phenomenon also tends to be framed in relation to childhood and family rather than with reference to the events that negatively impacted on the family.

The 1917 revolutions are relatively absent as a subject for memory (appearing only nine times as a memory, with one further reference to the 1905 revolution), doubtless reflecting the ages of the majority of survivors and writers. That, however, does not explain why revolution has such a minimal presence as a historical framework for the texts (see table 8.6). As the foundation of the regime that ultimately imprisoned the authors or their parents, one might expect it to be more prominent, yet it appears in only around 10 percent of initial passages. Its general exclusion from historical openings downplays the political dimension, as is also apparent in the small number of references to Lenin and Stalin in titles and prefaces and the recourse to the idea of fate rather than the agency of the perpetrators. By contrast, war, which is very minimally present as a subject of memory (the Great Patriotic War appears seven times, and World War One once), is significantly more prominent as a historical subject. In particular, the Great Patriotic War is positioned as the formative historical context, accounting for 81 percent of these references.[34] The emphasis on the Great Patriotic War may reflect the shift away from privileging the Great Terror and from the assumption that party members were the primary victims of Stalinism, which Solzhenitsyn's *The Gulag Archipelago* initiated. Moreover, placing the war in this dominant position removes these works from the purely personal realm to focus on the wider picture, beyond the Gulag, and even the Soviet experience.

The emphasis on the war, rather than the Soviet context, is also apparent in memoir introductions that focus on personal status and relationship of the author (or their family) to the state. Only 15 percent of these works focus on party membership or serving the revolutionary cause. In contrast, over 57 percent stress military service, almost all in the Great Patriotic War, endowing greater importance to saving the nation—broadly conceived—in the fight against a common enemy than to contributing specifically to the *Soviet* state. At the same time, nation appears in another context in relation to war service; for a significant subset of survivors who privilege this aspect of their lives, this overlaps with a national story. Twenty-seven of the forty-six memoir openings that emphasize nationality are by Kalmyks, all but one or two of whom detail their service in the war prior to their mass transfer to Shirokstroi. The emphasis on war service is on one level unsurprising, as most of these memoirs are from the 1994 collection *Shirokstroi—Shiroklag: A Collection of Memoirs of Kalmyk Military Participants in the Construction of the Shirokovskii Hydro-Electric Power Station* (*Sbornik vospominanii voinov-kalmykov, uchastnikov stroitel'stva Shirokovskoi GES*). Yet this emphasis is accompanied by a tendency to downplay the experience of transportation and reduce labor in Shiroklag almost to an afterthought. Frequently, a simple reference to the name of the camp (in the title of individual texts, as mentioned above) appears sufficient to signal the entirety of that experience. As a result, the vast majority of these short memoirs, both in this collection and elsewhere, represent the Kalmyks' national story as one not of victimhood or tragedy but of unrecognized service.[35] This is a very different national story than we see among other repressed ethnic and national groups. Memoirs by Lithuanians and Latvians deported at the beginning of the war tend to foreground aspects of the deportation itself. These often begin with arrest as the moment when their lives were uprooted or emphasize the length of the journey, the arrival in an alien landscape on the Yenisei River, and the sense of dislocation suffered by the whole group of deportees.[36] Crimean Tatars and Greeks, Chechens and members of other Caucasian peoples, by contrast, more frequently frame their memoirs abstractly as stories of national tragedy, focusing on the lost homeland, without reference to specifics of their own journey through the Gulag.[37] Thus the broader national story appears to dominate, the primary focus is directed beyond the author's own suffering, and the Gulag becomes a point of reference only where it is explicitly part of that story for particular groups.

Where authors focus their opening scenes primarily on their own experiences of repression, again it is little surprise that the majority choose to begin with the arrest itself or the events leading up to it, as table 8.7 shows. What is de-emphasized, however, may be of more significance. The number of memoirs that place interrogation in the primary position is dwarfed by practically every other aspect of the initiatory experience. This may be because of authors' feelings of shame at their own behavior during interrogation or to avoid placing blame on others. It could also relate to the fact

Table 8.7. Aspects of personal experience of the Gulag in the first five hundred words of memoirs

Personal Experience	Number of Texts
arrest	303
interrogation	24
prison cell	67
transport (individual)	62
labor camp/exile	128
release and rehabilitation	38
execution	11
dekulakization/collectivization	52
orphanhood	15
displacement/deportation (group)	96
reason for arrest (individual)	12
life before arrest	19
life after release	5
unconnected incident	13
general/other	7

that interrogation was the point where a new story and a new identity were imposed on the victim.[38] Eliding that experience allows the survivor's own identity to reemerge. A second area of comparative silence concerns the reasons for arrest or details of charges against individuals. This suggests that for those writing many years after the events they are depicting, the reasons—for the most part long since exposed as spurious in any case—no longer seem as important as the experience itself. But for many survivors, this absence appears again to be about defining the subject matter according to one's own categories and experience rather than with reference to those through which the authorities directed events and controlled the individuals involved. A very different picture is evident in narratives by members of national groups and dekulakized peasants. Where authors were part of a mass repression of a particular group, that is almost always explicit in their framing of the experience, as in the cases outlined above, which is one reason why family and national backgrounds and depictions of home tend to be more prominent in memoirs of the Stalin era than works devoted to the post-Stalin period. For those repressed as individuals under Stalin, arrest is usually depicted either as an arbitrary and essentially meaningless event or as a gradual and unstoppable process in which the writer was eventually caught up.[39]

CONCLUSION

Prefaces and other ruminations on the theme of writing indicate the extent to which the memoirs in the Sakharov corpus are self-consciously literary and aim to make their mark within Russian literature and life-writing more generally, as well as contributing to the tradition of carceral writing. This creates a tension between two aims that are apparent in many texts: on the one hand, the need to testify to the experience of the Gulag or the repressions, and on the other, the desire *not* to be confined solely to or identified solely with that experience. The elaboration of the latter imperative in memoirs, influenced by authors' backgrounds and membership in social and ethnic groups, enables survivors to reclaim identity and place it in the context no longer of victimhood but of family, nation, or service. It also moves Gulag memoirs away from being a homogenous genre, or one that can be entirely separated from other forms. Many of these texts operate *both* as Gulag memoir *and*, for example, family chronicle, spiritual journey, biography of place, or national myth. These other genres play an important role in shaping the material and its emphases and omissions. But this does not suggest that the Gulag has therefore been subsumed by or is being downplayed in relation to other elements. Rather, it is an indication of the extent to which the Gulag has been integrated into the wider picture and become a literary theme as well as a historical subject—a fact that is evident in the large number of fictional texts from the former Soviet Union and beyond that take the Gulag as their inspiration.[40]

Identifying authors' adherence to the tropes of other narrative and life-writing genres in no way suggests that the authority or sincerity of these works is in doubt, or that they therefore lack authenticity as witness testimony. Emily Johnson has rightly observed that the influence of literary models on Gulag narratives is so dominant that "one cannot take them as an exact, factual account of past events and conditions."[41] Yet the very presence of this literary landscape is one reason for the proliferation of Gulag narratives, as existing works become templates and stimulus for subsequent writers and the potential (or need) to contribute to the tradition in itself adds to the motivation for producing memoirs. That literary context plays a significant role in balancing the collective voice of victims with the uniqueness of individual experience. But it also means that just as the writers signal their awareness that they can tell stories only about their experience, so too must scholars be sensitive to the additions and lacunae those stories entail and the wider context in which individual ordeals are placed. Indeed, this represents a significant reason to further explore the corpus. In addition to helping us identify these personal and socially constructed choices about the form and framing of memoirs, it enables us to see beyond the limitations of narratives taken in isolation.

NOTES

1. Shalamov, *Sobranie sochinenii*, 5:157. In their contributions to this volume, Alan Barenberg and Josephine von Zitzewitz provide more detailed discussions of Shalamov's essay "O proze" and his efforts to create an appropriate prose form for writing about the Gulag.
2. Moretti, "Patterns and Interpretation," 2.
3. Sakharov Center, "Vospominaniia o GULAGe i ikh avtory." My thanks to John Levin for his work in bulk downloading and sorting the texts in order to construct the corpus, which made the present analysis possible.
4. Gullotta, "Trauma and Self in the Soviet Context," 74, 79–80.
5. Barenberg, *Gulag Town, Company Town*; Bell, "Was the Gulag an Archipelago?"
6. On the similar composite properties of Holocaust literature and the need to hear its collective voice, see Rosenfeld, *A Double Dying*, 34.
7. Amir, "Awakening to and from the Traumatic Lacuna," 305.
8. Dostoevskii, *Polnoe sobranie sochinenii*, 4:220.
9. Anthony, *AntConc*.
10. Alieva, "Zapakh fialki," in Alieva, ed., *Tak eto bylo*, 1:317–32.
11. Ignatov's "Dekulakized for 'Sabotage'" (*Raskulacheny za "sabotazh"*) is an example of a title focusing on cases and sentences. Experiences of the Gulag include uprisings and escape, as in Bezsonov's *Twenty-Six Prisons and Escape from Solovki* (*Dvadtsat' shest' tiurem i pobeg s Solovkov*). References to the Soviet leadership, the Bolshevik/Communist party, and the security services are included under "Soviet power"—for example, Khromushin's "My 'Stalinist Academy'" (*Moia "Stalinskaia akademiia"*). General references to the repressions and the Gulag include titles such as Vengerskii's "Memory of the Gulag" (*Pamiat' o Gulage*), where the subject matter is specified, but no further context or detail is supplied.
12. Abushinov, "Nevozmozhno vyrazit' slovami," in Neiachenko, Oglaev and Gladkova, eds., *Shirokstroi—Shiroklag*, 12–14.
13. Trezise, "Unspeakable."
14. The English titles of Nadezhda Mandel'shtam's memoirs, *Hope against Hope* and *Hope Abandoned*, were the choice of the editors, playing on the meaning of her given name, Hope.
15. Olitskaia, *Moi vospominaniia*, 7.

16. Akhtiamov, *Naperekor udarom sud'by*, 4.
17. Ratushnaia, "Etiudy o kolymskikh dniakh," 107.
18. Bulgakov, *Pis'ma iz iunosti*, 6. Italics in the original. This comment appears in Bulgakov's second preface, titled "Questions."
19. Morson, *Boundaries of Genre*, 4.
20. Holmgren, *Russian Memoir*, xxvii.
21. As Alan Barenberg's chapter in the present volume notes, the question of who had the authority to write about the camps was a pressing issue for survivors in the 1960s.
22. Marchenko, *Zhivi kak vse*, 11.
23. Polak, *Bylo tak*, 5.
24. Zatmilova, "Prinadlezhit istorii," 231.
25. Sats, *Zhizn'—iavlenie polosatoe*, 6.
26. Berger, *Krushenie pokoleniia*, 6.
27. Fink, *I—odna—moia—sud'ba*, 3.
28. Ratushnaia, "Etiudy," 107.
29. Vail', *Osobo opasnyi*, 9.
30. Polak, *Bylo tak*, 5–6; Gershman, *Prikliucheniia amerikantsa*, 7–9.
31. Levi, *Conversazioni e interviste*, 83–4. Cited in Agamben, *Remnants of Auschwitz*, 33. On the impossibility of shared experience of the Shoah and the challenge this represents to the reception of Holocaust narratives, see Felman and Laub, *Testimony*, 2.
32. For example, Amit, "Nikto ne zabyt, nichto ne zabyto," in Alieva, ed., *Tak eto bylo*, 3:74–120; Nikiforova, *Barzha na Obi*; Lopatina, "Vospominaniia o moem ottse"; Zakharov, ". . . i segodnia Noril'sk soediniaet nas."
33. Lisianskii, *Vospominaniia*, 3.
34. For example, Gavrish, *Pozovi menia v den' skorbi*; Ratsevich, *Glazami zhurnalista i aktera*.
35. See, for example, Dzhambinov, "Est' na Urale reka Kos'va," in Neiachenko, Oglaev, and Gladkova, eds., *Shirokstroi—Shiroklag*, 48–51; Tiurbeev, "Takoe ne zabyvaetsia."
36. As in N. Lial'kaite-Baikene, "Doroga v neizvestnost'" and K. Puodzhiuvene, "Gore-goriushko," in Merkite, *Litovtsy u Ledovitogo okeana*, 87–115 and 75–86 respectively.
37. For example, Abbas-Ogly, *Ne mogu zabyt'*; Aituganov, *Krugi ada*; Alieva, "Zapakh fialki," in Alieva, ed., *Tak eto bylo*, 1:317–32.
38. On the process of interrogation and the new identities created for those arrested, see Shentalinsky, *The KGB's Literary Archive*.
39. Examples of the first type include Aleksandrovskii, *Zapiski lagernogo vracha*; Durasov, "Eto bylo strashnym sobytiem"; of the second, Vaishvillene, *Sud'ba i volia*; Vaza, "Ia sprashivaiu sebia . . . ."

40. Prominent recent examples translated into English include Vodolazkin's *The Aviator*, Iakhina's *Zuleikha*, and Izmailov's *The Devil's Dance*.
41. Johnson, *Gulag Letters*, 12.

BIBLIOGRAPHY

Abbas-Ogly, A. Sh. *Ne mogu zabyt'*. Moscow: AST, 2005.
Agamben, G. *Remnants of Auschwitz: The Witness and the Archive*. Translated by Daniel Heller-Roazen. New York: Zone, 1999.
Aituganov, I. P. *Krugi ada*. Kazan': n.p., 1998. https://www.sakharov-center.ru/asfcd/auth/?t=book&num=1813.
Akhtiamov, Ia. A. *Naperekor udarom sud'by*. Cheliabinsk: n.p., 1997. https://www.sakharov-center.ru/asfcd/auth/?t=book&num=389.
Aleksandrovskii, V. G. *Zapiski lagernogo vracha*. Moscow: Vozvrashchenie, 1996.
Alieva, S. U., ed. *Tak eto bylo: Natsional'nye repressii v SSSR, 1919–1952 gody*. Moscow: Insan, 1993.
Amir, D. "Awakening to and from the Traumatic Lacuna." *The Psychoanalytic Quarterly* 87, no. 2 (2018): 303–21.
Anthony, L. *AntConc* (version 3.5.7). Tokyo: Waseda University, 2018. http://www.laurenceanthony.net/software/antconc/.
Ashkenazi, M. B. *I bylo v te dni: Ocherki, vospominaniia*. Nizhnii Novgorod: Volgo-Viat. kn. izd-vo, 1991.
Barenberg, A. *Gulag Town, Company Town: Forced Labor and Its Legacy in Vorkuta*. New Haven, CT: Yale University Press, 2014.
Bell, W. T. "Was the Gulag an Archipelago? De-Convoyed Prisoners and Porous Borders in the Camps of Western Siberia." *The Russian Review* 72, no. 1 (January 1, 2013): 116–41.
Belousov, V. (S. A. Vladimirov). *Zapiski dokhodiagi*. Ashkhabad: Turkmenistan, 1992.
Berger, I. (Isaak Zhelezniak). *Krushenie pokoleniia: Vospominaniia*. Translated by Ia. Berger. Florence: Aurora, 1973.
Bezsonov, Iu. D. *Dvadtsat' shest' tiurem i pobeg s Solovkov*. Paris: Impr. de Navarre, 1928.
Blok-Baers, R. M. "N'iu-Iork—Moskva—Sibir' po etapu." *Zvezda*, no. 9 (2001): 194–204.
Bogdesko, I. T. *Krug za krugom*. Edited by N. G. Bagrova. Kishinev: n.p., 2014. https://www.sakharov-center.ru/asfcd/auth/?t=book&num=2632.
Bolonkin, A. A. *Zapiski politzakliuchennogo*. New York: self-published, 1991. https://www.sakharov-center.ru/asfcd/auth/?t=book&num=1409.
Bulgakov, V. A. *Pis'ma iz iunosti*. Moscow: Nauka, 2005.
Dostoevskii, F. M. *Polnoe sobranie sochinenii v tridtsati tomakh*. Vol 4. 30 vols. Moscow and Leningrad: Nauka, 1972.

Durasov, S. G. "Eto bylo strashnym sobytiem: Vospominaniia o 1938–1940 gg." *Istoricheskii arkhiv*, no. 6 (1999): 69–84.

Ermolaev, S. A. *Zapiski "vraga naroda."* Edited by V. Molodniakov and Iu. Lazovskii. Moscow: In-t Obshchegumanitar. Issledovanii, 2004.

Felman, S., and D. Laub. *Testimony: Crises of Witnessing in Literature, Psychoanalysis, and History*. New York: Routledge, 1992.

Fink, L. A. *I—odna—moia—sud'ba: Vospominaniia, razdum'ia, polemika*. Samara: Biblioteka gazety "Tarbut," 1993.

Gavrish, M. M. *Pozovi menia v den' skorbi: Zapiski uznika XX veka*. Piatigorsk: Severo-Kavkaz. izd-vo "MIL," 2002.

Gershman, M. D. *Prikliucheniia amerikantsa v Rossii (1931–1990)*. New York: Effect, 1995.

Gridin, V. M. *My, kotorykh ne bylo...: Vospominaniia o GULAGe v stikakh i proze*. Odessa: Astroprint, 1996.

Gullotta, Andrea. "Trauma and Self in the Soviet Context: Remarks on Gulag Writings." *Avtobiografija* 1 (2012): 73–87.

Holmgren, B., ed. *The Russian Memoir: History and Literature*. Evanston, IL: Northwestern University Press, 2003.

Ignatov, M. D. "Raskulacheny za 'sabotazh.'" In *Pokaianie: Komi respublikanskii martirolog zhertv massovykh politicheskikh repressii*, edited by G. F. Dobronozhenko and L. S. Shabalova, 947–52. Syktyvkar: n.p., 2004. https://www.sakharov-center.ru/asfcd/auth/?t=page&num=5934.

Irshtein, M. (Mila Rubinshtein). "Tak eto bylo." *Neva*, no. 9 (2005): 183–94.

Johnson, E. D. Introduction to Arsenii Formakov, *Gulag Letters*. Translated by E. D. Johnson. New Haven, CT: Yale University Press, 2017.

Khromushin, O. N. "Moia 'Stalinskaia akademiia.'" In *Politicheskie repressii v Stavropole-na-Volge v 1920–1950-e gody: Chtoby pomnili...*, 272–76. Tol'iatti: Tsentr inform. tekhnologii, 2005.

Levi, P. *Conversazioni e interviste 1963–1987*. Edited by M. Belpoliti. Turin: Einaudi, 1997.

Lisianskii, V. Iu. *Vospominaniia*. Kaluga: n.p., 2003. https://www.sakharov-center.ru/asfcd/auth/?t=book&num=1450.

Lopatina, G. I. "Vospominaniia o moem ottse." In *Leningradskii martirolog. 1937–1938*, 4:617–18. St Petersburg: Izd-vo Rossiiskoi natsional'noi biblioteki, 1999.

Marchenko, A. T. *Zhivi kak vse: Moi pokazaniia; Ot Tarusy do Chuny; Zhivi kak vse*. Edited by L. I. Bogoraz. Moscow: Vest'-VIMO, 1993.

Marchenko, Z. D. *Semnadtsat' let na ostrovakh GULAGa*. Moscow: Vozvrashchenie, 1999.

Merkite, R., ed. *Litovtsy u Ledovitogo okeana*. Iakutsk: Bichik, 1995.

Mindlin, M. B. *Anfas i profil': 58–10*. Edited by S. S. Vilenskii. Moscow: Vozvrashchenie, 1999.

Moretti, F. "Patterns and Interpretation." *Stanford Literary Lab Pamphlets*, no. 15 (2017). https://litlab.stanford.edu/LiteraryLabPamphlet15.pdf.
Morson, G. S. *The Boundaries of Genre: Dostoevsky's Diary of a Writer and the Traditions of Literary Utopia*. Austin: University of Texas Press, 1981.
Neiachenko, R. V., Iu. O. Oglaev, and S. A. Gladkova, eds. *Shirokstroi—Shiroklag: Sb. vospominanii voinov-kalmykov, uchastnikov stroitel'stva Shirokovskoi GES*. Elista: Dzhangar, 1994.
Nikiforova, T. S. *Barzha na Obi: Novelly po pamiati*. n. place: n.p., 2006. https://www.sakharov-center.ru/asfcd/auth/?t=book&num=1957.
Olitskaia, E. L. *Moi vospominaniia*. 2 vols. Frankfurt/Main: Posev, 1971.
Polak, L. S. *Bylo tak: Ocherki*. Moscow: n.p., 1996. https://www.sakharov-center.ru/asfcd/auth/?t=book&num=1221.
Ratsevich, S. V. *Glazami zhurnalista i aktera: Iz vidennogo i perezhitogo*. Vol. 1. 2 vols. Narva: n.p., 2005. https://www.sakharov-center.ru/asfcd/auth/?t=book&num=1184.
Ratushnaia, L. P. "Etiudy o kolymskikh dniakh." *Ural*, no. 7 (1999): 107–35.
Rosenfeld, A. H. *A Double Dying: Reflections on Holocaust Literature*. Bloomington: Indiana University Press, 1980.
Sabinin, A. M. "Ostrova arkhipelaga GULAG v Kazakhstane." In *Stranitsy tragicheskikh sudeb: Sb. vospominanii zhertv polit. repressii v SSSR v 1920–1950-e gg.*, edited by E. M. Gribanova, A. S. Zulkasheva, and A. N. Ipmagambetova, 228–32. Almaty: Zhety zhargy, 2002.
Sakharov Center. "Vospominaniia o GULAGe i ikh avtory." Accessed June 5, 2021. https://www.sakharov-center.ru/asfcd/auth/.
Sats, N. I. *Zhizn'—iavlenie polosatoe*. Moscow: Novosti, 1991.
Shalamov, V. T. *Sobranie sochinenii v shesti tomakh*. Vol. 5. 6 vols. Moscow: Terra, 2004.
Shentalinsky, Vitaly. *The KGB's Literary Archive*. Translated by John Crowfoot. London: Harvill Press, 1995.
Shiller, F. P. *Pis'ma iz mertvogo doma*. Edited by V. F. Dizendorf. Moscow: Obshchest. akad. nauk. ros. nemtsev, 2002.
Siniagovskii, P. I. "Ia dolzhen rasskazat'." In *Kniga pamiati: Posviashchaetsia tagil'chanam—zhertvam repressii 1917–1980-kh godov*, edited by V. M. Kirillov, 141–44. Ekaterinburg: Nauka, 1994.
Tiurbeev, B. E. "Takoe ne zabyvaetsia." In *Bol' pamiati*, edited by P. O. Godaev, 61–72. Elista: Dzhangar, 2000.
Trezise, T. "Unspeakable." *Yale Journal of Criticism* 14, no. 1 (2001): 36–99.
Vail', B. B. *Osobo opasnyi*. London: Overseas Publications Interchange, 1980.
Vaishvillene, N. A. *Sud'ba i volia*. Magadan: MAOBTI, 1999.
Vaza, E. O. "Ia sprashivaiu sebia . . ." In *Pechal'naia pristan'*, edited by I. L. Kuznetsov, 370–75. Syktyvkar: Komi kn. izd-vo, 1991.

Vengerskii, E. "Pamiat' o GULAGe." *Novaia Pol'sha* 46, no. 10 (2003): 47–50.

Zakharov, Iu. V. "... i segodnia Noril'sk soediniaet nas." In *O vremeni, o Noril'ske, o sebe...: Vospominaniia*, edited by G. I. Kasabova, 4:334–57. Moscow: PoliMEdia, 2003.

Zatmilova, G. I. "Prinadlezhit istorii." In *Dodnes' tiagoteet: Zapiski vashei sovremennitsy*, edited by S. S. Vilenskii, 2nd ed., 1:231–54. Moscow: Vozvrashchenie, 2004.

Zubkovskii, S. R. "Ia pomniu, kak eto bylo." In *Tragediia Rossii—sud'by ee grazhdan: Vospominaniia o repressiiakh*, 40–60. Vladimir: Status kvo poligrafiia, 2004.

SARAH J. YOUNG is Associate Professor of Russian at the School of Slavonic and East European Studies, University College London. She is author of *Dostoevsky's "The Idiot" and the Ethical Foundations of Narrative* and translator and editor of *Writing Resistance: Revolutionary Memoirs of Shlissel'burg Prison, 1884–1906*.

NINE

RESEARCHING THE GULAG IN THE ERA OF "BIG DATA"

Commentary on the "Sources" Section

JUDITH PALLOT

OVER THE PAST FEW YEARS, it has become impossible to overlook how advances in computer technologies have revitalized many areas of humanities research. This scholarly intersection is commonly known as digital humanities. Russian studies have lagged behind other disciplines in the humanities and social studies in the application of these new technologies and, leaving aside the inevitable "good job too" comments, it is time now to ask what we can discover, or have confirmed, by the application of new digital and quantified methods to the history of the Gulag. I am certainly not arguing for a positivist turn in Gulag studies. Many advances in big data analysis can be used to support qualitative research, as the chapters by Grunewald and Young demonstrate. We should, however, not forget that counting has played a central role in the historical analysis of the Gulag and, given the politicization of debate about the Gulag in the Russian Federation today, will remain important in the future. As new sources of data become available, we can refine our understanding of the scale of the Gulag, as Mikhail Nakonechnyi's chapter demonstrates. In what follows, I discuss the three chapters in the "Sources" section in turn. I also note the possibilities that the different methods of data processing employed by Nakonechnyi, Grunewald, and Young offer for advancing knowledge of the Gulag.

I begin with Mikhail Nakonechnyi's contribution. His chapter speaks to the enduring debate about the quantification of the victims of the repression. It is not necessary to reprise the opposing views, except to observe that the early high estimates of the total camp population have been steadily revised downward, as have estimates of the total number of deaths. In response to the revisionist approaches that reshaped the field of history in the 1970s and 1980s, scholars began to pay more attention to defining variables and clarifying boundaries, which led to lower numbers. More rigor began to be applied to calculations of stocks and flows of Gulag inmates, to verifying the reliability of sources, and to justifying decisions about which categories of the repressed to include in the analysis. The declassification of documents in the 1990s has been especially helpful in showing that the estimates of the revisionists were a lot closer to the officially recorded totals than those of their opponents. The current provisional consensus is based on the estimates published in a landmark 1993 article by Arch Getty, Gabor Rittersporn, and Viktor Zemskov.[1] In the aftermath of the victory of the revisionist estimates, a new generation of scholars, some armed with the theoretical insights of poststructuralism and benefiting from further declassification of Gulag archives, has reengaged with the underlying existential questions the statistics pose. The differing views of the new generation of Gulag scholars, in turn, feed into the long-standing and highly politicized debate about the comparability of the Gulag to Nazi concentration camps and, for that matter, to the penal systems of China, North Korea, and the United States as well as to the Russian penitentiary system today.

The contribution that Mikhail Nakonechnyi's research makes to these debates is absolutely fundamental. His work demonstrates the importance of "keeping on counting" if we wish to address the deeper question of the motivations of the architects and practitioners of the Gulag. In his larger research program, Nakonechnyi has carefully recalculated Gulag mortality totals based on a comparison of regional camp-level and central statistics. He confirms the suspicions that excess deaths were underreported by the Gulag center.[2] In the contribution that he makes to this collection, Nakonechnyi examines how the system of *aktirovka*—the early release of terminally ill prisoners—was cynically manipulated by camp bosses to suppress mortality levels for their camps. In twenty-first-century prison systems, the early release of terminally ill prisoners can be a mark of humanitarianism that allows prisoners to go home to spend their last weeks or months in comfort, surrounded by their family. However, even today under the watchful eye of the UN Committee Against Torture or Council of Europe, the provision for early release can be put to nefarious purposes: to exert pressure and extort money from prisoners (by its denial) or to massage prison morbidity and mortality rates. This, sadly, is a feature of Russia's prison system today, although motive is always difficult to prove. Nakonechnyi shows that in the Soviet Gulag there was no ambiguity about aktirovka. A humane death surrounded by family did not await the prisoners who were released for health reasons from the Gulag; in fact, some of those released never made it out of the camp compound, and death en route was the fate of those who did make it to the local railway station. These releases-to-die must be added to excess mortality figures calculated on the basis of official inmate deaths. Nakonechnyi is the first scholar to precisely quantify how release-to-die was employed in major camps in the regions during crisis periods. His findings will force a recalculation upward of the current consensus surrounding the number of excess deaths in the USSR attributable to the Gulag and must undermine any residual confidence that might be placed in the accuracy of central NKVD statistics.

Nakonechnyi's chapter speaks to the current interest in Gulag biopolitics. The extent to which excess mortality in the Gulag can be understood as the purposive inducement of death or as a case of criminal neglect and irresponsibility has long divided historians and has been central to the comparative studies of the Gulag and Nazi death camps. The manipulation of aktirovka that Nakonechnyi describes can cast light on this disagreement. The story he tells is compelling and nuanced. Rich pickings in the regional archives allow him to reconstruct interactions between local-level officials involved in making and monitoring decisions about early release and higher administrative levels. The picture he paints is of a "façade of legality" behind which the procuracy, the courts, camp bosses, and other institutions, right up to the highest levels, were complicit in the manipulation of aktirovka to conceal Gulag deaths. The greater part of the chapter consists of evidence of this complicity drawn from handwritten marginalia or the body of reports and memos on the use of medical release to reduce mortality totals for this or that camp. However, the evidence shows that this was far from a monolithic, top-down, coordinated conspiracy, as has been argued by some. The process Nakonechnyi describes is mercurial and, moreover, highly place and time dependent. His numerical analysis shows that the pressure on the agencies and individuals involved in the use of aktirovka to suppress formal Gulag deaths was most intense during periods of national disasters, notably 1932–33, 1941–44, and 1946–47 and that it was felt more acutely in some camps than in others. During famines and the war and the immediate postwar years, the health of the labor force was at its worst, and the Gulag faced a mortality crisis. Medical release served as an "emergency measure" that could be used to conceal the elevated mortality statistics. As the figures in the chapter show, as soon as the situation reverted to what counted as normal in the Gulag, the necessity of tweaking the data receded. For Nakonechnyi, therefore, the central intervention in this process is better described as *situational cover-up* than as sustained collusion in the distortion of mortality data.

Nakonechnyi's research confirms, if any confirmation is necessary, the importance of research at the regional level if Gulag scholarship is to move forward. As already demonstrated in the groundbreaking studies of particular camps and regions conducted when the window of opportunity to work in regional archives opened after 1991, the examination of politics and everyday life at the local level often produces new directions in Gulag research and can shed light on old controversies. Nakonechnyi's chapter also reminds us that, even when focusing on numbers and their interpretation, it is important not to lose sight of the extraordinary inhumanity of the practices Gulag scholars are called on to identify, validate, and describe. He shows that a whole constellation of agents was complicit in a cruel system that subjected its victims to lonely deaths, without medication and with little prospect of reaching family, home, and friends. I have already observed that early release for reason of ill health is practiced for ostensibly humanitarian reasons in the Russian prison system today. Given the current leadership's penchant for historical revisionism, it is probably only a matter of time before the high level of aktirovka in Stalin's Gulag is presented to the Russian public as an early example of penal humanitarianism. I leave to moral philosophers the question of whether it is better to die a free man having been abandoned, scantily clad, at the local railway station or in captivity in one's own bunk or the overcrowded ward of a camp hospital.

Mikhail Nakonechnyi's chapter underscores the variability in the relationship between the Gulag's center and periphery. There was a differential response at the regional level to changes in the external environment and the signals received from above, depending on the particularities of time and place. In her chapter, Susan Grunewald takes the analysis of the location and timing of events connected with systems of forced labor further by employing the techniques of GIS, geographical information system mapping, to identify spatial patterns in the distribution of German prisoner of war camps. The challenge Grunewald faces is the manipulation of large data sets in a way that is productive of new knowledge. In taking up this challenge, she tells a story that hitherto has escaped the interest of historians of the Gulag and has remained "an unresolved mystery" of the Soviet Union's involvement in the Second World War.[3] She makes a strong case in her chapter for including prisoners of war in studies of Soviet repression. POWs are, moreover, already part of the Russian Federation's national mythmaking. In 2007, when I visited the museum of the Mordovian prison service, which administers the correctional colonies in the heart of what was—and still is—referred to by prisoners and local populations alike as Dubravlag, I found a display devoted to Italian prisoners of war. The central exhibit was photographs of Russian prison guards gathering berries in the forest to give to the Italian POWs so they did not suffer from vitamin C deficiency.

I agree with the editors that a chapter on POW camps belongs in this collection and also welcome the inclusion of Grunewald's chapter because my disciplinary background in geography has left me with a heightened sensitivity to poor cartographic representations in historical texts. Unfortunately, the major Gulag histories are all guilty of crimes against maps. Typically, the maps that are inserted to illustrate a five-hundred-page book (I suspect as an afterthought in the final stage of manuscript production) smother the USSR's landscape with watchtowers, each marking a major camp administration that existed at some point between 1930 and 1960. Alternatively, the maps show whole swathes of the country labeled, for example, as *area set aside for forced labor*. Rarely are data sources cited—a strange omission for historians who place particularly high value on footnotes. While it is true that the Soviet Union's size and uneven distribution of population present challenges for mapping social processes and their outcomes, there have long been a rich variety of techniques for manipulating the spatial representation of diverse data sets, from the familiar two-dimensional maps to cartograms, three-dimensional maps, and GIS. As has been demonstrated in the historiography of Holocaust studies, these tools are readily available and can be put to the service of visualizing terror landscapes in ways that reveal new meanings and suggest new directions for research.[4] The prime example is the Holocaust spatial history project based at Stanford University, which marries the archival and textual data of history with the spatial analytical tools of geovisualization. The Stanford project has identified new kinds of places that emerged as the Nazis imposed "a sweeping geography of oppression."[5] The temporal and geographic scales involved in dynamic mapping allow for the visualization of processes that can be described but not captured easily in a print format: movement through space, the relationship between center and periphery, and concentration and dispersion.

There have been various efforts to map the Gulag using geospatial analysis. I took some steps in this direction in collaboration with the historical and human rights society Memorial more than a decade ago, which resulted in the website *Mapping the Gulag: Russia's Prison System from the 1930s to the Present*. Sofiya Gavrilova, then a doctoral student in the Geography Department of the University of Oxford, played a key role in this project. It combined the use of GIS technologies with published and unpublished data provided by Arsenii Roginskii of Moscow Memorial and Andrei Suslov in Perm to produce a variety of large- and small-scale maps of camp administrations, their subdivisions, and special settlements for a number of regions. The aim of the map series was to convey visually the fluidity of the Gulag in time and space. The Moscow Memorial's *Guide to the Labor Camps of the USSR (Spravochnik ispravitel'no-trudovykh lagerei v SSSR)* provided the data for the interactive map of camps that is hosted on the website of the Museum of the Gulag and also for Seth Bernstein's series of maps produced in 2015, which demonstrated the varied ways GIS can be used (by heat maps and point maps, for example) to visualize temporal and spatial change in the Gulag between 1920 and 1960.[6] Thanks to the existence of *The Guide to the Labor Camps of the USSR*, maps of the main Gulag administrations are available online, and a start has been made in exploring camp locations across time with an eye to changing climatic and physical geographic conditions, transport networks, and population density. In the future, we can expect other relationships to be explored as new data become available, which will reveal new kinds of places for Gulag scholars to analyze.

Compared with such small-scale or national-level mapping, large-scale geospatial mapping showing the locations of camp subdivisions and the other spaces of repression including special settlements, correctional labor colonies, and prisoner of war camps is weakly developed. The challenges for regional-level mapping are much greater than for the macro level, as we discovered when we wished to map special settlements (*spetsposelnii*) in the Perm region and the camp subdivisions in a sample of regions for *Mapping the Gulag*. The first challenge is that, unlike for the main camp administrations, there is not a convenient published database recording camp subdivisions (*otdelenii*), let alone camp points (*lagpunkti*). Secondly, even when lists of places are assembled from local archives, settlement name changes and disappearances, failures in record-keeping, and the fact that many camp points were simply placed in virgin territory make the geocoding of locations often impossible. In order to locate the whole range of places of detention associated with the Stalin repression, different data-gathering methods are needed, including witness testimonies, remote sensing (as, for example, by drones), crowdsourcing, and expeditions. These forms of data collection must rely primarily on the efforts of people living in the main penal regions, although a Czech-led project by Stepan Cernousek to map places where Czech, Hungarian, and Polish victims were detained has taken to the skies and rivers of Siberia to record the GPS coordinates of camps in Siberia.[7] In Russia, Gulag mapmaking has also been stimulated by a new understanding that for the victims of the repression and their descendants, the precise placement of events has a special importance. It is as important in commemorating the victims of the Gulag as the collection of artifacts, letters and diaries, and video and audio recordings. Examples of this include Memorial Society's project *Eto priamo zdes'* ("it happened here"), which began in 2013 and has produced detailed large-scale maps of the capital's topography of terror, and St. Petersburg Memorial's reconstruction of the geography of Gulag necropolises under Irina Flige's direction.[8] Projects and expeditions run by local NGOs, local history (*kraevedcheskie*) museums, and individual enthusiasts with the aim of producing large-scale Gulag maps before the taiga and melting permafrost claim the last visible remnants of camps also represent part of this trend.

Grunewald's chapter concerns the national level and departs from existing scholarship on the spatiality of Soviet repression by focusing not on the camps and prisoners of the Gulag proper but on German POW camps that were technically administered separately. Grunewald makes a strong case for integrating the POW camp system into Gulag scholarship; POW camps were similar to standard Gulag camps in their material and organizational architecture and prisoner management (including, as we learn, the practice of aktirovka) and the performance indicators to which they were subject. Since both types of camp were under the NKVD and then later the MVD, their organizational and operational similarities are to be expected. Using GIS, the chapter illustrates that the POW camps were in a symbiotic spatial relationship with the Gulag, one that turned out to be necessary for the postwar reconstruction of the Soviet economy. For the purposes of national economic planning, Grunewald shows, Gulag camps and POW camps were treated as a single whole made up of spatially complementary parts.

Grunewald's principal data source is the archives of the Administration (later Main Administration) for the Affairs of Prisoners of War and Internees (UPVI/GUPVI). There is a large amount of data to geocode, as the total number of internment and POW camps rose to a staggering 4,313, with the flow of Germans detained in them reaching around the three million mark. GIS technology allows Grunewald to use these data to visualize patterns of labor deployment and its distribution in order to evaluate its contribution to postwar reconstruction. The four maps she produces undermine some of the common notions about how POW labor was used in the USSR. Unlike Soviet citizens confined within the Gulag system, POWs were not geographically isolated in the peripheries but were primarily used for high-priority reconstruction projects in major cities and key industries. POW camps had a more dispersed geography than the Gulag, the main camp complexes of which were concentrated in the Russian and Ukrainian SSRs. POW camps existed in all but one republic, including in regions that had been occupied during the war or incorporated into the USSR afterwards. Sixty-six percent of the total number of camps were located in the RSFSR, but the placement of these followed an inverse pattern to the location of Gulag camps in the postwar period. Despite the popular assumption that the German captives were sent to Siberia, POW camps were not placed in the more remote northern and eastern regions, clustering instead in the industrial centers in the European part of the country and the Urals and along the Trans-Siberian Railroad. The principal Asiatic destination of German prisoners of war was Kazakhstan, where they worked in the coal industry. The camps that were farther north avoided the harshest climatic regions. The distribution of the German POW camps Grunewald maps leads her to conclude that use of German labor was planned from the center at the highest level and was one cog in the universal war and postwar labor mobilization that also involved deported Volga Germans, Finns, and Baltic people.

Grunewald is exceptional in that she embodies the very different skills needed for the cartographic visualization of historical data: she is a good historian, able to navigate her way through the highways and byways of Russian archives and to locate her research interests in existing historical debates while also able herself to generate the cartographic images that have allowed her to make a significant interdisciplinary contribution to those debates. Keeping up with new technologies, especially when they seem to change so frequently, is difficult. Fortunately, the turn toward digital humanities has proved attractive to technophiles in search of new problems on which to test and refine their models. As a result, the environment at present is ripe for developing fruitful and productive collaborations.[9]

Sarah Young's contribution to this volume provides a very different model for applying the new methodologies than Grunewald's chapter. Young's data set is the testimonies and memoirs of Gulag survivors, collected and digitized by the Sakharov Center. As Young notes, this corpus consists of 43,800,000 words, which, she reasonably observes, is beyond the capacity of a single researcher to read (though modest in big data terms). The Sakharov corpus is but a fragment of all the known Gulag testimonies and, importantly, excludes some previously published and digitized classic memoirs, including works by Solzhenitsyn, Shalamov, and Ginzburg as well as other less obvious texts. The existing practice of researchers who have used testimonies in their historical and literary analyses has been to select a sample from the expanding volume of titles, making an intelligent guess about those most relevant to the question at hand. In much historical scholarship, extracts from testimonies have been used as illustrative materials or mined for objective data to triangulate with other sources. In the humanities, it is the authors' subjectivities and the character of the memoir genre itself that are the focus of research. It is into this category that Sarah Young's chapter falls. In the chapter, she uses the prefatory material of the texts included in the corpus of Sakharov Center to analyze the forms and conventions authors employed "to represent their experience of the Gulag and express their perspective on it." Her study focuses on the titles that authors choose for their narratives, authorial prefaces, and the opening paragraphs or first five hundred words of each text. Young uses this prefatory material to identify the generic forms that the authors reference and the themes that predominate in writing about the Gulag.

Young uses a program called AntConc, an off-the-shelf software program that is easy to use. AntConc allows researchers to conduct keyword searches of large collections of linguistic texts and then to find patterns, or collocations, surrounding particular target words. The program provides an accurate means of placing keywords in context, and the claim of its developer is that it performs this task more accurately than would be possible manually. The assumption underpinning linguistic collocation is that meanings do not reside in words but, rather, in how words relate to other words.[10] In her chapter, Young presents tables summarizing the word concordances she finds using AntConc. The use of this analytical tool confirms previous suppositions about Gulag memoirs, notably that most trace an individual's journey through the camps with particular emphasis on initial arrest (this, incidentally, is true also in interviews with prisoners in Russia today). However, Young's analysis also highlights more unexpected findings. Her "distant reading" of the prefatory materials in the Sakharov Center corpus shows that Gulag memoirs operate simultaneously as family chronicles, accounts of spiritual journeys, biographies of place, and national myth and that the conventions associated with these disparate genre forms play as much of a role in shaping the materials authors choose to include in their storytelling as their Gulag experiences do. There is thus a tension at the memoirs' heart that, in Young's view, is testimony to the memoirists' need to tell all about the Gulag but not be defined by it.

The use of linguistic concordance analysis is not confined to linguistic and literary specialists. Programs similar to the one used in the Young chapter have been applied by area studies specialists examining Soviet history and today's Russia. To date, such methods have been applied in digital humanities mainly for the automated analysis of texts scraped from social media platforms as well as news media and political and policy texts such as party manifestos, speeches, press releases, legislative proposals, and position papers. The difficult feature of the Gulag memoirs compared with many of these sources is that, unlike the run of a newspaper, for example, or Putin's speeches to the Federal Assembly, they do not constitute a single corpus. To create a single corpus out of Gulag testimonies demands complicated decisions about which texts to include and which not to include, a boundary question that Sarah Young foregrounds in her analysis. Such a project also requires the scholar to take on the time-consuming and potentially expensive task of making the chosen texts digitally compatible. Digitizing the many testimonies that are still available only in manuscript form, for example in the archive of Memorial in Moscow, would be expensive.

In my view, there can be no question of treating the findings of the machine learning analysis of one of the preexisting corpuses of memoirs as representative in the social science understanding of the word. The numerical values calculated for different clusters of words can only ever relate to that particular corpus of texts. But this does not mean we have to wait until a single complete corpus is created before employing new technologies to analyze the existing digital collections of memoirs to answer questions about the Gulag. It simply means we should resist the temptation to use them to make generalizations beyond that particular collection of texts and should keep in mind the inherent biases of that corpus when interpreting the meaning of the word collocations the models find—something that Young does ably here. Young's chapter suggests new avenues of research for our language and literature colleagues that complicate prior assumptions about labor camp survivor testimonies. All Gulag scholarship can benefit from such work.

Inspired by Sarah Young's analysis and by her previous conference presentations, I decided to engage the help of a machine learning expert who wanted to try out his models on Slavic language texts. In order to explore what machine learning technology might reveal for the historian or social scientist interested in mining the Gulag memoirs for empirical materials, we included the whole texts of the Sakharov corpus in the analysis and, rather than search for keywords, employed an algorithm designed to scan the corpus to detect the top fifty assemblages of words and phrases within them. In other words, the aim was to find the most common topics addressed in the memoirs without having me or my current research team read all the nearly forty-four million words. What resulted was a list of automatically clustered word groups and similar expressions that characterize this particular set of documents. Some of these assemblages made sense, and others appeared to be made up of random clusters of unrelated words and concepts (but maybe the machine knew better!). Of the clearly recognizable clusters, a number reproduced the linguistic concordances that Young found in the prefatory materials, but there were others that colocated concepts in unexpected but suggestive ways. The exercise confirmed that this particular corpus of testimonies covers an extraordinarily large range of topics, but with unexpected lacunae. Thus, there were several assemblages bringing together words about science, revered professors, academia, intellectual and artistic pursuits, *sharashki*, and the Russian nuclear program, which, no doubt, reflects the membership of the majority of authors in the intelligentsia. My current research interest is ethnicity and nationality in the Gulag, so I was disappointed that no obvious nationality or ethnicity assemblages emerged. Apart from the frequent appearance of the Chuvash in a number of clusters, a reflection of the overrepresentation in the Sakharov corpus of authors writing about *Shiroklag*, ethnicity and race surfaced primarily in assemblages of words relating to the Second World War.

The proposition is that by quickly identifying the main themes or topics in large corpuses of texts, linguistic concordance analysis can be useful to the researcher in the first stages of an investigation in suggesting lines of inquiry. Thereafter, if the researcher is inclined to continue down the machine learning or thematic modelling path, things begin to get complicated. I admire Sarah Young's first steps in this direction and agree with her that these technologies, used with circumspection, may help empirical historians, social scientists, and literature specialists working on the Gulag search and analyze large bodies of qualitative data.

Taken together, the three chapters on which I have been asked to comment could not be more different from one another. Bringing them together in a way that might be helpful to the reader has been a challenge. Each contribution originates in a different discipline—history, geography, literature—and is informed by epistemological assumptions specific to that discipline. Furthermore, the questions the authors ask of their sources and the methods by which they seek to answer them could not be much further apart. Of the three, Mikhail Nakonechnyi's is the most conventional in its epistemic underpinnings and method. He uses painstaking archival research to track down, in forensic fashion, the patterns and motives behind the use of aktirovka to suppress bad news about life expectancy in the Gulag. In doing so, he gives us a glimpse of the secrets the archives have yet to yield that have the potential to turn upside down some long-standing received wisdoms. I am sure I will not be the only commentator in this volume to bemoan the slowdown in the declassification of the archives, the destruction of some funds, and neglect of the conservation of others. By contrast with Nakonechnyi, Susan Grunewald and Sarah Young both demonstrate the use of new computer-based methodologies designed to analyze large data sets that are becoming available online. But there is no epistemological crossover between the two chapters; Susan Grunewald's deals with objective data placing each and every POW camp precisely at its geographic coordinates, from which she draws conclusions about the role of prisoners of war in the USSR's postwar reconstruction. Sarah Young's preoccupation, by contrast, is with subjective truths: how and why people told the stories they did about the place the Gulag occupied in their life experiences.

So how do we bring them together? The unity in these three chapters is that they demonstrate the different ways in which combining quantitative and qualitative analysis can be used to strengthen arguments. In this sense, all three scholars are engaged in triangulation. The use of more than one method to collect data on the same topic has acquired near talismanic status in the social sciences, but, as I believe these chapters show, such a strategy offers clear benefits. A mixed method approach can help researchers better establish the validity of their findings.

NOTES

1. Getty, Rittersporn, and Zemskov, "Victims of the Soviet Penal System."
2. Nakonechnyi, "Mortality, Disability, and Early Release."
3. The lack of scholarship on German POW camps is noted in Ventsel and Zhanguttin, "Prison Camp No. 29," as well as in the texts Grunewald lists. The same point is made for Japanese POW camps in Siberia in Dähler, "Japanese Prisoners of War in Siberia," and Kuznetsov et al, "Construction in Post-War Siberia." Citation from Ventsel and Zhanguttin, "Prison Camp No. 29," 9.
4. Knowles et al., eds., *Geographies of the Holocaust*, 34.
5. Hunter, "Geographies of the Holocaust," 156
6. Smirnov, ed., *Sistema ispravitel'no-trudovykh lagerei v SSSR, 1923–1960*; Muzei istorii Gulaga, *Karta Gulaga*; Bernstein, "Mapping the Gulag."
7. This project is described in *A Journey to the Gulag*, a film directed by Tomas Polensky and produced by Chernousek.
8. International Memorial, "Eto priamo zdes'"; Fond Iofe and the Scientific-Information Center of Memorial, St. Petersburg, "Nekropol' terrora i Gulaga."
9. In Isoaho, Gritsenko, and Mäkelä, "Topic Modeling and Text Analysis," the use of machine learning in the analysis of political policy making in Russia and the USSR is discussed, and the authors consider the limitations and conditions necessary for machine learning to be helpful in mixed method research.
10. Krippendorff, *Content Analysis*.

BIBLIOGRAPHY

Bernstein, Seth. "Mapping the Gulag over Time." *Abstractualized: A Blog about the Digital History of Russia and Eurasia*. Last modified October 19, 2015. http://www.abstractualized.com/2015/10/mapping-gulag-over-time.html.

Dähler, Richard. "The Japanese Prisoners of War in Siberia 1945–1956." *Internationales Asienforum* 34, no. 3–4 (2003): 285–302.

Fond Iofe and the Scientific-Information Center of Memorial, St. Petersburg. "Nekropol' terrora i Gulaga: Kartoteka zakhronenii i pamiatnikh mest." Accessed June 1, 2021. https://mapofmemory.org.

Getty, J. Arch, Gabor T. Rittersporn, and Viktor N. Zemskov. "Victims of the Soviet Penal System in the Pre-War Years." *American Historical Review* 98, no. 4 (October 1993): 1017–49.

Hunter, Richard. "Geographies of the Holocaust." *The AAG Review of Books* 4, no. 3 (2016): 156–58.

International Memorial. "Eto priamo zdes': Moskva, topografiia terrora." Accessed June 1, 2021. https://topos.memo.ru/page/about/.

Isoaho, Karoliina, Daria Gritsenko, and Eetu Mäkelä. "Topic Modeling and Text Analysis for Qualitative Policy Research." *Policy Studies Journal* (2019): 1–25.

Knowles, Anne Kelly, Tim Cole, and Alberto Giordano, eds. *Geographies of the Holocaust*. Bloomington: Indiana University Press, 2014.

Krippendorff, Klaus. *Content Analysis: An Introduction to Its Methodology*. Los Angeles: Sage Publications, 2018.

Kuznetsov, Sergey, Sergey Karasev, Evgeniy Drobotushenko, and Ugor Chapigin. "Construction in Post-war Siberia: Participation of German and Japan Prisoners of War." *IOP Conference Series: Materials Science and Engineering* 667, no. 1 (2019): 1–13.

Mapping the Gulag: Russia's Prison System from the 1930s to the Present. Accessed July 7, 2021. http://www.gulagmaps.org.

Muzei istorii Gulaga. *Karta Gulaga*. Accessed June 1, 2021. https://gmig.ru/projects/karta-gulaga/.

Muzei istorii Gulaga. *Moi GULAG*. Accessed June 1, 2021. https://mygulag.ru.

Nakonechnyi, Mikhail. "Mortality, Disability, and Early Release in the GULAG, 1930–1955." PhD diss., University of Oxford, 2020.

Polensky, Tomas, director. *A Journey to the Gulag*. 2019 film. https://journeytothegulag.com.

Smirnov, M. B., ed. *Sistema ispravitel'no-trudovykh lagerei v SSSR, 1923–1960. Spravochnik*. Moscow: Zven'ia, 1998.

Ventsel, Aimar and Baurzhan Zhanguttin. "Prison Camp No. 29 for Prisoners of War from the Second World War on the Territory of Kazakhstan between 1943–1949." *Folklore—Electronic Journal of Folklore* 63 (2016): 9–28.

JUDITH PALLOT is Emeritus Professor at the University of Oxford and Director of Research at the Aleksanteri Institute, Helsinki University. In 2018 she was awarded a European Research Council Advanced Grant focusing on the treatment of ethnic and racial difference in the Soviet and post-Soviet penal systems.

PART III

LEGACIES

TEN

THE ROLE OF NATURE IN GULAG POETRY

Shalamov and Zabolotsky

JOSEPHINE VON ZITZEWITZ

IN THE VERSE THAT THEY wrote during and after their time in the Gulag, both Varlam Shalamov (1907–82) and Nikolai Zabolotsky (1903–58) turned to nature themes. There are distinct similarities in the ways in which each poet uses nature, and they reveal—at least potentially—the influence of the camp experience on their work and thinking.

Neither Shalamov nor Zabolotsky need much introduction. Shalamov is the author of the *Kolyma Stories* (*Kolymskie rasskazy*), arguably the most powerful literary work to emerge from the Gulag. Perhaps surprisingly, he saw himself primarily as a poet. The poems he wrote during the latter part of his camp sentence and shortly afterward were published in their entirety as *Kolyma Notebooks* (*Kolymskie tetradi*, comprising 466 individual lyrics) only in 1994. To the reader who knows about their provenance, the labor camp setting is palpable. Yet suffering and everyday details are largely absent; the poems thus reveal a different, less discursive facet to Shalamov's writerly engagement with his experience as a prisoner. Zabolotsky, who became famous as a member of OBERIU (*Ob"edinenie real'nogo iskusstva*; Association for Real Art), the last avant-garde group of the 1920s, wrote only a handful of poems in which the camp features directly. However, the years he spent in captivity are a key factor in the transformation of his poetics during his later years.

Shalamov and Zabolotsky had been fascinated by nature as the subject of poetry long before they were imprisoned. One might assume that direct contact with nature during their labor assignments played a crucial role in deepening their fascination. In the camp, nature became a spiritual force and a source of both hope and humility: the natural world was elevated above the human cruelty that defined the prisoners' everyday experience, and the awe-inspiring landscape of the Russian north served as a reminder of humanity's frailty and insignificance. It is worth noting that both poets treat nature as the addressee of ultimate questions. However, the poems they wrote through the prism of their respective Gulag experiences stand out not just for their philosophical quality. They are also crucial to the formal evolution of these major twentieth-century writers. Both Shalamov and Zabolotsky are hailed as literary innovators—Zabolotsky for his pre-1930 poetry, Shalamov for his *Kolyma Stories*. Yet their camp-related nature poetry is conventional in formal terms, highlighting Zabolotsky's move away from the modernist aesthetic after his time in the camp and the fact that Shalamov seems to have reserved formal experimentation for prose that communicates the camp experience directly.

Shalamov and Zabolotsky belong among the many former Gulag prisoners who felt the need to write about their experiences. As a rule, written accounts of Gulag imprisonment are not literary, perhaps due to the fact that only a small number of those survivors who were psychologically healthy enough to put pen to paper were skilled writers.[1] Memoirs and lightly fictionalized accounts, such as Evgeniia Ginzburg's famous *Into the Whirlwind* (*Krutoi marshrut*), represent the dominant forms of camp writing, and researchers have tended to focus on such texts.[2]

Literary accounts that emerge from the Gulag are dominated by prose—including Shalamov's own *Kolyma Stories*—and descriptive verse.[3] Gulag poetry remains little studied; this is particularly true of poems like the ones written by Zabolotsky and Shalamov, which are lyrical and irreducibly individual. Such verse may hint at the ways in which educated, literate, and creative Gulag inmates more generally processed the trauma of the camps. Philosophical nature poetry inspired by the Gulag is located at the intersection of two important traditions. The first tradition is philosophical nature poetry. From Pushkin to Tiutchev, Pasternak, Zabolotsky, and others, Russian poets (and, of course, not only Russian ones) have created and manipulated images of the natural environment in order to explore and express the human being's inner state. The second, less well-known tradition is what I will call *contemplation of nature inspired by the camps*.

Imprisonment in Russia—prerevolutionary, Soviet, and post-Soviet—usually means exile to the far north or Siberia and labor in an austere northern landscape that is hostile to human life. These conditions have inspired countless prisoners to contemplate nature in written and visual artwork as well as the letters they sent to their loved ones. The prevailing mode of these accounts is lyrical, with a focus on individual expression as opposed to the use of nature imagery as part of a narrative or message. In practice, this means the everyday reality of the prison camp—cold, hunger, hard work, overcrowding, and violence—are absent or at least move into the background. The scope of this chapter makes it impossible to provide either a representative list of such accounts or close analysis of even a few select works. Suffice it then to list several different cases for the purpose of illustration. Fyodor Dostoevsky spent five years doing hard labor in a Siberian camp; in his *Notes from the House of the Dead* (*Zapiski iz mertvogo doma*, 1862), Russia's first "camp novel," the arrival of spring inspires in the narrator an extended meditation on freedom.[4] The priest, mathematician, and poet Pavel Florensky, arrested in 1933 and executed in 1937, became fascinated with frost, ice formations, and water plants while he was a prisoner first in the Far East and then in SLON, a camp on the Solovetskii Islands that is discussed by Jeff Hardy in his contribution to this volume. Florensky's letters to his family were often accompanied by detailed drawings, and he repeatedly mentioned the particular "transparency" and "unreality" of the natural environment on Solovki. Ice and its various shapes also feature as prominent metaphors in the dedication to the unfinished poem "Oro" (1936), written for his son Mik.[5] Another prominent victim of SLON, the meteorologist Aleksei Vangengeim, executed in 1937, turned his letters to his daughter Eleonora into lessons on the plant life on Solovki, explaining how different plants protected themselves against an adverse environment. These letters, now available online, are veritable artwork, complete with drawings and dried plant parts.[6] Another example of the centrality of nature to accounts of imprisonment in the Gulag is the catalogue *Art and Life in the Gulag* (*Tvorchestvo i byt Gulaga*), which features the Gulag art collection of the Memorial Society.[7] Some nature paintings specifically from Solovki are collected in the virtual exhibition of the Hunterian Museum in Glasgow *Beauty in Hell: Culture in the Gulag*.

It is not surprising that Gulag inmates should turn their attention to nature. As a rule, labor assignments would take them outside, into an environment often exhibiting a sublime beauty unlike anything intellectuals from the large cities were used to. While it was inimical to the prisoners, who were forced to do work for which they were ill prepared and ill equipped, the natural world also helped sustain them physically as well as spiritually, through activities such as berry gathering and hunting.[8] Moreover, in a world in which human beings and their accomplishments seemed so inherently fragile and there were so few constants in which one could trust, the harsh and seemingly immutable landscape of the north often emerged as an object of contemplation or source of consolation.

VARLAM SHALAMOV: NATURE AND POETRY AS UNIVERSAL LANGUAGES

In the heady 1920s, Shalamov left his hometown of Vologda for Moscow, where he immersed himself in the exciting cultural experiments of the young Soviet Union and took his first steps as a writer. Only a few short stories and journalistic pieces survive from this time.[9] His life, not to speak of his writing career, was cruelly interrupted by the Gulag. Having already served three years in a camp in the Urals between 1929 and 1932, he was arrested again in 1937 and sentenced to five years in Kolyma, later extended for a further ten years. By the time he was accepted into a training course as a paramedic in 1946, he was weakened by nine years of hard labor in the mines at -50 degrees Celsius, and it is reasonable to assume that the opportunity to change to less strenuous work indoors saved his life. On his release in 1953, he began writing his *Kolyma Stories*, but none was accepted for publication in the wake of the sensation caused by the publication of Solzhenitsyn's *One Day in the Life of Ivan Denisovich* in 1962. During Shalamov's lifetime, the stories circulated only in unofficial typescript versions (*samizdat*, literally "self-published"), and their piecemeal publication abroad triggered further reprisals. Located somewhere between fiction and documentary—Shalamov's own term is "prose that has been born through suffering, like a document" (*proza, vystradannaia kak dokument*)—these stories stand out among other literary accounts of the Gulag for their innovative literary form and strategy, which the author considered necessary in order to convey the experience of the Gulag.[10] He also produced about fifty short autobiographical pieces on the subject of his imprisonment.[11] However, most of Shalamov's early texts have been lost, including much of the poetry he wrote in the 1920s and 1930s, as his first wife burned all unpublished manuscripts after he was sentenced in 1937.[12]

The fact that none of Shalamov's pre-camp poetry survived makes it impossible to comment on the evolution of his nature imagery. We must therefore rely on his (retrospective) observations. In "Some of My Lives" (*Neskol'ko moikh zhiznei*), he specifies that he had written poetry since he was a boy and that a collection was planned for 1938.[13] We get a sense of the degree to which his identity as a writer hinged on poetry by comparing the number of short essays and reflections on poetry that he wrote to his statements about prose.[14] Because his reputation (most of it established posthumously, at least in his native Russia) rests mostly on his prose, there is comparatively little critical writing on his poetic oeuvre.[15] Shalamov always regarded himself as a nature poet: "I consider my place in Russian poetry ... as defined by my relationship to nature."[16] Shalamov's nature poetry was by definition camp poetry. The northern landscape provided him with images that allowed him to both express and sublimate suffering. However, the majority of Shalamov's Kolyma poems neither mention the camp nor hint at violence, suffering, or inhumanity. Where violence and death do feature, such as in "Burial" (*Pokhorony*) or "A Toast to the River Aian-Uriakh" (*Tost za rechku Aian-Uriakh*), the experience of suffering is embedded in nature imagery and never narrated as a singular event.

Nevertheless, Shalamov was acutely aware of the impact his situation had on his writing, noting, "My understanding of nature is very different from that of Pasternak, Fet, and Tiutchev. An understanding of nature born through suffering." It is significant that he used the adjective *vystradannoe*, the same neologism he used to describe the specific style of his *Kolyma Stories*.[17] For Shalamov—and other inmates, judging by the testimonies that have reached us—nature was a source of hope precisely because it does not depend on humans and their mutable concerns; the perpetual renewal that is evident in the seasonal cycles cannot be sullied by the reality of the Gulag. Shalamov's other source of strength was poetry itself: "And if the dead cold of evil / surrounds me once again, / In a new blizzard I will / light a campfire with my poems."[18] Here, both evil and poetry are described with the help of nature metaphors that are particular to the camp—evil is "cold" and poetry a warming flame the poet can fan to warm himself. Literature is thus a remnant of humanity wrenched from an environment inimical to this very humanity and an activity that helps the poet explore what it means to try to stay human. This is self-expression in the best sense of the word. And the pathway to self-knowledge that made the exploration of self through poetry possible in the first place was nature: "I tried to translate the voice of nature in its natural activity for myself, not for humanity in general."[19] Communicating a particular message was thus not important to Shalamov; he explicitly rejected the Soviet demand that literature exhort and teach: "When writing poetry, my need has always been to expound not some sort of issue in a Nekrasov-inspired sense, but certain thoughts and feelings I am not yet aware of myself."[20] This explains why the poetry is devoid of straightforward descriptions of camp life, in sharp contrast to Shalamov's prose. It follows that whatever the reader learns about life in the camps they learn indirectly, through the prism of the poet's emotions. Indeed, Shalamov asks his reader to participate in the creation of the poem rather than rely on the lyrical voice to explain the world: "there are no poems that are accessible to everyone; there are no poems that are completely accessible to the poet himself. Friends or time will finish writing them, and more importantly . . . finish feeling them."[21] It is thus the reader's responsibility to inquire into the meaning of the poet's images, and every individual reader will arrive at a different understanding.

In "The Poet from Within" (*Poet iznutri*), Shalamov remembered that "during work . . . everything poetic was knocked . . . out of my soul and body."[22] While he apparently wrote sporadically even when working in the mines, the bulk of his camp poetry, and virtually all surviving poems, were written after 1949. At this time, he was working as a paramedic, an opportunity that had saved his life.[23] His creative trajectory thus follows the one he described in his story "The Adage" (*Sententsiia*): the creative and spiritual faculties return only when the body has recovered, if at all.[24]

In order to appreciate the full scope of Shalamov's nature imagery, the reader needs to know some facts about prison camps. In the short poem "I live not by bread alone" (*Ia zhiv ne edinym khlebom*), the sky takes the place of the bread that is dipped in the watery soup served in the morning; thus the sky itself is presented as the prisoner's essential nourishment:

> I live not by bread alone.
> In the morning, when it's still cold,
> I take a small piece of dry sky
> And soak it in the stream.[25]

The first line is closely based on a Gospel quotation ("Man shall not live on bread alone," Matthew 4:4), reminding humans of the spiritual dimension of life. In the context of the camp, the effect of these words is very different. The poem is poignant because prisoners in Kolyma were constantly on the edge of starvation and obsessed with food. This is reinforced by the ambiguity of the word here translated as *sky*, in Russian *nebo*. Depending on which syllable is stressed, it can mean either *sky* or *palate*. In the face of the threat of physical annihilation, the poetic voice here defiantly asserts its independence from the scraps of food it is thrown and affirms the importance of spiritual integrity for physical survival.

Written in the same spirit is "He warms his frozen fingers" (*On pal'tsy zamerzshie greet*), which communicates the joy of a man who sits by the river in the biting frost and scribbles on a piece of paper:

> He warms his frozen fingers,
> Blowing breath onto his palm;
> The walking speed of his pencil
> Grows faster with every step.
>
> And so, moving his wooden legs,
> like a mannequin he walks

the way that's forgotten, through snow,
towards the river's bank.

...

And with hoarse, hacking laughter
He welcomes back his own strength.
Even the frost cannot stop him.
Frost happens in paradise.²⁶

This poem, published in 1966 in *Literaturnaia gazeta*, is one of the few lyrics that betray Shalamov's modernist roots. The estrangement technique of making a pencil "walk," the wooden mannequin in the second stanza, which alludes to Dziga Vertov's cinema, and the echo of Osip Mandel'shtam's 1909 poem "I was given a body" (*Dano mne telo*) in the line about the river's breath all reflect the influence of modernism.²⁷ Interestingly, Shalamov identifies this poem as "the most Kolyma-related poem of mine."²⁸ Ostensibly, the poem is about being outside on a winter's day and not feeling the frost for sheer joy of being. Only a reader who is familiar with Shalamov's biography will be able to sense some of the wonder the emaciated prisoner felt when he was able to elope to the bank of the river and write, removing himself from his relentless routine. For the reader familiar with the *Kolyma Stories*, the pencil might also trigger an association with the story "Graphite," written almost twenty years later, in which Shalamov uses an abundance of detail, including of burial practices, to explain why graphite—natural pencil—is the only writing instrument fit for the taiga.²⁹

Long before he had the opportunity to expound his poetics in essays and correspondence, Shalamov dedicated a number of poems to this topic.³⁰ Alongside lyrics that celebrate poetry as lifesaving, we find those that point to an essentially romantic understanding of the role of the poet. The feature singling the poet out among people is his ability to feel others' pain. This is the place to inquire into Shalamov's preference for poetry over prose and his enduring fascination with nature as a literary topic. In "To Poetry" (*Poezii*), Shalamov praises poetry as the force that sustains the captive writer's thirsting soul—the sound of the poem carries the soul along and dispels the fear of darkness.³¹ At the same time, the poet diagnoses an irreducible link between nature and poetry, as both of them possess all-encompassing qualities, stipulating "the contact with nature brought me to the conclusion that there is nothing within human affairs that nature could not replicate." Poetry is thus the only method suitable for inquiry into all aspects of existence: "Poetry is a universal language, the only denominator by which all phenomena of the world divide."³² This statement explains Shalamov's concept of the close relationship between poetry and nature. The belief that nature is superior to human existence because it is able to reproduce human experience, but not vice versa, echoes widely throughout Shalamov's lyric oeuvre. It finds expression not only in verses praising nature as the source of strength and hope but also in meditations on the transience of human life: "All human things—they pass, they pass. / Everything that happened was in vain. / Whole and indivisible / Are birdsong and sunrise alone."[33] It also culminates in the writer's doubt as to whether humans figure in God's plan at all: "Perhaps no cities exist at all / and no green gardens either / . . . / Perhaps in God's understanding / the world is only taiga."[34] As the sole thing capable of encompassing all human experience, nature is thus the natural subject matter of poetry.

While living in Moscow in the 1920s, Shalamov belonged for a time to the Young LEF, the Left Front of Art, which featured Futurists such as Mayakovsky among its founding members. However, this exposure to late modernism left very few traces in his poetics. The imagery in "He warms his frozen fingers" discussed above is one such trace. While we should not conflate innovation in form with innovation in language, and bear in mind that not all modernists were adventurous versifiers, Shalamov's conservative approach to rhyme and meter sets him apart. He adhered to the conventions of the nineteenth century, with perfect end rhymes and a preference for abab-rhymed quatrains and iambic meters, perhaps because he judged poetic *form* to be immutable in its universality. Shalamov seems to have believed that classical Russian verse would never exhaust itself, implying that classical Russian poetry was perfectly able to grapple with the experience of the camps.[35] This was the main difference between Shalamov's respective approaches to poetry and prose, the latter of which he judged in need of new forms in order to address the recent Russian past.[36]

This poetic philosophy underpins Shalamov's attitude toward the evolution of literary form. As we have seen, he regarded poetry as a universal means for exploring and expressing human experience. This universal language was not to be confused with ordinary language, into which it would never translate fully— just like the liturgical language of the Orthodox Church does not correspond to everyday language, a curious and probably subconscious parallel given that Shalamov grew up in a clergy household but was a staunch atheist himself. As he wrote, "The best poems are always based on allegory, circumlocution, subtext."[37] Such an understanding of poetry as pointing beyond itself seems to be a modernist tenet, but Shalamov's formal conservatism, and ultimately his lack of a coherent theory of poetic language, place him outside the modernist camp. We find a partial explanation for his formal conservatism in the evolution of his reading tastes. They seem to have evolved backward—his appreciation for the transrational poetry of Futurist Velimir Khlebnikov preceded his love for Alexander Pushkin, the founding father of the Russian classical tradition. Interestingly, Shalamov's ultimate favorite, the man he called "the zenith of Russian poetry," was Fedor Tiutchev, the master of nineteenth-century Russian nature poetry.[38]

Perhaps we can speculate a bit at this point: while there is no evidence that Shalamov, unlike Zabolotsky, ever wrote verse that can be deemed avant-garde, the evolution from avant-garde to nineteenth-century classical poetry *in his reading preferences* mirrors the evolution in Zabolotsky's style, away from avant-garde elements toward philosophical nature poetry in the spirit of the nineteenth century. Many researchers have commented on parallels and contrasts between Zabolotsky and Tiutchev.[39] Conversely, we can absolve Shalamov of the charge that he deliberately modified the formal properties of his poetry in order to fit in more easily with the changing official aesthetic, which discouraged formal experiments and stressed the importance of accessibility. This charge has been levied against Zabolotsky's post-camp poetry, perhaps because he, despite his prior involvement with a discredited avant-garde group, managed to resume his career on his return to Moscow in 1946. It is easy to understand why if we contemplate the distance between Zabolotsky's flamboyant early work and the much simpler post-camp verse. But perhaps the trajectory toward simplicity was inherent in his poetry from the very start.

ZABOLOTSKY: METAMORPHOSIS FROM SUPERIORITY TO UNITY

Nikolai Zabolotsky, born near Kazan, began his writing career in 1920s St. Petersburg. His literary fame predates his arrest in 1938: his work as a member of the avant-garde group OBERIU, whose manifesto he authored, as well as his contribution to Russian nature poetry are well researched.[40] His best-known collection of poetry, *Scrolls* (*Stolbtsy*), a series of satirical snapshots of everyday life in the 1920s, was published in 1929. Unlike in the case of Shalamov, we as researchers thus have the opportunity to chart the development of his nature imagery and identify changes potentially brought about by the Gulag.

The much-discussed "break" in Zabolotsky's aesthetics—that is, the turn away from the modernist absurd of OBERIU toward a measured, philosophical mode of exposition, transparent subject matter, classical poetic form, and growing preoccupation with nature—was clearly evident before the Gulag silenced the poet for more than half a decade. Arguably, even *Scrolls* already carried the seeds of Zabolotsky's later conservative poetics: the collection features conventional stanzas (iambic feet with perfect end rhymes, often to a ditty-like effect) that serve as a counterpoint to the grotesque subject matter, here contributing to the alienating effect of the poems that marks them as modernist. More importantly, the second volume of poems Zabolotsky unsuccessfully attempted to publish in 1932 was divided into a more experimental section, containing *Scrolls*, and a section for new nature poetry that sounded more conventional. It can thus be argued that later, in the poems he wrote after the camp sentence, he merely chose to pursue certain formal and philosophical aspects that he had already been developing at the expense of the avant-garde mode.[41] Zabolotsky's poetic trajectory is reminiscent of that of Pasternak, another modernist nature poet who turned to simplified formal properties and accessible imagery during the 1930s.[42]

On the other hand, the understanding of nature that characterizes Zabolotsky's nature poems of the early 1930s is clearly influenced by the official ideology of these years. As we know, the 1930s were the decade not only of mass repression but also of rapid industrialization and monumental building projects, often in inaccessible parts of the country where the natural environment was ill suited to human life and endeavor. Many of these projects were realized through the Gulag; entire mining towns in the Russian north and northeast, such as Vorkuta and Noril'sk, owe their existence to the camp system.[43] Official ideology presented nature as an inimical sphere that needed to be conquered. An extreme version of this view is the much-quoted 1934 statement by the biologist Ivan Michurin: "We cannot expect favors from nature, our task is to wrest these favors from her."[44] While Zabolotsky's understanding of nature was more organic, shaped as it was by a cosmic philosophy that understood humankind as nature's ordering principle, and ultimately yearned for unity, it was also based on an assumption of humanity's inherent superiority. This stance is exemplified in the poem "Everything that was in my soul" (*Vse, chto bylo v dushe*).[45] Here, the poet lies in a meadow reading a book on plant life in the hope to revive his anguished soul. Instead, it is nature that is stirred by the poet's presence and the words on the page. The lyric voice describes a process of thought gradually entering nature, ultimately triggering a new kind of music: "Unusual movement of thought trembled in the leaves, / this very effort of will that can't be conveyed." The poem features the memorable line "And the sad creature / began to sing mind's praise," implying that inferior, "creaturely" nature has found a way to acknowledge the superiority of human reason. The same hierarchical model is evident in "Yesterday, thinking about death" (*Vchera, o smerti razmyshliaia*) when the poet writes, "And I myself was not the child of nature / but I was her thought! I was her unsteady mind!"⁴⁶ The human being is clearly elevated above nature's purely physical processes and placed in a position to guide, direct, and form her. Reason imposes order on chaos, and by bringing nature's chaos into harmony, man changes his world.⁴⁷

Zabolotsky's pre- and post-camp verse is linked by the theme of metamorphosis. Critics including Goldstein, Sarah Pratt, and Elena Stepanian regard it as a key to Zabolotsky's nature poetry; indeed, one of his most intriguing nature poems is called "Metamorphosis" (*Metamorfozy*).⁴⁸ The cycles of nature, where old life continually generates new life, constitute a particular, nonpersonal form of immortality based on an essentially pantheistic vision of the world. Goldstein has argued that this is Zabolotsky's reading of nature and that it implies a negation of the authority of death.⁴⁹ More than thirty years later, Olga Sedakova would enter a curious dialogue with this feature of Zabolotsky's ecological utopia in her "The Grasshopper and the Cricket" (*Kuznechik i sverchok*)—a poem steeped in imagery suggesting that reunion with the earth is available for the price of physical death or the dissolution of personal identity. The poem, set in a stark northern landscape, takes as its starting point and refrain an epigraph by John Keats: "The Poetry of Earth is never dead."⁵⁰ This statement could serve as a motto for the direction in which Zabolotsky's poetry would develop after the camp. In its more abstract sense—that poetry *is* of the earth and therefore alive—the Keats epigraph also summarizes Shalamov's understanding of poetry and nature as universal language and subject matter.

Zabolotsky spent six years in Siberia (1938–44), doing hard labor in the forest and mines and working as a draughtsman in Vostoklag in Komsomolsk-na-Amure and in the Altailag complex, followed by two more years in exile in Kazakhstan. He thus spent much less time in the Gulag than Shalamov, and in less harsh conditions. The effect of the camp experience on his poetry was a seminal shift in his *attitude* toward nature. This shift concerns primarily the human being's place within creation; it is very hard to sustain a view of humanity as masters of nature in a situation that exposes the impotence and fragility of our physical being as starkly as the labor camp. Moreover, death was ubiquitous, and it is likely that this experience fueled Zabolotsky's preoccupation with the topic. That imprisonment was having a profound impact on Zabolotsky can be gleaned from a letter to his family, dated April 19, 1941: "If I could write now, I would write about nature. The older I grow, the closer nature becomes to me. And now nature is standing before me as a monumental topic."⁵¹ In the Gulag, Zabolotsky fell effectively silent. He wrote only two poems, "Lake in the Woods" (*Lesnoe ozero*, 1938/1944, during his transfer to Siberia) and "Nightingale" (*Solovei*, 1939/1944), as well as a short prose piece on the peculiar beauty of the taiga, entitled "Pictures of the Far East" (*Kartiny dal'nego vostoka*, 1944).⁵² His personal circumstances do not feature in any of these texts. A short autobiographical piece on his time in prison before he was transferred to Siberia, "The Story of My Time in Prison" (*Istoriia moego zakliucheniia*), written retrospectively, remained unfinished and was published only in 1988. It seems that during this period of quasi-enforced silence, a monumental shift in his worldview took place, which would come to fruition once he resumed writing verse.

Only four poems written after Zabolotsky's return to Moscow recognizably portray elements of the Gulag, "In the Taiga" (*V taige*) and "The Creators of Roads" (*Tvortsy dorog*) in 1947, "The Return from Work" (*Vosvrashchenie s raboty*) in 1954, and "Somewhere in a Field near Magadan" (*Gde-to v pole vozle Magadana*) in 1956. The first three display a clearly Socialist Realist penchant for romanticizing collective labor. Moreover, "The Creators of Roads" places the emphasis firmly on the human being as the active transformer of the natural environment, closely emulating Zabolotsky's stance from the early 1930s.

More relevant to this discussion are other post-camp nature poems that do not touch on the camp experience directly but display the full extent of the change in Zabolotsky's understanding of nature. The fascination with metamorphosis—the moment in which one state is replaced by another—remained a constant. But now nature appears as a reservoir of truth rather than a sphere to be transformed by human reason. In "Late Spring" (*Pozdniaia vesna*, 1948), the poet tries to penetrate the secret of spring and the nightingale's song (a symbol for poetry), only to discover that they are ultimately opaque: "Like ancient Copernicus, I destroyed / the Pythagorian song of the stars, / And in its very ground I discovered / Only babble and the music of wings."⁵³ In "Midday" (*Polden'*, 1948), the stirring of the writer's inquisitive mind is stilled by the midday sun: "a past flame // Dies away and wanders in my blood, / Stirring not the body, but the mind. // But by midday it will fall asleep," and the poet literally melts into his surroundings.⁵⁴ As we can see, the idea of mind and reason remains important to Zabolotsky, but the thrust of this imagery has changed now. In "I was educated by stern nature" (*Ia vospitan prirodoi surovoi*, 1953), "life as the flow of shimmering dust" emerges as fragile and transitory while the poet, no longer claiming to act as the "mind" of his environment, instead obediently follows along the line of thoughts that nature inspires in him: "I would lie here and think the thoughts / Of the endless fields and leafy groves."⁵⁵ The image of the poet as a "thought system" embedded in nature finally comes into its own in "Gomborsky Forest" (*Gomborskii les*, 1957), where the poet literally turns into the interior system of the nature he touches: "I became the nervous system of plants, / I became the thoughts of the rocky cliffs."[56] Here, we see how Zabolotsky continued to cherish the key images he used in the 1930s while moving away from a philosophical stance that emphasized domination toward a much humbler one that is sustained by faith in ultimate unity. It is easy to see how the experience of forced labor in the north would have contributed to this shift, debunking abstract dreams of domination as illusory. In Zabolotsky's post-camp poetry, humans are no longer either passive observers or active agents of transformation; instead they organically fuse with their environment. In "Morning" (*Utro*, 1946), people feature as normal parts of the morning scene, with nature clearly having primacy over human designs.[57] "Thaw" (*Ottepel'*, 1948) describes the beginning of spring from the moment when the snowstorm subsides to the first song of returning migratory birds.[58] Here we see another of Zabolotsky's old topics in a transformed fashion—namely, his fascination with nature's cycles.

Zabolotsky rarely voiced despair at his fate. But when he did so, it was, perhaps paradoxically, through images that emphasized the poet's unity with nature. In "The Thunderstorm" (*Groza idet*, 1957) the spectacle of a thunderstorm, expressed in majestic anapests, represents the poet recovering his verbal power after a period of creative drought; the unleashing of words mirrors the rain beating down:

> Sing me a song, oh tree of sorrow!
> Like you, I rushed towards the height,
> But I was only met by lightning
> And burned with flames during my flight.
>
> Why is it that, like you outside,
> I didn't die when split in two.
> My soul still feels the same fierce hunger
> And love, and songs to the very end![59]

The singing tree is explicitly likened to the poet, who extols their shared endurance in the face of hardship and their ultimate love for life. The focus on song, as well as the subdued reference to the violence of the camps through images of flight, pursuit, and wounding in the earlier stanzas and the image of death in the final stanza quoted here, brings to mind another poem, "In this Birch Grove" (*V etoi roshche berezevoi*, 1946), which hinges on an allegory of the poet's death and restoration to life/resurrection. The poet entrusts the story of his life to the oriole, whom he implores in almost the same words he uses to address the tree above: "Sing me a bleak song, oriole, / the song of my very own life." After he has been shot, the voice of the bird brings him back to life when "then your voice will start to sing / in my torn-open heart."⁶⁰ The poem's final image of rain and "happy" flowers is unashamedly anthropomorphic. Interestingly, in a letter to A. K. Krutetskii from 1958, Zabolotsky advances a similarly anthropomorphic picture of what poetry is: "A poem is like a person . . . it has its own face, mind and heart."⁶¹ It seems that ultimately, handing over his story to nature was a way for Zabolotsky to come to terms with his fate.

PARALLELS AND A CRUCIAL DIFFERENCE

One striking parallel between Shalamov and Zabolotsky is found in Zabolotsky's most iconic Gulag poem, "Somewhere in a Field Near Magadan" (1956). Magadan, a far eastern port city, was the major transit center for prisoners on the way to Kolyma, which, as D. V. Sapina notes, "assumed the significance of a symbol denoting the camp as such."⁶² In the poem, the reader witnesses the death of two old prisoners whose life is mirrored by "nature's images." Yet the poem's real focus is on the stars in the sky above. Initiated into the mysteries of the universe and representing freedom, they have become indifferent to human fate; the unity with nature, so palpably yearned for in other poems, is broken. The stars' elevated distance is contrasted with the fatal weariness in the bodies of the two men:

> Life took its course above them
> In the images of nature.
> Only the stars, symbols of freedom,
> No longer looked at humankind.
> The universe's marvelous mystery
> unfolded in the theater of the northern stars,
> But its fire, full of feeling,
> No longer reached humankind.

Death, witnessed only by the stars, comes as a relief to the men, liberating them from the persecution their fellow humans have visited on them:

> No longer will the guards catch up with them,
> No longer will the escort hunt them down,
> Only the constellations of Magadan
> Start to sparkle, high above their heads.⁶³

Zabolotsky's reformed view of humanity's role in nature constitutes the most significant parallel between his camp poetry and that of Shalamov. Human life in the camps as an aberration when seen against the "powerful health" of the surrounding landscape is the topic of Shalamov's short poem "From Lomonosov's Diary" (*Iz dnevnika Lomonosova*). Here, the contemplation of "immortal minerals"— a nonorganic entity—offers respite from the burden of human life, which might after all be "an illness . . . of nature."[64] Even closer to Zabolotsky's imagery of indifferent stars is Shalamov's "Campfires and Stars" (*Kostry i zvezdy*), permeated by a similar note of peaceful fatalism in the company of stars and rocks that remain utterly aloof toward the humans that fate has scattered into the northern landscape.

> Camp fires and stars. The blue light
> Of snow, settled in the ravine
> For thousands of years, it seems,
> After the blizzard's attack.
> . . . .
>
> And we—we look for silence,
> We look for peace and quiet,
> And, surrounded by rocky crags,
> We sleep in the snow.[65]

This poem presents a pared-down version of a human life that has peace and silence rather than, say, food and warmth as its basic necessity. A change in the basic markers of life can also be seen in Zabolotsky's "Somewhere in the Field. . . ." The prisoners' deaths mark their passing to a different level of existence where the camp no longer exists. Sleep fulfills a similar function in "Campfires and Stars." In such a context, stars and rocks, in their literal and figurative coldness, are ultimately a source of comfort, as they witness the existence of something much larger than human suffering.[66]

There are further parallels between the two poets in texts that hail nature as an irrepressible source of inspiration. We discussed several such poems by Shalamov above ("I live not by bread alone," "He warms his frozen fingers," and "Morning"). Among the poems Zabolotsky composed on his return, "The sun hasn't yet risen above the village" (*Eshche zaria ne vstala nad selom*, 1946) exhibits joyful motifs reminiscent of Shalamov: "I can feel the connection / Between my soul and this cold morning. // . . . / The living powers of our imagination / Appear before us more fully and more free."[67] Here, Zabolotsky celebrates a winter morning, rejoicing in his own strength and the (creative) freedom bestowed on him. In the eyes of Shalamov, nature is dominated by austere notes. And yet, sometimes, nature stoops down to console the poet, notably so in poems addressed to trees. In "The Dwarf Pine" (*Stlanik*), the tree is described in anthropomorphic terms that echo the language of Zabolotsky's "The Thunderstorm," discussed above.

> And it stretches its black, dirty hands
> Up to heaven, that place where
> There is neither sorrow nor suffering
> And no deadening, threatening ice.
>
> It rustles its emerald dress
> Above the white, deserted earth.
> And people's hope grows strong
> That spring will come very soon.[68]

The dwarf pine is a living thing whose branches reach for the sky, seeking to escape the suffering imposed by the "deadening, threatening ice"—the northern winter is as harsh on the tree as it is on humans. The tree's almost-human qualities—its branches are "hands," dirty and blackened, reminiscent of the hands of a laborer—combined with its evergreen "dress" and striving for higher things inspire in the prisoner the hope for spring, a symbol of new life.[69]

Shalamov's "Poem in Honor of a Pine Tree" (*Stikhi v chest' sosny*) is even more anthropomorphic, describing the "relationship" of the prisoner with a pine tree, with whom he is "more open than with my wife" and who is "always with me."[70] Here, nature emerges as a compassionate companion, and the human qualities the poet bestows on the tree, reminiscent of Mikhail Lermontov's approach in "In the wild North a lone pine tree stands" (*Na severe dikom stoit odinoko*, 1841), testify to the inalienable longing for human intimacy that the camp undermines. The image of the gentle pine that is privy to the deepest secrets of the poet's heart assumes particular poignancy if the reader knows that the long years of confinement and exile had irrevocably estranged Shalamov from his past life and family.

The communion with plants as the most constant and primal living organism is a surprising detail that Shalamov and Zabolotsky have in common. Plants, and trees in particular, offer respite, inspiration, and sometimes company. Precisely because of this commonality, these poems are ultimately also the best gauge for the fundamental difference that persists in the poets' respective attitudes toward nature.

For Shalamov, nature is comforting precisely because it remains separate from the realm of humans. Trees and their robust, patient vitality inspire the poet to work, to sing, to write poetry, to see the bigger picture, to carry on. Nature is thus an enduring reference point beyond personal experience and suffering, not explicitly friendly and certainly not offering a utopian perspective of unity and transformation; the poet remains separate from that which he contemplates. While Shalamov uses metaphor sparingly (e.g., in "The Dwarf Pine"), Zabolotsky's nature poems are replete with exuberant images where human thought can literally enter plants and the poet's voice fuses with the rain.

In the case of Zabolotsky, the camp experience changed the poet's understanding of the hierarchy between humanity and nature; being at the mercy of frost, wind, and darkness, and experiencing hunger and supply shortages, must have communicated the individual human's smallness and weakness before nature. Yet Zabolotsky continued to portray nature as receptive and permeable to human influence; an active, transformative exchange characterizes the relationship between poet and natural environment. When Zabolotsky communicates with plants, they "take over," integrating the poet into themselves and transmitting his song; thus they allow him to transcend his self and his finite form. These images are both surreal and philosophical, and they reach far beyond the natural world that has inspired them. In his Gulag poems, Zabolotsky remains a cognitive poet rather than a poet primarily seeking self-expression.[71]

CONCLUSION

The poetry of Shalamov and Zabolotsky oscillates between two different concepts of Gulag literature—some of it is poetry emerging from the labor camp itself, some of it is poetry defined by repression, and some of it is clearly both. But none of it describes the camp and the suffering in literal terms. The nature imagery the two poets employ can be read in different ways that are not mutually exclusive. The first would interpret the turn to nature as a reaction to trauma, focusing on the starkness of the imagery—Zabolotsky's preoccupation with the death motif and his utopian hope of literally dissolving his self into nature; Shalamov's bare landscapes in which the absence of human life emerges as the only source of hope—and then try to define more exactly, and with tools beyond literary criticism, what it was that the poets were reacting to.

A complementary second reading would stress the lyricism of the nature images, which is given even more weight by the Russian classical tradition. The austere natural environment was the only subject matter available to the poets that was not tainted by traces of the camp and a source of hope—hope for renewal in some instances, or comfort in the fact that there exists a living sphere that human cruelty cannot corrupt in those instances when the prisoner-poet's despondency is palpable. Lyric poetry is a medium for the deepest personal experience and as such an inherently individual genre. It was not a coincidence that under mature Socialist Realism, between the end of the war and Stalin's death, lyric poetry was in sharp decline, as it was very hard to reconcile with the prevailing ideology that favored the collective over the individual and discouraged the expression of subjective experience and emotion. The camp, too, as the most monstrous embodiment of Stalin's regime, sought to eliminate individuality, in very literal terms, by turning prisoners into identically clothed numbers who slept on communal bunks, undertook identical labor, and, as Irina Flige's chapter in this volume reminds us, rested in unmarked, often communal graves. Read in this vein, lyric poetry born out of the camp experience can be read as a courageous act of resistance.

NOTES

1. Throughout this chapter, the term *literary* refers to creative fiction and poetry only. For a different categorization that extends the term to include memoirs, see Sarah J. Young's chapter in this volume.
2. For a systematic discussion of these accounts, see Toker, *Return from the Archipelago*.
3. Compare, for example, Semen Vilenskii's anthology of Gulag poetry, *Poeziia uznikov GULAGa*.
4. Dostoevskii, *Zapiski iz mertvogo doma*, part 2, chap. 5.
5. Florenskii, *Pis'ma s Dal'nego Vostoka i Solovkov*.
6. Vangengeim, "Lagernye pis'ma."
7. Tikhanova and Okhotin, eds., *Tvorchestvo i byt Gulaga*.
8. Gathering firewood and berries is the theme of one of Shalamov's most haunting short stories, "Berries" ("Iagody") in *Sobranie sochinenii*, 1:399–406.
9. These pieces are collated on Shalamov.ru, a comprehensive website devoted to Shalamov and his work, as "Rasskazy 30-kh godov" and "Ocherki 30-kh godov."
10. Shalamov, "O proze," in *Sobranie sochinenii*, 5:157.
11. Collected in volume 4 of Shalamov, *Sobranie sochinenii*.
12. Shalamov deplores the loss of his unpublished writings in "Neskol'ko moikh zhiznei," 9.
13. Shalamov, "Neskol'ko moikh zhiznei," 3.
14. They are collated on Shalamov.ru as "Esse."
15. Collated under the tab "Tematicheskii katalog" on Shalamov.ru; note the prevalence of "memory" as the focus of research.
16. Shalamov, "Poezia-vseobshchii iazyk," 103.
17. Shalamov, 103.
18. "Here I used the first genuine poem..." (*Zdes' pervym iskrennim stikhom*). In Russian: "I esli mertvyi kholod zla / Opiat' stoit vokrug, / Ia snova—v novuiu

purgu— / Koster stikhami razozhgu." Shalamov, *Sobranie sochinenii*, 3:106. Other examples of this stance include "The Thunderstorm" (*Groza*), "Poems are pain and a defense against pain" (*Stikhi—eto bol' i zashchita ot boli*), and "To Poetry" (*Poezii*) in 3:110, 3:432, and 3:320 of the same edition.

19. Shalamov, "Poeziia-vseobshchii iazyk," 103.
20. Shalamov, "Poet iznutri," in *Sobranie sochinenii*, 5:164.
21. Shalamov, 171.
22. Shalamov, 165.
23. Shalamov, "Neskol'ko moikh zhiznei," 10–11.
24. Shalamov, "Sententsiia," in *Sobranie sochinenii*, 1:93–96.
25. Shalamov, Kolymskie tetradi, *Sobranie sochinenii*, 3:262. All translations are mine.
26. Shalamov, 3:127.
27. For example, Vertov's 1929 *The Man with the Movie Camera*. Mandel'shtam, *Sochineniia*, 2:68–69.
28. For Shalamov's commentary on the poem, see Shalamov, *Kolymskie tetradi*, in *Sobranie sochinenii*, 3:454–55.
29. Shalamov, "Grafit," in *Sobranie sochinenii*, 2:106–110.
30. For example, in "On Song" (*O Pesne*), "To the Poet" (*Poetu*), and "The Instrument" (*Instrument*) as well as several poems written after 1957 that are not part of the *Kolyma Notebooks*: "Poetry is for grey-haired men" (*Poeziia—eto delo sedykh*), "Poems are stigmas" (*Stikhi—eto stigmaty*), "Over Old Notebooks" (*Nad starymi tetradiami*), and "Some Characteristics of Rhyme" (*Nekotorye svoistva rifmy*), found in Shalamov, *Sobranie sochinenii*, 3:114, 3:143, 3:389, 3:370, 3:394, and 3:341 respectively.
31. Shalamov, *Sobranie sochinenii*, 3:320.
32. Shalamov, "Poezia-vseobshchii iazyk,"103.
33. "All human things—they pass, they pass" (*Vse liudskoe—mimo, mimo*), in Shalamov, *Sobranie sochinenii*, 3:156.
34. "Like Archimedes, catching the shadow" (*Kak Arkhimed, loviashchii na peske*), in Shalamov, *Sobranie sochinenii*, 3:54.
35. Solzhenitsyn lists several quotations by Shalamov that suggest this in "S Varlamom Shalamovym." Also see Shalamov, "Neskol'ko moikh zhiznei," 12.
36. For Shalamov's theory of prose, see "O proze," in *Sobranie sochinenii*, 5:144–57.
37. Shalamov, "Poezia-vseobshchii iazyk," 103.
38. Shalamov, "Neskol'ko moikh zhiznei," 4.
39. Notably Pratt, "Antithesis and Completion"; Milner-Gulland, "Zabolotsky: Philosopher-Poet"; Povlovskii, "N. A. Zabolotskii i F. I. Tiutchev."
40. For example, Mikhail Epshtein included Zabolotsky in his *Priroda, mir, tainik vselennoi....*, indexing him under "Nature as language," "Nature as a book," "The Philosophy of Nature," "Thought in Nature."

41. Goldstein, *Nikolai Zabolotsky*, chap. 3.

42. During his life, Zabolotsky published collections in 1937, 1948, and 1957; the latter had a print run of twenty-five thousand copies.

43. For an introduction to the economic role of the Gulag, see Applebaum, *Gulag. A History*, part 3.

44. Michurin, *Itogi shestidesiatiletnikh rabot*, 11.

45. Zabolotskii, *Polnoe sobranie stikhotvorenii i poem*, 197. All translations are mine.

46. Zabolotskii, 198.

47. Goldstein, *Nikolai Zabolotsky*, 114–16. Darra Goldstein identifies two sources for Zabolotsky's attitude toward nature pre-camp. The first is Friedrich Engels' *Dialectics of Nature* (1883, unfinished, first published 1925)—a text that heavily influenced Soviet ideology. According to Engels, dialectical development would ultimately reach a finite point at which the human being, embodying reason, would achieve a perfect relationship with nature. The second and perhaps stronger influence on Zabolotsky is Schelling's *Naturphilosophie* (1797–99), with its greater emphasis on human consciousness as nature's highest faculty and humanity's unity with nature. Exploring these influences—especially the influence of Schelling via the nature poetry of Tiutchev—is beyond the scope of this article.

48. Zabolotskii, *Polnoe sobranie stikhotvorenii i poem*, 205–6.

49. Goldstein, *Nikolai Zabolotsky*, especially chap. 3. On 114–15, she cites the poem "Lodeinikov" (1932) as exemplary of this stance.

50. Part of the collection *Vorota, okna, arki* (1983). In Sedakova, *Sobranie sochinenii*, 1:243–44. I owe this observation to Alexandra Smith.

51. Zabolotskii, *Pis'ma*, 114.

52. Zabolotskii, *Izbrannye proizvedeniia*, 2:224–27.

53. Zabolotskii, *Polnoe sobranie stikhotvorenii i poem*, 236.

54. Zabolotskii, 236–37.

55. Zabolotskii, 249–50.

56. Zabolotskii, 285.

57. Zabolotskii, 209–10.

58. Zabolotskii, 234–35.

59. Zabolotskii, 288.

60. Zabolotskii, 214–15.

61. Zabolotskii, *Izbrannye proizvedeniia*, 2:265. Also the essay "Mysl', obraz, muzyka" on 286 of the same volume.

62. Sapina, "Gulag v sud'be i tvorchestve N. Zabolotskogo," 116.

63. Zabolotskii, *Polnoe sobranie stikhotvorenii i poem*, 264.

64. Shalamov, *Sobranie sochinenii*, 3:157.

65. Shalamov, 23.

66. The indifferent stars are also a recurring image in Anna Akhmatova's *Requiem*, her monument to those who perished during Stalin's terror.

67. Zabolotskii, *Polnoe sobranie stikhotvorenii i poem*, 213–14.

68. Shalamov, *Sobranie sochinenii*, 3:230. This poem was published with five other poems from the *Kolyma Notebooks* as "Poems in the North" in the journal *Znamia* 5 (1957).

69. This presentation sharply contrasts with how Shalamov describes the same pine trees in the story "Dry Ration" (*Sukhim paikom*), as "dying lying down, like people" and having "their lives broken by the North." Shalamov, *Sobranie sochinenii*, 1:80–81.

70. Shalamov, *Sobranie sochinenii*, 3:284–87. Other poems in which Shalamov intimately communes with trees: "I complained to a tree" (*Ia zhalovalsya derevu*), "The woods are stooping under the wind's onslaught" (*Les gnetsia vetrovym udarom*), and "Once in autumn" (*Odnazhdyi osen'iu*), found in Shalamov, *Sobranie sochinenii*, 3:58, 3:87, and 3:159 respectively.

71. Milner-Gulland, "Zabolotsky and the Reader."

BIBLIOGRAPHY

Akhmatova, Anna. *Rekviem*. In *Sobranie sochinenii v shesti tomakh*, vol 3, 21–30. Moscow: Ellis Lak, 1998.

Applebaum, Anne. *Gulag. A History*. London: Penguin, 2003.

Dostoevskii, Fedor. *Zapiski iz mertvogo doma*. In *Polnoe sobranie sochinenii v tridtsati tomakh*, vol. 4. Leningrad: Nauka, 1972.

Epshtein, Mikhail. *Priroda, mir, tainik vselennoi. . . . Sistema peizazhnykh obrazov v russkoi poezii*. Moscow: Vysshaia shkola, 1990.

Florenskii, Pavel. "Oro." Accessed June 1, 2021. http://antology.igrunov.ru /authors/Florensky/1085583699.html.

———. *Pis'ma s Dal'nego Vostoka i Solovkov*. In *Sochineniia v chetyrekh tomakh*, vol 4. Moscow: Izdatel'stvo "Mysl'," 1998.

Goldstein, Darra. *Nikolai Zabolotsky: Play for Mortal Stakes*. Cambridge: Cambridge University Press, 1993.

Hunterian, The. "Beauty in Hell: Culture in the Gulag." Accessed June 1, 2021. https://www.gla.ac.uk/hunterian/visit/exhibitions/virtualexhibitions /beautyinhellcultureinthegulag/.

Lermontov, Mikhail. *Polnoe sobranie sochinenii v desiati tomakh*. Moscow: Voskresen'e, 1999–2002.

Mandel'shtam, Osip. *Sochineniia*. Two vols. Moscow: Khudozhestvennaia literatura, 1990.

Michurin, I. V. *Itogi shestidesiatiletnikh rabot po vyvedeniiu novykh sortov plodovykh rastenii*. Third edition. Moscow: OGIZ Sel'khozgiz, 1934.

Milner-Gulland, Robin. "Zabolotsky: Philosopher-Poet." *Soviet Studies* 22, no. 4 (April 1971): 595–608.

———. "Zabolotsky and the Reader: Problems of Approach." *Russian Literature Triquarterly* 8 (1974): 385–92.

Povlovskii, A. I. "N. A. Zabolotskii i F. I. Tiutchev." In *Nikolai Zabolotskii i ego literaturnoe okruzhenie*, edited by V. P. Muromskii and A. I. Mikhailov, 100–6. St. Petersburg: Nauka, 2003.

Pratt, Sarah. "Antithesis and Completion: Zabolockij Responds to Tiutcev." *Slavic and East European Journal* 2 (1983): 211–27.

———. *Nikolai Zabolotsky. Enigma and Cultural Paradigm*. Evanston, IL: Northwestern University Press, 2000.

Sapina, D. V. "Gulag v sud'be i tvorchestve N. Zabolotskogo." *Vestnik Voronezhskogo gosudarstvennogo universiteta*. Seriia: Filologiia. Zhurnalistika 2 (2010): 113–20.

Sedakova, *Sobranie sochinenii v 4 tomakh*. Moscow: Universitet Dmitriia Pozharskogo, 2010.

Shalamov, Varlam. "Neskol'ko moikh zhiznei." In *Vospominaniia*, 3–12. Moscow: AST, 2003.

———. "Poeziia-vseobshchii iazyk." *Literaturnoe obozrenie* 1 (1989): 100–4.

———. *Sobranie sochinenii v shesti tomakh*. Six vols. Moscow: Terra: Knizhnyi klub Knigovek, 2013.

Shalamov.ru (Varlam Shalamov, 1907 g.–1982 g). Accessed June 1, 2021. https://shalamov.ru.

Smith, Alexandra. "In the Shadow of Akhmatova and Tsvetaeva: Olga Sedakova and the Postmodern Writing of Melancholy." Unpublished paper delivered at the conference "Contemporary European Women Writers: Gender and Generation," University of Bath, April 2005.

Solzhenitsyn, Aleksandr. "S Varlamom Shalamovym." *Novyi mir* 4 (1999): 163–69.

Stepanian, Elena. "Metamorfosy zreniia." In *Polnoe sobranie stikhotvorenii i poem*, by Nikolai Zabolotskii, 5–30. St. Petersburg: Akademicheskii proekt, 2002.

Tikhanova, V. A., and N. G. Okhotin, eds. Tvorchestvo i byt Gulaga: Katalog muzeinogo sobraniia Obshchestva "Memorial." Moscow: Zven'ia, 1998.

Toker, Leona. *Return from the Archipelago: Narratives of Gulag Survivors*. Bloomington: Indiana University Press, 2000.

Vangengeim, Aleksei. "Lagernye pis'ma Alekseia Vangengeima k docheri." Accessed June 1, 2021. http://togdazine.ru/project/fatherletters/.

Vilenskii, Semen, ed. *Poeziia uznikov GULAGa*. Moscow: Mezhdunarodnyi fond "Demokratiia," 2005.

Vertov, Dzhiga, dir. *The Man with the Movie Camera* (Chelovek s kinoapparatom). 1929.

Zabolotskii, Nikolai. *Izbrannye proizvedeniia v dvukh tomakh*. Two vols. Moscow: Khudozhestvennaia literatura, 1972.

———. "Pis'ma N.A Zabolotskogo, 1938–1944 godov." *Znamia* 1 (1989): 96–127.

———. *Polnoe sobranie stikhotvorenii i poem*. St. Petersburg: Akademicheskii proekt, 2002.

JOSEPHINE VON ZITZEWITZ is the Marie Sklodowska Curie Fellow at UiT The Arctic University of Norway, Tromso. She is author of *Poetry and the Leningrad Religious-Philosophical Seminar 1976–1980: Music for a Deaf Age* and *The Culture of Samizdat: Literature and Underground Networks in the Late Soviet Union*.

ELEVEN

"I WOULD VERY MUCH LIKE TO READ YOUR STORY ABOUT KOLYMA"

Georgii Demidov, Varlam Shalamov, and the Development of Gulag Prose, 1965–67

ALAN BARENBERG

ON MAY 6, 1965, GEORGII Georgievich Demidov, a fourteen-year veteran of the Kolyma camps, penned a letter to Varlam Tikhonovich Shalamov, another former prisoner who had spent as many years as a prisoner in Kolyma. Warmly greeting his old friend as "the paramedic from the surgical [hospital]," Demidov initiated a correspondence that would last for the next two years.[1] Both in their late fifties, they were old camp comrades: after working together for several months in 1948–49 in the Kolyma central prison hospital in Debin, they had been separated and had only recently learned of each other's survival, more than a decade after release.[2] Now they were attempting to renew a camp friendship in much different circumstances. For the next two years, they would correspond regularly and meet rather irregularly whenever Demidov had the chance to visit Moscow from his home in Ukhta, Komi ASSR, in the European north of the RSFSR.

Demidov and Shalamov did not spend a lot of time playing catch-up for the lost years—although they did exchange information about their mutual friends and acquaintances from the Kolyma hospital. Instead, the conversation quickly turned to literary matters. Both, as it turns out, were actively writing about their camp experiences. Shalamov had been writing his *Kolyma Stories* for over a decade and by this time had completed the first three cycles of his stories (*Kolyma Stories*, *The Left Bank*, and *The Spade Artist*), in addition to poetry, essays, and a play.[3] Demidov, on the other hand, had been writing since the beginning of the 1960s and had several works (novellas and short stories) in various stages of completion. It quickly became apparent that the two men did not see eye to eye on literary matters, and by the end of 1965 their letters and personal meetings were consumed with intense and often bitter debate about how to represent the Gulag experience in prose. By the summer of 1967, their post-camp friendship had run its course, and the two men would have no further contact with each other, although Shalamov would live until 1982 and Demidov until 1987.

Why did Demidov and Shalamov, who clearly held deep respect for each other both as prisoners and as ex-prisoners, fall out so dramatically? On one level, this was simply a question of personality—Shalamov's difficult character, compounded by years of literary frustrations and worsening health, is well documented. One should note, for example, his rocky relationship with Solzhenitsyn, which was severely strained by 1964.[4] While Demidov did not share Shalamov's serious physical ailments, he was also stubborn and deeply opinionated. Thus, on one level this was a personality conflict. Yet to dismiss the correspondence as a mere argument would be to miss an opportunity to examine what the letters reveal about several important developments at a key juncture in Soviet history. It sheds light on the nature of ex-prisoner networks and the difficulties of maintaining relationships established in the camps in the challenging context of the early Brezhnev era. Further, the correspondence demonstrates how those ex-prisoners intent on representing their camp experiences saw the prospects for their writing in uncertain times after Khrushchev's ouster.

Demidov and Shalamov corresponded in the aftermath of one of the watershed political moments in Soviet history, the XXII Party Congress of 1961, where Khrushchev had renewed his public criticism of Stalin and the use of mass terror. In terms of the development of literature about the Gulag, the correspondence fell during a relatively poorly understood period—that between the appearance of two of Solzhenitsyn's landmark works: *One Day in the Life of Ivan Denisovich* (1962) and *The Gulag Archipelago* (1973). *Ivan Denisovich* and other works on the Gulag that appeared in the official Soviet press in 1962–64 opened new possibilities for literary examinations of the camps. However, it was widely understood that this was only a preliminary foray into the topic, and no paradigm for discussing the Gulag had yet been established. This would come with *The Gulag Archipelago*, a work that circulated illegally in the Soviet Union in unofficial typescript copies (*samizdat*, literally "self-published") and was published abroad without the permission of the Soviet state (*tamizdat*, literally "published there") beginning in 1973. Unlike earlier officially published works, *The Gulag Archipelago* provided a framework for most later memoirs and literary works on the Gulag.[5] Thus, while we are used to thinking about the mid- to late 1960s as the transition between "thaw" and "stagnation" following Khrushchev's ouster, this was not necessarily the case when it came to Gulag authors. While it was clear by 1965 that the window for publication of works on the Gulag was closing, the literary possibilities opened up by *Ivan Denisovich* and other published works on the Gulag were nevertheless inspiring for Demidov and, to a lesser extent, for Shalamov, both of whom continued to write camp prose into the 1970s, even when there were no prospects for publishing these texts within the Soviet Union.[6] Thus, examining the rocky relationship between these two writers, survivors, and friends at this crucial juncture reveals a great deal about ex-prisoners' social networks, discussions about representation of the camp experience in prose, and, more broadly, the place of the former prisoner in Soviet society in the years following the XXII Party Congress.

CATCHING UP FOR LOST YEARS

In the spring of 1965, having finally located one of his closest friends from his time in Kolyma, Georgii Demidov composed an enthusiastic letter to Varlam Shalamov. In their first direct contact in over fifteen years, a letter dated May 6, 1965, Demidov wrote, "You probably know practically everything about me."[7] Shalamov and Demidov had shared the most intimate details of their lives before the camps during the long nights working together at the Kolyma central camp hospital in Debin at the end of the 1940s, a friendship remembered by Elena Mamuchashvili, a nonprisoner surgeon who worked with both of them in Kolyma.[8] More than a decade after release, Shalamov had learned of Demidov's survival in the apartment of the translator Lidiia Maksimovna Brodskaia. During a visit by Shalamov to Brodskaia, a neighbor (Vera Linde) had stopped by to announce that Demidov was soon to visit Moscow, and Shalamov recognized the name of his old friend. Thus Shalamov learned of Demidov's survival and was brought up to speed on his post-camp fate by these mutual acquaintances.[9] It was Demidov, however, who wrote the first letter, presumably after Linde passed on Shalamov's whereabouts.

Born in 1908 in Petersburg to a working-class family, Demidov had become a rising star in Soviet physics in the 1930s. At the time of his arrest in 1938, he was working on his doctoral dissertation on electrophysics in the lab of renowned theoretical physicist Lev Landau at the Kharkov Institute of Physics and Technology. Arrested in February 1938 as part of widespread purges of the institute and its scientists, he was sentenced to eight years under article 58–10 and sent to Kolyma.[10] Demidov was held in various camps in Kolyma from late 1938 until approximately 1950, when his file was flagged during a search for nuclear scientists throughout the Gulag, and he was brought from Kolyma back to Moscow. However, once it was discovered that he had been working on electrophysics and not nuclear physics in Landau's lab in the 1930s, he was not transferred to an atomic *sharashka* (Soviet slang for prisons and camps set up to develop science and technology), where conditions would have been favorable.[11] Instead, Demidov was sent north to Minlag, a coal mining camp in Inta, Komi ASSR. He was released in 1953 or 1954, settled in nearby Ukhta, and began working as an engineer in a mechanical factory. Although he was rehabilitated in 1958, he remained in Ukhta until 1972, after which time he retired to Kaluga in central Russia, where he was able to buy an apartment in a cooperative.

Demidov's post-camp trajectory was, in most respects, fairly typical for former Gulag prisoners. Unable to simply return home because of formal legal restrictions on the movement of ex-prisoners who had not been rehabilitated, and facing potential informal discrimination, he had opted to settle near his former place of incarceration in an area with a high concentration of ex-prisoners and significant demand for skilled labor and expertise. Ukhta fit the bill well: it was a few hundred kilometers away from his last place of incarceration along a major rail line, was a fairly well-developed industrial town that had been built by prisoners, and was not on the list of cities where ex-prisoners were forbidden to settle.[12] What was perhaps unusual about Demidov's post-camp fate was that he was never permanently reunited with his family after release. His wife remained in Kharkov with his daughter, who had been born mere months before his arrest in 1938. He did, however, correspond regularly with his family, and his daughter visited him periodically in Ukhta. By 1965, Demidov was not particularly optimistic about his situation. As he related to Shalamov, "Of course, I don't plan to leave here for anywhere else, at least until my pension. This doesn't mean that I'm satisfied with my work, and even more, with the results. It's simply necessary to continue out of inertia." Instead of his official work, he valued his time spent writing above all else.[13] If his work was not what kept him in Ukhta, perhaps he stayed because of complicated family dynamics. Demidov and his wife, Aleksandra Mikhailovna Fainshtein, had been married for less than two years when both were arrested in 1938, and whereas she was released, he spent the next fifteen years in prisons and camps. Although they remained in contact while he was in Kolyma, Demidov attempted to cut off ties with his family after receiving a second sentence in 1946, going so far as to ask a friend to send a letter home telling his wife that he had died.[14]

In his first letter to Shalamov, Demidov asked to learn more about his old friend's life after the camps, details that he hadn't been able to learn from their mutual contacts in Moscow. As he wrote, "But I currently know only bits about you. Where are you working? In what genre are you working? What was your path after Kolyma?"[15] Shalamov, however, shared precious few personal details of his post-camp life with Demidov during the correspondence. Demidov, of course, was familiar with Shalamov's pre-camp life from time spent together in the camps. Shalamov had been born in Vologda in 1907, the son of an Orthodox priest and a schoolteacher. Although he had studied in the law faculty of Moscow University, his involvement in left-wing opposition to the Bolsheviks resulted in arrest in 1929, and he spent two years in the Vishera section of the Solovki camps (SLON).[16] Returning to Moscow in 1932, he worked as a journalist for a variety of publications. He was once again arrested in 1937 and would spend the next sixteen years in Kolyma—although he was released in 1951, he was not able to return to the "mainland" until 1953.[17]

As for Shalamov's post-camp fate, Demidov picked up some details from mutual acquaintances and from his personal visits to Shalamov in 1965–67. Shalamov's trajectory was in many ways typical of a member of the Soviet intelligentsia arrested in one of the capitals of Moscow and Leningrad.[18] He returned to the Moscow region in 1953, although he was not able to reunite with his family permanently in Moscow proper until 1956, when he received his official rehabilitation. His working life after the camps was in many ways even less satisfying than Demidov's. Despite his considerable talent and experience, he was never particularly successful in the Moscow literary scene. From 1957 he was a part-time correspondent for the journal *Moskva* and in 1959 moved on to what was a somewhat better position as an internal reviewer for the influential periodical *Novyi mir*. By virtue of his position, he became intimately familiar with much of what was being written about Stalinist terror and the Gulag at this time.[19] He struggled to get his work published and recognized, although he was ultimately admitted to the Moscow branch of the Writer's Union in 1972.[20]

Thus, when they began writing to each other in 1965, their post-camp experiences were already quite different. Demidov's tended to follow one model of ex-prisoners who remained at or near their former places of incarceration, finding some degree of acceptance and stability where discrimination (formal and informal) was less widespread. Shalamov, on the other hand, like many members of the Soviet intelligentsia from Moscow and Leningrad, was able to return to the city and settle permanently after some struggle. Yet they did share significant things in common: neither was particularly happy with his personal situation in 1965. Both were members of a similar generation who had already begun their professional lives before their arrests in the 1930s and returned from the camps having already reached middle age. This distinguished them from those who had been arrested during and after the war, who were often only in their thirties when released. Both had also broken with the families they had established before incarceration: Demidov never returned to his, whereas

Shalamov's marriage collapsed soon after his permanent return to Moscow in 1956. Like all ex-prisoners, they had struggled to readjust to Soviet life and found the readjustment process to require, in Shalamov's own words, "a long period of amortization."[21]

THE LITERARY LANDSCAPE OF 1965

The correspondence between Demidov and Shalamov was primarily concerned with how one should represent the prisoner experience in prose. This is not surprising, given that both were writing about the Gulag. Further, they were not doing so in a vacuum—the mid-1950s to the mid-1960s had seen a significant outpouring of writing about terror and, to a lesser degree, about the camps. This includes unpublished material that was ultimately destined for desk drawers and for samizdat and tamizdat circulation (such as Evgeniia Ginzburg's *Journey into the Whirlwind*) but also a small but significant body of publications that appeared in the Soviet press and thick journals. The most famous of these, of course, was *One Day in the Life of Ivan Denisovich*, the novella published in *Novyi mir* in 1962 after being personally approved by Khrushchev.[22] *Ivan Denisovich* became a literary sensation both at home and abroad and launched the career of Aleksander Solzhenitsyn.[23] But this story was only one among several that appeared in Soviet thick journals from 1962 to 1964. Taken as a whole, these published and unpublished works played a significant role in the debate between Demidov and Shalamov, in addition to influencing their writing.

One of Shalamov's chief criticisms of literature about the terror and the Gulag was that the bulk of it stopped short of talking about the camp experience. As he wrote to Demidov in an undated letter from the summer of 1965, "There is one curious aberration—those of our brothers who take up the pen for some reason start with the investigation and, not reaching the most important, the most frightening part [the camp experience], get tired."[24] Most manuscripts by Gulag survivors focused on arrest and terror rather than the camps. Shalamov was uniquely positioned to note this trend: he was relatively well connected to networks of former prisoners in Moscow, through which he had access to samizdat works, and he had also read a large number of unpublished manuscripts in his role as internal reviewer for the journal *Novyi mir*. In fact, by this time Shalamov had already read drafts of two of Demidov's stories, neither of which concerned the camp experience. Shalamov's works on Kolyma, then, were somewhat unusual in that he had begun writing directly about the camp experience immediately after his release in 1953.

The publication of *Ivan Denisovich*, however, significantly changed the landscape of writing about terror and the camps. Shalamov, as he wrote to Solzhenitsyn sometime in the winter/spring of 1964–65, initially thought that the novella would be an "icebreaker" that would open up the topic of the camp experience and lead to greater publication opportunities.[25] Indeed, the appearance of *Ivan Denisovich* was followed by several works that dealt directly with life and survival in the camps as their primary focus, among them Georgii Shelest's *Kolyma Notes*, Boris D'iakov's *The Story of My Experience*, and A. I. Aldan-Semenov's *Bas-relief in the Rock*.[26] In fact, one of Shelest's stories, "A Nugget," had appeared in the newspaper *Izvestiia* just days before *Ivan Denisovich* was published in November 1962, an attempt by its ambitious editor, Aleksei Adzhubei, to scoop *Novyi mir* and claim the distinction of being the first to publish a work on the camps in the mainstream press.[27] The camps also figured in Iurii Piliar's *People Remain People*, a novel about a soldier captured during World War II, which was published in serial form in the journal *Iunost'* in 1963–64, and in Aleksandr Gorbatov's sweeping military memoir *Years and Wars*, which was published in three parts in *Novyi mir* in 1964.[28]

Shalamov and Demidov, like many other ex-prisoners, found these publications about life in the camps to be highly problematic. As Demidov wrote to Shalamov in a letter dated July 27, 1965, "You are indignant at our writers who are developing the theme of the 'black years' for the fact that they 'start from the end.' You are right."[29] Both of these former camp comrades were in agreement that a central flaw of the stories was that they were written backward. Rather than attempting to explain what had led to the terror or what prisoners experienced, they were instead intended to legitimize the current Soviet system and its limited criticism of Stalinism. Shelest's description of life in Kolyma, for example, was meant to demonstrate that truly dedicated Communists stayed true to their beliefs even as they suffered in the camps. Piliar's story of a Red Army officer who endured both German and Soviet captivity confirmed that "people remained people" in camps, including not only prisoners but also many Soviet camp officials. Aldan-Semenov's tale of an Arctic camp suggested that the corrupt impulses of Stalinist camp bosses could be redirected into the heroic conquest of nature by honest officials. Even Gorbatov's memoir of arrest, interrogation, and life in the camps, which struck Shalamov as remarkably honest, was packaged as part of a narrative about how a wrongly accused army officer was able to remain true to his values, secure a lawful release, and go on to play a decisive role in the Soviet victory in the Second World War.[30] In essence, each story had its own "happy ending" that was intended to legitimize the system rather than investigating its potential flaws.[31]

The ending, in fact, was what rendered *Ivan Denisovich* truly exceptional in the context of the published literature on the "black years" of Stalinism. Although the main character was in many ways an ideal Soviet man, a hardworking former peasant who was able to lose himself in his work laying bricks, the novella ended in an open-ended fashion—not with death or release but with a deliberately ambiguous statement about how this particular day in the camp had been just one of "three thousand six hundred and fifty-three days like that in his stretch."[32] Thus, it was more about the experience of the camps than it was about legitimizing the Soviet project in the post-Stalin era.[33] Open-endedness and ambiguity were also omnipresent in both Demidov's and Shalamov's prose works.

REPRESENTING THE CAMP EXPERIENCE

In his second letter to Shalamov, dated June 30, 1965, Demidov admitted that he had begun writing directly about his experiences as a prisoner but expressed a lack of confidence about how it was turning out. As he stated, "I am currently writing a series of 'Kolyma stories.' They are somehow not turning out right."[34] Demidov also discussed the unwanted attention that his writing and his attempts to circulate it had attracted: apparently one of the leaders of the Komi Writer's Union had described his literary efforts as "scabies" that ought to be hidden. Throughout the correspondence, Demidov repeatedly discussed how unsure he felt of the results of his many hours spent writing. Whether or not this should be seen as false modesty, it is highly probable that Demidov was seeking encouragement, reassurance, and validation from a professional writer whom he respected enormously.

Shalamov, however, did not offer validation. Although Shalamov invited Demidov to share his work, writing, "I would very much like to read your story about Kolyma," he offered sustained criticism even before he had the opportunity to read the stories.[35] Shalamov took offense at the way that Demidov discussed writing, such as his expression that he was "indulging in writing" and "developing the Kolyma theme."[36] Before he had even read any of Demidov's camp material, Shalamov explained to Demidov how he ought to write. He urged him to adopt the most direct of styles, avoiding all "belle-lettre-ness" and "literariness."[37] Shalamov went on to elaborate on his own approach to writing about the camps, which he related in a letter from July 1965: "I am exploring some psychological laws, arising within society, whereby an attempt is made to transform a person into a nonperson. These new laws, new manifestations of the human spirit and soul, arise in conditions that should not be forgotten, and the recording of some of these conditions is the moral obligation of anyone who was in Kolyma."[38] Thus, Shalamov's approach was to focus on how the camps had been so destructive of the individual. He continued by observing that writing on the camps should be "not the prose of documents, but prose that has been born through suffering, like a document."[39] As Shalamov continued, "I am not writing memoirs, nor am I writing short stories. Rather I'm trying to write that which is *not* a short story, that which would be *not* literature."[40] Shalamov sent this categorical and strongly worded advice to Demidov even before reading any of his camp stories.

What exactly did Shalamov intend to convey with this advice? What did it mean to dispense with "literariness"? Here, it is useful to turn to his unpublished literary manifesto, "On Prose," which was written in 1965, for more guidance. Reflecting on what writing meant in an age that had seen war, revolution, Hiroshima, Auschwitz, and Kolyma, Shalamov argued that the novel was "dead." It was now the obligation of every writer to adopt what he called "new prose."[41] As Josefina Lundblad-Janjic has pointed out, Shalamov intended that many standard literary devices should be abandoned, including "conventional characters, character development, description of characters' exterior or landscape, superfluous details, any excess of language, etc." In their place, writers should include only "personal experience ('personal fate, personal blood'); a serious subject ('death . . . murder, Calvary'); simplicity and brevity of style; and a resurrection of 'feeling' and ultimately of 'life.'"[42] This would, of course, be extraordinarily difficult advice for any writer to follow, especially for Demidov, who was not only untrained but also just beginning his literary endeavors.

It is essential to point out that while Shalamov was categorical in his pronouncements about camp writings, his own works did not necessarily hold up to his lofty standards. First of all, his experimental ideas were reserved strictly for prose. As Josephine von Zitzewitz points out in her contribution to this volume, Shalamov wrote extensive nature poetry that was quite traditional. As she writes, "Shalamov seems to have believed that classical Russian verse would never exhaust itself, implying that classical Russian poetry was perfectly able to grapple with the experience of the camps." Further, the *Kolyma Stories* themselves are filled with what seems to fall under Shalamov's heading of "literariness." The very first story of the first cycle, "Trampling the Snow," dated 1956 (long before his pronouncements to Demidov), uses the metaphor of clearing a road through snow as an invitation to the reader.[43] Later stories did this as well: for example, the 1967 story "Graphite" is a meditation on the fact that both cartographers and gravediggers use the same instrument to record their work—hardly an "unliterary" approach.[44] When discussing what she calls

Shalamov's "late style," Lundblad-Janjic points out that the author continuously struggled to fulfill its promise.[45]

Demidov made it clear that he did not appreciate the lecture from Shalamov.[46] As he replied, "You ask me to not get angry. But who can like the dogmatism, peremptoriness in your instructions and the distant tone?"[47] He expressed understanding for Shalamov's position on writing about the Kolyma experience, and he agreed that the "canonical rules of writing" needed to be reexamined. But the question was, with what were they to be replaced? Could Shalamov's extreme position actually be followed in practice? Should all "literariness" be abandoned, and what would such writing even look like? In other words, Demidov found Shalamov's literary pronouncements not only offensive as one writer lecturing another but also in that they were entirely dismissive of any other approach to writing about the camp experience. He roundly rejected Shalamov's categorical pronouncements on the camps.[48]

The disagreement over literary style also spilled over into another issue that was central to camp survivors in the mid-1960s: who had the authority to write about the camps, and about Kolyma in particular? Length of time in the camps and depth of personal suffering were often understood as conferring authority and, by extension, the right and obligation to describe the horrors of the Gulag experience. Shalamov explained that he would simply have broken off correspondence with just about anybody else who had described writing about Kolyma as Demidov had in his letters. Rather sarcastically, he stated that he could excuse Demidov his transgression because of "the fact that you were not in Kolyma [mining gold]. You arrived only at the end of 1938.... Only the difference of our experiences could explain your objectionable and inappropriate expression."[49] Thus, while ostensibly "excusing" Demidov's choice of words, Shalamov was in fact attacking Demidov's authority to write about the camps on the basis of a purported lack of experience and suffering.

Not surprisingly, Demidov objected strongly to Shalamov's dismissal of his experiences. As he wrote in response just days later, on July 27, 1965,

> Who do you take me for? For a *pridurok* [camp trusty], floating on the surface of Kolyma camp life somewhere in Debin [the camp hospital where they met] or in some other comfortable spot? Do you really not realize that I was in Kolyma in 1938, in truth, from the fall. That I spent a few years in *Butugychag* [a notorious mining camp section], that I mined gold, and that of my fourteen years in Kolyma I spent nearly ten in general work? Even a person incapable of observation and comparison could not help but recognize the tragedy of this 'Auschwitz without the ovens,' a phrase for which, among other things, I received my second sentence in 1946. And this court case in Magadan

should be a sufficient reminder to you of how unacceptable it is to accuse me of superficiality and of not understanding the essence of Kolyma."[50]

As for the fact that one had to "personally feel" Kolyma in order to write about it, Demidov listed various maladies he now experienced thanks to his time as a prisoner. He now typed the majority of his correspondence rather than writing by hand because of the damage his fingers had sustained in the mines. He continued, "Ten times I was a 'goner' and twice was dying of hypothermia. With whom have you confused me, Varlam?"[51] Thus, in response to Shalamov's withering attack on his experiences, Demidov was quick to establish his bona fides as a long-serving and long-suffering veteran of Kolyma. Not only had he suffered, he had openly criticized the cruelty of the camps in 1946 and had received a second prison sentence for his trouble.

That Demidov described Kolyma as "Auschwitz without the ovens" in Kolyma in 1946 was remarkable, not just for the way that he openly criticized the Soviet camp system but because he did so by comparing the camps of Kolyma to Nazi death camps. How did Demidov know about Auschwitz, and what did he know about it? It may very well be that Demidov learned about the Holocaust from other prisoners in Kolyma, many of whom had been arrested during the war and so might have second- or third-hand knowledge of the camps. But it is also entirely possible that Demidov learned about Auschwitz from the official Soviet press, to which prisoners had some limited access. Auschwitz was first mentioned as a site of execution and imprisonment in both *Pravda* and *Izvestiia* on June 26, 1941, and it figured regularly in both publications throughout the war. A major feature on Auschwitz was published on May 7, 1945, in *Pravda*, and updates on the Nuremberg trials were a regular feature in the postwar Soviet press.[52] Of course, such articles described it as a site of mass death for Soviet citizens in general, never mentioning the fact that Jews, Roma, and members of other ethnic categories made up the vast majority of victims. This followed a general Soviet practice of rarely recognizing that certain groups were the specific targets of Nazi genocide.[53] Thus, Demidov may not have known in 1946 that Auschwitz was a death camp for Jews, and thus a comparison to Soviet camps (which generally lacked such a clear ethnic dimension) would have made sense.[54]

Shalamov responded to Demidov's furious defense of his reputation only a few days later, and his tone immediately mellowed. He wrote, "I haven't confused you with anyone, you are one of the few people in Kolyma who resisted the times."[55] Yet Shalamov did not entirely back down from his criticism of Demidov for not having adequately experienced the horrors of Kolyma. In the final paragraph of his letter, he described his own sufferings in the camps, pointing out that he had been imprisoned in 1929–31 as well. He listed his various experiences in Kolyma, including being on death row in the winter of 1938–39.[56] However, nothing that he experienced was quite as bad as the time from December 1937 until the fall of 1938, the period of the height of the "mass operations" of the terror, before Demidov had reached Kolyma. Although he apologized for having invoked 1938 in his previous letter, Shalamov still argued that his suffering was greater than Demidov's.[57]

Why did Shalamov and Demidov argue so bitterly about the harshness of their camp experiences? Why would Shalamov attack Demidov as not having sufficiently suffered, and why would Demidov see the need to defend himself so vigorously? Clearly, each saw his experience in the camps as fundamental to his identity and self-presentation, and what is more, they saw the need to defend it to each other. How else could former camp prisoners have their experiences and suffering acknowledged? Public discussions of the Gulag were highly circumscribed and ambivalent, and suffering was rarely acknowledged. The only official documentation of incarceration that prisoners might be able to obtain would be a certificate of "rehabilitation," a document that entitled a former prisoner to extremely limited financial compensation and some restoration of other political and social rights. Prisoners faced a wide variety of formal and informal discrimination in the mid-1960s, and thus their past was often a liability in their everyday lives. What was more, neither Demidov nor Shalamov could see themselves represented in the protagonists who appeared in the published literature on terror and the Gulag, a collection that by and large included only wrongly accused Communist Party members and army officers. Even *Ivan Denisovich*, which broke from this mold by depicting camp life from the perspective of an average peasant, did little to examine the experience of intelligentsia "politicals" like Demidov and Shalamov. Where else could they find affirmation of their experiences and suffering than in informal networks of former prisoners? Thus, the disagreement between Demidov and Shalamov was not just about who had the talent or background to "properly" represent prisoners' experiences. It was also about who had the moral authority to speak for ex-prisoners, particularly "politicals" who were struggling to counter widespread suspicion and discrimination against them, which had intensified by the middle of the 1960s.

It might be objected that there was one former prisoner voice who seemed to have this moral authority: Aleksander Solzhenitsyn. As is clear from Shalamov's correspondence with Solzhenitsyn, he had a great deal of respect for the writer and for *Ivan Denisovich* itself. While we know relatively little about what Demidov thought about the writer or the story, it seems that it had a significant influence on him. Valentina Georgievna Demidova, Demidov's daughter, recalls being "scolded" by her father for her naïve reaction to the story as a straightforward description of camp life that conflicted with the horrors he had told her about Kolyma.[58] *Ivan Denisovich* clearly influenced Demidov in at least two ways: first, it encouraged him to shift from writing about the experience of terror to that of the camps; second, the structure of the novella (describing a "day in the life" of a prisoner) was used by Demidov in one of his first camp stories, "The Stiff" (see below). But despite the respect for his work, Solzhenitsyn was a problematic figure to serve as a spokesperson for prisoners like Demidov and Shalamov. He belonged to a different generation; he had served in the Second World War and been arrested afterward. Perhaps even more importantly, he had not spent any time in the more far-flung camps of the system, including, for example, Kolyma, Noril'sk, or Vorkuta. In fact, he had spent a large portion of his sentence in the relatively mild conditions of a sharashka camp for scientific and technical development. In many ways, Solzhenitsyn appears to have been an unspoken presence in the debate about whose experiences and suffering gave them the authority to write about Kolyma. It is also apparent that Solzhenitsyn was aware that his own stature among former prisoners was lacking due to his relatively "mild" experience of incarceration. Thus, his decade-long project of gathering testimony from other prisoners, which resulted in *The Gulag Archipelago*, might be seen as an attempt to overcome his own relative deficit in experience and suffering. This was openly acknowledged in the preface to the second volume of his opus, where he wrote, "The whole scope of this story and of this truth is beyond the capabilities of one lonely pen.... In the *Kolyma Stories* of Shalamov the reader will perhaps feel more truly and surely the pitilessness of the spirt of the Archipelago and the limits of human despair."[59] Neither Shalamov nor Demidov saw the need to gather testimony from other prisoners to inform their work on Kolyma, yet the problem of establishing authority existed for them as well, as the testy back-and-forth described above suggests.

CONCLUSION

Demidov and Shalamov did finally meet sometime between August and December of 1965. Judging from Demidov's letter that followed the meeting, they had managed to patch over their disagreements, at least for a time. Demidov related to Shalamov that he had left a notebook of his stories with a mutual friend in Moscow and asked Shalamov to be "strict, but fair" in his judgment of them.

As Demidov wrote, meeting with Shalamov and his friends had "strengthened my belief in myself and in a reason to continue living."[60] Indeed, the period from 1965 to 1967 was a remarkably productive one for Demidov, as he completed several stories about terror and life in the camps. In 1966 he completed what has become his best-known work: "The Stiff." This short story, which describes an unusual day in the life of a prisoner, clearly exemplifies Demidov's emerging literary style. The narrator, who tells the story in first person, is saddled with an unpleasant job during a day off in a Kolyma agricultural camp section: digging a grave. Working in solitude outside the confines of the camp zone to bury a victim with whom he establishes an emotional connection, the narrator unearths feelings that had long been suppressed by the brutal daily routines of the camps. Feeling the need to somehow mark the grave, he fashions a makeshift cross, a symbolic attempt to prevent the body from being swallowed up by the harsh Arctic environment and the chaos of the universe The story ends with him leaving the sense of "spiritual illumination" evoked by the burial and "returning to the camp, and vulgarity, callousness, and the adulteration of thoughts and feelings."[61] The text clearly violated Shalamov's rules for "new prose" in fundamental ways, including as it did long descriptions of nature and discussion of the narrator's internal development as well as a premise that was not so much a discussion of suffering and survival as an opportunity for the author to reflect on the emotional challenges of imprisonment.

"The Stiff" was likely one among several of Demidov's stories that Shalamov read during their correspondence, and the latter's response deepened the conflict between the two men about their approaches to writing about the Gulag. Indeed, although they seem to have patched up their friendship after meeting in 1965, the relationship continued to sour in 1966–67. As Valentina Demidova stated in a 2011 interview, she recalls her father raging as they walked back to central Moscow after a tumultuous meeting with Shalamov in the latter's apartment near the Moscow hippodrome. Reacting to Shalamov's condemnation of the subject matter of his stories, Demidov told his daughter that they had indeed lived through "frightening, impossible hard labor. There [in Kolyma] very few survived after general work, but regardless—people lived there. These people loved, had friendships. . . . And I can't *not* write about that" [emphasis mine].[62] In this matter, Demidov stood his ground. Although his stories certainly did not avoid the themes of death and survival, they were hardly free of the "literariness" that Shalamov had grown to despise. What was more, Demidov embraced the challenge of trying to examine the experience of the camps from the perspectives of a variety of characters: this included prisoners with a wide variety of ages and backgrounds but also camp guards and officials. While such attempts were not uniformly successful, they demonstrate that the narrow approach to discussing the camps espoused by Shalamov was not the only one in circulation in the mid-1960s.[63]

Demidov and Shalamov exchanged their final letters in the late summer of 1967. Reacting to yet another lecture by Shalamov on writing, Demidov offered the following statement: "It is bad when correspondents are on levels of capacity for understanding and perception that are too different. It is even worse when one of them considers the other to be a fool on the basis of superficial and preconceived notions."[64] Although each writer would live into the 1980s, it appears this was the end of their post-camp relationship, though certainly not of their literary work on the camp experience. Shalamov continued to work on his poetry and prose throughout the 1960s and 1970s, and some of the *Kolyma Stories* began to appear in tamizdat beginning in 1966 in the New York–based *Novyi zhurnal*, a fact of which Shalamov was apparently aware by June 1967.[65] However, the author was deeply upset by the fact that the versions of his stories abroad were sometimes heavily edited and usually published piecemeal rather than as part of the completed cycles, as they had been intended. A public renunciation of these publications followed in a letter to *Literaturnaia gazeta* in 1972.[66] Shalamov was admitted to the Writer's Union that year, and a fourth collection of his noncamp poetry was published (previous volumes had been published in 1961, 1964, and 1967). However, it would not be until perestroika that the complete cycles of the *Kolyma Stories* would be published in Russia. For his part, Demidov also continued to write about the camps and was active until his manuscripts were confiscated by the KGB in 1980, at which point he was too demoralized to continue.[67] The first publication of his work was "The Stiff," which appeared in the journal *Ogonek* in 1990, some three years after his death.[68]

What can we say, then, about the broader significance of this correspondence between Demidov and Shalamov? Let us begin with the most obvious: in the decade that separated *Ivan Denisovich* from *The Gulag Archipelago*, there was significant discussion of representations of the prison camp experience among ex-prisoners in the Soviet Union. At this point, very little literature on the Gulag experience was available: aside from *Ivan Denisovich*, there was only a handful of published works. There was also unofficial literature circulating, like Demidov and Shalamov's poetry and stories, as well as Ginzburg's *Journey into the Whirlwind*. But in the absence of a major published work on the Gulag as a whole, much about Gulag literature was still very much up for grabs, leaving questions like acceptable subjects, authorial authority, and genre open to debate. Here, it is worth noting that one of the most frequently repeated responses by prisoners to *Ivan Denisovich* was to ask for more. Ex-prisoner after ex-prisoner pointed out to Solzhenitsyn that his story had described only one day—thus, it was still necessary to tell the story of all the other days.[69] By the time that *The Gulag Archipelago* was circulating in the 1970s both inside and outside the Soviet Union, there was a publication purporting to tell the story of the rest of those days. This didn't mean that others could not write about their experiences, but those who did would now have to contend with a powerful model and metaphor. When Demidov and Shalamov were discussing how to represent the camp experience and who ought to represent it, the stakes were relatively high for precisely the reason that there was not yet an established model.

Further, one should not conclude that the mid-1960s were generally discouraging for Gulag writing among ex-prisoners. Shalamov may have seen doors closing on his opportunities to publish by the time he began corresponding with Demidov in 1965, having experienced repeated rejections from Soviet journals and publishing houses. But Demidov clearly did not feel this way. For him, seeing stories about the Gulag in print encouraged him to spend every free moment at the typewriter, working out the stories he had long been telling in oral form.[70] And again, if we return to the responses by ex-prisoners to *Ivan Denisovich*, it's clear that Demidov was not alone in feeling encouraged. Khrushchev's ouster and greater limitations on artistic expression surely dampened this enthusiasm but hardly extinguished it. Shalamov himself continued to write about the Gulag after 1965, and the latter three cycles of his *Kolyma Stories* were completed after this time.

This correspondence, when seen against the backdrop of a string of publications about the camps in Soviet "thick journals" from 1962 to 1964, also highlights the question of identity and authority among ex-prisoners. Disagreements between Demidov and Shalamov reached the highest level of rancor when the two were discussing their respective prisoner biographies. Why was it so important for both of them to prove and defend their bona fides? In an environment where experiences of former prisoners could be discussed only very narrowly in public, and when one's status as a former prisoner (particularly as a "political") was a genuine liability in everyday life, recognition by a fellow former prisoner was one of the only ways to have one's experience affirmed. What was more, the way that Demidov and Shalamov measured each other's experiences suggested that they saw a clear hierarchy of suffering that was determined by a variety of factors such as type of conviction, when one was arrested, length of sentence(s), where one was incarcerated, and what kind of work one did while in the camps. Although they squabbled over the details of their particular biographies, both men shared the notion that survivors of Kolyma, especially those who had been arrested before the Second World War, had a special obligation to write about their experiences given the degree to which they had suffered. Although they did not mention him by name, Solzhenitsyn hangs over this conversation as a writer who was immensely talented yet was considered lacking in terms of authority because his experiences had been "milder" than those of Demidov and Shalamov. Solzhenitsyn himself understood his own deficiency in authority and experience—a deficiency he attempted to overcome by collecting the experiences of scores of other prisoners for his opus *The Gulag Archipelago*.

Strangely enough, while Shalamov questioned Demidov's authority in the correspondence, Demidov had been, and continued to be, a highly respected presence in Shalamov's writing. Before the correspondence began, Demidov had appeared by name in two stories in the *Left Bank* story cycle, as a minor character who behaved in an absolutely principled fashion.[71] Shalamov had dedicated his camp play *Anna Ivanovna* to Demidov and had praised him alongside Enrico Fermi in a 1964 letter to Solzhenitsyn.[72] Yet it was at the end of their correspondence in 1967 that Shalamov finally immortalized Demidov as the central character in one of his stories, "The Life of Engineer Kipreev"—a story that would become part of his cycle *The Resurrection of the Larch*.[73] Changing Demidov's name to Kipreev (likely to protect his friend now that he was certain he was alive), it told the story of Demidov-Kipreev's life from arrest through his reunion with the narrator ten years after release. In contrast to the detached, documentary tone of most of Shalamov's stories, "Kipreev" reads practically like a hagiography. Indeed, as Sarah Young has noted, the Russian title of the story (*zhitie*) uses a word typically reserved for saints' lives.[74] A central part of the story is a retelling of an incident also related as part of his 1962 story *Ivan Fedorovich*. Demidov-Kipreev, one of the few characters in Shalamov's stories who is willing and able to stick to a moral code, refuses a lend-lease American suit given to him as a reward for his role in setting up a light bulb recycling factory in Kolyma. But in the later retelling, Shalamov adds a further detail, which is Demidov-Kipreev's public declaration that Kolyma is like "Auschwitz without the ovens" (an incident that Demidov had reminded him of during their correspondence). In the story, Demidov-Kipreev is condemned for these courageous acts to a second sentence in Kolyma, after which he ceased contact with his family, going so far as to have another prisoner send a fake death notice to his wife. Thus, in "Engineer Kipreev," the principled heroism of Demidov from the earlier stories becomes something akin to martyrdom. Although Shalamov had attacked Demidov's authority to write about the camp experience in their

"I WOULD LIKE TO READ YOUR STORY ABOUT KOLYMA" 237

correspondence, the prisoner from his memory was elevated even further as a singular individual whose behavior had been beyond reproach. In the process, Shalamov had once again violated some of the key principles of his own idea of "new prose."

The correspondence between Demidov and Shalamov thus reveals a great deal about the fragility of post-camp networks and relationships. Both men characterized their friendship in the camps as intense, and they obviously shared a great deal of mutual respect. Yet friendship established in the conditions of the camps could not necessarily be sustained in the circumstances of the mid-1960s. The challenges and pressures that the two faced in trying to live their lives as ex-prisoners were obviously considerable and likely weighed heavily on any attempt to maintain friendship. Both experienced a significant degree of social isolation in their post-camp lives. Both were largely estranged from families that had been established in the late 1930s. Shalamov had to some degree been able to reestablish his Moscow social networks on his return, but Demidov was living in semi-exile in the former camp town of Ukhta. While many former prisoners were able to successfully construct new social networks in their post-camp lives, the relationship between Demidov and Shalamov suggests that there were many factors complicating these attempts.

NOTES

Drafts of this article benefited from discussion at the 2017 Canadian Association of Slavists (CAS) conference and at the 2017 Association for Slavic, Eastern European, and Eurasian Studies (ASEEES) annual convention. In particular, the author wishes to thank Wilson Bell, Heather Coleman, Sean Kinnear, Tyler Kirk, Diane Nemec-Ignashev, Alison Smith, and Sarah Young for their advice and suggestions. The author also wishes to acknowledge the Department of History, the Office of the Provost, and the Institute for Peace and Conflict (all of Texas Tech University) for their generous support. Special thanks are due to the late Semen Vilenskii, whose "instructions" led to this article, and Valentina Georgievna Demidova, who generously shared stories about her father.

1. Shalamov, *Novaia kniga*, 752–63. The correspondence can also be found at Shalamov.ru (https://shalamov.ru/library/24/33.html). The original documents are held in the Russian State Archive of Literature and Art (RGALI), fond(f.) 2596, opis'(op.) 2, delo(d.) 141. In total, the archive preserves seven letters from Demidov to Shalamov and four going in the other direction. It is clear that some letters from Shalamov to Demidov were not preserved.

2. Shalamov, "Anna Ivanovna," 3; *Valentina Georgievna Demidova ob ottse*.

3. Toker, *Return from the Archipelago*, chap. 6.

4. On Shalamov's relationship with Solzhenitsyn, see Esipov, *Shalamov*, 243–64, 290–309.

5. On the key role of *The Gulag Archipelago* in establishing a paradigm for memoirs in literature, see Toker, *Return from the Archipelago*, chap. 4.

6. Toker, *Return from the Archipelago*, 161.

7. Shalamov, *Novaia kniga*, 752.

8. Mamuchashvili, "V bol'nitse dlia zakliuchennykh."

9. "'Budushchemu na prokliatoe proshloe ... ,'" 63. An alternative version of this meeting is that the neighbor recognized Demidov's name in the dedication of Shalamov's camp play, *Anna Ivanovna*. Shalamov, "Anna Ivanovna," 3.

10. On the purge of this institute, see Pavlenko, Raniuk, and Khramov, *"Delo" UFTI 1935–1938*.

11. On the Stalinist *sharashka*, see Siddiqi, "Scientists and Specialists in the Gulag."

12. On formal and informal discrimination against former prisoners, see Barenberg, *Gulag Town, Company Town*, chap. 6; Elie, "Les anciens détenus du Goulag."

13. Shalamov, *Novaia kniga*, 752.

14. *Valentina Georgievna Demidova ob ottse*; Shalamov, *Sketches of the Criminal World*, 180. Much of this biographical material is also covered in Toker, "Testimony and Fictionality."

15. Shalamov, *Novaia kniga*, 752.

16. This experience is described in his "anti-novel" *Vishera*. Shalamov, *Sobranie sochinenii*, 4:149–294.

17. Esipov, *Shalamov*, 219.

18. On the fate of former prisoners from the intelligentsias of Moscow and Leningrad, see Adler, *The Gulag Survivor*; Adler, *Keeping Faith with the Party*.

19. Esipov, *Shalamov*, 240.

20. Esipov, 310.

21. Shalamov, *Kolyma Stories*, xviii.

22. Taubman, *Khrushchev*, 525–28.

23. On the response to the novella in the Soviet Union and abroad, see Kozlov, *The Readers of Novyi Mir*; Tiurina, "Dorogoi Ivan Denisovich!"; Jones, "The 'Thaw' Goes International."

24. Shalamov, *Novaia kniga*, 755.

25. Shalamov, 665.

26. Shelest, "Kolymskie zapisi"; D'iakov, "Povest' o perezhitom"; Aldan-Semenov, "Barel'ef na skale."

27. Shelest, "Samorodok." On the reactions of Tvardovskii and Solzhenitsyn to being scooped by *Izvestiia*, see Solzhenitsyn, *The Oak and the Calf*, 44; Tiurina, "Dorogoi Ivan Denisovich!," 20–25.

28. Piliar, "Liudi ostaiutsia liud'mi"; Gorbatov, "Gody i voiny."
29. Shalamov, *Novaia kniga*, 759.
30. Shalamov, 669–73.
31. This is explored at length in Tolczyk, *See No Evil*, 217–26.
32. Solzhenitsyn, *One Day in the Life of Ivan Denisovich*, 139.
33. As Tolczyk has written, it was "the only work that neither provides nor suggests clear authorial resolutions of the ethical problem inherent in the camp experience." Tolczyk, *See No Evil*, 256.
34. Shalamov, *Novaia kniga*, 754.
35. Shalamov, 755.
36. Shalamov, 756–57.
37. Shalamov, 755.
38. Shalamov, *Novaia kniga*, 757.
39. I use von Zitzewitz's translation of the key phrase "*Ne proza dokumentov, a proza, vystradannaia, kak document.*" See chapter 10 of this volume.
40. Shalamov, *Novaia kniga*, 757.
41. Shalamov, *Sobranie sochinenii*, 5:157.
42. Janjic, "Writer or Witness," 23.
43. Shalamov, *Kolyma Stories*, 3. As multiple reviewers have pointed out, the most recent English translation of the collection misreads the metaphor entirely. See, for example Young, "Huddling on the Ground."
44. Shalamov, *Sketches of the Criminal World*, 116–20.
45. Janjic, "Writer or Witness."
46. Leona Toker has made a similar point, arguing that "Shalamov slipped into a mentor's tone which alienated Demidov." Toker, "Testimony and Fictionality," 300.
47. Shalamov, *Novaia kniga*, 758.
48. Shalamov, 758.
49. Shalamov, 757.
50. Shalamov, 758.
51. Shalamov, 758–59.
52. See, for example, "Soobshchenie Chrezvychainoi gosudarstvennoi komissii."
53. Gitelman, "History, Memory and Politics."
54. The Soviet state did target specific nationalities for deportation, and these national groups experienced significant mortality due to ethnic cleansing operations carried out from the late 1930s until the early 1950s. On Soviet ethnic cleansing, see Martin, "The Origins of Soviet Ethnic Cleansing."
55. Shalamov, *Novaia kniga*, 760.
56. As described in "The Lawyer's Conspiracy." Shalamov, *Kolyma Stories*, 179–97.
57. Shalamov, *Novaia kniga*, 759–60.
58. "'Budushchemu na prokliatoe proshloe . . . ,'" 66.

59. Solzhenitsyn, *The Gulag Archipelago*, vol. 2, preface. Thanks to Sarah Young for alerting me to this quotation.
60. Shalamov, *Novaia kniga*, 760–61.
61. Demidov, *Five Fates from a Wondrous Planet*, 49–50.
62. "'Budushchemu na prokliatoe proshloe...'" 63–64.
63. For a more involved discussion of Demidov's literary approach, with a special eye to how it compared to Shalamov's, see Toker, "Testimony and Fictionality."
64. Shalamov, *Novaia kniga*, 762.
65. Klots, "Varlam Shalamov," 155.
66. On the letter and the controversy surrounding it, see Esipov, *Shalamov*, 299–300.
67. "'Budushchemu na prokliatoe proshloe...,'" 69–72.
68. Demidov, "Dubar'."
69. See, for example, letter from A. V. Movsesian to Solzhenitsyn, December 6, 1962, in Tiurina, *Dorogoi Ivan Denisovich*, 140–41.
70. "'Budushchemu na prokliatoe proshloe...,'" 65.
71. See "Ivan Fiodorovich" (1962) and "Special Order" (undated) in Shalamov, *Kolyma Stories*, 254–66, 387–89.
72. Shalamov, "Anna Ivanovna"; Shalamov, *Novaia kniga*, 660.
73. Shalamov, *Sketches of the Criminal World*, 174–88.
74. Young, "Recalling the Dead," 358.

BIBLIOGRAPHY

Adler, Nanci. *Keeping Faith with the Party: Communist Believers Return from the Gulag*. Bloomington: Indiana University Press, 2012.

———. *The Gulag Survivor: Beyond the Soviet System*. New Brunswick: Transaction, 2002.

Aldan-Semenov, Andrei. "Barel'ef na skale." *Moskva* no. 7 (1964): 68–154.

Barenberg, Alan. *Gulag Town, Company Town. Forced Labor and Its Legacy in Vorkuta*. New Haven: Yale University Press, 2014.

"'Budushchemu na prokliatoe proshloe...' Interv'iu s Valentinoi Demidovoi." In *Shalamovskii sbornik* 4:60–77. Moscow: Litera, 2011.

Demidov, Georgii. "Dubar'." *Ogonek* no. 51 (1990): 10–14.

———. *Five Fates from a Wondrous Planet*. Translated by Diane Nemec Ignashev. Moscow: Vozvrashchenie, 2015.

D'iakov, Boris. "Povest' o perezhitom." *Zvezda* no. 3 (1963): 177–96.

Elie, Marc. "Les anciens détenus du Goulag: Libérations massives, réinsertion et réhabilitation dans l'URSS poststalinienne, 1953–1964." PhD diss., Ecole des Hautes Etudes en Sciences Sociales (EHESS), 2007.

Esipov, V. V. *Shalamov*. Moscow: Molodaia gvardia, 2012.
Gitelman, Zvi. "History, Memory and Politics: The Holocaust in the Soviet Union." *Holocaust and Genocide Studies* 5, no. 1 (January 1, 1990): 23–37.
Gorbatov, A. V. "Gody i voiny." *Novyi mir* no. 3 (1964): 133–56; no. 4 (1964): 99–138; no. 5 (1964): 106–53.
Janjic, Linnea Josefina Lundblad. "Writer or Witness: Problems of Varlam Shalamov's Late Prose and Dramaturgy." PhD diss., University of California, Berkeley, 2017.
Jones, Polly. "The 'Thaw' Goes International. Soviet Literature in Translation and Transit in the 1960s." In *The Socialist Sixties. Crossing Borders in the Second World*, edited by Anne E. Gorsuch and Diane Koenker, 121–47. Bloomington: Indiana University Press, 2013.
Klots, Yasha. "Varlam Shalamov between Tamizdat and the Soviet Writers' Union (1966–1978)." In "Russia—Culture of (Non)Conformity: From the Late Soviet Era to the Present," edited by Klavdia Smola and Mark Lipovetsky, special issue, *Russian Literature* 96–98 (February–May 2018): 137–66.
Kozlov, Denis. *The Readers of Novyi Mir: Coming to Terms with the Stalinist Past*. Cambridge: Harvard University Press, 2013.
Mamuchashvili, Elena. "V bol'nitse dlia zakliuchennykh." In *Shalamovskii sbornik*, 2:78–88. Vologda: Grifon, 1997.
Martin, Terry. "The Origins of Soviet Ethnic Cleansing." *The Journal of Modern History* 70, no. 4 (1998): 813–61.
Pavlenko, Iu. V., Iu. N. Raniuk, and Iu. A. Khramov. *"Delo" UFTI 1935–1938*. Kiev: Feniks, 1998.
Piliar, Iurii. "Liudi ostaiutsia liud'mi." *Iunost'*, no. 6 (1963): 7–37; no. 7 (1963): 25–48; no. 8 (1963): 38–74; no. 3 (1964): 6–29; no. 4 (1964): 40–62; no. 5 (1964): 47–63.
Shalamov, Varlam. "Anna Ivanovna." *Teatr* no. 1 (1989): 3–22.
———. *Kolyma Stories*. Translated by Donald Rayfield. New York: NYRB Classics, 2018.
———. *Novaia kniga. Vospominaniia. Zapisnye knizhki. Perepiska. Sledstvennye dela*. Moscow: Eksmo, 2004.
———. *Sketches of the Criminal World: Further Kolyma Stories*. Translated by Donald Rayfield. New York: NYRB Classics, 2020.
———. *Sobranie sochinenii v shesti tomakh*. Six vols. Moscow: Terra: Knizhnyi klub Knigovek, 2013.
Shalamov.ru (Varlam Shalamov, 1907 g.–1982 g). Accessed June 1, 2021. https://shalamov.ru.
Shelest, Georgii. "Kolymskie Zapisi." *Znamia*, no. 9 (1964): 164–80.
———. "Samorodok." *Izvestiia*, November 5, 1962.
Siddiqi, Asif. "Scientists and Specialists in the Gulag: Life and Death in Stalin's Sharashka." In *The Soviet Gulag: Evidence, Interpretation, and Comparison*, edited by Michael David-Fox, 87–113. Pittsburgh: University of Pittsburgh Press, 2016.

Solzhenitsyn, Aleksandr Isaevich. *The Gulag Archipelago, 1918–1956*. Three vols. New York: Harper and Row, 1974.

———. *The Oak and the Calf: Sketches of Literary Life in the Soviet Union*. Translated by Harry Willetts. New York: HarperCollins, 1980.

———. *One Day in the Life of Ivan Denisovich*. Translated by Eric Bogosian. Reprint edition. New York: Berkley, 2009.

"Soobshchenie Chrezvychainoi gosudarstvennoi komissii." *Pravda*, May 7, 1945.

Taubman, William. *Khrushchev: The Man and His Era*. New York: W. W. Norton, 2003.

Tiurina, G. A, ed. *"Dorogoi Ivan Denisovich!...": Pis'ma chitatelei 1962–1964*. Moscow: Russkii put', 2012.

Toker, Leona. *Return from the Archipelago: Narratives of Gulag Survivors*. Bloomington: Indiana University Press, 2000.

———. "Testimony and Fictionality in Georgy Demidov's Gulag Stories." *Partial Answers: Journal of Literature and the History of Ideas* 17, no. 2 (June 2019): 299–318.

Tolczyk, Dariusz. *See No Evil: Literary Cover-Ups and Discoveries of the Soviet Camp Experience*. Russian Literature and Thought. New Haven, CT: Yale University Press, 1999.

Valentina Georgievna Demidova ob ottse. Last modified February 28, 2016. https://www.youtube.com/watch?v=buUVU5FBVO8&list=WL&index=1.

Young, Sarah J. "Huddling on the Ground: The Most Powerful Writer to Emerge from Stalin's Gulag." *Times Literary Supplement*, June 22, 2018.

———. "Recalling the Dead: Repetition, Identity, and the Witness in Varlam Shalamov's Kolymskie Rasskazy." *Slavic Review* 70, no. 2 (2011): 353–72.

ALAN BARENBERG is the Buena Vista Foundation Associate Professor of History at Texas Tech University. He is author of *Gulag Town, Company Town: Forced Labor and Its Legacy in Vorkuta*.

TWELVE

THE NECROPOLIS OF THE GULAG AS A HISTORICAL-CULTURAL OBJECT

An Overview and Explication of the Problem

IRINA FLIGE, TRANSLATED BY
JOSEPHINE VON ZITZEWITZ

THE TWENTIETH CENTURY BEQUEATHED US a new historical-cultural object—the "Necropolis of the Gulag," which consists of mass burial sites holding the remains of those shot during Soviet state terror, prison and labor camp cemeteries, the cemeteries of deportees and special settlers, and the graves of exiles.[1] I used this concept for the first time in 2004 and began to promote its use soon afterward when the Research and Information Center (RIC) of Memorial, St. Petersburg started cataloguing the burial sites of Soviet terror victims.[2] Those buried in the Necropolis of the Gulag died in captivity—they were executed or murdered or died from cold, hunger, and backbreaking labor. A key characteristic of the Necropolis is anonymity: secret burial sites for those who were killed, nameless graves for those who died, as well as sites that were unrecorded or incompletely recorded, so that we have lost all information about them.

Secret sites include the graves of victims of "judicial" or "quasi-judicial" killings. Practically everything related to capital punishment was kept secret; at one point this included the fact that someone had been sentenced to death. But even when a death sentence was made public, the execution was not public.[3] The method and site of execution remained secret, as did the place of burial. Other secret burial sites include the graves of individuals who died while under investigation as well as unmarked graves in town cemeteries and on special NKVD firing ranges. Mass burial sites that were not secret, but about which no information was recorded, include some special settler cemeteries at transit and distribution points; many burial sites from the war years, such as the mass graves of those conscripted into labor gangs (*trudkolonii*); and the graves of camp inmates who died during epidemics and famines (burials in common graves and trenches). A number of labor camp cemeteries at remote camp outposts and temporary sites also belong to this category, as do the burial sites of prisoners and special settlers who died in transit.

Burial sites about which data was recorded but later lost include labor camp cemeteries and the cemeteries of prisons in which convicts served sentences (as opposed to remand prisons and prisons where the condemned were held prior to execution). Prisoners who died in prison were buried in special cemeteries bordering on ordinary civilian burial places. Camp cemeteries sprang up in the immediate vicinity of all labor camps, always beyond the perimeter of the camp zone. These cemeteries existed for as long as the camp to which they were attached. When a camp closed down, its cemetery was not liquidated. Rather, it became gradually overgrown, and the grave markers decayed and fell to the ground. Where a settlement emerged around a camp, the camp cemetery would gradually fill up with graves of free citizens marked by ordinary gravestones, thus becoming a town or village cemetery; the old numbered graves were not preserved, and new decedents were interred on top of them.

The most numerous cemeteries within the Gulag are those of the so-called special settlers. The way in which peasants as well as national and social groups were exiled was distinct from all other forms of repression in that they were deported as entire families, including underage children and old people. The presence of these age groups drove up mortality rates during transit and during the first months in new settlements. As a rule, those who died during the journey (in railway carriages or at transit points) were buried in mass graves. But even if a family managed to bury their dead independently and place a marker on the grave, they had no opportunity to visit the site for many years, by which time it would have become impossible to find the actual grave. Once the settlers arrived at their designated site, ordinary village cemeteries with individual graves would emerge close to the settlement. However, the mortality of "the first year" or "the first winter" (terms frequently used in memoirs) remained catastrophically high, and people were often buried in common graves. In the years that followed, burial procedures normalized as conditions improved; settlers tried to bury their dead in accordance with family tradition and national rituals. However, for various reasons the cemeteries of special settlers were abandoned, graves were not visited for decades, and so the cemeteries once again acquired the defining characteristics of Gulag burial sites.

We do not have a corpus of statistical data that is complete and precise enough to allow us to determine the exact number of victims of the terror and the Gulag. However, research published in recent decades enables us to approximate the number of people who were executed and died in captivity between late 1917 and the end of the 1950s. At least 1,100,000 people were shot; at least 1,700,000 people died in camps and prisons; and at least 1,200,000 died during deportation and in special settlements. Thus, the underground part of the Necropolis of the Gulag comprises at least 4,000,000 individuals.[4] The main characteristic of the Necropolis of the Gulag is the initial absence, contingency, or transience of its aboveground part along with the substitution of a technical procedure for burial rites.

DEATH AND BURIAL DOCUMENTATION IN CASES OF EXECUTION

We do not have enough information to fully document execution procedures for the entire Soviet period. However, historians and archivists have found individual documents that show the process by which specific death sentences were carried out and how executed individuals were buried, as well as how reports were made confirming that executions had taken place. These sources enable us to reconstruct, with varying degrees of accuracy, execution procedures and the associated document flow in particular periods.

The first normative act known to us that establishes the procedure for burying executed individuals is a special decree of the Supreme Tribunal of the All-Russian Executive Committee [VTsIK] from 1922: "The body of the executed individual is not to be handed over to anyone and is to be committed to [the earth] without any formalities or ritual, fully dressed in the clothes in which they were shot, at the execution site or another uninhabited place and in such a fashion as to disguise the grave."[5] In early 1924, regional prosecutors, tribunal chairmen, and provincial judges received a similar decree from the People's Commissariat of Justice "on the procedure for execution," which stipulated that executions must not be carried out "in public," that the convict's "body must not be handed over," that the sentence "must not be carried out in such a way as to cause unnecessary suffering to the convict," and that "the body must not be stripped of clothing and shoes, etc."[6] The standards set in the decrees of 1922 and 1924 were observed until 1937. Execution protocols from two different regions show how these standards worked in practice:

> We, the undersigned, ... carried out the decision of the Troika of the OGPU Plenipotentiary Representation for the Northern Territory in relation to [a list of nine names follows]:
> ... Who **were shot in the woods** behind Kirul' sloboda **at 23hrs** on 2 March 1931. **The bodies were buried on site.** ...[7]

> Upon arrival at the *domzak* [prison; 1920s usage—translator] it was explained to convict SELIVERSTOV in the presence of the director of the *domzak*... that his petition for an individual amnesty... had been declined and the sentence... was due to be carried out, upon which convict Seliverstov was **transported beyond the town boundaries** and at **21hrs**, after two shots from a revolver of the "Nagan" make were fired into the head of convict Seliverstov, the latter showed no signs of life and his body was **committed to the earth**, and this protocol was compiled.[8]

An execution protocol usually bears the signatures of the officials who were present at the execution: the prison governor, a representative of the judicial or extrajudicial agency that passed sentence, the prosecutor (infrequently), or a doctor (very rarely). Burials were carried out by members of the firing squad, or, alternately, after an execution on NKVD premises, the bodies were handed over to a cemetery director with instructions to bury them. In those cases, an "official memorandum" (*sluzhebnaia zapiska*) recording the transfer of the bodies was filed.[9]

In Leningrad from 1923 onward, bodies were handed over for burial to the morgue of the Obukhov Hospital (today the clinical section of the S. M. Kirov Army Medical College).[10] In Kharkov between August 9, 1937, and March 11, 1938, 6,865 people were buried in the Jewish cemetery on the basis of orders that the UNKVD commander for Kharkov region issued to its director.[11] The mechanisms and practices underlying the mass-scale operations of the Great Terror are well researched; however, we have less information on the flow of documents related to executions and burials. Operational order no. 00447, which launched the so-called mass operations of the Great Terror in July 1937, describes the procedure for executing death sentences in general terms:

> 1. Sentences are to be executed by individuals appointed by the chairmen of troikas, that is, NKVD commissars for the republics or heads of the directorate or regional branches of the NKVD.... 2. Sentences of the first category are to be executed at sites and in accordance with the procedure established by People's Commissars of Internal Affairs, or directors of the administration or regional branches of the NKVD. The time and place of the execution are to be kept strictly confidential at all times. Documents attesting to the execution of the sentence are to be placed in a separate envelope and added to the investigative file of each of the condemned.[12]

As point two of the order indicates, regional branches of the NKVD implemented this procedure in accordance with local conditions. For example, on August 4, 1937, I. P. Popashenko, head of the UNKVD for Kuibyshev region, sent the head of the Ulianovsk town branch of the NKVD instructions that ordered him to equip "a suitable room in the NKVD building" for service "as a special prison cell for executions by shooting" and outlined local procedures for summoning prisoners for execution and for preparing the pits used for their burial. This document noted specifically that executions were to be carried out at night, as was usual for Soviet executions, and emphasized the importance of secrecy: every effort, Popashenko noted, must be made to "ensure the strictest confidentiality regarding the place, time and technical means by which the sentence of capital punishment was carried out" and to disguise the burial site.[13] Similarly, during preparations for an operation, before order no. 00447 was issued, S. N. Mironov (Korol'), UNKVD head for the Western Siberian territory, instructed the heads of the operative sectors as follows:

> Find an execution site and a site for burying the bodies. If this site is located in the woods, you must ensure that the turf is cut beforehand and afterwards used to cover up the site so as to keep the place where the sentence was carried out completely secret—because all these sites can attract counter-revolutionaries and church people who want to display their religious fanaticism. The [regional UNKVD] apparatus must not under any circumstances know either the execution site or the number of individuals executed, they must not know anything at all, because our own apparatus could become the source that spreads such information.[14]

Thus, the procedure for execution and burial remained strictly secret at all times, even if the death sentence itself had been announced publicly. There were standards regulating the execution itself and others for the burial of executed individuals. These standards included the practice of carrying out executions at night and burying the bodies in secret. The choice of execution site depended on local conditions: either in a specially equipped room inside a prison, followed by transportation of the bodies for burial in a cemetery, or in a designated remote location where the bodies were buried on site (in a forest, on a firing range, on the territory of an NKVD dacha, etc.). All those involved in an execution, including NKVD staff, drivers, and guards, had to sign a pledge of secrecy.

A variety of documents were created in connection with executions. As a rule, instructions (*predpisaniia*) were issued by the agency that had passed sentence, signed by one of the senior heads of that agency, and addressed to the individuals responsible for carrying out the sentence. They were printed on official letterhead or blank sheets of paper and had a fairly standardized format. They stated which agency had passed sentence and when, gave the order to execute by shooting, and listed those sentenced, stating their full names, sometimes ages or years and places of birth, and, rarely, the article according to which they had been sentenced to death. Instructions for the executions of large groups after mass-scale operations often did not correspond to this standard form: in some cases, they noted only the number of those condemned and where they were held, but copies of the execution protocols were attached.

Protocols (*akty*) on the execution of orders sometimes appeared as notes on the reverse of the order (or even on the front if the record was relatively short). Alongside the standard formula that the sentence had been carried out, the full version of the report listed the names of those shot while the short version specified only the number of individuals shot. In some cases, there was only a laconic notation: "carried out." The exact date and often also the time of the execution were always noted; sometimes death was ascertained. As a rule, the exact place of the execution was not specified.[15] These reports were signed by those who carried out the execution (for the most part, individuals named in the order) and also by the wardens of NKVD prisons who had witnessed the execution (fairly rarely), representatives of the public prosecutor's office or the statistics departments of the OGPU-NKVD, and, very rarely (and only when sentences were being carried out that they had passed themselves), representatives of a court or tribunal. In the overwhelming majority of cases, no doctors attended, and death was ascertained by representatives of the public prosecutor's office or, if none were present, by members of the firing squad. These reports were sent together with the order to the director of the First Special Section of the UNKVD of the region or territory and also to the Special Archive of the First Special Section of the NKVD of the USSR.

Protocols on the execution of a particular prisoner's sentence were appended to the archival investigation file of the executed individual. Neither my colleagues nor I have found any such protocols in those archival investigation files from the 1920s and early 1930s that we had a chance to view. However, I cannot confirm that no such documents existed during that period. In 1937–38, they were compiled according to a single pattern (regional differences are minor) and in a single copy, on a printed template, completed in typescript or sometimes by hand. They contain the following information: sentence (agency, date), full name of the convict, date the sentence was carried out; sometimes additionally, in both typewritten and handwritten versions, a note indicating who ordered the execution (date, rank, and surname) and, rarely, the time of the execution. The document would be signed by the head of the firing squad (a commander or deputy commander of the NKVD directorate) and certified by a stamp. As a rule, it was added to the archival investigative file in a separate envelope. Sometimes the "protocol" was replaced by documents that were similar in content such as an "excerpt from the protocol" (undated and not certified by a stamp, but often stating the time of the execution) or a "certificate" of the execution of the sentence (dating to the 1950s and probably issued during the rehabilitation process). Both documents sometimes specified where the protocol on the execution of the order was held.

Separate documents relating to burial exist only in cases when the burial was not carried out by the firing squad itself and took place in a civilian cemetery. Such documents include a requisition issued by the commander or individual in charge of the agency that carried out the sentence to the director of the cemetery or crematorium to accept "for immediate burial" (or cremation) a specific number of bodies and a receipt that the order was carried out. Generally, both types of documents are dated and kept together with the relevant orders and the protocols on their execution.

The description I have provided here does not cover the entire period of the Soviet terror. Procedures for execution and burial during the period of the Red Terror (1918–21) were much more varied and are less well documented than those of the later period. This is also true of the extrajudicial executions and burials of the 1920s and early 1930s that were carried out by the Special Purpose Sections (ChON), detachments of the GPU-OGPU, and special branches in those subdivisions of the Red Army that suppressed peasant and national uprisings. Finally, I know little about procedures after 1953.

THE DOCUMENTATION OF DEATH IN CAMPS AND PRISONS

For every individual arrested, a "prisoner's personal file" was opened immediately. From that moment the person turned into a statistical unit of the camp and prison system. Once sentence was passed, the personal file would accompany the convict from the remand prison to the prison camp or prison where they would serve their sentence. A prisoner's death was recorded in the prisoner's personal file (death certificate; certificate attesting to the medical examination of the body; postmortem certificate, if a postmortem was carried out; burial certificate or certificate confirming that the body was handed over to the next of kin; and reports of accidental death were also common) and also on the registration card that was kept inside the prisoner's personal file. In addition, the death was also noted on the registration cards (*kartochka po forme* no. 2) that were maintained on each individual prisoner in the registration indexes of the camp division, the central camp administration, and the Information

Center of the Ministry of Internal Affairs of the USSR. In this way, the death was recorded at every level of the Gulag accounting system, although I am not familiar with the mechanism for recording deaths at higher-ranked agencies. Moreover, I cannot verify whether these records contained falsifications as these card indexes are not accessible to researchers.

The procedure for registering a death is outlined in order no. 00674 of the NKVD of the USSR, dated July 11, 1939 (similar documents existed earlier, too).[16] According to this order, the administration of the relevant camp or prison is to inform the regional registry office of the death of a prisoner—not the registry office local to the Gulag institution in which the death occurred but that of the region where the deceased lived before their arrest (it was only possible to register a death with the local registry office in the absence of information about the prisoner's home address). The order specifies that the record must not contain any signs that the deceased was in captivity. Deaths in camps and prisons "are accounted for in the general report of municipal and regional registry offices," thus becoming part of the overall death statistic of the region where the person was arrested and as such unrecognizable.

In addition, according to the instructions issued on burial procedures, the camps kept "cemetery books" (my expression), which provided basic information regarding the prisoner's circumstances, cause and time of death, the name of the cemetery, and the number of the grave. These books were kept in the administrative section of the camp subdivision; whether they survived and where they were kept after the closure of the camp is unknown. In all the accounts of the discovery of such documents that I have heard, they were found by chance.

In the 1920s and early 1930s, as well as during the war years, a complete set of documents recording the death of a prisoner in their personal file was the exception rather than the rule. In the second half of the 1930s and the years after the war, the personal files of deceased prisoners always contained a full set of "death documents"—that is, a medical certificate, death certificate, burial certificate, and confirmation that a registry record had been made.

Burial procedures for the period of the 1920s–1930s can be reconstructed with the help of the content of certificates and the memories of camp inmates. Deceased prisoners were buried in coffins and in separate graves with wooden tablets featuring the prisoners' names. Figure 12.1 shows the remains of such a camp cemetery with wooden markers that are now unreadable. Apart from the signatories of the burial certificate, burial squads consisting of prisoners who held a special permit that allowed them to leave the camp perimeter conducted burials. Prisoners knew where the cemeteries were located but were, as a rule, unable to visit them.

Figure 12.1. Grave markers at the cemetery of camp subsection 5 in the village of Abez', Komi republic. Photograph by Irina Flige, 2009.

Mikhail Nakonechnyi discovered and published a number of documents from the war period regulating prisoner burials during years of extremely high mortality, when ordinary burial procedures were suspended.[17] These documents—instructions, orders, and clarifications that the Gulag administration published between July 1941 and January 1943—permit burials (a) without coffins, (b) without the bodies being wrapped in sheets, (c) without underwear, and (d) in mass graves; in addition, they instructed that graves be marked by columns bearing numbers.[18] Regardless of the fact that the period concerned is fairly short, precisely these camp burial practices came to dominate the public imagination of death and burial in the Gulag. Moreover, we can use them to infer (by reverse analogy) a certain amount of information about burial procedures during the prewar years.

An instruction issued by the Gulag administration on September 21, 1946, abolished these emergency burial procedures: deceased prisoners were once again buried in coffins and separate graves and no longer left naked.[19] However, the burial procedures of the 1920s–1930s did not resume completely. A certain amount of anonymity remained in the form of numbered graves and numbered cemeteries. The abovementioned "cemetery books" made it theoretically possible to identify a grave with the help of the number on the wooden tablet that was affixed to the column on the grave, as the records in these books included personal information about the person buried and the number of the grave; however, these kinds of documents survived in even smaller numbers than the columns and tablets erected on the graves themselves. On the whole, the existence of such documents was hardly more conducive to the identification of individual graves than affixing to each body (!) "a wooden marker specifying the surname and initials of the prisoner, alongside the number of their personal file"—a measure mandated by the same instruction of the Gulag administration.

In literature and memoirs, we often come across the claim that the number on the wooden tablet on a prisoner's grave corresponded to the prisoner's identification number. This claim is incorrect. The number on the tablet was the number of the burial, corresponding to the number of a grave in the register of a civilian cemetery. And yet this idea is essentially correct: the presence of a number instead of a name on the grave marker implied that in practice the number became associated with the prisoner after death, signifying ultimate depersonalization.

In terms of its content, the set of documents confirming a death in the camp is analogous to the one used in civilian life. However, the Gulag worldview afforded internal record keeping absolute priority. Herein lies the reason for two characteristic peculiarities of Gulag documentation. The first is the careless manner in which the documents were compiled and the incompleteness or even absence of certain information that is important from a human point of view but not essential from the point of view of record keeping. For example, cause and place of death are recorded in those documents that are part of the personal file (and even there they might be absent) but not on the registration cards that were maintained in the camp system's registration indexes. As a rule, the burial certificate, if it exists at all, does not specify the cemetery's location. One of the least reliable records is the date of death. We see an administrative and police-state mindset at work in this: the date marked on the registration card in the registration index, as well as on the registration card in the prisoner's personal file, could well be the date the prisoner was removed from the register as opposed to the date they died. Thus, the record "died on such-and-such date" ought to be read as follows: "removed from the register on such-and-such date, reason for removal: deceased."[20]

The second distinctive characteristic is the dissemination of incomplete or incorrect information about a prisoner's death to other institutions outside the camp system. In addition to documenting deaths internally, the Gulag had to provide information to the "outside world," if only because the death of a person led to certain changes in the civil and legal status of their relatives. G. V. Kuzovkin discovered a number of normative documents relevant to the process of informing relatives of the death of a prisoner in the State Archive of the Russian Federation (GARF). They demonstrate that in the 1930s, it was permitted to inform relatives of the death of an inmate serving their time in prison only at the relatives' request, and not in writing.[21]

DOCUMENTATION OF DEATH IN SPECIAL SETTLEMENTS

According to the provisional regulations on the rights and obligations of special settlers and on the administrative functions of the settlement administration that L. Kogan, the head of the OGPU Camp Administration, signed on October 25, 1931, the registration of acts of civil status was to be carried out according to generally established rules and practices.[22] This standard was applied to all groups of deportees between the 1930s and the early 1950s. However, the information on which registry records were based was provided by staff of the special settler warden's office (*spetskomendatura*) and not by the family of the deceased. Family members were obliged to inform the warden of the settlement of any death. The warden would enter information about the death on the individual's personal and family cards and in their personal file and would also mark the death in the special settler register. Afterward, he would send notice of the death to the registry office; this would trigger the creation of a registry record and a "death certificate." The registry office would send the death certificate to the warden, who would place it into the personal or family file of the special settler. The death certificate was not issued to the family.

The Gulag's record-keeping agencies themselves (the Section for Special Settlers [OSP] of the Gulag; after 1941, the Section for Labor and Special Settlements [OTSP]) recorded only the number of deceased individuals. The reports of the special warden's office were based on the overall number of special settlers, and there were several different columns for recording a decrease in numbers, all of them signifying that a person had been removed from the register: deceased, escaped, transferred to a different warden's office. Researchers compiling statistics on mortality rates among special settlers often come across unreliable data in the accounts. For example, N. Ignatova discovered cases of deliberate falsification of mortality data depending on what kind of data would look best in a given report (the deceased could be passed off as escaped and vice versa).[23] Be that as it may, details about the death of a concrete individual were not passed on to the OSP-OTSP.

Death certificates for special settlers note the deceased's full name, age (or date of birth), date and cause of death, and place of death (precise down to the name of the village council). They were issued by a staff member of the registry section (OAGS) at the time the registry record was made and sent to the warden's office. They were not issued to the deceased's family but were appended to the personal file by the warden. An exception was made for deported Polish citizens in the years 1940–41. It is likely that this exception is linked to the amnesty for all Poles that was issued on August 12, 1941: they presumably received these documents on their release. In any case, death certificates have been preserved in Polish family archives but are missing in the relevant individuals' personal files.[24]

Registry records from registry offices documenting the deaths of special settlers are an important source but unfortunately incomplete and imprecise. Their incompleteness can be explained by the ignorance of the wardens as well as the poor organization of record keeping in general. For example, there are no registry records at all for individuals who died before a family file was opened. In 1933, family members who were not special settlers at the moment in time when the family file was opened were not recorded in it.[25] To the best of my knowledge, no research has been conducted into the degree of incompleteness of registry records, but complaints made by relatives after they were released from administrative oversight show that the registries are incomplete and often feature incorrect death dates.

DOCUMENTATION OF THE DEATH AND BURIAL OF PRISONERS AND SPECIAL SETTLERS WHO DIED IN TRANSIT

Fragmentary sources allow us to reconstruct the procedure for registering the deaths of both prisoners and deportees who perished during transit; however, it is worth noting that this procedure was violated more often than in the case of the registration of the death of individuals who were executed or died in camps and prisons. An instruction by Genrikh Iagoda, vice chairman of the OGPU, dated February 2, 1930, orders the wardens who accompanied the special trains transporting "kulaks" to surrender the bodies of those who died "to the closest agency of the OGPU's territorial branch for burial with appropriate documentation."[26] Analogous orders can be found in the rules regulating the transport of prisoners into the NKVD's corrective labor camps, which came into force on April 29, 1935.[27] The procedure for burying bodies taken off the train and creating the corresponding documentation remains unknown.

The deaths of prisoners and deportees who perished during prisoner transport were recorded in the reports and acts of transfer made by the head of the guard detail once the transport had reached its final destination. As a rule, however, these reports and records contained information about the number of deceased individuals but not their personal data.[28] Individual death records for prisoners and deportees who died during transit were made out in several copies and signed by the head of the special train and/or the head of the guard, and sometimes even by the special train's doctor. One copy of the record was handed over, along with the body, to the administration of the train station where the body was offloaded and was likely used for documenting the burial. The second copy remained with the head of the special train and was, in all likelihood, added to reports related to assuming and transferring custody of those on the transport. The third copy (if the person on the transport was a prisoner) was appended to their personal file.

MEMORY IN THE FAMILIES OF SPECIAL SETTLERS

We do not need to ask whether special settlers knew about the death of a relative. As a rule, families remained together, and the dead were buried by relatives, fellow villagers, and compatriots. What did the funerals look like? Except in cases of death in transit, people usually tried to bury their dead according to their customs. However, during the first winter, when mortality was very high, this was not always possible, as the citations below demonstrate.

> The Rysmukhametov family was deported from Bashkiria together with a one-hundred-year-old grandmother. In the sultry heat she became very weak and eventually died. The Rysmukhametovs hid the body of their dear mother and grandmother under straw so the guards wouldn't see it and force them to throw her into some pit. They managed to take her all the way to Cheremkhovo and bury her like a human being.[29]
>
> According to Muslim tradition, women must not be at the cemetery during the funeral. Our grandfather was buried by strangers. And I could not remember his grave, I could not show it to my grandmother and mama—there were hundreds of identical graves. And so we could not honor tradition and erect a headstone with an epitaph or saying from the Quran.[30]
>
> My sister and I went to take our mama's measurements. She was lying on the floor in the shed, completely naked, stiff. Her hands placed on her chest, her hair shaved off. Next to a man. We took her measurements with a shoelace and my sister took them to her workplace.... They gave her a horse, a sledge,

a coffin and some rope. We went to this morgue in the form of a shed and with some difficulty managed to place mama into the coffin. Under her head we placed a folded towel, then we covered her with a lacy night shirt. And then we nailed the coffin shut as best we could. The coffin consisted of three planks. The fourth plank was the lid. All the planks were raw. The grave was hacked into the frozen ground.... We used the rope to lower the coffin into the grave and covered it with bits of frozen earth. Then we went home. We were glad that we had managed to bury mama.[31]

In the narratives of deportees, a funeral constitutes a family tragedy: to die in alien lands from cold, hunger, and disease is in itself already a catastrophe, but that is not all. The breakdown of traditional burial customs and the impossibility of carrying out the ritual in its entirety are catastrophic, too. This is why details, such as how the coffin was made and how the grave was dug, assume such importance when the death of a family member and the funeral are described. Moreover, every success is underlined; individual ritual and symbolic details such as "we were glad that we had managed to bury mama," "we covered her with a lacy night shirt," and "we made a little flower wreath" traditionally form part of the formula "we buried them well."[32]

After the settlers arrived at the location of settlement and made it through the first harsh winters, their circumstances improved somewhat. Life gradually assumed more or less routine features and death and burial traditional forms; commemorative practices became focused on the local cemetery (grave maintenance, memorial dates). However, the local cemetery could never become home—in the absence of ancestral graves, it remained alien and temporary. Later, these cemeteries would become overgrown and gradually turn into nameless burial sites that were not really different from the mass graves born out of the extreme circumstances of the first winters. This happened to the cemeteries of the peasants exiled in the early 1930s and those of the national groups deported in the 1940s–1950s.

Let us consider the visual evidence—that is, funeral photographs dedicated to the last farewell of family members, neighbors, and compatriots at the open coffin, during the funeral procession at the cemetery, and at the grave. I would suggest that the large number of funeral photographs taken in exile, in spite of limited technical resources, indicates that the death of a loved one in captivity assumed very great significance. According to Nikolaev, in the everyday life of peasants, funeral photos are testimony that a relative was "buried well." What did "burying well" mean for special settlers? Special settlers who had been deported from a village setting stayed within the framework of peasant traditions. City dwellers, on the other hand, often started to return to the roots and ritual

Figure 12.2. The funeral of the child of exiled Soviet ethnic Germans. The child's father, Bertkhol'd Ivan Khristianovich, and other family members surround the coffin. The German-language inscription beneath the photo reads, "Dear parents, good night!" Aktiubinsk, 1957. From the collection of the Omsk Kraevedenie museum.

practices of their ancestors for support and protection; this was a self-protective mechanism. "To bury well" while in exile also signifies the triumph of life and tradition over catastrophic external conditions. And funeral photographs, such as figure 12.2, record this triumph—that is, the victory of the family or clan over terror, violence, and, to some degree, death.

For deported Lithuanians, there was often yet another level of documentation besides photographs taken at the funeral—namely, the "farewell to the graves" photographs they took in Siberia before returning to their homeland. As a rule, these were group photographs taken in the deportee cemetery (see fig. 12.3). Sometimes the ritual of saying farewell to the graves included the erection of a common memorial to "those who did not return"; in those cases, a picture was taken with the memorial in the background.

At the same time, funeral photographs carry an additional message. They are evidence of a catastrophe, and as such they constitute the visual dimension of historical knowledge and serve to actualize memory of the terror. In the photo

Figure 12.3. Deported Lithuanians at the cemetery in the special settlement of Barun (Khortinskii region, Buryatia) to bid farewell to the graves before returning to their homeland. A general monument "to those who did not return" occupies the center of the frame. 1957. From the collection of the LGGRTC the Museum of Occupations and Freedom Fights.

archives of families who returned from exile, funeral and farewell photos are kept in albums (or files or boxes) dedicated to the "Siberian" period in the life of the family. These photographs not only actualized the memory of loved ones who died in captivity but also served as reminders of incomplete funerals. Neither the graves and crosses in a Siberian cemetery nor the funeral photographs were final. They did not mark the completion of the funeral rite but its suspension. In narrative and everyday speech, people would say that these graves "were left behind in alien soil." For Lithuanian deportees, "to bury well" meant "to rebury in our native land"; this opportunity would arise only decades later. When, in the late 1980s, the descendants of those who had died as special settlers began traveling to Siberia to collect the remains of their loved ones for reburial in churchyards at home, photographs of these trips were added to family albums, becoming the ultimate sign of a normalized death. Alongside personal dates, commemorative practices began to include the common national dates of remembrance—that is, the deportation dates. At the same time, the memory of the graves of those who did not return was transformed from a private family memory into a public and national memory: funeral photos were prominently displayed in museum exhibitions.

MEMORY OF THOSE WHO DIED IN THE CAMPS

What did the relatives of an arrested individual know about their fate once they had been led out of the house? What could they know? How did they find out about their loved one's death? During the first years of the Soviet regime, the machinery of terror was not yet running smoothly. The arbitrariness of arrests, sentences, and executions coexisted with the possibility of intercession and personal petitions as well as many different, unregulated contacts with the world outside prison. Moreover, prisoner turnover was high, and those who were released would pass on news to the families of others still under arrest. Alongside fanatical secret service agents, the apparatus of the Cheka included many who had joined the prison administration or service staff more or less accidentally; in the fervor of the revolutionary sense of justice, the Cheka had not yet adopted the practice of making staff sign a pledge of secrecy.

From the mid-1920s, opportunities for receiving unofficial information about the course of the investigation, the sentence, and the transfer to a camp gradually narrowed, and toward the beginning of the Great Terror they disappeared altogether. The only place to receive any information at all was the "hatch" for handing over parcels or the information point. There were more or less regular opportunities for communicating with those who had already been sentenced and sent to various camps; they included letters, parcels, and sometimes meetings. I will not discuss the details of changes in procedure over the years; for my topic, another fact is paramount: when a prisoner died, their family would find out—often with significant delay, but nevertheless—either from a letter written by a fellow prisoner or from the reply to a request filed when correspondence stopped. They were informed of the event of death and even of the cause, and sometimes of certain accompanying circumstances.

As a rule, information about the date of death was distorted in both letters from fellow inmates and official replies. Relatives would know that the deceased was buried in the camp cemetery but not the location of this cemetery. Cases where family members went to visit a grave were exceedingly rare. For example, in June 1928, during a typhoid epidemic, a teacher from Kharkov (sentenced to three years in 1926) died at the Solovetskii Camp's transit point in Kem'. On her grave is a marble headstone with the inscription "Raisa Pankrat'evna Truba. Died 7 June 1928 at the age of 25. Sleep my beloved, my young martyr. Mama."[33] We do not know who told Raisa's mother of her death or how she found her daughter's grave and erected the headstone (see fig. 12.4). In the 1990s, the locals remembered how the old lady would come and visit the grave even after the war; eventually the visits stopped, probably because she had died.

Figure 12.4. The grave of Raisa Pankrat'evna Truba (1902–28) in the cemetery of the Kem' Transfer Point, Solovetskii labor camp, with the monument erected by her mother. Photograph by Lev Krylenkov, 2013.

For the "inhabitants" of the Gulag, the death of a fellow inmate and bunk neighbor was an "abnormal norm" and an event they experienced keenly. It was important to inform their friend's family, to tell them how much the deceased had loved and missed that family, and of course to share their own feeling of loss and loneliness. Letters to the family constituted not only a notification of a death but also a form of obituary. Below I cite, in abbreviated form, one such obituary:

> Vera!
> ... I was very close to Iurii (we slept and ate together and shared our joys and sorrows). Iurii loved you very much and dreamed about being with you and your daughter in the near future.... We, his close friends, lost an exceptionally unselfish companion and irreplaceable friend. This loss is with us every day and every hour. For you, this loss will be all the more hard and painful. But Vera, because of Iurii's immense love for you and your daughter we, his friends and your well-wishers, are firmly convinced that you will endure this blow as staunchly as you have endured, in the name of that very same love, the deprivations and loneliness of the last years.... Allow me

Figure 12.5. Vladas Shimkunas, a former inmate of the Abez' camp, at the grave of Ionas Iuodishius (1892–1950). Camp cemetery in village of Abez', Komi republic. July 1956. From the collection of the LGGRTC the Museum of Occupations and Freedom Fights.

to express my deepest sympathy in the grief that has befallen you.... Over the 2.5 years of talking with Iurii about the past and the future, I started considering his wife and daughter to be my close friends.[34]

We know of cases in which fellow inmates managed to mark the grave of a deceased friend. In July 1956, just after he was released, Vladas Shimkunas, a former political prisoner in Minlag (a "special" camp in Inta, Komi ASSR), took care of the graves of General Ionas Iuodishius and philosopher Lev Karsavin, who had died in the Abez camp for invalids. He dug round the grave mounds and raised them and planted fir trees. Then he had his photo taken next to the grave marked "D-40," in which General Iuodishius lay buried (see fig. 12.5). In

Figure 12.6. Lithuanian inmates and exiles at the funeral of the inmate Vaisnora Vytautas (1920–55). Inta, September 1955. From the collection of the LGGRTC the Museum of Occupations and Freedom Fights.

some cases, groups of former prisoners and exiles were able to gather for the funerals of camp comrades, as was the case when Vaisnora Vytautas was buried in September 1955 in Inta, Komi ASSR (see fig. 12.6).

MEMORY OF EXECUTED INDIVIDUALS

How and what did relatives find out about a death sentence, the execution, and the place of burial? Before the start of the Great Terror, the passing of a death sentence was not secret and sometimes was even announced publicly. The family would be informed that the execution had taken place, albeit orally and without a precise date, and/or from the newspapers. Here is a fragment from the diary of N. S. Tagantsev. The Tagentsev family found out about the execution of several loved ones from the papers a few days after it took place, and they were told the date and approximate site by an unofficial source:

> Thursday, 1 September . . . just now I received the news that they killed both Volodya and Nadya—they shot them.[35]
>
> The execution took place at dawn between 24 and 25 August on the Irinovskaya railway where they buried, or rather dumped, their bodies. It is

likely that we will find out more details, given that a source has been found, who witnessed the execution.³⁶

In the autumn of 1921, Mariya Spiro, a staff member of the Geological Committee, was arrested near the graves of the executed. The Petrograd Cheka sentenced her to six months of imprisonment "for visiting the site where the participants of the 'Petrograd Combat Organisation' [*Petrogradskaia boevaia organizatsiia*] were executed." This burial site continued to be visited. Anna Akhmatova remembered, "My acquaintances had a laundress whose daughter was a prosecutor. She, that is the laundress, told them and even showed them the site, based on her daughter's words. They had gone there immediately and seen earth trampled down by boots. I found out nine years later and went there too."³⁷ Toward the end of the 1980s, knowledge of this place had almost disappeared from memory, but it was recalled, and the site was memorialized in 1997.³⁸

An office memorandum of the Ulyanovsk town branch of the OGPU provides a similar example:

> We have established that the relatives (wife and two daughters) of one of the men we executed ... about 2–3 days after his execution, i.e., 27–30 April [1930], after finding out that he had been shot and coming to the cemetery where sentences are carried out, bribed the guard and established the location of the grave where Milkov and two others were buried and with the help of the same guard opened the grave, removed the body of the executed Milkov and placed him into a new grave they had dug themselves in that same cemetery and placed a cross on it....
>
> Under interrogation the guard ... stated that information about executions and execution sites is allegedly passed on by a certain woman who lives in the courtyard of the *domzak*, and that afterwards they contact him with the request to show them the grave of a certain executed person or other, and that this has happened several times.... He explained that he determined the location of the grave where the body of the executed Milkov was buried based on the date of the execution given to Milkov's family.... For this, the cemetery guard received 30 rubles from Milkov's family.³⁹

Such examples were exceptional, though more could be cited. What do these exceptions tell us? They tell of love, of courage, of the natural human need to bury a loved one, but that is not all—they tell us that the secrecy of burial sites was relative and that people knew about these sites.

Things are different when it comes to the memory of those who were shot during the Great Terror. The fate of those executed during the mass-scale operations of the NKVD remained unknown for decades. Relatives received the reply "not on our lists" and later, from the end of 1937, oral information amounting to "sentenced to 10 years imprisonment without the right to correspondence." And from this moment, the individual would disappear forever. For the family, this disappearance was already like a death, but a death unknown, without a date, place, body, funeral, or grave. From the fall of 1945, the usual reply to inquiries by the family was that their husband, son, brother, or father had died in the camp from tuberculosis, a stroke, or pneumonia. If relatives insisted on an official document, they were issued a fake death certificate. In 1955, this practice was confirmed by a special directive.[40] From the early 1960s, it was permitted to orally inform the family that their relative had been shot—but only if the file contained no earlier inquiries that had led to the family being issued fake documents.[41] Truthful information about the fate of those individuals about whom lies had been spread became officially available only in 1988.[42] Whenever a new instruction appeared, changes were made to the previous record—the date and cause of death changed, and the family was issued a new death certificate.

WITNESS STATEMENTS ABOUT BURIALS

The testimony of people who accidentally saw burial sites became publicly known only in the late 1980s. But long before that, those accidental witnesses, silent or whispering, had a decisive impact on ideas about the Necropolis of the Gulag. Here are two examples of witness testimony:

> I remember, we went there. . . . We went back and told our father: we found dead people there, buried. You can see their heads. They took shovels, went to dig them up, to see what is there. . . . The guard made a phone call. . . . The answer was: "Get out of there, never set foot there again. If not, you'll end up there yourselves." After that everyone became afraid, they had been warned. . . .[43]
>
> The following image stood before our eyes: tire tracks that stopped about three meters away from a black rectangle, filled up to edge, and there was loose earth all around. Fear gripped us all. . . . I have no recollection at all how and by which way we retreated back then, whether we ran into the woods or home.[44]

These testimonies, which accumulated terrible details during subsequent retellings, encouraged the emergence of a mythologized idea of a "terrible place": a place you must not visit, about which you must not talk (and if somebody talked regardless, they would warn, "Don't go there, don't talk about it"). Later, the tale of the "terrible place" would be supplemented with stories about how people who had gone there and talked about it disappeared. Naturally, the mythological consciousness of the twentieth century was confused. Unlike the traditional folkloric consciousness, it did not distinguish between *terrible, bad, spellbound,* and *cursed.* Yet even in this form, the laws of folkloric consciousness contributed to the depersonalization of the victims and fostered the absolute conviction that it was forbidden to look for these places.

At the same time, the idea of the "terrible place" coexisted peacefully with the domestication of human remains and the disappearance of taboos surrounding death. If people found a burial site when digging up a garden, building a house, or laying a road or pipes, the uncovered graves were not marked, and the bones were thrown away like rubbish. "We discovered a special zone but established what it contained only once we began planting potatoes there and then rooted out the shrubs to make space for Kolkhoz fields. The soil was full of bones."[45]

"I worked in the Vologda region, in a planning group.... We saw skulls with round holes in them. This sand, with the bones and remains in it, was used to fill up the hollows in the wall of lock No 5."[46] At first glance, in terms of their culture, these stories seem to contradict the first group of testimonies and reveal emotional and psychological callousness and a lack of respect for human remains, testifying to everyday vandalism and dehumanization on a mass scale. However, there is no contradiction. In both cases the burials did not fall under the concept of a sacred, protected space, such as a cemetery, and the result is either revulsion (fear) or devaluation (rubbish).

Gradually, the formula "this town was built on bones" (and the variation "under every railway tie here") entered everyday speech, demonstrating not only how people rejected knowledge about Gulag burials but also referring us, via a rhetorical turn of phrase, to an absolutizing mythologeme, which replaces the proscription of knowledge about the graves of Gulag victims with a statement that these graves do not exist. In the practice of remembrance, all these formulas—"the terrible place," "useless rubbish," and "the city built on bones"—coalesced into a categorical rejection of the memory of a given place, of emotional experience, of responsibility, and, of course, of the personification of the victims.

Families and loved ones who had accepted the absence of a grave for their loved one ("he vanished in the camps") were gradually prompted by their memory of those they had lost to erect cenotaphs in ordinary town cemeteries, beginning in the late 1950s and early 1960s. As a rule, children would erect such a cenotaph to their executed father (more rarely, a father who died in the camps) after the death and funeral of their mother. The gravestone would feature two names, that of the father as well as the mother; thus, a traditional family grave was created. Later, these children would take their own children and grandchildren to the cemetery to commemorate their grandparents; when they died, they were buried there themselves. Such a "funeral" for the father brought a chapter of family history to a conclusion. However, such a materialization of individual memory by way of normalizing a traumatic death also entailed a rejection of the memory of the terror and the Gulag, and in any case a rejection of publicity. Here's an example:

> When my mama died [1984], I felt a strong urge to find my father's grave and bring some soil to my mother's grave. My parents were Orthodox believers and so am I. So, the question was: "Can I place soil from father's grave into my mother's grave and have a headstone made in both their names?" . . .
> But, of course, there is no grave; he died from typhus in 1929 [in the camp]. The priest explained to me that even if I brought soil from a garden in Kem' this would mean the same as if it came from the grave. . . . The headstone is engraved with the names of my mother and father. I have done my duty.⁴⁷

CONCLUSION

In its triune form that includes memory below the ground, memory above the ground, and ceremonial memory, the Necropolis of the Gulag represents the cross contamination of the actions of three groups of actors: the creators of the Necropolis (the "executioners," as common interpretation would have it), those who remember, and the witnesses. They pursue paradoxical intentions that are fundamentally opposed, such as hide versus find, ignore versus commit to memory and mark, and fear versus remember, and this created the common sociocultural perception that these victims had no graves.

Toward the end of the Soviet period, a holistic conception of the Necropolis of the Gulag as a sociocultural object took shape based on three separate, traumatic topics: the executions during the Great Terror, mass-scale death of special settlers during the "first winter," and mass-scale death in the camps during the war years. These generalized concepts gave birth to turns of phrase that are striking because they leave time, circumstances, and location undefined: "they took him away," "he vanished in the Gulag," "he did not come back from the Solovky/Vorkuta/Kolyma," and "he remained in Siberia."

There is no scope in this chapter for a detailed history of the search for mass burial sites in the late 1980s and the 1990s, a description of new forms by which memory is materialized, or the ceremonies and commemorative practices for the Gulag victims that have become established. There is only one thing I want to add: the impulse, at the very end of the 1980s, to actualize the memory of the executed as well as search for their graves was the moment when the families received truthful information about the date sentence was passed and the date of death (but not about the execution or burial site). These notifications and new death certificates actualized the deaths not just of those who were executed but of all those who died in captivity, although the memory of the victims of the Great Terror remained dominant. The new information was experienced as a new death and thus demanded a funeral. People gathered for thousands of rallies, demanding the opening of the Cheka-OGPU-NKVD-KGB archives and carrying placards reading "Where are the graves of our fathers?!" The search for burial sites assumed postcatastrophic significance that found expression in the formula "to bury them like human beings" (a transformed variation of the traditional formula "to bury well"). When, after the first post-Soviet decade, the archives were still not opened and most graves not found, with those that were found largely speculative, the Necropolis of the Terror returned to its basic state: unknown burials of unknown victims.

NOTES

This article provides a preview of my current book project. I thank my colleagues, A. Daniel, T. Morgacheva, O. Nikoleav, M. Rogachev, and N. Sokolov for their support.

1. The terminology used for deportees and the settlements where they were forced to reside varied over time: between 1930 and 1934 and after 1944, they were called *special settlers* or *special resettlers* (*spetsposelentsy, spetspereselentsy*) and their localities *special settlements* (*spetsposeleniia* or *spetsposelki*); between 1934 and 1944, they were called *labor settlers* (*trudposelentsy*) and their localities *labor settlements* (*trudposeleniia* or *trudposelki*). Throughout this chapter, I use the terminology of the first period for all periods.

2. See the Necropolis section of the "Virtual Museum of the Gulag" and "Map of Memory."

3. Executions based on sentences passed by military tribunals in the regular army during the war years and public hangings under the Decree of April 19, 1943, constitute exceptions.

4. Bezborodov, Bezborodova, and Khrustalev, introduction to *Naselenie Gulaga*, 50–56; Zemskov, *Spetsposelentsy v SSSR*, 280–81. This figure does not include those who died in the NKVD's special camps for POWs, internees and Soviet soldiers in "filtration" camps, or those who died in the camps of the Main Administration for the Affairs of POWs and Internees (GUPVI).

5. Telpliakov, *Protsedura*, 6.
6. Krylenko, "Tsirkuliar o rasstrelakh."
7. Poleshchikov, *Za sem'iu pechatiami*, 31–32.
8. Protocol [akt] dated March 23, 1931. Upravlenie gosudarstvennoi arkhivnoi sluzhby.
9. See, for example, Tikhonova, *Rasstrel'nye spiski. Vyp.1*, 201–3.
10. Vinogradov and Lukin, *Bol'shoi terror*, 1:49–50.
11. See the letter from the director of the UKGB for Kharkov region, N. G. Gibadulov, to the chairman of the KGB of the Ukrainian Soviet Socialist Republic, N. M. Golushko, dated August 19, 1989.
12. Khaustov, Naumov, and Plotnikova, *Lubianka*, 273–81.
13. Zolotov, *Kniga pamiati*, 797–98.
14. Uimanov, *Bol' liudskaia*, 5:110–11.
15. Protocols from Karelia and Western Siberian territory, which list the closest inhabited location in almost all cases, represent exceptions.
16. Kokurin, Petrov, and Shostakovskii, *GULAG*, 115–16.
17. GARF f. R-9414, op.1, d. 2762, ll. 190–190ob.; GARF f. R-9414, op. 1, d. 2785, ll. 18–19.
18. Erofeev, "Osobstroi-Bezymianlag."
19. Bezborodov, Bezborodova, and V. M. Khrustalev, eds., *Naselenie Gulaga*, 534–35.
20. Flige, "Gulag kak sozdatel' biograficheskogo istochnika."
21. Kuzovkin, "Prinuzhdenie k ischeznoveniu," 116–30.
22. Danilov and Krasil'nikov, *Spetspereselentsy v Zapadnoi Sibiri*, 74.
23. Ignatova, "Smertnost' spetspereselentsev," 48.
24. Kobryn and Kobryn, *Wspomnienia Sybirakow*, 102; Kobryn and Kobryn, *Wspomnienia Sybirakow. Czesc 2*, 37
25. Krasil'nikov, Salamatova, and Ushakova, *Korni ili shchepki*, 34–42.
26. Kishkin, "Instruktstiia."
27. OGA SBU f.9, d. 4-sp (provided by S. B. Prudovskii).
28. See, for example, Guri'ianov, *Repressii protiv poliakov*, 114–36.
29. Gabidullina, "Tun Seber erende," 4–5.
30. Amit, "Nikto ne zabyt," 3:88.
31. Kalsnava, 1:883.
32. The expression "to bury well" (*pokhoronit' khorosho*), which is common in narratives about burial according to the peasant tradition, was introduced into academic language by O. P. Nikolaev, "Traditsionnye formuly."

33. Truba's registration card lists her death date as June 9, 1928; in her personal file there are several records that give conflicting dates. I am sure that her mother ascertained the real date of death and inscribed it on the memorial. Arkhiv ITs MVD Respubliki Kareliia. Uchetnaia kartoteka.

34. Prilipp, Letter to V. Levanda.

35. On September 1, 1921, *Petrogradskaia Pravda* published a list of those executed in connection with the case of the Petrograd Combat Organization. V. N. Tagantsev, geographer, professor. His wife, N. F. Tagantseva, doctor.

36. Tagantsev, "Dnevnik," 146.
37. Chukovskaia, "Zapiski ob Anne Akhmatovoi," 46–47.
38. Iofe, "Pervaia krov'," 128–37.
39. Zolotov, *Kniga pamiati*, 758.
40. Artizov, *Reabilitatsiia*, 1:254–55.
41. Artizov, 2:417–19.
42. Artizov, 3:117.
43. Pelgagen, interview.
44. Verzhbitskaia, "Iz vospominanii."
45. Mikheeva, "Byvshii poselok NKVD."
46. Volkov, recording.
47. Vasil'eva, "U ottsa."

BIBLIOGRAPHY

Amit, E. "Nikto ne zabyt, nichto ne zabyto: Vospominaniia." In *Tak eto bylo: Natsional'nye repressii v SSSR, 1919–1952 gody: в 3 t.*, edited by Svetlana Alieva, vol. 3, 74–120. Moscow: Insan, 1993.

Artizov, Andrei. *Reabilitatsiia—kak eto bylo: Dokumenty Prezidiuma TsK KPSS i drugie materialy*. 3 vol. Moscow: Mezhdunarodnyi fond "Demokratiia," 2000–2004.

Bezborodov, A. B., I. V. Bezborodova, and V. M. Khrustalev, eds. *Istoriia Stalinskogo Gulaga*. Vol. 4, *Naselenie Gulaga: Chislennost' i usloviia soderzhaniia*. Moscow: ROSSPEN, 2004.

Chukovskaia, L. "Zapiski ob Anne Akhmatovoi. T. 2. 1952–1962." *Neva* no. 9 (1993): 6–122.

Danilov, V. P., and S. A. Krasil'nikov. *Spetspereselentsy v Zapadnoi Sibiri, vesna 1931—Nachalo 1933 goda*. Novosibirsk: Ekor, 1993.

Erofeev, Valerii. "Osobstroi-Bezymianlag." Accessed June 1, 2021. https://goo.gl/kKYQ5k.

Flige, Irina. "Gulag kak sozdatel' biograficheskogo istochnika. Biografii Gulaga: Norma i marginal'nost'." In *Pravo na imia. Materialy Vtorykh chtenii pamiati Veniamina Iofe*, 84–108. St. Petersburg: NITs Memorial, 2005.

Gabidullina, F. "Tun Seber erende zaldy enkesemden kebere." *Kyzyl tan.* no. 27 (2006): 4–5. Quoted in Allamuratova, L. Kh., and F. M. Suleimanov. "Raskulachennye krest'iane Baimakskogo raiona v spetsposelenii Cheremkhovo Irkutskoi oblasti." In *Nauchnye doklady regional'noi konferentsii "Nedelia nauki-2009,"* 159–62. Ufa: RITs BashGU, 2009.

Gibadulov, N. G. Letter to N. M. Golushko, August 19, 1989. Published by Allinn777 (K. Boguslavskii) under the title "KGB USSR o mestakh zakhoroneniia zhertv repressii v Khar'kove." LiveJournal. Arkhivnoe. Accessed March 3, 2021. http://allin777.livejournal.com/367308.html (site discontinued).

Guri'ianov, A. E. *Repressii protiv poliakov i pol'lskikh grazhdan.* Moscow: Zven'ia, 1997.

Ignatova, N. M. "Smertnost' spetspereselentsev v Severnom krae v 1930-e gody: Prichiny, masshtab, statisticheskii uchet." *Novyi istoricheskii vestnik* no. 2 (2011): 42–52.

Iofe, V. V. "Pervaia krov': Petrograd, 1918–1921." In *Granitsy smysla: Stat'i, vstupleniia, esse,* 128–37. St. Petersburg: Memorial, 2002.

Kalsnava, Anustra (Penka). In *Deti Sibiri: My dolzhny byli ob etom rasskazat'....* 2 vols. Edited by Dzintra Geka and Aivars Lubanietis, 1:883–85. Riga: Fonds Sibirijas berni, 2014.

Khaustov, V. N., V. P. Naumov, and N. S. Plotnikova. *Lubianka. Stalin i Glavnoe upravlenie gosbezopasnosti NKVD. 1937–1938.* Moscow: Mezhdunarodnyi fond "Demokratiia," 2004.

Kishkin. "Instruktsiia Komendantam po soprovozhdeniiu eshelonov pri perevozke krest'ian-kulakov i ikh semei." Published by Corporatelie (Mikhail Nakonechnyi). Accessed June 1, 2021. https://corporatelie.livejournal.com/128938.html. GARF, f. R- 9414, op.1, d. 1944, ll. 51–60.

Kobryn, Jerzy and Janusz Kobryn. *Wspomnienia Sybirakow: zbior tekstow zrodlowych.* Bystrzyca Klodzka: Ko-lo Zwiazku Sybirakow, 2008

———. *Wspomnienia Sybirakow: zbior tekstow zrodlowych.* Cz 2. Bystrzyca Klodzka: Ko-lo Zwiazku Sybirakow, 2010.

Kokurin, A. I., N. V. Petrov, and V. N. Shostakovskii. *GULAG (Glavnoe upravlenie lagerei). 1918–1960.* Moscow: Mezhdunarodnyi fond "Demokratiia," 2002.

Krasil'nikov, S. A., M. S. Salamatova, and S. N. Ushakova. *Korni ili shchepki. Krest'ianskaia sem'ia na spetsposelenii v Zapadnoi Sibiri v 1930-kh–nachale 1950-kh gg.* Moscow: ROSSPEN, 2010.

Krylenko. "Tsirkuliar o rasstrelakh. 1924 g." Published by Allinn777 (K. Boguslavskii). LiveJournal. Arkhivnoe. Accessed August 28, 2020. https://allin777.livejournal.com/321485.html (site discontinued). GATO, f. R-224, op. 4, d. 40, l. 46.

Kuzovkin, G. V. "Prinuzhdenie k ischeznoveniiu: Po materialam vedomstvennykh instruktsii NKVD-MVD (1930–1950-e)." In *Pravo na imia. Materialy Vtorykh chtenii pamiati Veniamina Iofe,* 116–30. St. Petersburg: Memorial, 2005.

"Map of Memory." Accessed on June 1, 2021. https://mapofmemory.org.

Mikheeva, S. "Byvshii poselok NKVD prevrashchaetsia v "dolinu nishchikh." SM Nomer odin (Irkutsk). February 13, 2006. http://babr24.com/irk/?IDE=27843.

Nikolaev, O. P. "Traditsionnye formuly krest'ianskoi kul'tury na slome epokh." *Problemy, filologii, kul'tury* (2012): 358–70.

Pelgagen, D. D. Interview recorded by Tatiana Kosinova. St. Petersburg, 1997. Archive of the RIC "Memorial."

Poleshchikov, V. M. *Za sem'iu pechatiami. Iz arkhiva KGB*. Syktyvkar: Komi knizhnoe izdatel'stvo, 1995.

Prilipp, P. I. Letter to V. Levanda. Magadan oblast', Iagodinskii region, Spornyi settlement, July 31, 1940. Personal archive of Iu. M. Virovets.

Tagantsev, N. S. "Dnevnik, 1920–1921." *Zvezda*. no. 9 (1998): 130–57.

Telpliakov, A. G. *Protsedura: Ispolnenie smertnykh prigovorov v 1920–1930-kh godakh*. Moscow: Vozvrashchenie, 2007.

Tikhonova, V. *Rasstrel'nye spiski. Vyp. 1. Donskoe kladbishche, 1934–1940*. Moscow: Memorial, 1993.

Uimanov, V. N., ed. *Bol' liudskaia*: Kniga pamiati tomichei, repressirovannykh v 30–40-e i nachale 50-kh godov. 5 vol. Tomsk: Izdatel'stvo Tomskogo universiteta, 1999.

Upravlenie gosudarstvennoi arkhivnoi sluzhby Samarskoi oblasti. "Vystavka k 100-letiiu Gosudarstvennoi arkhivnoi sluzhby Samarskoi oblasti." Akt. March 23, 1931. http://www.regsamarh.ru/info_act/exhibitions/100letie_arhivnoi/PlotiRepressii/.

Vasil'eva, T. P. "U ottsa na mogile." Archive of the RIC "Memorial." Donated in 1994–95.

Verzhbitskaia, G. D. "Iz vospominanii." Martirolog Minusinskogo raiona. December 3–4, 2008. http://xn--80agomcobmbs.xn----8sbahmlpvellwoag7lzb.xn--p1ai/?mode=intro-memories.

Vinogradov, O., and E. Lukin. *Bol'shoi terror v Leningrade/Leningradskii martirolog: 1937–1938*. Vol. 1. St. Petersburg: Rossiiskaia natsional'naia biblioteka,1995.

"Virtual Museum of the Gulag." Accessed June 1, 2021. http://www.gulagmuseum.org.

Volkov, K. G. Recording of his memories. St. Petersburg, 2005. Archive of the RIC "Memorial."

Zemskov, V. N. *Spetsposelentsy v SSSR, 1930–1960*. Moscow: Nauka, 2003.

Zolotov, Iu. M. *Kniga pamiati zhertv politicheskikh repressii: Rossiiskaia Federatsiia, Ul'ianovskaia oblast'*. Ulianovsk: Dom pechati, 1996.

IRINA ANATOLIEVNA FLIGE graduated from Leningrad State University in 1988 with a specialization in historical geography. She began working with the

Memorial movement in 1988 and has been Director of the Academic-Information Center of Memorial since 2002. She has written more than forty academic works on the history of the Gulag and the culture of memory.

JOSEPHINE VON ZITZEWITZ is the Marie Sklodowska Curie Fellow at UiT The Arctic University of Norway, Tromso. She is author of *Poetry and the Leningrad Religious-Philosophical Seminar 1976–1980: Music for a Deaf Age* and *The Culture of Samizdat: Literature and Underground Networks in the Late Soviet Union*.

THIRTEEN

SITES AND SOUNDS OF THE CAMPS

Commentary on the "Legacies" Section

ALEXANDER ETKIND

RESPONDING TO THE COMPLEXITY OF the Gulag as a political institution and cultural phenomenon, these three essays present vastly different perspectives. Irina Flige demonstrates the scale of the internal empire of the camps and the process of its displacement from cultural memory. Though much lower than the inflated numbers produced by Solzhenitsyn and other authors of the Cold War era, Flige's count of the victims is still enormous. Her simple but eloquent classification of the memorial phenomena as under- and above-the-ground helps us visualize the dynamics of remembrance and forgetting. In regard to this, all cultural phenomena are inherently political, though the opposite was not true. While I am writing, the person who did more than anyone else to uncover the underground—buried, displaced, forgotten—dimension of the Gulag, the lay archeologist, historian, and sculptor Yuri Dmitriev from Petrozavodsk, is waiting his fate in prison in northern Russia. In his case, the criminal police, high court, and other state bodies have combined forces to suppress the memory of the Gulag and its victims. The fight to remember the victims and perpetrators of the Gulag seems long if one dates the beginning of this struggle to Nikita Khrushchev's revelations about the Gulag in 1956. Dmitriev's case demonstrates that this fight is not over. This is a fight in which every effort counts—scholarly, cultural, and memorial; and this volume also contributes to the fight.

Flige introduces a helpful concept of the Necropolis of the Gulag. It is appropriately broad—much wider than the sites of memory, or even their imaginary sum if such a thing exists, because many of these sites of death and burial have not been remembered, and it only partially overlaps with cemeteries because many of the Gulag dead were buried in the woods or along the railroads or else were not buried at all. These dead have left two sets of traces—physical ones such as skulls and bones found nowadays in the dirt and symbolic ones such as names of the victims found in the archives. Again, these two sets of traces overlap only partially, and it takes a tremendous effort to match them. In painstaking detail, Flige depicts the typical life processes of the Gulag Necropolis—protocols of execution, burial, disappearance of the remains because of their decomposition, destruction of the grave markers or displacement of the dead by new corpses. She documents the consistent efforts undertaken by the NKVD, the KGB, and the FSB authorities to conceal the specific sites of the Necropolis, physically by hiding or destroying them, or symbolically by presenting them as burial sites of civil persons or victims of war. She also lists the approved procedures that the perpetrators used for concealing or distorting the identity of the victim. Only from the early 1960s did the Soviet government permit its clerks to orally inform the family of the victim that their relative had been shot, and only if the file contained no earlier inquiries that had led to the family being issued fake documents. Even when the state acknowledged the horrible crime of the state-supported execution of an innocent victim, it was still concerned about the bureaucratic consistency of its false records.

The scale of the Gulag contrasted with its futility. Economic historians have reached a rare consensus: with some exceptions that are usually connected to rare metals or other raw materials for Stalin's military industries, everything that the camps actually delivered could have been produced with lower costs, lower death rates, and fewer personnel by using free labor. This includes the skyscrapers in Moscow, the highways of Kolyma, the canals in Karelia, and the coal mines in the Southern Urals. Moreover, much of what the Gulag made was, like the White Sea Canal (*Belomorkanal*), not needed and of minimal value. The system worked as if its main purpose was to fill up its "underground part" (Flige) and creating things aboveground was of secondary importance.

In his revealing essay, Alan Barenberg brings to the fore Georgii Demidov, a survivor of the Gulag and a multitalented physicist, engineer, and writer. Forgotten now, Demidov was a friend and correspondent of the much better-known Varlam Shalamov, and Barenberg's work focuses on their changing relationship. Already in 1946, Demidov compared the Nazi and Soviet camps. As Harriet Murav recently demonstrated, Soviet intellectuals learned about the Holocaust, and trusted what they learned, earlier than their American counterparts.[1] Developing the same comparison in 1950, Hannah Arendt wrote about the antiutilitarian character of both Nazi and Soviet labor camps. Speaking about this kind of system, she noted that from a commonsense point of view, "neither the institution itself . . . nor its political role makes any sense whatsoever." It was "the complete senselessness" of the camps that surprised Arendt. Solving the puzzle, Arendt described the camps as "laboratories in the experiment of total domination," which could be achieved only in a "human-made hell."[2] Subjecting the documents written by the survivors of this hell to a close and compassionate reading, Barenberg's essay reveals the emotionally charged atmosphere of the post-Gulag era, with accidental meetings between the former colleagues in suffering, or between them and their torturers, becoming a routine of life. What Barenberg calls "a hierarchy of suffering" was a sort of constructed ladder or pyramid that gave priority in witnessing to those who had suffered more and offered some mutually recognized ways of verifying the quality of this suffering. This is a peculiar phenomenon that, I guess, is typical for many postcatastrophic situations of memory.

In *Warped Mourning*, I summarized the main point of Arendt's argument in the following terms: it was not the logic of production that organized life and work in the Gulag but the logic of torture. Hunger, hard labor, untreated illnesses, freezing temperatures, separation from families, isolation from the world, and vulnerability to violent attacks by fellow inmates combined to cause overwhelming pain.[3] Causing this pain was the purpose of the institution and not a collateral effect or unforeseen consequence. In her classic analysis of torture, Elaine Scarry defines the practice as consisting of acts "in which pain destroys a person's world." Pain, Scarry argues, has a unique ability to destroy language by degrading speech to the sounds anterior to language and thereby eliminating a person's world as it is expressed and contained in speech. If pain destroys the sufferer's world, torture adds an additional element: it expands the torturer's self and their self-perceived power. "The torturer's growing sense of self is carried outward on the prisoner's swelling pain."[4]

Indeed, suppression of the survivors' speech and victims' memory—of all traces of the former camps that remain above the ground, to use the dichotomy established in Flige's chapter—was an essential task of the Gulag system. But in fact, the system failed, and many survivors kept their voices or could speak out even more strongly after serving their terms. As Josephine von Zitzewitz notes in her chapter for this volume, "Lyric poetry born out of the camp experience can be read as a courageous act of resistance." Indeed, Gulag survivors demonstrated both the need and the ability to use poetry and other genres of high culture to memorialize their experiences. Surviving Soviet camps and prisons shaped professional historians such as Dmitrii Likhachev and, two generations later, Arsenii Roginskii; novelists and lay historians such as Aleksander Solzhenitsyn and Andrei Siniavsky; visual artists such as Boris Sveshnikov and Ernst Neizvestny; and poets such as Nikolai Zabolotsky. It is through their eyes and ears that we see the colors of the Gulag and hear the debates among the prisoners. Arguably, the most important among all those figures was Varlam Shalamov; his impact on the cultural memory of later generations has been crucial.

A "goner" who was saved by a camp doctor and became a paramedic, Shalamov described his peers as semicorpses whose suffering from hunger and humiliation deprived them of any decency or hope. While Solzhenitsyn presented his experience of survival as a moral lesson for mankind, Shalamov denied any value in the Gulag experience. Individual survival could be a matter of luck, or it could be earned by means of tricks or denunciations; for Shalamov, the vanity of survival was as absurd as the whole Gulag system. Terror had no positive meaning or function; the assertion of any such function bordered on justifying the senseless suffering. Shalamov did not buy Solzhenitsyn's appreciation of the survival skills of his protagonist, Ivan Denisovich, nor did Shalamov believe in any attempt at rational justification on economic or political grounds—for example, of the system that he called "senseless." Shalamov's readers did not appreciate this radical position, which underscored the author's rejection of the moralism and teleology of the late Soviet intelligentsia. Shalamov's intellectual roots were unusual: his father, Tikhon Shalamov, was a missionary of the Russian Orthodox Church in Alaska (1893–1904) who later became an activist involved in a large-scale church reform.[5] Tikhon Shalamov had unique experience with and strong opinions on everything from the most distant outpost of Russia's external colonization to the most sensitive aspect of the country's internal governance; probably, his influence on his only son was decisive. Born in 1907, a few years after Tikhon completed his service on the Aleut Islands and moved to provincial Vologda, Varlam grew up in an atmosphere permeated by colonial memories, religious debates, and revolutionary prophecies. Such was the background for Shalamov's radical take on resistance, meaning, and senselessness.[6]

Theoretically, nothing was more foreign to Shalamov than glorifying survival. The system was senseless, and the outcome that it was producing, suffering, had no meaning or use. In practice, however, resistance to the system was important to Shalamov, and collaboration with it would also define a person. The system was senseless, but surviving it secured dignity, developed virtue, and required gratitude. Betraying his stoic—or existentialist—principle of "senselessness," Shalamov tended to evaluate others on the relentless scale of survival. Revealed in the correspondence between Shalamov and Demidov as well as in the better-known polemic between Shalamov and Solzhenitsyn, this snobbery caused many conflicts in the narrowing circle of Gulag survivors.

Demidov hated Shalamov's yardstick for measuring their relative suffering, though he did not see that it contradicted the basic premises of Shalamov's prose.

In fact, after Stalin's death and the collapse of the Gulag, being a survivor became a prestigious asset, at least in intellectual circles. A graduate student of history in the late 1950s, Liudmila Alexeyeva described her "company" at the time—a group of friends that included recent returnees from the camps and future writers, bards, and human-rights activists. In the next decade, some of these people went on to become cultural stars and some political prisoners.[7] Two young and ambitious authors, Yuly Daniel and Siniavsky, both of whom, as it would later turn out, were smuggling their works abroad at the time, were at the center of this network. Siniavsky's student, Vladimir Vysotsky, entertained their mutual friends by singing camp songs, some of them authentic: "Vysotsky did not compose his own songs at that time. He sang old camp songs ... but he sang them in such a way, slow and passionate, that they felt new and tragic, like those songs that he would compose in the future."[8] Using first-person narration and singing in the low, hypermasculine voice of a convict and drunkard, Vysotsky inserted into his songs references to the geography of the Gulag and a recognizable aesthetics of this folkish genre. It was a time when the intelligentsia was preoccupied with the victims of the Soviet system and longed for art that would express this preoccupation. In early songs such as "Not Everyone Was Admitted to Our Circle" (*V nash tesnyi krug ne kazhdyi popadal*, 1964), Vysotsky told the story of a victim whose friend had turned out to be an informer. Now in a prison or camp, the narrator was contemplating revenge.[9] In 1977, a group that included Vysotsky, the star poet Yevgeny Yevtushenko, and several scientists went on a guided tour through the ruins of the Kolyma camps. In a veritable pilgrimage, they visited a makeshift camp cemetery where wooden boards bearing the personal identification numbers of the dead convicts written in indelible pencil marked the graves spreading over the permafrost to the horizon. Yevtushenko took one of these boards as a souvenir and kept it on his desk in his house near Moscow. Vysotsky wrote several songs about Kolyma. His plans to make a film about the camps never came to fruition, but he did coauthor a novel about them, *The Black Candle* (*Chernaia svecha*). One of his most popular songs takes its name and setting from the Vacha River, not too far from Shalamov's camp, and contains the refrain "I go to the Vacha weeping, I return from the Vacha grinning" (*Pro rechku Vachu i poputchitsu Valiu*, 1977).[10] This bohemian agitation about the Gulag and the sudden popularity of its sites and sounds weirdly contrasted the Soviet state's negligence of the survivors, the multiple obstacles to their full "rehabilitation," the miserable pensions that they were receiving, and their destroyed relationships with their families.

As Demidov's example, Grossman's novel *Everything Flows*, and myriad other cases demonstrate, many prisoners of the Gulag survived their pain, but family bonds did not. The reasons were multiple, but one of them was a sharp incongruence between lived experience in the camps and in the rest of the Soviet state—a conflict that was especially profound when a survivor returned to the relatively prosperous circles of the intelligentsia. Deadly painful, this experience was culturally productive. It was precisely because the torture camps destroyed a person's world and speech while letting the physical person survive and eventually go that the lyric poems written by the survivors—ordered, understandable, shared pieces of speech that communicated bygone worlds—worked as effective, popular acts of resistance.

In her innovative essay, Josephine von Zitzewitz explores Gulag poetry and the role of nature in this verse. Focusing on two survivors, Shalamov and Zabolotsky, she reveals key themes—nature, poetry, metaphor—that were important for the nineteenth-century romantic critics but later forgotten by their descendants, who were more interested in social or structural issues. Because of our contemporary concerns, we are again increasingly sensitive to nature and texts about nature. Though the vast majority of the camps were set in industrial cities, mining regions, or construction sites where nature was largely destroyed, much Gulag poetry was addressed to nature. There is no mystery here. What else could these "soon-to-be-dead" victims write about in the absence of sexual partners, with a lack of food or sleep, surviving in the most primitive social arrangements and in absence of any contact with their native culture? Quiet, reliable, and noninterfering, nature contrasted with everyday life in the barracks. Exploring the poetry of Shalamov and Zabolotsky, von Zitzewitz demonstrates the relevance of nature for these two survivors of the camps and the polarly different individual responses that nature evoked in their post-Gulag poetry. For the survivors who later wrote down their memories during the Thaw, bygone years and new impressions provided many other themes, but nature was still safe and poetry about it publishable. However, even nature or the classics acquired political undertones in extreme conditions, when writers were anticipating arrest, serving sentences in camps, or trying to adjust to a new life after release. The dead became trees in many of Zabolotsky's poems—this particular image of death is one of the central motifs of his poetry. In fact, such an allegorical reading had been much earlier proposed by Nikolai Lesiuchevskii in his 1938 denunciation: "Masking as a naturalist who observes wild nature, Zabolotsky paints a terrifying, nightmarish, oppressive picture of

Soviet life."[11] As it happened, this denunciation was the main reason why Zabolotsky was arrested, tortured, and imprisoned.

Appreciating the analytical work accomplished by von Zitzewitz, I wish to add another example from my work that has not been published in English—an analysis of "The Night Garden" (*Nochnoi sad*), a poem that Zabolotsky published in Moscow in 1937, about a year before his arrest.[12] In the poem, we see the garden (or the forest) of death, and its trees embody the dead. But the garden is alive; it is compared to a pipe organ and a caravan, images of movement. During the day, when the hunt was taking place, this garden shook and rumbled; but now it is night, and the garden is asleep, though untamed: "the souls of linden trees raised their hands, All voting against the crime." The forest mourns the victims of the hunter whose fate was determined in the past, but the trees are voting, in the continuous present, against those and new crimes.[13]

A classical source for Zabolotsky was the epic poem by the sixteenth-century Italian poet Torquato Tasso. In this poem, the knight Tancred kills his beloved Clorinda while she is disguised in the armor of the enemy. After her burial, he finds himself in an enchanted forest that strikes the Crusader with terror. At the height of his grief, he slashes with his sword at a tree. "I was Clorinda, now imprisoned here," says the tree. Now, this tree is not Clorinda but rather her ghost, who—as happens with ghosts—has a very different body but the same old voice. In contrast to psychoanalytic readings that present this scene as the paradigm of obsessive compulsion (Tancred is killing his lover again and again), I see in Tancred's story a beautiful image of his mourning for Clorinda. The grammatical tense in which the tree tells Tancred, "I *was* Clorinda" is crucial: he cannot kill her again, she is not there, the tree was her but not anymore. Rather than repeating the murder, Tancred reimagines it and ascribes to the dead new ghostly and monstrous features. This is how mourning works; like Zabolotsky who followed him, Tasso cultivated an enchanted forest and situated the process in it.[14] As a professional translator, Zabolotsky definitely knew Tasso's poem, which had been translated into Russian many times.

In March 1938, Zabolotsky was arrested. After four days of sleep deprivation and continuous beating, interrogators sent him to the psychiatric ward. After recovering, he spent eight years in Siberian camps. Almost unavoidably, readers have perceived "The Night Garden" in the light of these subsequent events. This is how Nikita Zabolotsky, the son and biographer of the poet, wrote about this poem. Seeing in the poem "the themes of grief, anxiety, and confusion," he asserts that the phrase "Iron August" is a reference to Stalin and the poem depicts the Stalinist terror, in the midst of which it was written.[15]

When he wrote this poem, Zabolotsky did not know that he would be arrested a year or two later, though he anticipated such an arrest. The poem's past tense narration and its quiet, mournful melody support the idea that it reflects the author's grief about events that had already transpired when he was writing, rather than his anticipation of the future. I see this poem as a record of grief rather than anxiety. These two emotions, grief and fear, often work together, particularly in the time of terror. But they should be distinguished on both theoretical and ethical grounds. Grief addresses the past, and fear addresses the future. In our grief, we mourn for others, but we fear for ourselves. Mourning is connected with memory, fear, with imagination. Fear is humiliating; mourning is sublime.

There is external, biographical evidence for connecting mourning, as expressed in "The Night Garden," with real-life events. We know that Zabolotsky wrote this poem in 1936, while living with his family in a rented summer home in Ukraine. His son, Nikita, talks about that summer:

> We ate an extraordinary delicious Ukrainian borsch that a local peasant, Marfa, brought for us daily. Having set the table, she ... told us about the horrible events that recently desolated Ukrainian villages. From her, Nikolai Alekseevich [Zabolotsky] learned about the relentless famine among the Ukrainian peasants in 1932–1933.... Marfa told how the agents came from the city to confiscate all the grain, how potatoes were eaten during the winter, how mice and even worms were eaten during the spring ... and then the worst started—cannibalism. Marfa said that one woman from her village had her daughter stolen and eaten, and this woman was still alive.... Marfa managed to flee from the village despite the military patrols, and she survived.[16]

A skillful biographer, Nikita Zabolotsky juxtaposed Marfa's testimony about the famine with her delicious borsch. It took the poetic talent of his father to convert this horrifying story of collectivization into the sublime, strangely beautiful poem about the trees that vote against the crime. But Marfa's story was also the source for another picture of the Ukrainian famine—arguably, the most eloquent and mournful description of it ever written in the Russian language. That was Grossman's *Everything Flows*.

In Grossman's novel, Ivan Grigorievich, a survivor of the Gulag, hears the story of the Ukrainian famine from its survivor, Anna Sergeevna, who becomes his girlfriend after his release. There was a complex real-life connection between these parallel fictions, Zabolotsky's story that he heard from Marfa and put into verse in "The Night Garden" and Grossman's novel. As it happened, in 1956, years after Zabolotsky returned from the Gulag and reunited with his family, his wife, Ekaterina, left him for Grossman. They lived together for about a year while Grossman was working on his *Life and Fate*. Then Ekaterina returned to her husband, who would die a few months later. She related Marfa's story to Grossman, and it reappeared, in recognizable forms, both in *Life and Fate* and in its sequel, *Everything Flows*.

For his part, Zabolotsky kept composing his poetic amalgams that connected universal nature to the very specific history of his land. Von Zitzewitz mentions several of these beautiful poems—for example, "In this Birch Grove" (*V etoi roshche berezovoi*, 1946) and "Somewhere in a Field near Magadan" (*Gde-to v pole vozle Magadana*, 1956); both feature typical references to trees, fields, and stars. But if the former carries a postwar sense of victory—"a triumph that will last forever"—the latter depicts two old men who have been just released from the camp.[17] Wandering across the Siberian land, gazing at the stars—"symbols of freedom"—and freezing to death in the end of the poem, these two survivors of terror closely resemble Ivan Grigorievich, the protagonist of Grossman's *Everything Flows*, and the real-life survivors, Shalamov and Demidov.[18]

NOTES

1. Murav, *Music from a Speeding Train*, 111–208.
2. Arendt, "Social Science Techniques," 233, 240–41.
3. Etkind, *Warped Mourning*, 27.
4. Scarry, *The Body in Pain*, 56.
5. Klein, "Novoe ob ottse Shalamova."
6. Shalamov's itinerary is comparable to the story of Ivan Grigorievich in Vasilii Grossman's short novel *Everything Flows* (1955–63). We find Ivan Grigorievich returning from the northern camps of the Gulag, where he spent twenty-nine years of his life. He visits Moscow and Leningrad, the cities of his youth, and then settles in a provincial town in southern Russia. Born in the Caucasus, Ivan Grigorievich frequently revisits his childhood in dreams that are narrated in the novel. His father was a colonial administrator in the land populated by the Circassians, a rebellious tribe that led the militant resistance against Russian domination. Comparing the Gulag experience to his childhood in the colony, Ivan Grigorievich describes both his shame for the past and his premonition of the future. Grossman himself was born and raised in Berdichev, one of the centers of the Jewish Pale of Settlement. For a deeper analysis of *Everything Flows*, see my *Warped Mourning* (31–34, 52–54), though I did not pursue there the plausible idea that Shalamov was a prototype for Ivan Grigorievich.

7. Alexeyeva and Goldberg, *The Thaw Generation*, 71.
8. Golomshtok, "Vospominaniia starogo pessimista."
9. Often published with the title "Pesnia o stukache." Vysotskii, *Sobranie sochinenii*, 1:92.
10. Vysotskii, *Sobranie sochinenii*, 4:78–80.
11. Lesiuchevskii, "O stikhakh N. Zabolotskogo," 10.
12. For a more detailed reading, see Etkind, "Zheleznyi avgust."
13. Zabolotskii, *Stikhotvorenii*, 118.
14. Tasso, *Liberation of Jerusalem*, 247.
15. Zabolotskii, "Golosuia protiv prestuplenii."
16. Zabolotskii, *Zhizn' Nikolaia Zabolotskogo*, 233.
17. Zabolotskii, *Stikhotvorenii*, 147–48.
18. Zabolotskii, 241–42.

BIBLIOGRAPHY

Alexeyeva, Ludmilla and Paul Goldberg. *The Thaw Generation. Coming of Age in the Post-Stalin Era*. Boston: Little, Brown, 1990.

Arendt, Hannah. "Social Science Techniques and the Study of Concentration Camps" [1950]. In Hannah Arendt, *Essays in Understanding*, 232–47. New York: Schocken, 1994.

Etkind, Alexander. *Warped Mourning: Stories of the Undead in the Land of the Unburied*. Stanford, CA: Stanford University Press, 2013.

———. "Zheleznyi avgust, ili pamiat' dvoinogo naznacheniia." *Novoe literaturnoe obozrenie* no. 4 (2012): 337–58.

Golomshtok, Igor'. "Vospominaniia starogo pessimista." *Znamia* no. 3 (2011). https://magazines.gorky.media/znamia/2011/3/vospominaniya-starogo-pessimista-2.html.

Grossman, Vasilii. *Everything Flows*. Translated by Robert and Elizabeth Chandler and Anna Aslanyan. New York: New York Review of Books, 2009.

———. *Life and Fate*. Translated by Robert Chandler. New York: New York Review of Books, 2006.

Klein, Lora. "Novoe ob ottse Shalamova." Accessed June 1, 2021. https://shalamov.ru/research/54.

Lesiuchevskii, Nikolai. "O stikhakh N. Zabolotskogo," *Literaturnaia Rossiia* no. 10 (1989): 10.

Murav, Harriet. *Music from a Speeding Train: Jewish Literature in Post-Revolution Russia*. Stanford, CA: Stanford University Press, 2012.

Scarry, Elaine. *The Body in Pain: The Making and Unmaking of the World*. New York: Oxford University Press, 1985.

Tasso, Torquato. *The Liberation of Jerusalem*. Translated by Max Wickert. New York: Oxford University Press, 2009.
Vysotskii, Vladimir. *Sobranie sochinenii v piati tomakh*. Tula: Gulitsa, 1993.
Vysotskii, Vladimir and Leonid Monchinskii. *Chernaia svecha*. Moscow: Moskovskaia mezhdunarodnaia shkola perevodchikov, 1992.
Zabolotskii, Nikita. "Golosuia protiv prestuplenii," *Vestnik* no. 11 (322), May 28, 2003. http://www.vestnik.com/issues/2003/0528/win/zabolotsky.htm.
———. *Zhizn' Nikolaia Zabolotskogo*. Moscow: Soglasie, 1988.
Zabolotskii, Nikolai. *Stikhotvoreniia*. Moscow: Sovetskaia Rossiia, 1985.

ALEXANDER ETKIND is Professor of History at the European University Institute at Florence. He is author of *Eros of the Impossible: The History of Psychoanalysis in Russia*; of *Internal Colonization: Russia's Imperial Experience*; *Warped Mourning: Stories of the Undead in the Land of the Unburied*; *Roads Not Taken: An Intellectual Biography of William C. Bullitt*; and most recently of *Nature's Evil: A Cultural History of Resources*.

FOURTEEN

AFTERWORD

ALAN BARENBERG AND EMILY D. JOHNSON

WHEN NOBEL LAUREATE ALEKSANDR SOLZHENITSYN passed away in Moscow on August 3, 2008, he was given what amounted to a state funeral. On August 5, a civil ceremony and daylong public viewing were held in the ceremonial hall of the Russian Academy of Sciences. Despite a driving rainstorm, thousands streamed through to pay their last respects to the writer, including leading cultural and political figures. Vladimir Putin, at the time Russia's prime minister, arrived at the viewing at 1:00 p.m., laid a large bunch of roses on the grave, and stopped to offer personal condolences to Solzhenitsyn's widow and children.

Perhaps because he was scheduled to leave for China the next day, Putin did not attend the Orthodox funeral rites that were held on August 6 in Moscow's Donskoi Monastery. Russian president Dmitri Medvedev and a host of other prominent political figures, however, did and were photographed crossing themselves and offering condolences to the writer's family. After the religious ceremony, a goose-stepping honor guard and a uniformed military officer bearing a huge portrait of the writer escorted Solzhenitsyn's casket from the monastery's main cathedral to its cemetery for burial and then lined up to fire rifles in salute before the writer's coffin was lowered into the grave. Press coverage of the funeral service cited Putin's praise of Solzhenitsyn as a person who "lived through great tragedy and repression along with the common people and, through his life and work, gave our society a significant inoculation against all forms of tyranny." Putin, it was widely reported following the funeral, had asked Russia's minister of education Andrei Fursenko to ensure that Solzhenitsyn's work was prominently featured in Russia's school curriculum.[1] On the day of Solzhenitsyn's burial, President Medvedev issued a state order on the preservation of the writer's memory that called for memorial efforts in cities where the writer had lived.[2] Since Solzhenitsyn's death, the Russian state has made a concerted effort to implement this decree. In 2018, on the hundredth anniversary of Solzhenitsyn's birth, Putin personally opened a new monument to the writer in Moscow on what, since 2008, had been known as Aleksander Solzhenitsyn Street.[3] Monuments to the writer have also opened in Vladivostok, Belgorod, and other locations, and Solzhenitsyn museums appeared in Moscow, the village of Mezinovskii in the Gus' Khrustal'nyi region, Kislovodsk, and Riazan.

The state honors accorded to Solzhenitsyn upon his death in many ways represented the culmination of a larger process of rapprochement between the writer and Russian state authorities that took place in the last years of Solzhenitsyn's life. In interviews with both Western and Russian journalists in the 2000s, Solzhenitsyn praised Putin for restoring order and glory to the Russian state after what he viewed as the disastrous decline of the Gorbachev and Yeltsin years. When asked specifically about Putin's service in the Soviet-era KGB in a 2007 interview, Solzhenitsyn answered that Putin "was not a KGB investigator, nor was he the head of a camp in the gulag"; he was a foreign intelligence officer, and "that is not a negative in any country." Although Solzhenitsyn had declined awards offered to him by both the Gorbachev and Yeltsin administrations, he accepted the State Prize of the Russian Federation from Putin in 2006.[4] Putin and Solzhenitsyn met several times in the 2000s, and detailed coverage of their discussions appeared in the press, on television, and online.[5] After Solzhenitsyn's death, Putin remembered these meetings warmly and noted the writer's "boundless love for his fatherland" and unwillingness to tolerate Russophobia while in exile in the West.[6] One might argue that for the Putin administration, the memorialization of Solzhenitsyn offered an important opportunity to acknowledge the darker chapters in Soviet history without undermining legacy power structures from the Soviet period such as the FSB (Federal Security Bureau), the successor to the Soviet-era KGB, or risking the kind of instability that had characterized the Khrushchev, Gorbachev, and Yeltsin periods. Solzhenitsyn's espousal of Russian nationalist sentiments meshed well with the new forms of patriotism that the Putin regime was actively cultivating in Russia's citizens.

The rapprochement between Solzhenitsyn and the Russian state is part of an important shift in the politics of memory and memorialization of the Gulag over the past decade and a half. Although reports by Russian activists and foreign journalists often paint a grim picture of the commitment of the Russian state to commemorating the Gulag and other crimes of Stalinism, in fact, significant state resources have been provided to such efforts. Doubtless, the most significant sign of the Russian state's willingness to fund the study and commemoration of the Gulag and Stalinist terror was the opening of a new Museum of Gulag History in Moscow on October 30, 2015. Strictly speaking, this was not a new museum—a precursor institution had been established under the same name in 2004. Directed by the former dissident and Gulag survivor Anton Antonov-Ovseenko and funded by the Moscow city government, it was small and rather chaotically organized and suffered from both very low visitor numbers and obvious neglect. The revamped museum that opened in 2015 is housed in a completely renovated four-story structure (albeit in a relatively sleepy residential neighborhood) and pitches itself as a national museum of the Gulag. Like Western trauma museums such as the US Holocaust Memorial Museum and Yad Vashem in Israel, the new Museum of Gulag History does more than host visitors and tour groups. It houses a library and archive, engages in outreach activities, offers material aid to survivors and their families, and provides consultations to those searching for information about relatives in state archives. It also coordinates with other Gulag museums in Russia's regions, preserving and documenting the ruins of Gulag camps, and is actively engaged in gathering testimony of survivors and their families, particularly through the ambitious "My Gulag" video series, which has recorded and posted more than one hundred film interviews with both victims and perpetrators of the Gulag.[7] Unlike staff members at the Moscow branch of Memorial, the employees of the Gulag History Museum are generally not associated with Gulag survivor networks or the remnants of the Soviet dissident movement/human rights world, which have so often clashed with the Putin regime on civil rights issues in recent years. Its director, Roman Romanov, comes from a background of theater and museum work. His leadership has helped the museum to achieve high curatorial standards and advance cutting-edge educational and scholarly initiatives even as it has challenged long-standing associations between efforts to preserve the memory of the Gulag and the traditions of protest and dissent represented by human rights organizations such as Memorial.

There have been other positive signs of state investment in Gulag memorialization and study in recent years. This includes the opening of new Gulag monuments in Moscow and in other major Russian cities. In 2017, a long-planned monument by the late sculptor Ernst Neizvestny, "Masks of Sorrow: Europe-Asia," was opened to the public at the Memorial Complex for the Victims of Political Repression in Ekaterinburg, the second in a planned trilogy of monuments to victims of the Gulag that had been in the works since the 1990s.[8] In Moscow, the "Wall of Grief" (*stena skorbi*), a monument to victims of Stalin-era political repression in the form of massive curved wall, one hundred feet long and twenty feet high, featuring human figures, was built by presidential decree, funded both by the state and by private donors. The monument is notable for its size, its location in central Moscow on a busy corner of the Garden Ring Road, and the fanfare with which it was opened on October 30, 2017. Both President Putin and Patriarch Kirill, the top official in the Russian Orthodox Church, were present at its opening.[9]

Yet even as the Russian state has supported some officially sanctioned efforts to memorialize the victims of Stalinist repression and opened new avenues for those interested in learning more about the terror and labor camps, it has also clamped down on other more independent initiatives spearheaded by Russian NGOs. Most notably, it has cracked down on the labor camp survivors' and human rights network Memorial, branding it as a "foreign agent" and subjecting its branches to fines and periodic raids. In one particularly notorious incident, Iurii Dmitriev, a local historian in the Karelia region who worked with other Memorial activists to locate the killing fields of Sandarmokh, where thousands of victims of Stalinist terror were shot and buried in the 1930s, was arrested in 2016 on what were widely regarded as false charges of manufacturing child pornography. After multiple appeals, Dmitriev was ultimately sentenced to thirteen years in confinement. While he awaited trial, Dmitriev saw his life's work challenged. Iurii Kilin and Sergei Verigin, military historians from Petrozavodsk State University, began to press a revisionist narrative: the killing fields in Sandarmokh might hold Soviet POWs executed by the Finns during the Second World War in addition to some victims of Soviet terror and should be re-excavated in the light of this hypothesis. Although Kilin and Verigin offered little evidence to support their thesis, state-controlled press organs began promoting this theory and cast aspersions on Memorial's work. Support among local politicians in Karelia for the annual day of remembrance, which had taken place at Sandarmokh since 1998 and regularly drew thousands, disappeared.[10] The Sandarmokh site had, since its discovery in 1997, functioned as a public memorial: handmade plaques honoring those shot and letters to parents and grandparents lost to the camp system were pinned to tree trunks; shrines honoring the dead of specific nationalities such as Ukrainians and Tatars dotted the landscape. New excavations conducted by the Russian Military History Society in 2018 and 2019 with the aim of finding evidence to support Kilin and Verigin's controversial theory were seen as desecrations by many activists and relatives of Gulag inmates known to have been shot at Sandarmokh.[11]

Even before Dmitriev's arrest and the re-excavations at Sandarmokh, another Gulag memorial site run by a Memorial branch, the Memorial Museum of the History of Political Repression at Perm-36, had been taken over by a rival group with ties to local political authorities, and its displays had been extensively reworked. Material on the political repression of Soviet dissidents and the Stalinist terror disappeared; new displays highlighted the contributions of the camp to the war effort and depicted those who served sentences as anti-Soviet saboteurs and common criminals.[12]

Attacks in recent years on Memorial branches and projects may have been motivated by the organization's involvement in contemporary Russian human rights issues as much as by the organization's historical work on the Soviet labor camp system and terror. Memorial is a broad-profile civil rights organization and has acted in defense of freedom of speech and assembly throughout the post-Soviet period. It regularly protests new Russian laws and official actions that it perceives as threats to civil rights and maintains ties with human rights organizations and educational institutions in many foreign countries.

How should we understand the seeming contradiction between the state's attacks on Memorial and other NGOs and its simultaneous efforts to memorialize the Gulag? One might argue that Russian state officials accept that the human rights abuses of the Stalin period cannot be entirely denied or ignored but want to control the way this topic is presented to the public so that memorial efforts do not undermine patriotic pride in what they view as the great achievements of the Soviet period (industrialization, victory in the Second World War), suggest connections to current Russian political realities, or inspire spontaneous mass action. Effectively, the Russian state is imposing a near monopoly on the memorialization of the Gulag in order to contain discussion and cast the topic as largely closed, something that belongs to Russia's past. By means of such efforts, it attempts to ensure that remembering the Gulag and the crimes of Stalinism cannot be a potential source of new revelations or challenges to the existing order.

The fact that Soviet repression occupies a central place in the foundational historical narratives of many of Russia's closest neighbors doubtless also contributes to the Russian state's desire to manage this historical topic carefully. In countries such as Latvia, Lithuania, Estonia, and Ukraine, museums, monuments, and historical texts often depict Communist purges of local citizens as equivalent to the worst horrors perpetrated by Nazi occupiers and reject the notion that the Soviet army constituted a liberating force even in the context of the Second World War. Current displays at sites like Perm-36 and the new Museum of Gulag History in Moscow can be read as rebuttals of the anti-Soviet and anti-Communist historical narratives of Russia's neighbors. They acknowledge that human rights abuses occurred in the Soviet period but are largely silent on the question of how these events are connected to twentieth-century Soviet and Russian history more broadly. Where possible, as at Sandarmokh, regime-friendly revisionists may try to recast some of those executed by Stalin as victims of fascist atrocities, much as Soviet leaders once blamed the Germans for the murder of the Polish officers buried at Katyn.

In some respects, the current wave of Gulag commemoration reads as a variation on two previous attempts to come to grips with the crimes of the Stalin era, destalinization and glasnost', launched by Khrushchev and Gorbachev respectively. In both of those cases, the state sought to reckon with past crimes as a way to build support for the current leaders and their agendas. There are, of course, key differences—unlike Khrushchev and Gorbachev, Putin is not seeking to launch a significant program of reform; in fact, he seeks to preserve the status quo. Nevertheless, the recent wave of state-sponsored efforts to commemorate the Gulag shares with both previous campaigns the desire to come to terms with the repressive legacies of Stalinism without calling into serious question the significant accomplishments that accompanied terror, particularly the Soviet victory in the Second World War and the transformation of the USSR/Russia into a global superpower. It seeks to bracket out particular transgressions and relegate them to the past without limiting the repressive power and imperial aspirations of the current Russian state. Managing the historical narrative in this fashion avoids deeper critiques of the Russian state and its connections to Soviet legacies.

RESEARCHING THE GULAG IN PUTIN'S RUSSIA

As many of the chapters included in this volume have noted, the current political climate presents challenges to both Western and Russian researchers working on topics connected with the Soviet labor camp and prison system. Some archival funds in both central and regional archives in Russia and Kazakhstan that were open to researchers in the early 1990s have become largely or entirely inaccessible, a process that Mikhail Nakonechnyi has aptly called an "archival counterrevolution."[13] Few scholars currently expect Russia's state archives to make large caches of new materials available in the near term. The FSB archives, which have never been accessible on a broad scale, seem likely to remain entirely closed for the foreseeable future. As a result, in coming years, Gulag researchers will doubtless make increased use of archives in former Soviet republics such as Ukraine, Latvia, Lithuania, and Estonia. Because critiques of Soviet power and Russian imperialism are important to contemporary politics and the construction of longer-term national narratives in these states, archival access and transparency on the crimes of the Soviet era are excellent. Western repositories such as the Hoover Institution and Harvard University that purchased microfilms of funds from GARF and other Russian archives in the immediate post-Soviet period also represent important resources: sometimes scholars can use these collections to access documents that have since been reclassified. Yet, it is also important to note that, as the historical studies in the present volume demonstrate, archival funds in Russia that remain open have hardly been exhausted: there is plenty more for scholars to learn through painstaking work in these collections.

Much of what scholars have learned since the archival revolution of the 1990s has concerned the variability of the Gulag experience. As Lynne Viola points out in her commentary on the first section of this volume, recent research shows that there was no universal Gulag experience. The Soviet prison, labor camp, and settlement system was large, complex, and chaotic, and both confinement sites and the detainee population varied widely. It is no longer useful to think of the camp of the Great Terror era as the institution that most Gulag inmates experienced or to try to reconstruct a "typical" prisoner experience, as done fictionally by Solzhenitsyn in his landmark novella *One Day in the Life of Ivan Denisovich*. We now know that prisoners and exiles were held in a wide variety of institutions and geographic locations and were subject to different regulations and conditions depending on the time period. "Bolshevik" may have been the lingua franca for the Gulag, but the meanings of the words (as well as their inflections) depended on both speaker and listener. Understanding the contexts and meanings of what was spoken and unspoken will be a priority for future research as scholars continue to explore the particular conditions that defined life in the Gulag's varied outposts in specific historical periods.

New theoretical models and tools, often developed in other fields, can be enormously useful as we work to explore the complexity and variability of the Gulag in a nuanced way. As Judith Pallot reminds us in her commentary chapter, Gulag studies may be a latecomer to the turn toward digital humanities, but such approaches offer enormous promise as a means of broadening and deepening our understanding of the Soviet carceral system. New digital mapping tools represent a significant enhancement over old static maps of camp locations across the USSR. They allow us to visualize large and complex population movements across space and time and thereby provide a better understanding of Solzhenitsyn's "archipelago" or, to borrow another of his metaphors, of the circulation within the Stalinist Soviet Union's "sewage disposal system." By that same token, machine learning and other techniques for examining large volumes of texts promise to reveal new patterns and lines of inquiry in even well-known primary sources such as memoirs and archival reports. "Big data" will never substitute for close reading in the humanities, but it will allow scholars to make new connections and discoveries.

As many of the chapters in this volume demonstrate, the legacies of the Gulag, both in the USSR and present-day Russia, are enormously complex. Studies of literary responses to the experience of terror and incarceration, reflections on how and why we memorialize particular events and yet ignore others, examinations of the visual politics and placement of monuments, analysis of museum displays, and work on the symbolism underlying burials, exhumations, and reburials are all part of a wave of scholarship that considers the afterlife of the Gulag. In part, this intense scholarly interest in the memorialization of the Gulag is a product of the on-again, off-again nature of the USSR/Russia's struggles to come to terms with its Stalinist past, a process that has waxed and waned ever since Stalin's death. The current political climate, which combines a crackdown on NGOs like Memorial with limited official memorialization of the Gulag, seems to have brought such scholarly interest to a peak. Yet scholarly and popular concern with how to process past crimes and traumas is far from a uniquely Russian phenomenon, nor is it limited to authoritarian states. For example, a reading of news headlines in the United States during the year 2020 suggests that examining and processing the legacies of past injustices is a universal challenge and that neither strong democratic conditions nor pluralism guarantee a healthy reckoning with past traumas. Comparison also suggests that while societies can and do make progress in coming to terms with past injustices, the goal of such efforts should not be an artificial endpoint but rather a continuous process of reexamining the past. Thus, while Russian officials may seek to advance a unitary interpretation of the Gulag and its place in Russian/Soviet history, this volume makes clear that such efforts serve neither academic nor public interests. We hope that *Rethinking the Gulag* has made important contributions to the larger process of understanding the Gulag and its place in the Soviet Union and post-Soviet states, no matter how modest.

NOTES

1. Larin, "Put' k poslednemu priiutu."
2. "Ukaz prezidenta Rossiiskoi Federatsii ot 6-ogo avgusta 2008 g."
3. "Putin nazval Solzhenitsyna istinnym patriotom Rossii."
4. "Spiegel Interview."
5. "Vstrecha Putina s Solzhenitsynym"; "Vladimir Putin vstretilsia s Aleksandrom Solzhenitsynym."

6. "Putin nazval Solzhenitsyna istinnym patriotom Rossii."
7. Hardy, "Commemorating and Forgetting Soviet Repression"; *Moi GULAG*.
8. Davies, "New Monument to Stalin's Victims Unveiled after 27-Year Wait."
9. On the planning, construction, and reception of the memorial site, see Smith, "A Monument for Our Times?"
10. Yarovaya, "Rewriting Sandarmokh."
11. Nuzov, "The Kremlin Is Trying to Whitewash Russia's Stalinist Past."
12. Danilovich, "Revamped Perm-36 Museum."
13. Nakonechnyi, "Archival Counterrevolution."

BIBLIOGRAPHY

Danilovich, Mikhail. "Revamped Perm-36 Museum Emphasizes Gulag's 'Contribution to Victory.'" *Radio Free Europe; Radio Liberty*. Last modified July 25, 2015. https://www.rferl.org/a/russia-perm-gulag-museum-takeover-contribution-to-victory/27152188.html.

Davies, Katie Marie. "New Monument to Stalin's Victims Unveiled after 27-Year Wait." *The Calvert Journal*. Last modified November 20, 2017. https://www.calvertjournal.com/articles/show/9241/monument-stalin-victims-repression-Neizvestny.

Hardy, Jeffrey. "Commemorating and Forgetting Soviet Repression: Moscow's State Museum of GULAG History." In *Museums of Communism: New Memory Sites in Central and Eastern Europe*, edited by Stephen M. Norris, 274–303. Bloomington: Indiana University Press, 2020.

Larin, Vladimir. "Put' k poslednemu priiutu: v sredu v polden' Rossiia prostilas' s Aleksandrom Solzhenitsynom." *Rossiiskaia gazeta*. Last modified August 7, 2008. https://rg.ru/2008/08/07/solzhenicyn-put.html.

Muzei istorii Gulaga. *Moi Gulag*. Accessed July 23, 2021. https://mygulag.ru.

Nakonechnyi, Mikhail. "'Archival counterrevolution': Why Are GULAG Regional Archives So Important?" *Peripheral Histories*. Last modified September 14, 2020. https://www.peripheralhistories.co.uk/post/archival-counterrevolution-why-are-gulag-regional-archives-so-important.

Nuzov, Ilya. "The Kremlin Is Trying to Whitewash Russia's Stalinist Past: Driven by the Desire to Forge a Strong National Identity, the Authorities are Excavating the Graves of Victims of Soviet Repression." *Moscow Times*. Last modified August 30, 2019. https://www.themoscowtimes.com/2019/08/30/the-kremlin-is-trying-to-whitewash-russias-stalinist-past-a67096.

"Putin nazval Solzhenitsyna istinnym patriotom Rossii." *RIA Novosti*. Last modified December 11, 2018. https://ria.ru/20181211/1547797642.html.

Smith, Kathleen E. "A Monument for Our Times? Commemorating Victims of Repression in Putin's Russia." *Europe-Asia Studies* 71, no. 8 (September 14, 2019): 1314–44.

"Spiegel Interview with Aleksandr Solzhenitsyn: 'I Am Not Afraid of Death.'" *Spiegel International*. Last modified July 23, 2007. https://www.spiegel.de/international/world/spiegel-interview-with-alexander-solzhenitsyn-i-am-not-afraid-of-death-a-496003.html.

"Ukaz prezidenta Rossiiskoi Federatsii ot 6-ogo avgusta 2008 g. N. 1187 'Ob uvekovechenii pamiati A. I Solzhenitsyna," *Rossiiskaia gazeta*. Last modified August 8, 2008. https://rg.ru/2008/08/08/solzhenizyn-dok.html.

"Vladimir Putin vstretilsia s Aleksandrom Solzhenitsynym." Last modified June 12, 2007. http://kremlin.ru/events/president/news/40495.

"Vstrecha Putina s Solzhenitsynym." Last modified September 20, 2000. https://www.youtube.com/watch?v=eotw8kUnHTM.

Yarovaya, Anna. "Rewriting Sandarmokh: Who Is Trying to Alter the History of Mass Executions and Burials in Karelia, and Why? Published in English Translation on 'The Russian Reader.'" Last modified December 29, 2017. https://therussianreader.com/2017/12/29/anna-yarovaya-rewriting-sandarmokh.

ALAN BARENBERG is the Buena Vista Foundation Associate Professor of History at Texas Tech University. He is author of *Gulag Town, Company Town: Forced Labor and Its Legacy in Vorkuta*.

EMILY D. JOHNSON is the Brian and Sandra O'Brien Presidential Professor of Russian at the University of Oklahoma. She is author of *How St. Petersburg Learned to Study Itself: The Russian Idea of Kraevedenie* and editor and translator of *Gulag Letters* by Arsenii Formakov.

INDEX

Italicized page numbers refer to figures or tables.

Abbas-Ogly, A. Sh., 161
Abez camp (Komi ASSR), 261
Abrosimov (Unzhlag procurator), 126n61
Abushinov, 161
"Adage, The" [*Sententsiia*] (Shalamov), 202
Adzhubei, Aleksei, 226
agriculture, collectivization of, 5
Aituganov, I. P., 167
Akhmatova, Anna, 217n66, 263
Akhtiamov, Ia. A., 162, 164
Aldan-Semenov, A. I., 226
Aleksandrovskii, V. G., 160
Alexeyeva, Liudmila, 277
Alexopoulos, Golfo, 72–73, 104, 105, 122, 123; on Gulag medical discharge data, 106; on mortality rates in medical release, 113, 121, 135
Alieva, Svetlana, 159
Altailag complex, 207
ALZHIR [Akmolinsk Camp for Wives of Traitors to the Motherland] (Kazakhstan), 160
amnesties, 13n5, 59, 246, 254
And It Was in Those Days [*I bylo v te dni*] (Ashkenazi), 161
Andreev, Gennadii, 24
Andreevskii (lay Josephite), 31, 33, 34
Anna Ivanovna (Shalamov), 236, 238n9
AntConc software, research using, 158, 189

anthropology, 10
antitheft laws (1947), 3, 146
Antonii, Archbishop, 34
Antonov-Ovseenko, Anton, 286
Applebaum, Anne, 132
archives, as memoir theme, 164, *165*
archives, Soviet and post-Soviet, 2, 6, 12–13; "archival counterrevolution," 289; central and local, 106; declassification of documents, 182, 191; FSB, 289; KGB, 170; NKVD, 44; non-Russian, 60–61; opening of (early 1990s), 19; partial opening of, 7, 92, 184; regional, 289; secret police, 267
Arendt, Hannah, 274–75
Arkhlag camp, 114
Armenia, German POWs in, 134, 142
arrests, 3, 6, 9, 12, 170, 189; as focus of Gulag manuscripts, 225; in memoirs, 173–74, *173*; "prisoner's personal file" and, 249
Art and Life in the Gulag (*Tvorchestvo i byt Gulaga*) catalogue, 199
Ashkenazi, M. B., 161
atheism, 20, 204
Auschwitz, 228, 229, 230, 236
autobiography, as genre marker in memoir titles, *163*
Aviator, The (Vodolazkin), 177n40
Azerbaijan, 118, 119, 134

295

Baikal-Amur Mainline, 137
Balakhlag camp, 53
Balkarians, 4
Baltic republics, 50, 58, 79, 188. *See also* Estonia; Latvia; Lithuania
Barenberg, Alan, 12, 104, 131, 135, 141, 274, 275; on porousness of labor camp system, 156; on Vorkuta and coal mining, 142
Barnes, Steven, 8, 47, 84, 141; on "coddling of the thieves," 74; on reliability of official statistics, 104
Bas-Relief in the Rock (Aldan-Semenov), 226
Beauty in Hell: Culture in the Gulag (virtual exhibition, Hunterian Museum), 199
Belarus, 4, 50; German POWs in, 134, 141, 142
Belbaltlag (Medvezh'ia gora) camp, 60
Bell, Wilson, 121, 135, 141, 156
Belousov, V., 160
Beria, Lavrentii Pavlovich: labor mobilization of POWs and, 130, 133–37, 145, 147, 150n51; medical release process (*aktirovanie*) and, 110, 111; practice of using prisoners as guards and, 98n13
Berman, Matvei Davydovich, 108, 109, 112
Bernstein, Seth, 185–86
"Berries" [*Iagody*] (Shalamov), 214n8
biographies, 156, *163*
Bitches' War (1948–53), 75
Black Candle, The [*Chernaia svecha*] (Vysotsky and Mochinskii), 277
black markets, 71, 82, 95
blatnye (career criminals), 3, 10, 70, 82; governance by, 76; as managers of information, 71, 86n18; privileges of, 73–74; signatures of, 75. *See also* criminals, common; thieves
blocs, as threat to thieves' hierarchy, 79–80
Blok-Baers, R. M., 159
Bogdesko, I. T., 167
Bolonkin, A. A., 160
Bolshevik regime, 31, 32, 33, 34; Bolshevik ideology, 7–8; improvised policies toward religious inmates, 20–25, 26; nationalities policy of, 59–60; penal procedures and non-Russian languages, 47–48
Branesti colony (Moldova), 82

Brezhnev, Leonid, 221
Brodskaia, Lidiia Maksimovna, 222
Bubnov (procurator of Sevpechlag), 114, 115
Bulgakov, Viktor, 165
Bulganin, Nikolai, 136
bureaucracy, Stalinist, 106
"Burial" [*Pokhorony*] (Shalamov), 201
bytoviki (petty offenders), 3, 71

Camp Cultural Education Sectors, 7, 11
"Campfires and Stars" [*Kostry i zvezdy*] (Shalamov), 211
Cancer Ward [*Rakovyi korpus*] (Solzhenitsyn), 157
card games, criminal culture and, 68, 70, 75
caste system (inmate hierarchy), 68, 70, 74, 85n4; in post-Soviet prisons, 78–79; as reputation system, 75–76; separation of castes, 80–81; supported by bulk of common criminals, 71
Catholic inmates, 21
Caucasus, punished peoples of, 4
cell phones, in prisons, 81, 95
cemeteries, 12, 250, *251*, 273; cenotaphs to executed family members, 266; of deportees, 257, 258. *See also* graves/burial sites
censorship: delays in mail delivery and, 51; military, 54, 55; protocols in different penal categories, 52; self-censorship, 106; shifts in language usage over time and, 56; stamps and blacking, 44–45, 47, 53, 57, 62n8; translation and, 48, 49, 50
Central Asia, 4, 5, 56
Cernousek, Stepan, 186, 192n7
Chalidze, Valery, 77
Chechens, 4, 172
Cheka, 259, 263, 267
Chekhranov, Pavel, 22, 26–27
chekists (secret police), 28
Chernezkii (Dmitlag deputy procurator), 115
Chernyshev, Vasilii Vasil'evich, 111, 112, 136
Chernysheva (OITK head), 111–12
Chernyshevsky, Nikolay, 62n23
China, penal system of, 182
Ciliga, Ante, 92
Circle after Circle [*Krug za krugom*] (Bogesko), 167

Circles of Hell [*Krugi ada*] (Aituganov), 167
cities, German POW camps near, 134, *139*
civil war, Russian, 20, 47
Clarke, Roger A., 149n39
class enemies, 19, 21
coal basins, German POW camps and, 142, *144*, 145
Cold War, 130, 146, 273
collectives (teams of workers), 73, 95
collectivization, 3–4, 9, 132
Communist Party, 20, 97, 231
Conquest, Robert, 6, 132
construction projects, large-scale, 132–33
corruption, 71, 72, 77, 95; inability to fulfill centralized plans and, 98; ubiquity of, 73; underfunding of prisons and, 84
Council of Europe, 182
"Creators of Roads, The" [*Tvortsy dorog*] (Zabolotsky, 1947), 208
Cricova No. 15 colony (Moldova), 80
Criminal Russia (Chalidze, 1977), 77
criminals, common, 67, 71, 131–32, 288; culture of, 68; divide with political prisoners, 84; in Solovki, 25, 28, 35. See also *blatnye* (career criminals); thieves
Cultural Education Sector, 46
Cyrillic alphabet, 54

Daniel, Yuly, 277
data-gathering methods, 186, 192, 192n9
David-Fox, Michael, 123
Death and Redemption (Barnes, 2011), 8, 148n11
death rates. *See* mortality/death rates
Decembrist revolutionaries, 168
dekulakization, *173*
"Dekulakized for 'Sabotage'" [*Raskulacheny za "sabotazh"*] (Ignatov), 175n11
Demidov, Georgii Georgievich, 220, 274, 278; end of friendship with Shalamov, 221; literary landscape after *Ivan Denisovich* and, 225–27; as physicist, 222–23; post-camp life of, 223; as prisoner in Kolyma, 222, 230, 233; Shalamov's correspondence with, 220–24, 226–30, 232, 234–37, 276; "The Stiff," 232, 233
Demidova, Valentina Georgievna, 232, 233

deportations, 4, 170, 172, *173*, 188, 239n54; of families, 244; funerals and memory among deportees, 255–58, *257*, *258*. See also exiles
detachment (*otriad*) system, 76, 82, 95
"detective story," as genre marker in memoir titles, 162, *164*
Devil's Dance, The (Izmailov), 177n40
D'iakonov, Vladimir Pavlovich, 114, 115
D'iakov, Boris, 226
Dialectics of Nature (Engels, 1925 [1883]), 216n47
diaries, 8, 105, 156, 158, *163*
Dmitlag camp, 49, 60, 94, 115
Dmitriev, Iurii, 273, 287
Dobronravov (chief of directorate of camp courts), 112
documentary, as genre marker in memoir titles, 162, *163*
Dombrovskii, Iurii, 62n12
Dostoevsky, Fyodor, 157, 165, 167, 168, 199
Dray-Khmara, Mikhailo, 56
Dreimanis, Janis, 62n8
drug dealers, in prisons, 81–82
Dubravlag, 184
"Dwarf Pine, The" [*Stlanik*] (Shalamov), 211–12, 213

Eastern Europe, 93, 94
ego documents, 105
Egorov (prisoner released with TB), 117
Eikhmans, Fedor, 26
Ekibastuz camp (Kazakhstan), 160
"elephants" [*slony*] (prisoners resistant to thieves' system), 79
Emets (Siberia region director), 107–8, 112
Engalychev (ULLP deputy head), 111
Engels, Friedrich, 216n47
epidemics, 29, 243, 259
E. P. Peshkova: Aid for Political Prisoners, 49
Epshtein, Mikhail, 215n40
Ermolaev, S. A., 160
escapes, 97–98, 175n11
Estonia, 9, 74, 288; archives in, 289; German POWs in, 134, 141
Estonian language, 50, 59
Estonians, 4

ethnic cleansing, Soviet, 239n54
Etkind, Alexander, 10, 12
Eto priamo zdes' ("It happened here") project (Memorial Society), 186
Everything Flows (Grossman, 1955–63), 278, 280–81, 281n6
"Everything that was in my soul" [*Vse, chto bylo v dushe*] (Zabolotsky), 206
executions, 8, 267n3; documentation of death and burial, 245–49, 254; extrajudicial, 246, 249; memory of executed individuals, 262–64; secrecy of, 243, 247; as theme of Gulag memoirs, 173
exiles, 3, 4, 5, 8, 290. *See also* deportations

Fainshtein, Aleksandra Mikhailovna, 223
Falevich, Petr, 22
family, as memoir theme, 164, 165, 170, 173, 174
famines, 5, 106, 182, 243, 280
Fate and Will [*Sud'ba i volia*] (Vaishvillene), 162
Federovich (UITLiK procurator), 115
Feldman, A. E., 56
Feodosii, Archimandrite, 24, 25, 26, 27, 31
Fet, Afanasy, 201
fiction, 1, 6, 13
"filtration" camps, 268n4
Filtzer, Donald, 121–22, 138
Fink, Lev, 166
Finland, 129
Finns, 4, 138, 188, 287
First Circle, The [*V kruge pervom*] (Solzhenitsyn), 5, 157
five-year plans, 9
Flige, Irina, 6, 12, 186, 214, 273, 274
Florensky, Pavel, 199
forced labor, 5, 131, 185, 209; economic gains through, 9; five-year plans and, 9; of German POWs, 131–38; in Tsarist period, 131
Forced Labor in Soviet Russia (Dallin and Nicolaevsky), 6
Formakov, Arsenii, 43, 54
Formakova, Anna Ivanovna, 43
Frolov (chairman of Azerbaijani UITLiK camp court), 118, 119–20

"From Lomonosov's Diary" [*Iz dnevnika Lomonosova*] (Shalamov), 211
FSB (Federal Security Service), 93, 274, 285, 289
Full Face and Profile: [Article] 58–10 [*Anfas i profil': 58–10*] (Mindlin), 159
Fursenko, Andrei, 284
Futurism, 204, 205

Gambetta, Diego, 74
gangs, prison, 69–70, 80
GARF (State Archive of the Russian Federation), 49, 106, 252, 290
Gavrilova, Sofiya, 185
gender, 96, 158
Georgia, 68; German POWs in, 134; reputation system in post-Soviet prisons, 78, 83
German language, 50, 257
Germans, Soviet, 4, 257
Gershman, M. D., 167
Getty, Arch, 182
Ginzburg, Evgeniia, 6, 157, 167, 188, 198. *See also Journey into the Whirlwind* [*Krutoi marshrut*]
Ginzburg, Isaak Grigorievich, 108
GIS (geographic information system) mapping, 12, 131, 184, 185, 186, 187
glasnost', 289
Goldstein, Darra, 207, 216n47
"Gomborsky Forest" [*Gomborskii les*] (Zabolotsky, 1957), 208–9
Gorbachev, Mikhail, 285, 289
Gorbatov, Aleksandr, 226
Gorshenin, Konstantin Petrovich, 116–17
Granovskii, German Markovich, 112
"Graphite" (Shalamov), 203, 228
"Grasshopper and the Cricket, The" [*Kuznechik i sverchok*] (Sedakova), 207
graves/burial sites, 12, 233, 243–45, 266–67; "to bury well" (*pokhoronit' khorosho*) as tradition, 256, 257, 258, 268n32; Christian burials, 29, 38–39n51; documentation of death in camps and prisons, 249–53, 251; documentation of death in special settlements, 253–54; documentation of deaths in transit, 254–55; executions

and, 245–49; memory of those who died in camps, 259–62, 260–62; special settler cemeteries, 243, 244, 258; witness statements about burials, 264–66. *See also* cemeteries; mortality/death rates

Great Terror (1937–38), 3, 132, 171, 231, 246, 290; executions during, 263; secrecy and, 259, 262

Greeks, Crimean, 172

Gridin, V. M., 161

Grigorii, Bishop, 31

Grinev, Mitrofin, 22

Grinevich, Archpriest, 30–31

Grossman, Vasilii, 167, 278, 280–81, 281n6

Grunewald, Susan, 12, 181, 184–85, 187–88, 191

guards, 8, 71, 233; failure to separate prisoners by category, 72; inmates as, 97, 98n13; processing of new arrivals, 82

Gubanov (UITLiK camp court chairman), 120

Guide to the Labor Camps of the USSR [*Spravochnik ispravitel'no-trudovykh lagerei v SSSR*] (Moscow Memorial), 185, 186

GUITU (Main Administration of Corrective-Labor Establishments), 107, 108, 121

Gulag [*Glavnoe upravlenie lagerei*] (Main Administration of Camps), 1, 6, 9, 105; broadened definition of, 91–92; camps linked by transportation arteries, 74; capital construction projects and, 132–33; chronology and context in relation to, 96–97; creation of (1929), 131; as defining experience of the Soviet Union, 162; economic role of, 5, 9–10, 76, 116, 123, 132, 274; lack of formal control in camps, 72; legacies of, 10, 12, 13, 84, 291; medical release practices and, 104, 105; Nazi camp system compared with, 91–97, 182, 230, 236, 274; number of staff, 97; poor functioning of, 96; Procuracy and, 121; record-keeping agencies of, 253–54; rehabilitation as goal, 76; SANO (Sanitary department), 107, 108, 112, 115; SLON as predecessor of, 19; symbiotic relationship with GUPVI network, 12; Third Department, 74; as underfunded system, 122–23

Gulag Archipelago, The (Solzhenitsyn, 1973), 1, 6, 10, 91, 157, 234, 235; authorial prefaces' references to, 166, 167, 168; as framework for later Gulag memoirs, 221; on the Great Terror, 171; illegal circulation in the Soviet Union, 221; preface, 2; subtitle of, 155; testimony of prisoners and, 232

Gulag Maps project, 8

Gulag studies, 2, 67, 157, 290; computer technologies and, 181; evolution of, 6–10; interdisciplinary, 11; POW camp system integrated into, 187

Gullotta, Andrea, 156

GUPVI (prisoner of war) network. *See* UPVI/GUPVI

Hardy, Jeffrey, 11, 74, 92–94, 98, 113, 199

Healey, Dan, 123

Heinzen, James, 73, 74

"He warms his frozen fingers" [*On pal'tsy zamerzchie greet*] (Shalamov), 202–3

Hirsch, Francine, 46, 59

history, as memoir theme, 164, 165, 169

Holmgren, Beth, 165

Holocaust, 274; memoirs of, 168; spatial history project at Stanford, 185; US Holocaust Memorial Museum, 286

hooliganism, 72, 132, 148n9

Hoover Institution, 290

Hope Abandoned (Mandel'shtam), 175n14

Hope Against Hope (Mandel'shtam), 175n14

Hunterian Museum (Glasgow), 199

Iagoda, Genrikh, 254

Iakhina, Guzel, 177n40

"I Ask Myself" [*I sprashivaiu sebia*] (Vaza), 161

I Cannot Forget [*Ne mogu zabyt'*] (Abbas-Ogly), 161

identity, national, 2, 4, 9, 45, 49, 79; cultivated by Soviet state, 60; persistence and erosion of, 94

"I live not by bread alone" [*Ia zhiv ne edinym khlebom*] (Shalamov), 202

"Impossible to Express in Words" [*Nevozmozhno vyrazit' slovami*] (Abushinov), 161

"I Must Tell" [*Ia dolzhen rasskazat'*] (Siniagovskii), 161
In Defiance of the Blows of Fate [*Naperekor udarom sud'by*] (Akhtiamov), 162
industrialization, 3, 132, 206; forced labor and, 5; seen as achievement of Soviet Union, 288
informants/informers, 8, 50, 84, 277; "goats" (*kozly*), 79; in post-Soviet prisons, 78, 83; ubiquitous presence of, 71, 74, 76, 95
information/communication, 68–70, 71, 76, 95; across state borders, 81–82; central remand prisons as switchboards, 80–81; credibility of, 75, 81, 85; documentation of death and, 259; "polyopticon" (mutual monitoring among prisoners), 73, 83; reputation system and, 78; thieves' code and, 74
Ingush, 4
intelligentsia, Soviet, 224, 231, 276
interrogation, 1, 4, 172–73, *173*
"In the Taiga" [*V taige*] (Zabolotsky, 1947), 208
"In the wild North a lone pine tree stands" [*Na severe dikom stoit odinoko*] (Lermontov, 1841), 212
"In this Birch Grove" [*V etoi rochche berezevoi*] (Zabolotsky, 1946), 209–10, 281
I Remember How It Was [*Ia pomniu, kak eto bylo*] (Zubovskii), 160
"irregulars" [*neputi; neputevye*] (thieves' code breachers), 79, 81
Irshtein, M., 161
"Islands of the Gulag Archipelago in Kazakhstan" [*Ostrova arkhipelaga GULAG v Kazakhstane*] (Sabinin), 167
Iusoshius, General Ionas, 261, *261*
Ivan Fedorovich (Shalamov, 1962), 236
Ivanova, Galina, 116, 121, 124n4, 131
"I was educated by stern nature" [*Ia vospitan prirodoi surovoi*] (Zabolotsky, 1953), 208
"I was given a body" [*Dano mne telo*] (O. Mandel'shtam, 1909), 203
Izmailov, Hamid, 177n40

Jakobson, Michael, 131
jargon/slang, criminal, 46, 68, 70, 75, 82, 95
Jewish inmates, 21
Johnson, Emily D., 11, 93–94, 98, 174
Joseph, Metropolitan, 33
Journey into the Whirlwind [*Krutoi marshrut*] (Ginzburg), 157, 198, 225, 234
Journey to the Gulag, A (film, dir. Polensky), 192n7

Kaganovich, Lazar, 136
Kakhovskaia, Irina, 166
Kalmyks, 4, 172
Karachai, 4
Karelia (Karelo-Finland), 134, 268n15, 274, 287
Karlag camp (Kazakh SSR), 8, 60, 94
Karvasin, Lev, 261
Katyn, murder of Polish officers at, 289
Kazakhstan, 4, 8, 58, 207; German POWs in, 133, 141, 142, 145; Karaganda region, 51, 60, 160; regional archives in, 289; Western Kazakhstan UITLiK camp court, 120
Keats, John, 207
Kengir camp (Kazakhstan), 160
KGB (Committee for State Security), 170, 234, 267, 274
Khalmuradov, Sagdulla Khalmuradovich, 56–58
Kharkhordin, Oleg, 73
Khasanov, Mirsaid Mustafich, 55
Khelemskii, Mikhail Isaevich, 114, 115
Khlebnikov, Velimir, 205
Khlevniuk, Oleg, 72, 73, 131, 135
Khristianovich, Bertkhol'd Ivan, 257
Khrushchev, Nikita, 3, 113, 225, 273, 285; destalinization launched by, 289; ouster of, 221, 235; Stalin criticized by at XXII Party Congress, 221
Kilin, Iurii, 287
Kirill, Patriarch, 287
Kiselev-Gromov, Nikolai, 25
Kizsi, Lyafitova Sakkina Abbas, 118
Klinger, Anton, 21, 24, 32
knowledge, subcultural, 75
Kogan, L., 253
Kolyma camp system, 5, 157, 210, 228, 233; as "Auschwitz without the ovens," 229, 230, 236; *Butugychag* (mining section),

229; referenced in memoir titles, 159; representation of the camp experience, 227–32; Shalamov as prisoner in, 200, 220, 231; Vysotsky songs about, 277
Kolyma Notebooks [*Kolymskie tetradi*] (Shalamov, 1994), 197
Kolyma Notes (Shelest), 226
Kolyma Stories [*Kolymskie rasskazy*] (Shalamov), 197, 198, 201, 203, 220, 232; "Berries," 214n8; "Dry Ration," 217n69; *The Left Bank* (second cycle of *Kolyma Stories*), 220, 236; piecemeal publication abroad, 200, 234; *The Spade Artist* (third cycle of *Kolyma Stories*), 220; "Trampling the Snow," 228; writing of, 227, 235
Kolyma: The Arctic Death Camps (Conquest), 6
Komi ASSR, 55, 115, 220, 261; Lithuanian exiles in Inta, 262; Minlag coal mining camp, 223, 261
Kondrashev (Novosibirsk procurator), 115
Konovalev, Aleksander, 84
Kopka, 72
Kotkin, Stephen, 11
Krasnov, Simeon, 22
Krasnoyarsk camp, 72, 75
Krivosh-Nemanich, Vladimir, 48
Kruglov, S., 137
Kruketskii, A. K., 210
Krylov, Hegumen Pitirim, 26
Kudriashov, M. M., 117
kulaks (wealthy peasants), 3–4, 5, 96, 132, 254
Kutiavin, Nikolai Grigor'evich, 52–55, 63n45
Kutsenko, Grigorii Petrovich, 45, 62n11
Kuznetsov (commander of Vladimirskaya oblast' labor colonies), 112
Kyiv Society of Political Prisoners and the Repressed, 45
Kyrgyzstan, 68; German POWs in, 142; reputation system in post-Soviet prisons, 78, 79–84, 95

labor army (*trudovaia armiia*), 109, 110
labor camps, 2, 3, 7, 91, 96; language policy in, 44; peasants in, 93; presentation albums for visiting dignitaries, 8; projects produced at, 5; as sites of Russification/Sovietization, 60; transfers and, 74

labor colonies, 2, 3, 77, 91; censorship protocols in, 52; projects produced at, 5; translators and, 74
"Lake in the Woods" [*Lesnoe ozero*] (Zabolotsky, 1938/1944), 207
Landau, Lev, 222, 223
"Late Spring" [*Pozdniaia vesna*] (Zabolotsky, 1948), 208
Latvia, 9, 288; archives in, 289; Museum of the Occupation of Latvia (Riga), 44, 45
Latvian language, 44, 45, 54
Latvians, 4, 172
law merchants, medieval, 69, 70
LEF (Left Front of Art), 204
Leliukhin, Deacon, 31
Lenin, Vladimir, 171
Leningrad Affair, 3
Leninism, 164, 167
Leonardovich, Mechislav, 29
Lermontov, Mikhail, 212
Lesiuchevskii, Nikolai, 278–79
letters, 13, 156, 158, *163*
Letters from the House of the Dead [*Pis'ma iz mertvogo doma*] (Shiller), 167
Levi, Primo, 168
Life and Fate (Grossman), 281
"Life of Engineer Kipreev, The" (Shalamov), 236
Likhachev, Dmitrii S., 34, 92, 275
Linde, Vera, 222
Lisianskii, Valerii, 162, 170
literary studies, 10
Lithuania, 9, 68, 288; archives in, 289; German POWs in, 134, 141; reputation system in post-Soviet prisons, 78, 79, 83
Lithuanian language, 44, 45
Lithuanians, 4, 172, 257–58, *258*
Living (Renovationist) Church, 21–22, 30, 32, 33, 93
Lobov, Zakharii, 22
local history (*kraevedcheskie*) museums, 186
"Lodeinikov" (Zabolotsky, 1932), 216n49
Lozina-Lozinskii, Vladimir, 28
Lundblad-Janjic, Josefina, 228–29
Lutheran inmates, 21

machine learning technology, 190–91, 192n9, 290
Magadan, 210, 229–30

Malenkov, Georgii, 136
Mal'sagov, Sozerko, 25
Mamedov, Hussien Guli Aga Ogly, 119
Mamuchashvili, Elena, 222
Mandel'shtam, Nadezhda, 156, 162, 175n14
Mandel'shtam, Osip, 203
Mapping the Gulag: Russia's Prison System from the 1930s to the Present (website), 141, 185, 186
Marchenko, Anatolii, 166
Marchenko, Zoia, 159
Martin, Terry, 59
Marushin, Petr Maksimovich, 118
Marxism, 21
"Masks of Sorrow: Europe-Asia" (Neizvestny), 286
Mayakovsky, Vladimir, 204
medical release process (*aktirovka* or *aktirovanie*), 12, 103–5, 120–23, 184, 191; diagnoses by number and percentage, *118*; "façade of legality" and, 105–6, 110, 116, 120; Ministry of Justice (MIu) and, 116–20; NKVD and, 107–13; Procuracy and, 113–16; red tape and, 113, 116–17, 120, 121; registered death index and, 108; "release to die" practice, 104, 114, 122, 182–83; situational cover-up and, 122, 183. See also mortality/death rates
Medvedev, Dmitri, 284–85
memoirs, 1, 6, 8, 13, 46, 291; of camp bosses and guards, 8; on correspondence in non-Russian languages, 43; distant reading of, 155–56, 189; fictional forms associated with, 165; of German POWs, 142; machine learning technology applied to study of, 190–91; negative view of common criminals in, 67; online database of, 156; by ordinary people, 92; of political prisoners, 84–85, 94–95; on politicals' interaction with thieves, 71; published since fall of Soviet Union, 93; of SLON inmates, 21, 36n10; of Soviet officials, 105; on speech forms in mixed-ethnicity barracks, 56
memoirs, framing of, 155–58, 174–75; authorial prefaces and, 164–68, 188; opening scenes and, 168–74, 188–89; prefatory materials and, 158; Russian literature as context, 168, 174; titles and, 158–62, *163–64*, 188
Memorial (human rights network), 47, 55–57, 186, 286; Gulag art collection of, 199; revisionist narratives opposed to, 287–88, 291
memory, 31, 237; of executed individuals, 262–64; in families of special settlers, 255–58, *257*, *258*; Gulag displaced from cultural memory, 273; of people who died in the camps, 259–62, *260–62*; Russian state and memorialization of the Gulag, 285–86; as theme in authorial prefaces to Gulag memoirs, *165*, 166; as theme in Gulag memoirs, *169*, 170–71; in titles of Gulag memoirs, 159, 160–61
"Memory of the Gulag" [*Pamiat' o Gulage*] (Vengerskii), 175n11
messages (*ksiva, maliava,* or *progon*), 75, 81
"Metamorphosis" [*Metamorfozy*] (Zabolotsky), 207
Michurin, Ivan, 206
"Midday" [*Polden'*] (Zabolotsky, 1948), 208
Mikhailov (procurator of Birlag), 114
Milgrom, Paul, 69
Mindlin, M. B., 159
mining, 5, 206, 223, 278; arrests of mining engineers, 9; POW labor and, 145
Ministry of Justice (MIu), 104, 105, 116–20
Minlag camp (Komi ASSR), 223, 261
Mironov, S. N., 247
Mitrotskii, Archpriest Mikhail, 23–24
Moldavians, 4
Moldova, 68; German POWs in, 134, 141, 142; reputation system in post-Soviet prisons, 78, 79, 80, 81, 82, 83, 95
Molotov, Vyacheslav, 136, 137, 147
Monakhov, Viktor, 77
Moretti, Franco, 155
"Morning" [*Utro*] (Zabolotsky, 1946), 209
Morson, Gary Saul, 165
mortality/death rates, 2, 6, 96, 103, 106, 274; archival information about, 7; downwardly revised estimates, 181–82; "façade of legality" and, 105, 110; fake documents issued to families, 264, 274; of German POWs, 135, 149n26; manipulation/

distortion of, 2, 113–14, 116, 119, 122; of medically discharged invalids, 103, 117–21, 118; reliability of official figures, 104; secrecy and euphemisms involving, 106, 124n13; of special settlers, 244, 253; in war years, 109, 133. *See also* graves/burial sites; medical release process
Morukov, Mikhail, 148n16
Moscow Memorial, 185, 190
mourning, 279–80
Murav, Harriet, 274
Museum of Gulag History (Moscow), 286, 288
Museum of the Gulag website, 185
Museum of the Occupation of Latvia (Riga), 288
muzhiki (common prisoners), 71, 79, 80
MVD (Ministry of Internal Affairs), 44, 77, 112, 116, 118; labor mobilization of POWs and, 137, 147, 187; Prison Section (*Tiuremnyi otdel*), 51; red tape in, 120
"My 'Stalinist Academy'" [*Moia "Stalinskaia akademiia"*] (Khromushin), 175n11
My Testimony [*Moi pokazaniia*] (Marchenko), 166
MZ [*mesta zakluchenia*] (prisons and colonies), 108

Nakonechnyi, Mikhail, 11–12, 133, 135, 181–84, 191; on "archival counterrevolution," 289; on documentation of prisoner burials, 251
Nasedkin (Gulag director), 109, 110–11, 112
national groups, deportations of, 4
nationalism, among prisoners, 79
national minorities, 10, 49, 94
national theme/story, in memoirs, 164, *165*, *169*, 172, 174
Naturphilosophie (Schelling, 1797–99), 216n47
Nazis, 105, 129, 138, 184, 230, 274, 288
Nechaev (URO inspector), 111
Necropolis of the Gulag, 12, 186, 245, 264, 266, 273–74. *See also* graves/burial sites; mortality/death rates
Neizvestny, Ernst, 275, 286
Nekrasov, Nikolai, 201

"New York—Moscow—Siberia under Convoy" [*N'iu-Iork—Moskva—Sibir' po etapu*] (Blok-Baers), 159
NGOs, Russian, 186, 287, 288, 291
nicknaming, in prison culture, 68, 70, 75
"Night Garden, The" [*Nochnoi sad*] (Zabolotsky, 1937), 279–80
"Nightingale" [*Solovei*] (Zabolotsky, 1939/1944), 207
Nikodim, Father, 28
Nikolaev, O. P., 256, 268n32
NKU (Commissariat of Justice), 107–8, 121
NKVD (People's Commissariat for Internal Affairs), 44, 47, 72, 105, 268n4; archives of, 267; burial sites concealed by, 274; documentation of death and, 250, 254; executions by, 243, 246–48, 263; German POWs and, 134, 142, 147, 187; in Gulag staff during war years, 97; medical release practices and, 104, 107–13, 115, 117–18, 122; Procuracy in relation to, 113; records of, 104; special settlements created by, 132. *See also* secret police; OGPU; UPVI/GUPVI
Nogtev, Aleksandr, 25, 26
Noril'sk camp system, 159, 206, 232
North, Douglass, 69
Northern Camps of Forced Labor, 21
North Korea, 182
Notes from the House of the Dead [*Zapiski iz mertvogo doma*] (Dostoevsky, 1862), 157, 165, 199
Notes of a Camp Doctor [*Zapiski lagernogo vracha*] (Aleksandrovskii), 160
Notes of a Goner [*Zapiski dokhodiagi*] (Belousov), 160
Notes of an "Enemy of the People" [*Zapiski "vraga naroda"*] (Ermolaev), 160
Notes of a Political Prisoner [*Zapiski politzakliuchennogo*] (Bolonkin), 160
"Not Everyone Was Admitted to Our Circle" [*V nash tesnyi krug ne kazhdyi popadal*] (Vysotsky song, 1964), 277
Novosibirsk, city of, 5
Novyi mir (journal), 224, 225, 226
"Nugget, A" (Shelest, 1962), 226
Nuremberg trials, 230

OAGS (registry section), 254
OBERIU [*Ob'edinenie real'nogo iskusstva*] (Association for Real Art), 197, 205
Ogly, Tagiev Hussien Aga Mamed, 118–19
OGPU (Joint State Political Directorate), 107, 245, 248, 254; archives of, 267; civil status of special settlers and, 253; secrecy of burial sites and, 263; Special Purpose Sections (ChON) of, 249
Olitskaia, E. L., 164
One Day in the Life of Ivan Denisovich (Solzhenitsyn, 1962), 6, 91, 157, 200, 221, 222; Demidov influenced by, 232; ex-prisoners' responses to, 234–35; literary landscape of 1960s influenced by, 225–27; perspective of peasant in, 231; publication approved by Khruschchev, 225; "typical" prisoner experience in, 290
"On Prose" [*O proze*] (Shalamov), 155, 228
oral histories/testimony, 6, 13, 92, *163*
organized crime, 77
"Oro" (Florensky, 1936), 199
Orthodox clergymen, as inmates, 19–20, 22, 35–36, 92–93; abuse of religious sensibilities and, 25; Church hierarchy and, 30–35; "Epistle of the Solovetskii Bishops," 32–33; "Josephites" and "Sergiusites," 33–35, 36, 39n71; labor imposed on, 24; memoirs of, 22, 24; religious practice in SLON and, 26–29; repression viewed as test of faith, 23–24. *See also* Russian Orthodox Church
OSP (Section for Special Settlers), 253
OTSP (Section for Labor and Special Settlements), 253
Otto, Robert, 134
outcasts (*obizhennye*), 70

Pallot, Judith, 8, 11–12, 68, 141, 290
Partisan mine/camp, 56
Pashutina (head of directorate of camp courts), 116, 117, 119–20
Pasternak, Boris, 198, 201
Päts, Helgi-Alice, 59
peasants, 93, 96, 231; "to bury well" (*pokhoronit' khorosho*) as tradition, 256, 257, 258, 268n32; deported as families, 244; kulaks (wealthy peasants), 3–4, 5, 96, 254; Ukrainian famine and, 280
Pechorlag camp, 72, 73
People Remain People (Piliar, 1963–64), 226
People's Commissariat of Justice, 21
Perm-36 camp, memorial museum at, 287–88
Petr, Archbishop, 28, 29
Piacentini, Laura, 73
"Pictures of the Far East" [*Kartiny dal'nego voztoka*] (Zabolotsky, 1944), 208
Piliar, Iurii, 226
Pirozhenko, Iliia, 22
"Poem in Honor of a Pine Tree" [*Stikhi v chest' sosny*] (Shalamov), 212
"Poet from Within, The" [*Poet iznutri*] (Shalamov), 202
poetry, nature and, 1, 156, 197–99, 216n47, 228; lyric poetry, 213–14; nature as enduring reference point, 212; nature as source of hope, 201; Russian classical poetry, 205; of Shalamov, 197, 200–205, 278; of Zabolotsky, 205–10, 278–79
Pokrovka colony, 81
Polak, Lev, 166, 167
Poland, Soviet invasion of (1939), 129
Polensky, Tomas, 192n7
Poles, 4, 254
political offenders, 19, 74, 78, 235; forced labor and, 132; inmate caste system and, 70; medical release of, 110; as minority of Gulag population, 2–3, 13n5; personal accounts by, 7; reputation system and, 76, 84–85; in strict regime camps (*osobye lageri*), 91; as translators and censors, 50
Political Red Cross, 48
polozhentsy (prison leaders), 78
Pol'skii, Archpriest, 26, 28, 32–33
Popashenko, I. P., 246–47
Popov, Ivan, 26, 32
Pospelov, Archpriest, 31
post-Soviet states, 13
poststructuralism, 182
POWs (prisoners of war), German, 5, 129, 148n4, 184–85; in factories, 135–36; forced-labor mobilization of, 131–38, 147; mapping of POW camps, 138, *139–40*, 141–42, *143–44*, 145–46, 147, 149–50n43,

187–88; population density of camps, *144*, 145, 150–51n53; reconstruction of Soviet Union and, 130–31, 133, 134, 136–38, 145–47, 191; repatriations of, 134–35, 142, 147, 149n26, 150n51; Western nations' pressure on USSR to release, 146, 151n57

Pratt, Sarah, 207

prisoner mail, in non-Russian languages, 43–47, 51–56, 93–94; Arabic script, 55; camp rules and procedures relating to, 47–51; censors and, 44–45, 47, 62n8; delays in circulation, 51, 63n41; emotion conveyed in non-Russian languages, 45, 52, 53–54, 55, 94; forgetting of native language, 59; shifts in language usage over time, 56–59, *57*; Soviet Latinization campaign and, 55; Soviet "prison of peoples" and, 59–61; translators and, 44, 48, 49

prison-industrial complex, 107, 108

prisonization, 67

prisons, 2, 3, 7; remand prisons, 80, 81, 84, 244, 249; as sites of Russification/Sovietization, 60; underfunding of, 47, 82, 84

prison transfers, 57, 71, 74, 95; decrease in post-Stalin period, 77; of Orthodox clergymen, 20; in post-Soviet period, 84; translators and, 50; wartime increase in, 74

Procuracy, 104, 105, 113–16, 121

property rights, 70, 95

Protestant inmates, 21

Pushkin, Aleksandr, 168, 198, 205

Putin, Vladimir, 189, 284, 285, 287, 289

"quarantine" (reception unit of prison colony), 80, 81, 82

railroads, German POW camps near, *140*, 141, 150n45, 188

Ratushchnyi, Major-General, 136

Ratushnaia, L. P., 164–65, 166

Razgon, Lev, 167

record-keeping, 253

Red Terror (1918–21), 249

reeducation, 20, 22, 132, 146, 148n11

refashioning, ideological, 132, 146, 148n11

rehabilitation, 76, *173*, 224, 277; certificate of, 231, 249; multiple obstacles to, 277

religious inmates, 10, 11, 35

representation, problem of, 155, 168

reputation systems, 68–71, 84–85; emergence and expansion of, 72–78; faking of reputation, 75; in globalized illegal markets, 77; in post-Soviet prisons, 78–84

Requiem (Akhmatova), 217n66

Research and Information Center (RIC), 243

Resurrection of the Larch, The (Shalamov), 236

"Return from Work, The" [*Vosvrashchenie s raboty*] (Zabolotsky, 1954), 208

revolution, as theme in Gulag memoirs, 171, *171*

Rittersporn, Gabor, 182

Roeder, Bernhard, 71

Roginskii, Arsenii, 185, 275

Romanov, Roman, 286

RSFSR (Russian Soviet Federative Soviet Republic), 108; Criminal Code of, 21, 105; German POWs in, 134, 136, 141, 142, 187; Gulag camps clustered in north of, 141; Komi ASSR, 55, 115, 220, 223, 261–62, *261*, *262*

Russian Federation, 4, 47; debate about the Gulag in, 181; memorialization of Gulag in, 286–88; POWs and national mythmaking of, 184; prison system of, 182, 184; researching the Gulag in, 289–91; State Archive (GARF), 49, 106, 252, 290; state honors for Solzhenitsyn, 285

Russian language, 43, 280; criminal slang, 46; incomplete command of, 45, 58; as lingua franca in multiethnic camps, 46, 56, 94; mixed with non-Russian languages in Gulag correspondence, 54, 55, 57, *57*

Russian Orthodox Church, 204, 275, 287; "black clergy," 30–31; "Catacomb Church," 33, 34; schism of mid-1920s, 19, 20; Solzhenitsyn funeral and, 284; "white clergy," 31. *See also* Living (Renovationist) Church; Orthodox clergymen, as inmates

Russification, 45, 94

Rysmukhametov family, 255–56

Sabinin, A. M., 167

Sakharov Center (Moscow), 156, 157, 164, 170, 174, 188, 189

samizdat ("self-published") literature, 200, 221
Sandarmokh killings, revisionist account of, 287, 289
SANO (Sanitary department of Gulag), 107, 108, 112, 115
Sapina, D. V., 210
Sats, Nataliia, 166
Scarry, Elaine, 275
"Scent of Violets, The" [*Zapakh filiaki*] (Alieva), 159
Schelling, Friedrich Wilhelm Joseph, 216n47
Scrolls [*Stolbtsy*] (Zabolotsky), 205–6
secret police, 20, 21, 24, 28, 32. *See also* Cheka; KGB; NKVD; OGPU; VChK/GPU
Sedakova, Olga, 207
Sederkhol'm, Boris, 25
Sergius, Acting Patriarch, 20
Sergius, Metropolitan, 32, 33, 34, 35, 39n71
Seventeen Years on the Islands of the Gulag [*Semnadtsat' let na ostrovakh GULAGa*] (Marchenko), 159
Sevpechlag camp, 114, 115
sexuality, 25, 67, 278
Shalamov, Tikhon, 275
Shalamov, Varlam, 6, 12, 85, 155, 167, 188, 200–205; Demidov's correspondence with, 220–24, 226–30, 232, 234–37, 237n1, 274, 276; end of friendship with Demidov, 221; formal conservatism of, 204–5; LEF (Left Front of Art) and, 204; life after incarceration, 224–25; literary landscape after *Ivan Denisovich* and, 225–27; Moscow literary scene and, 224; nature themes and, 197–98; pre-camp life of, 224; as prisoner in Kolyma, 200, 220, 231; representation of camp experience and, 227–32; Solzhenitsyn's relationship with, 221, 231, 236, 276; on suffering and survival, 275; Zabolotsky in comparison with, 210–13
Shalamov, Varlam, prose of: *Anna Ivanovna* (camp play), 236, 238n9; "Graphite," 203, 228; *Ivan Fedorovich* (1962), 236; "The Life of Engineer Kipreev," 236; "From Lomonosov's Diary," 211; "On Prose," 155, 228; *The Resurrection of the Larch*, 236. See also *Kolyma Stories*

Shalamov, Varlam, poems of: "The Adage," 202; "Burial," 201; "Campfires and Stars," 211; "He warms his frozen fingers," 202–3; "I live not by bread alone," 202; *Kolyma Notebooks* (1994), 197; "From Lomonosov's Diary," 211; "The Dwarf Pine," 211–12, 213; "Poem in Honor of a Pine Tree," 212; "The Poet from Within," 202; "To Poetry," 203, 215n18; "Some of My Lives," 200; "A Toast to the River Aian-Uriakh," 201
Shaufel'berger, Arnol'd, 26
Shelest, Georgii, 226
Shiller, F. P., 167
Shimkunas, Vladas, 261, *261*
Shiraev, Boris, 28
Shiroklag (Perm region), 159–60, 191
Shirokstroi—Shiroklag: A Collection of Memoirs of Kalmyk Military Participants [*Sbornik vospominanii voinov-kalmykov*] (1994), 172
Shirovskii hydroelectric power station, 159
Shishkin, Aleksei, 22
shortages, 73
Siberia, 35, 48, 131, 187, 198; eastern, 4, 5; Lithuanian deportees in, 257, 258; mapping of camps in, 186; western, 5, 141; Zabolotsky in, 207, 208. *See also* mortality/death rates
Siniagovskii, P. I., 161
Siniavsky, 277
"skiers" [*lizhniki*] (prisoners resistant to thieves' system), 79
Slade, Gavin, 3, 11, 60, 73, 94–98
Slezkine, Yuri, 46, 59
SLON [Solovki] (Solovetskii Special Purpose Camp), 4, 5–6, 35–36, 92–93, 96; administrators of, 22, 25; blasphemy by guards and inmates in, 25; creation of (1923), 21; Kem' transfer point and, 22, 23, 27, 28, 259, *260*, 266; mandatory labor imposed at, 24; medical institutions, 29; monastery complex as location of, 22, 23; Orthodox Church hierarchy and, 30–35; prisoners' meditations on nature, 199; referenced in memoir titles, 159; religious practice in, 26–29; secret police at, 24; Shalamov in Vishera section, 224

smotriashchie (overseers), 78–79, 83
Socialist Realism, 208, 213–14
sociology, 10
Solonevich, Boris, 35
Solovetskii Islands, 19, 22, 23, 27, 92
Solovki camp. *See* SLON [Solovki]
Solzhenitsyn, Aleksandr, 5–6, 74, 91, 156, 188, 225, 275; death and memorialization of, 284–85; Gulag system named by, 1; on lack of access to archives, 2; memoirists' references to, 166, 167–68; moral authority and, 231, 235; on numbers of Gulag inmates, 273; political prisoners emphasized by, 132; Shalamov's relationship with, 221, 231, 236, 276; Soviet archives and, 12. See also *Gulag Archipelago, The*; *One Day in the Life of Ivan Denisovich*
"Some of My Lives" [*Neskol'ko moikh zhiznei*] (Shalamov), 200
"Somewhere in a Field near Magadan" [*Gde-to v pole vozle Magadana*] (Zabolotsky, 1956), 208, 210, 211, 281
songs, in prison culture, 68, 75
Sovietization, 11, 45, 94
Soviet studies, 11
Soviet Union (USSR), 1, 94, 95, 234; collapse of, 78, 79; constitution of, 21, 22; ethnic and linguistic identity in, 46; fall of, 10, 93; five-year plans, 9, 145, 147; forced labor pervasive in, 129; "guarantee of religious liberty" in, 22, 92; historical contingency and, 96; human rights movement in, 156; industrialization targets, 5; Ministry of Internal Affairs, 249–50; minority languages of, 45; Politburo, 131, 151n57; transformation into global superpower, 289; XXII Party Congress (1961), 221, 222
"speaking Bolshevik," 11, 46, 93, 290; resisted by criminal culture, 95; in written appeals to authority, 96
special settlements, 2, 6, 9, 91, 267n1; dispossessed kulaks in, 132; documentation of death in, 253–54; escapes from, 97–98; mapping of, 186; peasants in, 93
special settlers, 44, 243, 267n1; death in transit, 244, 254–55; mass-scale deaths during "first winter," 266; memory in families of, 255–58, 257, 258. *See also* deportations
spiritual journey, memoir as, 174
Spiro, Mariya, 263
Stalin, Joseph, 7, 8, 35, 59, 91, 274; death of, 3, 213–14, 277; five-year plans, 9; Gulag camps as embodiment of Stalin regime, 214; Khrushchev's criticism of, 221; labor mobilization of POWs and, 130, 133, 135, 136, 137, 145, 147, 150n51, 151n54; poetic reference to, 279; referred to in memoir titles, 159, 167, 171; revisionist accounts of, 12
Stalinism, 106, 113, 164, 224, 289; "black years" of, 227; as a civilization, 11; limited criticism of, 226; memorialization of crimes of, 285–87, 288; Party members seen as primary victims of, 171; Russia's reckoning with, 291
Stalin period, 44, 50, 51, 156, 186; arrests described in memoirs of, 173–74; human rights abuses of, 13; "socialist legality" in, 122
starvation, 106, 202
State Military Archive, 106
Stepanian, Elena, 207
"Stiff, The" (Demidov), 232, 233
STON (Solovetskii Special Purpose Prison), 4
Story of My Experience, The (D'iakov), 226
"Story of My Time in Prison, The" [*Istoriia moego zakliucheniia*] (Zabolotsky, 1988), 208
strict regime camps (*osobye lageri*), 91, 97
subcamps, 97–98
subjectivity, Soviet, 7, 11
"suits" (*masty*), 79–80
"Sun hasn't yet risen above the village, The" [*Eshche zaria ne vstala nad selom*] (Zabolotsky, 1946), 211
Suslov, Andrei, 185
Suzdal camp, 49
Sveshnikov, Boris, 275
Sykes, Gresham, 23

Tagantsev, N. S., diary of, 262–63
Tajikistan, 138

tamizdat ("published there" [abroad]), 221, 225, 234
Tamm, Milja, 50
Tasso, Torquato, 279
Tatar ASSR, 55
Tatars, Crimean, 4, 172
tattooing, prison culture and, 68, 70, 75, 95
terror, Stalinist, 8
testimony, of witnesses/survivors, 2, 6, *163*, *164*, 167, 174, 232; about burials, 264–66; digitization of, 189–90; Gulag Maps project and, 8; mapping of detention centers and, 186; in Sakharov Center corpus, 188; of secondary importance, 7; "unspeakability" of trauma and, 166
text mining, 11, 12, 158
"Thaw" [*Ottepel'*] (Zabolotsky, 1948), 209
"thick journals," 235
thieves: mutual aid fund (*obshchak*) of, 79; as opponents of Soviet system, 71; in post-Soviet prisons, 78–84; thieves-in-law (*vor-v-zakone*), 11, 70, 77, 85, 94; thieves' world, 68, 77; "uncrowning" (*razkoronovanie*) of, 75. See also *blatnye*; criminals, common
thieves' code, 81, 83; Bitches' War (1948–53) and, 75; informers and, 74; as prisoner self-governance, 67
"This Cannot Be Forgotten" [*Takoe ne zabyvaetsia*] (Tiurbeev), 161
"This Is How It Was" [*Tak eto bylo*] (Irshtein), 161
"Thunderstorm, The" [*Groza idet*] (Zabolotsky, 1957), 209, 212
Tikhon, Patriarch, 20, 21, 30, 93; death of, 32, 35; moderation of anti-Soviet stance, 33
Titov, Archbishop Prokopii, 30, 32
Tiurbeev, B. R., 161
Tiutchev, Fedor, 198, 201, 205, 216n47
"Toast to the River Aian-Uriakh, A" [*Tost za rechku Aian-Uriakh*] (Shalamov), 201
Toker, Leona, 239n46
"To Poetry" [*Poezii*] (Shalamov), 203
torture, 1, 23, 275
totalitarian model, 91, 96
transit points, 22, 23, 26, 77, 210, 243, 259
Trans-Siberian Railroad, 141, 150n45, 188
trauma, 10, 96, 155, 157, 170, 291; Holocaust memoirs and, 168; legacy of, 12; linguistic amnesia and, 59; trauma museums, 286; "unspeakability" of, 161, 166
Trifil'ev, Aleksii, 22
Troitskii, Archbishop Ilarion, 27, 28, 30, 39n71; in group portrait, 22; Josephite–Sergiusite split and, 33, 34
Truba, Raisa Pankrat'evna, 259, *260*, 269n33
Tsarist imperial period, 47, 70
Tsyrul'nikov, L. E., 49
Turkmenistan, German POWs in, 142
Twenty-Six Prisons and Escape from Solovki [*Dvadtsat'shest' tiurem i pobeg s Solovkov*] (Bezsonov), 175n11

Udmurt language, 45, 52, 53–54
UITLiK (Administration of Camps and Colonies), 114, 115, 116, 120
Ukhta-Pechora camp, 72
Ukraine, 9, 50, 288; archives in, 289; famine in, 280; German POWs in, 134, 141, 142, 145; nationalist prisoners from, 79; western, 93
Ukrainian language, 45, 52, 56
Ukrainians, 4, 63n41
ULLP (Main Administration of Forestry Camps), 111
Umniagin, Viacheslav, 36n10
United Nations, 146, 151n57, 182
United States: legacy of past injustices in, 291; penal system of, 182; prison gangs in, 69–70, 95
Unknown Gulag, The (Viola, 2007), 9
untouchables (*obizhennye*), 79, 80, 81
Upmane, Antonina, 62n8
Upmanis, Bernards, 62n8
UPVI/GUPVI (Administration of Prisoners of War and Internees), 5, 6, 129, 136–37, 146, 187; climate and location of POW camps, 141, *143*; overwhelmed by number of German POWs, 130; Stalin and, 133; statistical manipulation by officials, 135; symbiotic relationship with Gulag system, 12
Urals, 4
Urbaitis, Ignas, 54, 61n2
urki (violent career criminals), 3

URO/OURZ (Allocation and Distribution department), 107, 109, 111, 112, 115
Uzbekistan, 81; German POWs in, 133, 134, 142; Uzbek SSR, 56

Vail', Boris, 167
Vaishvillene, N. A., 162
Vangengeim, Aleksei, 199
Varese, Federico, 74
Vasilenko, Vasilii Kharitonovich, 52
Vaza, E. O., 161
VChK/GPU, 48
Verigin, Sergei, 287
Verkhne-Ural'sk prison, 57, 58
Vertov, Dziga, 203
Vetlag camp, 53
Viktor, Bishop, 31, 33–34
Vincent, Mark, 67, 70
Viola, Lynne, 9, 10, 11, 290
violence, 83, 85, 168, 257; absent or subdued in nature poetry, 199, 201, 209; from camp administration, 73, 76; decrease in post-Stalin period, 77; gang reputations and, 70; lack of formal governance and, 71, 72; reputation system in post-Soviet prisons and, 80, 95; social status and, 74; in Solovetskii, 24
Vladimir Central, 4
Vodolazkin, Eugene, 177n40
Volga-Don Canal, 137
Volga Germans, 109, 110, 188
Volkov, Oleg, 30
Vologurin, Vladimir, 22
Vorkuta camp complex, 72, 135–36, 141, 159, 206, 232
Vostoklag, 207
VTsIK (All-Russian Executive Committee), 245
Vysotsky, Vladimir, 277

"Wall of Grief" [*stena skorbi*] (Moscow), 286–87
Warped Mourning (Etkind), 10, 275
We, Who Didn't Exist [*My, kotorykh ne bylo*] (Gridin), 161
Weingast, Barry, 69
West Germany, 146, 151n57
Wheatcroft, Stephen, 104, 105

White Sea–Baltic (Belomor) Canal, 132–33, 148n16, 274
Winter War, 129
women: among Gulag staff, 97; religious belief in the Gulag and, 93; in women's and mixed-gender camps, 96
work brigades, 5, 56
World War, First, 171
World War, Second (Great Patriotic War), 6, 52, 106, 184, 232; amnesty at end of, 59; Battle of Stalingrad, 129–30; bitches' participation in, 75; composition of Gulag staff during, 97; decrease in incarcerated population during, 3, 13n5; forced labor projects during, 133; Gulag death rates during, 109; Gulag inmates released to fight in Red Army, 130–31, 133, 146; national deportations during, 4; Nazi invasion of the Soviet Union, 129; prisoners of war, 5; Soviet losses of population and assets, 138, 147; Soviet victory in, 226, 288, 289; as theme of Gulag memoirs, 171, *171*
Writer's Union, 224, 234

Yad Vashem (Israel), 286
Years and Wars (Gorbatov, 1964), 226
Yeltsin, Boris, 285
"Yesterday, thinking about death" [*Vchera, o smerti razmyshliaia*] (Zabolotsky), 206–7
Yevtushenko, Yevgeny, 277
Young, Sarah, 12, 181, 188–90, 236

Zabolotsky, Nikita, 279, 280
Zabolotsky, Nikolai, 12, 216n42, 275; Gulag experience of, 207; metamorphosis as theme in poetry of, 205–10; nature themes and, 197–98; Shalamov in comparison with, 210–13
Zabolotsky, Nikolai, poems of: "The Creators of Roads: (1947), 208; "Everything that was in my soul," 206; "Gomborsky Forest" (1957), 208–9; "I was educated by stern nature" (1953), 208; "Lake in the Woods" (1938/1944), 207; "Late Spring" (1948), 208; "Lodeinikov" (1932), 216n49; "Metamorphosis," 207; "Midday" (1948), 208; "Morning" (1946), 209; "The Night

Zabolotsky, Nikolai, poems of (*Cont.*)
  Garden" (1937), 279–80; "Nightingale"
  (1939/1944), 207; "Pictures of the Far
  East" (1944), 208; "The Return from
  Work" (1954), 208; "Somewhere in a Field
  near Magadan" (1956), 208, 210, 211,
  281; "The Story of My Time in Prison"
  (1988), 208; "The sun hasn't yet risen
  above the village" (1946), 211; "In the
  Taiga" (1947), 208; "Thaw" (1948), 209;
  "In this Birch Grove" (1946), 209–10, 281;
  "The Thunderstorm" (1957), 209, 212;
  "Yesterday, thinking about death," 206–7
Zaikin (captain of state security), 109–10
Zaitsev, Ivan, 23, 25, 26
Zatmilova, G. I., 166
zeks [*zakliuchennyi*] (prisoners), 1, 2
zemliachestvo (compatriot support networks),
  60, 79, 80, 96
Zemskov, Viktor, 103, 182
Zernov, Archbishop Evgenii, 22, 30, 32
Zhdanov, Andrei, 150n51
Zhizhilenko, Bishop Maksim, 29, 31, 33,
  38n49
Zitzewitz, Josephine von, 12, 228, 275, 278,
  281
Znamenskii, Archpriest Sergei, 23
"zonification," 72, 83
Zotov, Vladimir, 28
Zubkovskii, S. R., 160
Zuleikha (Iakhina), 177n40
Zverev, Archbishop Petr, 30, 31

www.ingramcontent.com/pod-product-compliance
Lightning Source LLC
Chambersburg PA
CBHW030607230426
43661CB00053B/1885